MOSCOW-LENINGRAD HANDBOOK

INCLUDING THE GOLDEN RING

D0168258

MOSCOW-LENINGRAD HANDBOOK

INCLUDING THE GOLDEN RING

BY MASHA NORDBYE

MOON
PUBLICATIONS, INC.

MOSCOW-LENINGRAD HANDBOOK
Including The Golden Ring

Please send all comments,
corrections, additions,
amendments, and critiques to:

**MASHA NORDBYE
c/o MOON PUBLICATIONS
722 WALL STREET
CHICO, CA 95928 USA**

PRINTING HISTORY
First Edition 1991

Published by
Moon Publications Inc.
722 Wall Street
Chico, California 95928 USA
tel. (916) 345-5473

Printed by
Colorcraft Ltd., Hong Kong

Library of Congress Cataloging in Publication Data

Nordbye, Masha, 1955-
    Moscow-Leningrad Handbook Including the Golden Ring / by Masha Nordbye
        p. cm.
    Includes bibliographical references and index.
    ISBN: 0-918373-61-1 : $12.95
    1. Moscow (R.S.F.S.R.)—Description—Guide-books. 2. Leningrad (R.S.F.S.R.)—
        Description—Guide-books. 3. Russian (S.F.S.R.)—Description—Guide-books.
        I. Title.
DK587.N67
914.7'31204854—dc20   90-25180
                                                        CIP

Printed in Hong Kong

Cover photo by Pat Lanza

to Moshka and The Lenin Sisters

ACKNOWLEDGEMENTS

Finnair & Ilkka Mitro; Lindblad; Angliiski Misha; James "Toshiba" Burke; Robert Trent Jones, II; Jeff Kriendler, Pan American; Herb Caen; Jando; Eleanor, Len, Gorsky & Karen; Lyoni Craven; Bolshoi Bob McDougal; "Multimate" Winters; Dan Hays; Belka; Babushka Anna & Dedushka Mitro; Leningrad Circus & Nikulin; Sasha, Tanya & Andrei–The Frishkadelkamis; Tolya Valushkin & Katya Jharkovskaya; Shigeru-san; Valentin, Volodya & Viktor; Slava; Govard Green & Vatrushka; Ivan "Lodka"; Markski; Yuko & Ari, Dave Pleiman; Andy; Geriakaka; Muffett Kaufman; Carlichka Gottlieb; Rich Neill; Bashkaus Bill; Karen Montgomery; John Porterfield; David Fineman; Peggy Burns; Matt Valencic; Dywa Puziri Mashahari and Medvyed Philip. Special thanks to Dikii Deke, Tovarish Tobias and Magnus Bartlett.

CONTENTS

INTRODUCTION..................................1
  History 6
  Government 19
  The Russian Language..............21
  Religion 28
  Art...30
  Russian Music...........................35
  The Golden Age of Russian Literature 39
  Youth and Culture 40
  Holidays and Festivals...............45
  Planning Your Trip.....................47
  Getting There 50
  Getting Around..........................52
  Accommodations 55
  Food...56
  Shopping...................................64
  Health.......................................67
  Money and Measurements........68
  Communications and Conduct 70
  Useful Addresses......................72

MOSCOW 75
  Introduction 75
  Sights 82

  Practicalities..............................111
  Vicinity of Moscow 120

THE GOLDEN RING....................125
  Introduction 125
  Zagorsk 127
  Pereslavl-Zalessky...................131
  Rostov Veliky 134
  Yaroslavl.................................137
  Kostroma.................................142
  Ivanovo...................................143
  Palekh 144
  Vladimir 145
  Suzdal 150

LENINGRAD 157
  Introduction 157
  Sights 161
  Practicalities............................163
  Vicinity of Leningrad.................191

BOOKLIST 199

INDEX...203

LIST OF MAPS

Golden Ring...126
Kremlin/Red Square.................................86
Leningrad...................................158-159
Leningrad Metro.....................................188
Leningrad, Vicinity of.............................191
Moscow...76-77
Moscow Metro..80
Moscow, Vicinity of.................................121

Pereslavl..131
Rostov Veliky..135
Soviet Union on the Globe.......................2-3
Suzdal...151
Vladimir...146
Western USSR and Eastern Europe..............16
Yaroslavl...138
Zagorsk..128

LIST OF CHARTS

Basic Russian Vocabulary.....................21-26
Clothing and
   Shoe Size Conversion........................67
Cyrillic Alphabet with
   Approximate Pronunciation.................27
International Trains from Moscow.................51

Menu Vocabulary................................60-64
Metric System, The...............................69
Terms for Local Stores...........................65
Trans-Siberian Railroad..........................54
Useful Addresses and
   Phone Numbers..............................72-73

PHOTO AND ILLUSTRATION CREDITS

Photos by the author appear on pages: 17, 19, 28, 41, 43, 45, 82, 85, 88, 110, 112, 116, 117, 119, 120, 132, 140, 145, 150, 153, 155, 163, 165, 168, 172, 175, 184, 193

Illustrations by Robert Race appear on pages: 32, 33, 47, 50, 53, 57, 58, 75, 79, 95, 111, 123, 125, 129, 182, 185

IS THIS BOOK OUT OF DATE?

Travel information is continually changing, especially in the Soviet Union. We have endeavored to make the information in this book as accurate as possible at the time it was published, and we will continue to update it. You can help. If you spot information that is no longer valid, please let us know. If you discover places that could have been included, share them with fellow travelers by informing us about them. We especially appreciate feedback from women travelers, local residents, outdoor enthusiasts, and special-interest or special-needs travelers. We also like hearing from experts in the field as well as local business owners who wish to serve travelers.

If you have photos or drawings that you feel could be used in this guide, please send them to us. Send only high-quality duplicates and be aware that the publishers cannot undertake to return any materials unless you include a self-addressed, stamped envelope. If your material is used you will be mentioned in the credits; Moon Publications, Inc. will own the rights to all material submitted. Address your letters to:

Masha Nordbye
c/o Moon Publications, Inc.
722 Wall Street
Chico, CA 95928

INTRODUCTION

Perhaps no other place in the world has ever so captivated the traveler's imagination as the Soviet Union. Throughout the centuries, visitors to Russia reported phenomenal and fanciful scenes: from golden churches, bejewelled icons and towering *kremlins* to mad-cap czars, wild Cossacks and prolific poets. Russia was an impressive sight for any beholder. A travel writer in the early 20th century remarked that Russia's capital, Moscow, "embodies fantasy on an unearthly scale.... Towers, domes, spires, cones, onions, crenellations filled the whole view. It might have been the invention of Danté, arrived in a Russian heaven." Today the Soviet Union is an equally, if not more, fascinating, intriguing and perplexing land.

Largest country in the world, the USSR, or as the Soviets refer to their homeland, SSSR, (CCCP in Cyrillic), Soyuz Sovyetskikh Sotsialisticheskikh Respublikh, spreads across 11 time zones and two continents from Europe to Asia, encompassing one-sixth of the planet's total land area. Its inhabitants number 289 million in 15 republics, and speak over 200 different languages and dialects. Russian, the official language, unites 92 different nationalities. It would be impossible to take in the diversity of the entire country on one (or even two or three) visits alone, but there's no better way for a more insightful glimpse into the Russian character and way of life than with a trip to Moscow and Leningrad.

"I love my native land . . . my heart reawakens.
To her life in tales and myth and out the dim past taken . . .
Her rolling steppes, at once so chill and soundless,
Her wind-swept, rustling groves and forests boundless . . .
I love to bump along a country road at night,
To see the smoke coiling over the village light . . .
Young birches perched atop a mound,
Carved wooden shutters, roofs of thatch, grain blanketing the ground . . .
All, all within me wakes of feeling of joy!"

–Mikhail Lermontov

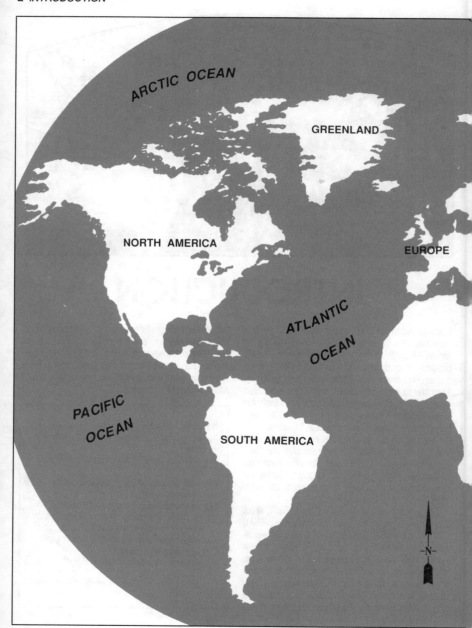

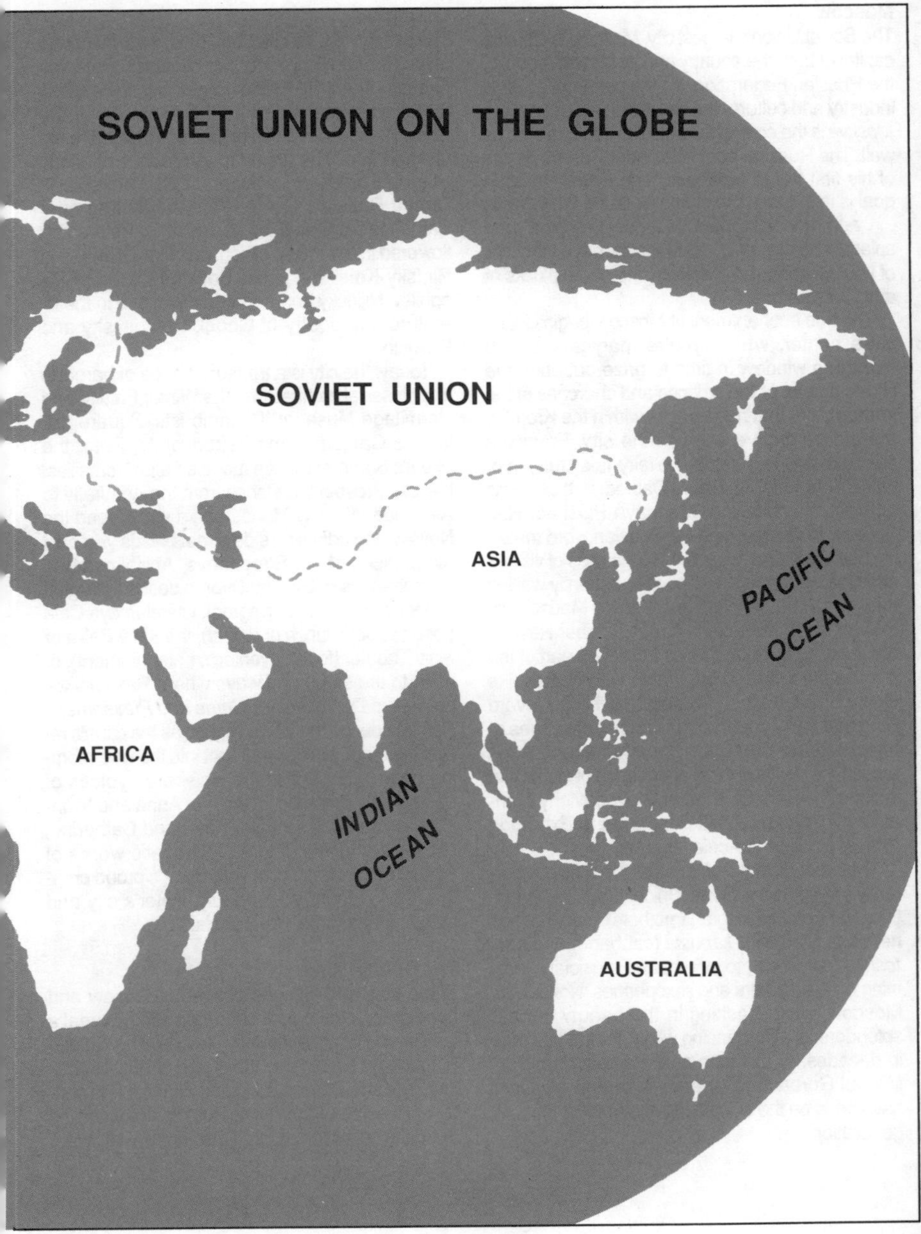

SOVIET UNION ON THE GLOBE

SOVIET UNION

ASIA

PACIFIC OCEAN

AFRICA

INDIAN OCEAN

AUSTRALIA

Moscow

The Soviet Union's largest city, Moscow is also the capital of both the country and its largest republic, the Russian Federation. It's the center of politics, industry and culture, the heart of this giant nation. *Moskva* is the core of the Russian spirit, *dusha*, as well. The Russian poet Alexander Pushkin wrote of his first trip to Moscow: "And how at last the goal is in sight: in the shimmer of the white walls . . . and golden domes, Moscow lies great and splendid before us. . . . O Moscow, have I thought of you! Moscow, how violently the name plucks at any Russian heart!"

The true enchantment of Moscow begins in the city's center, where you're magically pulled through a window in time to gaze out upon the gilded domes of the palaces and churches of the former czars that rise up from within the Kremlin, the old protective walls of the city. From the citadel, paths lead out to the fairy-tale creation of Ivan the Terrible, St. Basil's Cathedral, that looms up from the middle of Krasnaya Ploshad, Red Square. *Krasnaya* is an old Russian word meaning both "red" and "beautiful." Huge lines of visitors stretch around the Kremlin walls, patiently waiting their turn to be admitted into Lenin's Mausoleum to view the "Father of the Great October Revolution." Jutting out like arteries from the heart of the city are the long thoroughfares with names like Gorky Street, Kalinin Prospect and the Boulevard Ring that carry you through various passages of history to the present. These lanes and rings around the city lead to an abundance of sights that include the Bolshoi Theater, Novodevichy Monastery, Tretyakov Art Gallery and the Exhibition Park of Economic Achievements.

The Arbat district embodies all the changes currently sweeping the Soviet Union. You'll find everything from *babushki* (grandmothers), carrying their net bags filled with *kapusta* (cabbage) and *kartoshka* (potatoes), to long-haired musicians jamming on their guitars and saxophones. Nowadays, Moscow, while basking in the beauty of past splendors, is also dancing wildly, for the first time in decades, to the tune of a different drummer. Mikhail Gorbachev's *perestroika* and *glasnost* have become the scintillating symbols for the new generation.

Leningrad

The second largest city, Leningrad, was the capital of the Russian Empire for two centuries. Peter the Great founded St. Petersburg, a city so beautiful that it was referred to as the "Babylon of the Snows" and the "Venice of the North." Voltaire exclaimed that "The united magnificence of all the cities of Europe could but equal St. Petersburg!" During Russia's Golden Age, beginning after Catherine the Great, the genius of St. Petersburg flowered in the music of Tchaikovsky, Glinka, and Rimsky-Korsikov; in the Ballets Russes of Diaghilev, Nijinsky and Anna Pavlova; and in the literature and poetry of Gogol, Dostoevsky and Pushkin.

Today, the city is a treasure house of baroque and classical architecture: the Winter Palace and Hermitage Museum, Decembrists' Square, St. Isaac's Cathedral and Petrodvorets, Peter the Great's Summer Palace modeled after Versailles. Nevsky Prospekt stretches from the Admiralty to Alexander Nevsky Monastery; a stroll along the Nevsky and adjoining side streets leads you past the palaces of the Stroganovs, Anichkovs and Sheremetevs to Gostiny Dvor (oldest and largest shopping arcade in Leningrad), Literaturnaya Cafe (for a delicious lunch or dinner), the Kirov Ballet or Maly Theater (for an evening's entertainment), or even to the small alleyways where Raskolnikov roamed in Dostoevsky's *Crime and Punishment.* Perhaps during the White Nights, as the canals reflect the magical iridescent light into the wee morning hours, you'll hear the whispered voices of Leningrad's romantic lovers—of Anna and Vronsky, Tatyana and Onegin, Peter and Catherine, Nicholas and Alexandra. The poetic words of Pushkin linger on: "I love you, Peter's proud creation. . . . Flaunt your beauty, Peter's city and stand, unshakable, like Russia."

The Golden Ring

The towns and villages between Moscow and Leningrad, known as the Golden Ring, reveal a quieter and quainter country lifestyle. The Golden Ring area is considered the cradle of Russian culture. The small towns, including Zagorsk (the center of Russian Orthodoxy), Rostov, Vladimir and Suzdal (the most ancient Russian towns), were built between the 10th and 17th centuries and are still magnificently preserved. Antiquated villages, onion-domed churches, the frescoes and icons of the 15th-century artist Andrei Rublev, colorful wooden *dacha* (country homes) and endless groves of birch trees provide a lovely contrast to the bigger cities. The serene sites rekindle a Tolstoyan portrait of Russia's past.

Memorable And Rewarding

With this dawning of Gorbachev's "second revolution" comes a virtual explosion in communication, culture and national awareness—there has never been a more interesting and exciting time to visit the Soviet Union. In what's been termed the new Russian Renaissance, Soviet people are experiencing greater freedoms than ever permitted throughout the entire history of post-revolutionary Russia. Yet aside from all the new and stimulating developments, the Soviet Union is still a place filled with paradoxes and limitations, and a traveler cannot anticipate the same relaxing or luxurious holiday familiar to most Westerners. "First-class, socialist style" can be a little different from what you may imagine; it doesn't include piña coladas by the pool or sumptuous breakfasts in bed!

Most travelers enter the USSR through the Soviet Tour Agency, Intourist, which provides hotels, meals and sightseeing. Even though the USSR, through the years, has boasted large-scale productions of rockets and ballets, it hasn't yet produced the simplest surplus of food or clothing, let alone stocked a warehouse full of tourist amenities. Creature comforts for the Soviets don't include a variety of fruits and vegetables, nor sometimes even the very basics, such as toilet paper or soap. The average Igor must still stand in long lines to buy most things, including ice cream, and there's currently a rationing of the most common items such as sausage, sugar and tea. So, in a moment of slight frustraton, remember that the traveler is receiving all that the country can readily provide, and it's likely this is much more than is available to the average citizen. A sure remedy for the lack of certain supplies is to simply bring anything you can't do without—from prescription drugs to peanut butter.

If you don't read Cyrillic or speak the Russian language, bring a Russian phrasebook; it's amazing how far a smile, some patience and the knowledge of a few Russian words will go. So far, in fact, that you may even find yourself being invited to someone's home for dinner, where you'll quickly discover that Russians are some of the warmest, most hospitable and friendliest people that you'll ever meet.

The country has come a long way from being "a riddle wrapped in a mystery inside an enigma," as Winston Churchill once observed. The ingredients to understanding Russia have changed. Now with just an added dash of your own *glasnost* (openness), and curiosity toward the Russian culture, your trip to the the Soviet Union will surely be one of the most rewarding, fascinating and memorable adventures of your life.

HISTORY

THE EARLY SETTLEMENTS

Slavs

In the 7th century B.C., nomadic Scythians migrated north into fertile Russian territories. Herodotus the Greek, who visited southern Russia in the 5th century B.C., observed that "Some tribes cultivated the land; the builders of the Parthenon would have gone hungry without Russian wheat; but the ruling element remained nomads, living in tents, yet not altogether eschewing the arts of civilization." These people also began trading furs and honey with Constantinople; eventually, the merchants acted as middlemen between other settlements in the far north (inhabited by Finnish tribes) and the Roman Empire. As these early Slavic people began to cultivate the land, villages and towns sprang up, protected by wooden citadels, or *kremlins,* cut from the abundant forest timber. The inhabitants gradually occupied an area from what is now Leningrad to Kiev and spoke a language (originating from Greek) quite similar to modern Russian.

Varangians

The numerous tribes were united in the 8th and 9th centuries, when the Scandinavians, Vikings known as Varangians, migrated south and began establishing trade settlements with the Slavs, along with their own strongholds. Many of these settlements were situated along the Neva River and Lake Ladoga. When the Norseman Rurik defeated the strongest Slavic settlement, Novgorod, in A.D. 862, the Varangians became the rulers of northern Russia. In the south, the Slavic Prince Kii had formed the Kievan territory. In 880, Rurik's successor, Oleg, conquered the Slavic-ruled Kiev and made the city his capital two years later. With the two areas united, the State of Rus (derived from the Viking word *ruotsi,* meaning "oarsman") became one of the largest kingdoms in the world.

Christianity

Rus was still a pagan state when Prince Vladimir succeeded to the throne in 978. To further unify his large kingdom, the Prince decided to select a monotheistic religion for his people. One of the first Russian chronicles, *The Story of the Passing Years,* describes the experiences of the Russian

Cossacks writing a mocking letter to the Turkish sultan *by Ilya Repin*

ambassadors in Constantinople: "We did not know whether we were in heaven or earth for upon earth there is no such sight or beauty; we only know that there, God is present among men." In 988, Prince Vladimir introduced Byzantine Christianity to Russia. It had an overwhelming effect on the country: along with a new religion came Byzantine art, architecture and culture.

By the 11th century, the two most important towns in Russia were Kiev and Novgorod. The seats of the Grand-Prince and the Metropolitan of the Orthodox Church were in Kiev, where all the splendors of Constantinople were recreated. Novogorod was the northern commercial and religious center. Even though Russian culture was greatly influenced by Byzantium, it took many years to spread the new religion through the pagan states of the north. After the Mongols, headed by Batu Khan (grandson of Genghis), sacked Kiev in 1240, the Russian rulers and church leaders shifted their kingdoms to the north. Through the next few centuries, the Golden Ring towns of Rostov, Vladimir, Suzdal and Zagorsk became the secular and religious capitals during the Golden Age of Rus.

EARLY DAYS OF MOSCOW

As Kiev declined, Russia's northern principalities grew in political and economic importance. The governing ruler of Russia, Kievan Grand-Prince Yuri Dolgoruky (Long Arms), wanted to extend and strengthen his rule over the northern territories. For the first time in centuries, his father, Vladimir Monomakh, had succeeded in reuniting the north and south. In 1125, Dolgoruky declared Suzdal his northern capital and made himself the Prince of the region. Between the Volga and Oka rivers, on the banks of the Moskva River, Dolgoruky established a protective outpost for the Rostov-Suzdal principality. The first reference to Moscow appeared in the *Chronicle Ipatyev*, in 1147, when it mentioned that Prince Yuri Dolgoruky hosted a feast in Moscow to honor the Prince of Novgorod. In 1156, Dolgoruky built the first wooden *kremlin* and added a church within the settlement. Since the settlement lay along important trade routes to the Baltic in the north, the Black Sea in the south, and later to Europe in the west, Moscow slowly grew in size and signifi-

cance, and eventually became the capital of the Moscovy principality.

Mongols

In the beginning of the 13th century, the Mongols, under the leadership of Genghis Khan, set out to conquer Asia and Europe. The great Khan believed that his people "were intended by Heaven to rule the world." In 1237, Batu Khan, grandson of Genghis, invaded Russia from the south, and with a vengeance sacked and burned every town from Kiev to Moscow. The people of Russia were subjugated under the Golden Horde. For the next 250 years, Russia was cut off from the outside world; the Khans appointed the princes, controlled the government and collected taxes on the lands.

Except for the provinces of Novgorod and Moscovy, most of the other areas of Russia were completely devastated. Many people fled to the more isolated areas around Moscovy to escape the pillage of their cities. In 1240, the Scandinavians again invaded from the North, but the Prince of Novgorod, Alexander Nevsky, defeated the Swedes on the banks of the Neva River. The Khan appointed Nevsky Grand-Prince and his son, Daniil, the Prince of Moscow. In 1299, the Metropolitan of the Russian Orthodox Church fled the ruined city of Kiev and took up residence in Vladimir, seat of the Grand-Prince since 1157.

Ivans I, II, And III

In 1328, the Prince of Moscow, Ivan I, was appointed Grand-Prince by the Khan. Ivan I (1328-40) had a strong economic hold over the other principalities. Since Ivan collected large tributes for the Mongols from the northern territories, he became known as Ivan Kalita or "Moneybags." At this time, both seats of the Grand-Prince and the Church Metropolitan were transferred from Vladimir to Moscow.

During the rule of Ivan II (1353-59), the Mongol yoke was weakened and the Khans lost their right to appoint the Grand-Prince. Ivan II's son, Dmitri, became the first Russian leader to defeat the Mongols, in the decisive battle of Kulikovo on the Don in 1380. Grand-Prince Dmitri Donskoi (of the Don) increased his domain by annexing the Vladimir-Suzdal principality to Moscow.

In 1453, the Ottoman Turks conquered Constantinople, which released the Russian Orthodox Church from Byzantium's domination. Eight years later the Orthodox Church changed the title of the Metropolitan of Kiev to the Patriarch of Moscow and All Russia. For the first time, the Church was run by the Grand-Prince in Moscow, which further enhanced the power of Moscovy.

Grand-Prince Ivan III (1462-1505) married the niece of the last Byzantine Emperor in 1472 and adopted the Byzantine crest of the double-headed eagle for Russia. Ivan refused to pay any further tributes to the Khans. With Russian armies conquering the remaining Tatar hordes, two centuries of Mongol oppression came to an end. Ivan III, who became known as *Veliky* (the Great), also annexed Novgorod to the Moscovy principality and rebuilt the city of Moscow. He summoned foreign architects to build elaborate churches and palaces within the Kremlin walls. The city grew to such splendor that the Patriarch declared Moscow the new Constantinople. In the early 16th century, a monk wrote that "two Romes have already fallen, but the third remains standing and a fourth there shall not be."

THE CZARIST EMPIRE

Ivan The Terrible

In 1547, for the first time in Russian history, Ivan IV (1533-84), grandson of Ivan the Great, was crowned Czar of All Russia ("czar" was derived from Caesar) in the Kremlin's Uspensky Cathedral. In addition, Moscow became the capital of the Holy Russian Empire. Ivan ruled with a deep-seated paranoia and ruthlessness; it's said that he gouged out the eyes of the architects who built St. Basil's so that a similar cathedral of such beauty could never be copied. The Czar's power became absolute when Ivan, now called "the Terrible," succeeded in conquering the remaining independent principalities. He confiscated the property of the *boyars* (ruling class nobles) and granted state property to those who served him. Since the soldiers were tenured to the state for life, their land grants became hereditary. The state also assigned a master to the peasants who worked the lands around an estate; this, in a sense, paved the way for serfdom. Ivan the Terrible organized the Streltsy (members of the army elite) to govern his districts and the Oprichniki (the first police force) to suppress *boyar* rebellions. In 1582, after the Livonian War with Poland and Sweden, Russia

lost her far northern territories and her access to the Baltic. In the same year the Czar also killed his son Alexcei in a fit of rage. When Ivan the Terrible died in 1584, Moscovy was left in a state of almost total political and economic ruin.

Time Of Troubles

Ivan the Terrible's last son, the feeble-minded Fyodor, inherited the crown. Fyodor's brother-in-law, Boris Godunov, was elected Regent and virtually governed the country. In 1598, when Fyodor died (and with him the House of Rurik), Godunov, who wasn't even a member of the higher nobility, was elected to the throne by the Imperial Assembly, which consisted mainly of the discontented gentry. Godunov's reign (1598-1605) ushered in the Time of Troubles: famines swept the land and there was increasing unrest among peasants, Boyars and Cossacks.

In 1591, the youngest son of Ivan the Terrible, Dmitri, mysteriously died. But in 1604, a false Dmitri (claiming he had escaped an assassination attempt) turned up in Poland and claimed to be the rightful heir of Moscovy. Supported by the Russian *boyars*, gentry (who thought the Poles respected the rights of noblemen), and a Polish army (which also had an eye on the territory), Dmitri advanced on Moscow. Boris Godunov died before Dmitri reached the city, paving the way for Dmitri to claim the throne. He was murdered shortly thereafter. A second false Dmitry attempted to gain control of the city with the remaining Polish army. Russian forces united in fear of a Polish invasion. Headed by the rugged Cossacks, this army emerged victorious. The Council of All Russia elected Mikhail Romonov, from an influential *boyar* family, their new czar in 1613. The Romonov Dynasty would rule over Russia for the next 150 years.

In 1652, Nikon, during the rule of Mikhail's son, Alexcei I (1645-76), became Church Patriarch. Nikon immediately set out to reform Russian Orthodoxy. This resulted in a violent schism within the Orthodox Church. Those in favor of reform assembled under Nikon. Those opposed called themselves the Old Believers and were led by the monk, Avvakum. Those who rejected the reforms were tortured and hanged; many of the Old Believers fled into the northern woods to escape persecution.

When Alexcei's eldest son, Fyodor, died in 1682 after only six years as Czar, a struggle broke out for the throne. Ivan V and his half-brother Peter I were proclaimed joint czars, with their older sister Sophia acting as Regent. When Ivan died, Peter the Great became sole ruler and Emperor of All Russia. Moscow, capital of the Russian Empire for almost two centuries, was fated, as Pushkin described, "to bow to a new capital [St. Petersburg] as the Queen Dowager bows to a young Queen."

ST. PETERSBURG

Peter The Great

Shortly before the Neva River flows into the Gulf of Finland, it branches into smaller tributaries that weave their way around a cluster of 44 islands. Upon these islands and marshes arose one of the most extraordinary and exquisite cities ever devised by man. In 1703, when the Russian army won a decisive battle against the Swedes in the Baltic, Peter the Great decided to protect his newly acquired seaport with a fortress on the Neva delta. On May 16, 1703, the Czar declared, "Here shall

Peter the Great

be a town." As Peter stood on Zayachi Ostrov (the Isle of Hares), he laid the first stone in the foundation of Peter and Paul Fortress.

Only Peter (a man who loved the sea and learned to sail at the age of 12) among Russian rulers wanted to bring his landlocked nation to the sea. The isolated and windswept area of marshes and bogs (*neva* is the Finnish word for swamp) was subject to frequent fogs and floods, and this northern city was said to be "built on human bones"—up to 100,000 workers died from the horrendous conditions. Even so, it emerged a showplace modeled after Venice and Amsterdam.

Peter the Great was the first ruler to extensively travel outside of Russia; he visited England, Germany, France and Holland. He was greatly impressed by Western ways and resolved to bring Russia up to a status equal with her European neighbors. Peter named his city Sankt Pieterburkh, after Christ's first apostle, his patron saint. Nine years after its founding in 1712, Peter made his beloved city the capital of the Russian Empire; it remained so for 206 years.

Golden Age

Peter I introduced Western culture, commerce and technology, and constructed the first buildings of the city, which included an Admiralty and shipping yards. Every structure had to be made from stone; builders of wooden structures risked banishment to Siberia. Peter immediately brought in 1,000 aristocratic families, 500 families of the best merchants and traders, and 2,000 artisans and craftsmen. Foreign architects designed some of the most splendid buildings that Russia had ever seen. Both Westerners and Russians flocked to the new capital. By 1725, the year of Peter's death, St. Petersburg had over 75,000 inhabitants.

Over the next 150 years, especially during the reign of Catherine the Great, St. Petersburg became the host to Russia's Golden Age and a mecca to some of the world's greatest dancers, artists, composers and scientists. It was the home to Lomonosov, Mendeleyev and Pavlov, and distinguished architects such as Montferrand, Rossi and Rastrelli. As the catalyst for Russia's Renaissance, St. Petersburg paved the way for the poetry of Pushkin, Lermontov, Blok and Akhmatova, and the novels of Gogol, Dostoevsky, Gorky and Nabokov.

REVOLUTIONARY TIMES

Decembrists
St. Petersburg was also destined to become the cradle of the Russian Revolution. The first general strikes in Russia occurred in 1749 under Empress Elizabeth. After Napolean was defeated in 1812 during the reign of Alexander I, secret societies sprang up throughout the country calling for the abolition of serfdom. One of these movements, known as the Decembrists (a group of dissatisfied nobles), also petitioned for the end of autocracy. On 14 Dec. 1825, they marched into Senate Square with other soldiers who had refused to swear allegiance to the new Czar, Nicholas I. The uprising was crushed within a few hours and the conspirators immediately hanged. Pushkin, whose personal censor was the Czar himself, composed a poem about the event: "He was made emperor, and right then displayed his flair and drive: Sent to Siberia 120 men and strung up five."

Petrashevists
Twenty-three years later in 1848, another revolutionary circle, known as the Petrashevists, was sparked into action by the writings of Belinsky. Fyodor Dostoevsky became a member of this group. The aim of the society was to prepare for an uprising and the members secretly printed material that advocated emancipation. But the secret police uncovered their plot, and on 22 April 1849, Count Orlov, Chief of the Gendarmes, had all of them arrested and imprisoned in Peter and Paul Fortress. With the earlier Decembrist revolt in mind, Nicholas I exiled them to penal servitude in Siberia. But before the prisoners were to hear their sentences, Nicholas I set up a mock execution. Dostoevsky, along with five others who spent eight months in solitary, were led outside expecting to be executed. Only at the last minute were they informed that the Imperial Majesty had granted them their lives. In a letter to his brother, Dostoevsky wrote: "Today, December 22, we were driven to Semyonovsky Parade Ground. There the death sentence was read to us all, we were given the cross to kiss, swords were broken over our heads, and our final dress was arranged. Then we were set against the posts so as to carry out the execution."

Freedom Group
In 1861, under increasing pressure and protests, the next Czar, Alexander II, signed a decree abolishing serfdom. This action, however, fell far short of revolutionary goals. Words by the Russian poet Nekrasov show that the people were still disenchanted with their way of life. "Do not rejoice too soon! 'Tis time to march ahead. Forget your exultation. The people have been freed. But are the people happy?" With the publication in Russia of Karl Marx's *Das Kapital* in 1867, the first Marxist groups were formed within the country. Revolu-

The Arrest of a
Propagandist
by Ilya Repin

tionary activities mounted and on 1 March 1881, the Narodnaya Volya (People's Will or Freedom Group) succeeded in assassinating Alexander II—but not in stopping czarist oppression. The country remained in a state of turmoil. Six years later, five students, including Lenin's older brother, tried to kill Alexander III, but their attempt failed. All were hung in the Kronstadt Fortress.

Bloody Sunday

Czar Nicholas II, fated to be the last czar, began his reign by marrying Alexandra, granddaughter of Queen Victoria. Nicholas, a weak and superstitious man, held a paranoia and deep dislike for the intelligentsia and politicians. Proletarian organizations continued to gather. The Social Democratic Labor Party was founded in 1898. In 1903, the Labor Party Congress split into two factions: the Mensheviks, led by Martov, and the Bolsheviks, headed by Lenin. Two years later Nicholas presided over Russia's defeat in the Russo-Japanese War. In the same year, 1905, Russia's first revolution received a bloody baptism. On 9 Jan. a huge procession of dissatisfied workers, headed by Father Gapon, marched into Palace Square. By carrying icons and chanting "God Save the Czar," the protestors hoped to get Nicholas's attention. In the Czar's absence, the director of the police dept. commanded his men to open fire on the group. Hundreds were massacred. This watershed event is remembered as Bloody Sunday.

A tide of strikes and protests ensued, and the Czar was forced to establish a limited consultative parliament called the State Duma. The Soviet (Council) of Workers and Soldiers became the organ of the proletariat. To gain some control, Nicholas appointed Stolypin his premier, who proved ruthless in suppressing any further revolutionary activities. From 1907-09, at least 2,000 people were executed. Stolypin himself was shot to death in the Kirov Theater in 1911. Nicholas's hold on the country was further weakened by the outbreak of World War I in 1914. Due to anti-German sentiment, the city's name was Russianized to Petrograd. The notorious Rasputin, brought into the court to heal the Imperial Family's hemophiliac son, had a strong influence over Nicholas and Alexandra and practically ran the country for a few years until his death in 1916.

Vladimir Ilyich Ulyanov: Lenin

The Revolution

In February 1917, a revolution finally overthrew the monarchy and a provisional government led by Kerensky was established. After 10 years of forced exile abroad, Lenin returned by train to Petrograd and planned the Bolshevik takeover. On 24 Oct. 1917, Lenin gave the command from the Smolny Institute, headquarters of the Red Guard, for the start of the Great October Revolution. The battleship *Aurora* sailed up the Neva and fired a blank shot near the Hermitage that signaled the famous beginning of what American writer John Reed termed "the ten days that shook the world." Red Army troops stormed the Winter Palace and the Bolsheviks took control of the new Soviet State. Trotsky, Lenin's main ally, wrote that "without Lenin the October Revolution would not have been won." Vladimir Ilyich Lenin was elected the first chairman of the Union of Soviet Socialist Republics. In 1918, Nicholas and his family were executed in the Ural town of Sverdlovsk; that same year, Lenin moved the capital of the Soviet Union to Moscow. When Lenin died in 1924, the city of Petrograd was renamed Leningrad in his honor.

STALIN AND HITLER

The Great Terror

The Secretary of the Communist Party who followed Lenin was Iosif Vissarionovich Dzhugashvili, who adopted the last name of Stalin, meaning steel. Stalin ruled for almost 30 years, up to his death in 1953. In 1928, Stalin initiated the first five-year plan and collectivization of agriculture. Two years later, he began industrialization of the cities. Collectivization, the grouping of all farmlands under State control, proved such a radical departure from the self-ownership rights given to the peasants after the revolution, that many chose to burn their crops rather than give up their land. Along with the devastation caused by the Revolution, civil war and World War I, a widespread famine swept the nation, which eventually killed 10 million people.

The assassination in 1934 of Sergei Kirov, Leningrad Party Chief, signaled the beginning of the Great Terror. Between 1935 and 1941, Stalin persecuted anyone thought to be against him or the state. Suspects were arrested and, without proper trial, either shot or sent to prison camps. Following Stalin's orders, the head of the secret police, Lavrenti Beria, and his officers rounded up every suspect of society: old Bolsheviks, new party members, Red Army corps, intellectuals and *kulaks* (prosperous peasants). Leningrad party leader, Andrei Zhdanov, in his campaign of "Zhdanovshchina," persecuted Leningrad's writers and artists in what is known as the "Leningrad Affair." Eventually the poets Mayakovsky and Yesenin committed suicide. Zhdanov permitted only the art of "Socialist Realism," which he said "aided the process of ideological transformation in the spirit of socialism." No one escaped the purges; even Zhdanov fell from Stalin's grace and was executed in 1948. Of approximately 20 million that were arrested, seven million were immediately shot and the others sent off to the *gulag* camps for rehabilitation. The purges and prisons are described in Alexander Solzhenitsyn's *A Day in the Life of Ivan Denisovich* and *The Gulag Archipeligo*. Stalin wiped out the whole ruling class of Bolsheviks. Half the delegates of the 17th Party Congress were arrested between 1934-39, along with 90% of the military's generals. Within a few decades, the Soviet Union lost an entire generation of its most courageous, creative and devoted citizens—the brains and soul of the nation.

Invasion

In 1941 Hitler invaded the USSR, which now had no more than a skeleton army and a starving, terrorized population. The crippled country battled against the invading German forces; World War II (The Great Patriotic War as it's called in the USSR) lasted for four years. Leningrad was surrounded and cut off from the outside world for 900 days. Today, a monument on the outskirts of Moscow (seen on the way into town from the airport) shows how close the Germans came from capturing the city. Every tenth inhabitant of the USSR was killed, more than 20 million people. One must understand the turmoil experienced by this generation to comprehend why the war continues to play such a significant part in people's lives today.

> "I heard a voice. It promised solace.
> 'Come here,' it seemed to softly call.
> 'Leave Russia, sinning, lost and graceless,
> Leave your land, pray, for good and all. . .'
> With even, calm deliberation
> I raised my hands to stop my ears,
> Lest the ignoble invitation
> Defile a spirit lost in tears.
>
> —Anna Akhmatova

KHRUSHCHEV

Nikita Khrushchev succeeded Stalin in 1953. During the 20th Party Congress in 1956, Khrushchev gave a secret speech, never published, denouncing Stalin. In 1954, after Beria's fall, Khrushchev founded the KGB, Committee for State Security, to establish party control over the secret police. Under the de-Stalinization program, the KGB didn't have the power to hold its own trials and Party officials were exempt from arrest. Khrushchev's new "thaw" campaign attempted to shed light on Stalin's atrocities and challenge the Party's position. He opened up the prison camps and brought home five million people. The political thaw was accompanied by an intellectual and cultural one, with greater freedom of expression for artists and writers. But at the same time, two-thirds of the Orthodox churches and monasteries were closed down.

Khrushchev tried to undo the damage of collectivization by implementing new reforms, but he caused havoc several times by again eradicating the peasants' private plots and ordering the widespread planting of maize.

In 1961, Khrushchev met with U.S. President Kennedy. The same year, the Soviets sent the first man, Yuri Gagarin, into space. Congress also voted to remove Stalin's body from its place of honor alongside Lenin in the Kremlin Mausoleum. Khrushchev began to rebuild Moscow, finally, 15 years after the war. Large-scale housing projects (with communal living residencies), the Palace of Congresses, Kalinin Prospect, and the Rossiya, largest hotel in the world with 6,000 rooms, were constructed. He also turned the Kremlin buildings into a museum that was opened to the public.

Because of his inconsistent policy changes, economic blunders and the Cuban Bay of Pigs fiasco, in 1964 the Party demanded Khrushchev's resignation. His downfall was accelerated by his introduction of Rule 25: No party official should have more than three terms or 15 years in office. The majority of Party members were ready to hold their positions for life. Thus the first inner-Party coup toppled a leader whose insightful ideas weren't realistically considered or implemented until Gorbachev came to power.

BREZHNEV

Khrushchev's successor, Leonid Brezhnev, was said to have plotted the coup with the Party's ideologist, Mikhail Suslov. Brezhnev immediately amended Rule 25. Thanks to the discovery of large gas and oil reserves and the reinstatement of the peasants' private plots, the first part of Brezhnev's term brought the largest boom to the economy since the Revolution. The new détente permitted Western trade, tourists, exchange students and journalists to enter the Soviet Union through Moscow.

But as the wages for blue collar, industrial and farm workers nearly doubled, they failed to increase for the white collar workers and professionals. Consumer goods couldn't keep pace with increasing demands and huge waiting lines appeared for housing and cars. By the mid 1970s, poor planning, mismanagement and lack of incentive led to a crisis in the economy. Rampant corruption also affected every facet of Soviet society. (In 1988, Brezhnev's son-in-law, Yuri Churbanov, Minister of the Interior, was sentenced to 15 years in prison for taking bribes. Yuri's wife Galina had a lavish and scandalous affair with circus manager Boris the Gypsy. Brezhnev himself had a huge collection of antique foreign cars.) In 1968, the Soviet army entered Czechoslovakia. In 1979, military spending was further increased when forces invaded Afghanistan.

As people continued to grow disillusioned with their way of life, alcohol consumption increased (quadrupled since Khrushchev). Further repressions stimulated the dissident and *samizdat* movements. The dissident writers Sinyavsky and Daniel were arrested in Moscow under Article 70 of the criminal code for "spreading anti-Soviet propaganda."

An invalid for many of his last years in office, Leonid Brezhnev died in 1982. The former head of the KGB (1967-82), Yuri Andropov was appointed the new General Secretary. He immediately employed anti-corruption tactics. An illness kept him away from the public eye during his last six months in office. He died in February 1984.

The Soviet playwright, Viktor Rosov, gives this account of his country's leaders: "Stalin created a society as primitive as an iron tomb, where fear was the overriding element. But he decorated this heavy construction with beautiful pictures, flowers and belly dancers. Then Stalin died, and his successor, Khruschev, threw away all the pictures and all the flowers, and tried to move the object. But it was too heavy for him. Then Brezhnev came and made himself very comfortable around the tomb. He put up new pictures. For many, it was very convenient. He had his own people everywhere, and people took bribes. And people should have been prosecuted for that, because there were rules at the time. And now Gorbachev wants to break up the tomb. Whilst Khrushchev inherited a disciplined society, Gorbachev has inherited a corrupt society, and now this is our main grief and sorrow. The society doesn't want to lose its priviliges; that's why the fight is going on and I can't see who will win. I hope Gorbachev will win."

Brezhnev's 72-year-old protégé, Konstantin Chernenko, was elected to replace Andropov. His Prime Minister was 79-year-old Nikolai Tikhonov. His Foreign Minister was 74-year-old Andrei Gromyko, who helped draft postwar agreements in Yalta with Stalin, Roosevelt and Churchill. Chernenko died one year later in March 1985.

GORBACHEV

Radical Reforms
On 11 March 1985, 54-year-old Mikhail Sergeyevich Gorbachev was elected the new General Secretary of the Communist Party. Following in the footsteps of such past rulers as Ivan the Terrible, Peter the Great, Stalin and Brezhnev, Gorbachev inherited a stagnating economy, an entrenched bureaucracy and a population that had lived in fear and mistrust of their previous leaders. Gorbachev's first actions were to shut down the production and sale of vodka and ardently pursue Andropov's anti-corruption campaign; one of the first to go was Leningrad party boss, Grigory Romanov.

On 25 Feb. 1986, the 27th Party Congress endorsed new party programs, changes in the selection methods of officials and elected a new Central Committee. No other Soviet leader in history had consolidated power in the Politburo as quickly as Gorbachev. In 1986, he introduced the radical reform policies of *perestroika* (restructuring), *demokratizatsiya* (democratization) and *glasnost* (openness) that have now become household words. Gorbachev emphasized that past reforms hadn't worked because they didn't stress the "involvement of the people in modernizing and restructuring the country." *Perestroika* implemented more profit motives, quality controls, private ownership in agriculture, decentralization and multi-candidate elections. Industry concentrated on measures promoting quality over quantity; private businesses and cooperatives were encouraged; farmers and individuals could now lease land and housing from the government and keep the profits made from selling produce grown on private plots; hundreds of ministries and bureaucratic centers were disbanded. A law was passed that allowed individuals to own small businesses and hire workers so long as there is "no exploitation of man by man." In the campaign for *demokratizatsiya*, open elec-

Mikhail Gorbachev

tions were held. *Glasnost* let truths surface from the Stalin and Brezhnev years.

Integrating The Russian Character
When Gorbachev came to power, people were instilled with a lack of incentive and morale, and a fear of expression that carried over from the difficulties of past decades. An entire generation had led a two-faced life—one face for the State and the other for themselves. For the first time in decades, Gorbachev worked on integrating the Russian character. Andrei Sakharov and other political prisoners were released from internal exile. (After winning the 1975 Nobel Peace Prize, Sakharov, the physicist and human rights activist, was banished for nearly seven years to the city of Gorky. He died in Moscow on 14 Nov. 1989.) One hundred Soviet dissidents from 20 cities were allowed to form the "Democratic Club," an open political discussion group. *Glasnost* swept like a tidal wave through all facets of Soviet life.

For the 40 million Russian Orthodox and people of other religious beliefs, Gorbachev stated that "believers have the full right to express their convictions with dignity." On 1 Dec. 1989, Gorbachev became the first Soviet leader to set foot in the Vatican. In a historic meeting with Pope John Paul II, Gorbachev promised to open diplomatic relations with the Vatican and that the government soon would pass a law guaranteeing freedom of religion for all believers. In one of his speeches in Rome, Gorbachev expressed that: "We need spiritual values; we need a revolution of the mind. . . . No one should interfere in matters of the individual's conscience.

"Christians, Moslems, Jews, Buddhists and others live in the Soviet Union," he said. "All of them have a right to satisfy their spiritual needs—this is the only way toward a new culture and new politics that can meet the challenge of our time."

Modernization

As Peter the Great had understood, modernization means Westernization, and Gorbachev reopened the window to the West. With the fostering of private business, about five million people are now employed by over 150,000 cooperatives. After 1 April 1989, all enterprises were allowed to carry on trade relations with foreign partners. This triggered the development of joint ventures. Multimillion dollar deals have been established with Western companies such as Chevron, Pepsico, Eastman-Kodak, McDonald's, Time-Warner, and Occidental.

At the 1986 Iceland Summit, Gorbachev proposed to sharply reduce the Soviet stockpile of ballistic missiles. In December 1987, Gorbachev and U.S. President Ronald Reagan signed a treaty at the Washington Summit to eliminate intermediate nuclear missiles. "I do think the winter of mistrust is over," declared Premier Nikolai Ryzhkov. In January 1988, plans to withdraw all forces from Afghanistan were announced. Nine months later Andrei Gromyko retired and Gorbachev was elected President of the Supreme Soviet.

During a visit to Finland in October 1989, Gorbachev declared that "the Soviet Union has no moral or political right to interfere in the affairs of its East European neighbors. They have the right to decide their own fate." Soviet spokesman Gennadi Gerasimov added that Moscow has adopted the "Sinatra Doctrine, 'I Did It My Way.' " And that they did! By the end of 1989, every country throughout Eastern Europe saw its people protest-

ing openly for mass reforms; not in this century has there been such sweeping political change. The Iron Curtain crumbled, symbolized most poignantly by the demolishing of the wall between East and West Berlin.

In December 1989, Gorbachev met with U.S. President George Bush at the Malta Summit, where they agreed that "the arms race, mistrust, psychological and ideological struggle should all be things of the past." An additional summit was held in the United States in the spring of 1990.

ELECTIONS

On 26 March 1989, in the Soviet Union, the first general elections for the new Congress of People's Deputies were held. This was the first time since 1917 that the people actually had a chance to vote in a national election. Fifteen hundred delegates were elected and joined by 750 others, who were elected by other public organizations. This 2,250-delegate body elected 542 members to form a new Supreme Soviet.

Ousted a year earlier from his Politburo post for criticizing the reforms, the Congress candidate Boris Yeltsin won 89% of the Moscow district vote to make a historic comeback. As Moscow crowds chanted, "Yeltsin is a man of the people" and "Down with bureaucrats," a surprising number of bureaucrats had, in fact, lost to people like the Church Metropolitan of Leningrad. Andrei Sakharov was also elected. For the first time in Soviet history, those running unopposed could lose. In the beginning of 1990 the people once again headed for the polls to elect their own regional and district officials. For the first time in seven decades, the voters had the opportunity to chose from other independent and pro-democracy movements. Scores of Communist Party candidates suffered defeat to former political prisoners, adamant reformers, environmentalists and strike leaders. Yeltsin, this time, was voted in as President of the Russian Federative, the Soviet Union's largest republic, which has more than half the country's population and Moscow as its capital. In June 1990, Yeltsin resigned from the Communist Party, stating that "I am announcing my resignation in view of my . . . great responsibility toward the people of Russia and in connection with moves toward a multi-party state. I cannot fulfill only the instructions of the Party."

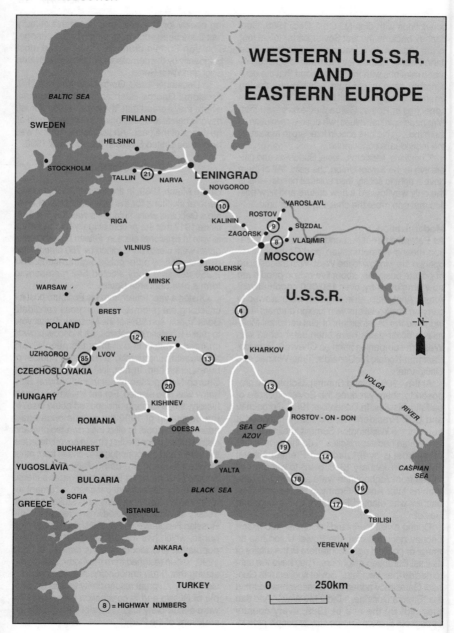

WESTERN U.S.S.R. AND EASTERN EUROPE

BALTIC SEA

SWEDEN

FINLAND

HELSINKI

STOCKHOLM

TALLIN (21) NARVA

LENINGRAD

NOVGOROD

YAROSLAVL

(10)

ROSTOV

RIGA

KALININ (9) SUZDAL

ZAGORSK (8) VLADIMIR

MOSCOW

VILNIUS

(1) SMOLENSK

U.S.S.R.

WARSAW

MINSK

POLAND

BREST

(4)

(12) KIEV

KHARKOV

UZHGOROD (85) LVOV

CZECHOSLOVAKIA

(13)

HUNGARY

(20)

(13)

KISHINEV

ROSTOV - ON - DON

ROMANIA

VOLGA

RIVER

BUCHAREST

ODESSA

SEA OF

AZOV

YUGOSLAVIA

YALTA

(19)

(14)

CASPIAN

SEA

BULGARIA

(18)

(16)

GREECE

SOFIA

BLACK SEA

(17)

ISTANBUL

TBILISI

YEREVAN

ANKARA

-N-

TURKEY   0   250km

(8) = HIGHWAY NUMBERS

ECONOMY

However, for all the unprecedented reforms and innovative policies, Gorbachev hasn't been able to bring the country's economy out of stagnation and he's losing his popularity at home. In an extensive poll conducted in the Soviet Union, the survey found more than 90% considered the economic situation in the country critical. Some of the disheartened have commented that "*glasnost* has produced more copies of Solzhenitsyn than salami." Food and fuel are in critically low supply and the population is expecting the worst food shortages since World War II. Ration coupons are being issued for meat, sugar, tea and soap. After a recent launching of a probe to Mars, graffiti in Moscow appeared, exclaiming "To Mars for Soap!" Modernization doesn't approach Western standards—there are few computers and most areas still use the abacus. It's estimated that 40% of the crops are wasted because of poor storage, packing and distribution methods. Many Soviets express that their living conditions have worsened. "We live like dogs. The leash has become longer but the meat is a bit smaller, and the plate is two meters further away. But at least we can now bark as much as we want," goes a joke in Moscow.

Gorbachev is also faced with a budget deficit of over 100 billion rubles. The severe shortages have created a virtual black-market economy. Up to 85% of the population get many of their goods from the black market. There's an increasing number of black marketeers, the *fartsovshiki,* (many of whom exchange goods only for foreign currency), prostitutes, and Mafia gangs. On 1 Nov. 1989, the government drastically cut the bank ruble exchange rate by 90% in order to curb black-market exchanges (up to 20 times above the official rate) and to bring the ruble closer to an open exchange on the world market. The Prime Minister has stated that 43 million people (15% of the population) live below the poverty level. There're also an estimated 23 million unemployed, the new paradox of modern Soviet society.

On top of failing measures and political contradictions, a series of disasters struck that have cost the nation billions: Chernobyl, the earthquake in Armenia, ethnic unrest, and extensive strikes in mines and factories across the country (a 1989 law legalized strikes). But Gorbachev remains confident and presses on with *perestroika.* "This is a turbulent time, a turbulent sea in which it's not easy to sail the ship. But we have a compass and we have a crew to guide that ship, and the ship itself is strong."

We can't forget, as one Westerner observed, that "the amazing thing about *perestroika* is not that the Soviets are doing it well, but that they are doing it at all." One Soviet ideologist pointed out that "Gorbachev has removed our ideological

a Moscow market

blinders. From the time of Stalin through Chernenko, we viewed the world basically as being in a state of transition from capitalism to communism. Now we see that that was an illusion." At the United Nations in December 1988, Gorbachev called for a foreign policy between nations that is based on interdependence, no longer regarded as a capitalist-socialist struggle. "We have abandoned the claim to have a monopoly on the truth; we no longer think that we are right, or that those that disagree with us are our enemies."

THE SOVIET UNION TODAY

A New Order

Mikhail Gorbachev has unleashed the forces of change and, in a country of 289 million people, it will take years to witness the full effects of his reforms. "Empty store shelves and housing problems," stated a Soviet economist, "have made the process difficult, but something absolutely vital has taken place in Russian terms: a change in our way of thinking."

Time magazine named Mikhail Gorbachev the "Man of the Decade," calling him "the Copernicus, Darwin and Freud of Communism all wrapped in one" and the man responsible for ending the Cold War. On 7 Feb. 1990, after 72 years of Communist rule, the Soviet Communist Party's Central Committee voted overwhelmingly to surrender its monopoly of power. On 15 March 1990, the Soviet Congress of People's Deputies amended Article Six, which had guaranteed the Communist Party as the only "leading authority" in government. In its revised form, Article Six states that the Communists, together with "other politcal parties" and social organizations, have the right to shape state policy. During the 28th Party Congress, the Party voted to reorganize its ruling body, the Politburo, to include Communist Party leaders from each of the 15 republics, in addition to the top 12 Moscow officials; it is expected to grow to as many as 23 voting members. Instead of being selected by the Central Committee, the Party in each republic will choose its own leaders, guaranteeing a voice in the Party to even the smallest republic.

Vladimir Ivashko from the Ukraine was elected the first Deputy General Secretary, a new position created to assist the General Secretary.

Other amendments revised the Marxist view that private property is incompatible with socialism. Individuals may now own land and factories as long as they do not "exploit" other Soviet citizens. New economic policies plan to replace direct central planning, instill new price reforms and even create a stock exchange; farmers may soon sell their produce on the open market. Additional new laws decree that "the press and other mass media are free. Censorship of the mass media is forbidden," and "all political movements will have access to the airwaves with the right to establish their own television and radio stations." The Communist Party no longer has a monopoly on the state-run radio and television. These historic votes pave the way for a multiparty democracy and a free-market economy.

Executive President

In one of the most important changes in this country's political and economic system since the 1917 Bolshevik Revolution, Mikhail Gorbachev was elected by the Congress as the Soviet Union's first executive President. This new post, over the old honorary chairman of the Supreme Soviet, has broader constitutional powers; the President now has the right to propose legislation, veto bills passed by Congress, appoint and fire the Prime Minister and other senior government officials and declare states of emergency (with the republics' approval). In a speech to the Congress after he was sworn in, Gorbachev stated that "the need for a more radical *perestroika* is obvious, and I shall use my presidential powers first of all to achieve this."

Gorbachev himself summarized the results of all his policies. "Having embarked upon the road of radical reform, we have crossed the line beyond which there is no return to the past. . . . Things will never be the same again in the Soviet Union," or, for that matter, in the whole socialist world. Gorbachev's second revolution has become one of the most momentous events in the second half of the 20th century.

GOVERNMENT

Communist Party

The Bolshevik Party, formed by Lenin, began as a unified band of revolutionaries. The 8,000 members organized the mass strike of the 1905 St. Petersburg revolt. By October 1917, the proletariat movement had over 300,000 members. Many of these became the leaders and planners for the newly formed Soviet State. Lenin changed the name Bolshevik to Communist, the only political party then allowed in the State. In the 1930s, membership grew to 3.5 million. Today there are 20 million Party members, seven percent of the total population (30% of whom are women). Membership is open to any citizen who "does not exploit the labor of others," abides by the Party's philosophy, and gives three percent of their monthly pay as dues to the Party. Members are also required to attend several meetings and lectures every month, provide volunteer work a few times a year and help with election campaigns. Of the 20 million, one percent, or about 200,000, are full-time officials, *apparatchiks,* who are paid by the Party. The Komsomol, Communist Youth Organization, has 40 million members. Twenty-five million school children belong to the Young Pioneers. Eligibility for party membership begins at age 18.

The Communist ideology of Marxism-Leninism unites the Party. Under Lenin's "democratic-centralism" policy, the proletariat is led by the Party, which can help set policies, standards and guidelines, but cannot pass laws.

Democratic Socialism

For over seven decades, the Communist Party was, under Article Six of the Constitution, the sole "leading and guiding force" in Soviet society. It was headed by the General Secretary. About every five years the Party Congress elected a 200-plus-member Central Committee, which in turn elected the Politburo and Secretariat. The 12 members of the Politburo headed the Central Committee. The Party Congress met a few times a year to determine Party policy. The numerous departments were run by the Secretariat, which executed Party policy and handled the day-to-day administrative details. Over two million regional and local deputies carried out Party policy, organized members and ran party functions, from districts down to each individual workplace.

During a historic meeting of the Congress of People's Deputies in March 1990, the Communist Party lost its monopoly on power; Article Six was amended to read that the Communists and "other

May Day celebration

politcal parties" now have the right to shape policies of the state. During the 1990 28th Party Congress in Moscow, the Soviet Communist Party voted to transform its ruling body, the Politburo, into a broader-based group. For the first time, the reorganized Politburo will include Party representatives from each of the 15 republics, along with other top Moscow party officials. Instead of being appointed by the Central Committee, each republic will elect its own representative. The new position of Deputy General Secretary was also created; this person will assist the General Secretary in Party duties.

The Party wants to break with the "authoritarian-bureaucratic system" and develop a "humane democratic socialism." With multiparty elections, the Communist Party will no longer be the sole authority in governing the nation. The planned overhaul of the political system transfers power from the Communist Party to the executive and legislative branches of government.

In the first six months after the government allowed the formation of new political parties, taking away the monopoly of the Communist Party, over 200,000 members (including Boris Yeltsin, President of the Russian Federation) quit the Communist Party. Tens of thousands of people have participated in mass demonstrations outside the Kremlin calling for their comrades to defect from

it ranks. Such a split in the beliefs of the people hasn't been felt nor expressed this widely and openly since the Party originally split into the Bolshevik and Menshevik sides during the 1917 Revolution.

Congresses

The center for the country's governing bodies is in Moscow. The 2,250-delegate Congress of People's Deputies (now voted for by the public) elects members to the 542-member Supreme Soviet. This legislative body is divided into two chambers: the Soviet (or Council) of the Union and the Soviet of Nationalities. The Supreme Soviet is now headed by the new office of Executive President. The People's Congress meets a few times a year to discuss and decide upon broad policies; the Supreme Soviet is in session about eight months a year. In between sessions of the Supreme Soviet, the Presidium assumes the power to govern. The Council of Ministers presides over each of the individual ministries and state committees.

The Congress of People's Deputies acts as a parliament and the Supreme Soviet mandates the law. The Council of Ministers functions as the executive of the laws and policies. The President, now with broader executive powers, acts as the head of government.

THE RUSSIAN LANGUAGE

History

In the late 9th century, two Greek brothers, Methodius and Cyril (both renowned scholars from Macedonia), converted vernacular Slavic into a written language so that teachings of Byzantine Orthodoxy could be translated for the Slavs. Many of the letters were derived from the Greek—the Slavic alphabet was called Cyrillic, after Cyril. When Prince Vladimir brought Christian Orthodoxy into Kievan Rus in the 10th century, Slavonic became the language of the Church. Church Slavonic, written in the Cyrillic alphabet, remained the literary and liturgical language of Russia for over seven centuries.

In 1710, Peter the Great simplified Church Cyrillic into the "civil alphabet" *(grazhdansky shrift),* a written form used in secular books. The two types of writing, the older script of the Church and Peter's revised version, were both employed in Russia up to the time of Lomonosov and the poet Pushkin, who were largely responsible for combining the two into a national language for the Russian people. The alphabet that is used today was further simplified after the October Revolution.

Letters And Words

Russian is the official language of the Soviet Union. Even though English is spoken in major hotels and on tour routes, it's not widely spoken anywhere else. Everything, everywhere is written in the Cyrillic alphabet, with few translations.

Therefore, it's recommended that you learn letters of the Russian alphabet before your trip. This way you can sound out and recognize many of the words, and feel much more at ease in the new environment. Besides, it's fun to walk down the streets and identify many of the signs and shops.

Once you can recognize Cyrillic letters, you can then work on Russian vocabulary and phrases. You'll be surprised how simple it really is to communicate without a common language! A few gestures and simple Russian expressions can go quite far and bring smiles to many faces! Purchase a comprehensive Russian phrasebook that you can show to the non-English speaking people whom you meet. For example, a Berlitz pocket-size language guide with sections on everything from dining to dentists can be found in most bookstores.

Pronunciation

Russian sounds correspond to many of the English ones, but sometimes the letters for these sounds are different. For example, a Russian B is an English V, C is S, U is pronounced E, and a P is an R sound. Many sounds are written the same, as A, O, K and M. There is no English W (water) sound in Russian; a "W" is a "SH" sound. Thus Masha is written MAWA and Sasha CAWA. Viktor is BUKTOP. For an introduction to the spoken language, buy a few introductory Russian language tapes.

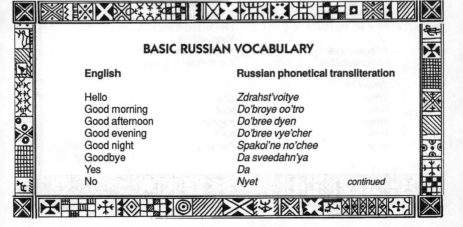

BASIC RUSSIAN VOCABULARY

English	Russian phonetical transliteration
Hello	*Zdrahst'voitye*
Good morning	*Do'broye oo'tro*
Good afternoon	*Do'bree dyen*
Good evening	*Do'bree vye'cher*
Good night	*Spakoi'ne no'chee*
Goodbye	*Da sveedahn'ya*
Yes	*Da*
No	*Nyet*

continued

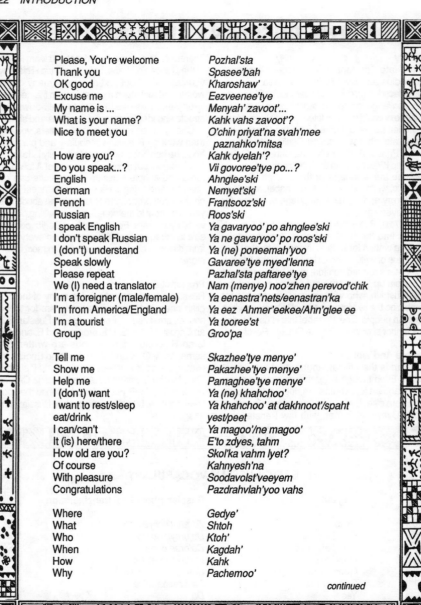

English	Russian
Please, You're welcome	*Pozhal'sta*
Thank you	*Spasee'bah*
OK good	*Kharoshaw'*
Excuse me	*Eezveenee'tye*
My name is ...	*Menyah' zavoot'...*
What is your name?	*Kahk vahs zavoot'?*
Nice to meet you	*O'chin priyat'na svah'mee paznahko'mitsa*
How are you?	*Kahk dyelah'?*
Do you speak...?	*Vii govoree'tye po...?*
English	*Ahnglee'ski*
German	*Nemyet'ski*
French	*Frantsooz'ski*
Russian	*Roos'ski*
I speak English	*Ya gavaryoo' po ahnglee'ski*
I don't speak Russian	*Ya ne gavaryoo' po roos'ski*
I (don't) understand	*Ya (ne) poneemah'yoo*
Speak slowly	*Gavaree'tye myed'lenna*
Please repeat	*Pazhal'sta paftaree'tye*
We (I) need a translator	*Nam (menye) noo'zhen perevod'chik*
I'm a foreigner (male/female)	*Ya eenastra'nets/eenastran'ka*
I'm from America/England	*Ya eez Ahmer'eekee/Ahn'glee ee*
I'm a tourist	*Ya tooree'st*
Group	*Groo'pa*
Tell me	*Skazhee'tye menye'*
Show me	*Pakazhee'tye menye'*
Help me	*Pamaghee'tye menye'*
I (don't) want	*Ya (ne) khahchoo'*
I want to rest/sleep	*Ya khahchoo' at dakhnoot'/spaht*
eat/drink	*yest/peet*
I can/can't	*Ya magoo'/ne magoo'*
It (is) here/there	*E'to zdyes, tahm*
How old are you?	*Skol'ka vahm lyet?*
Of course	*Kahnyesh'na*
With pleasure	*Soodavolst'veeyem*
Congratulations	*Pazdrahvlah'yoo vahs*
Where	*Gedye'*
What	*Shtoh*
Who	*Ktoh'*
When	*Kagdah'*
How	*Kahk*
Why	*Pachemoo'*

continued

How much/many	Skol'ka
How much does it cost?	Skol'ka stoi'eet?
I	Ya
He	Ohn
She	Ahna'
It	Ahno'
You-informal	Tii (Like German Du and French Tu)
We	Mii
You-formal/plural	Vii (Like German Sie and French Vous)
They	Ahnee'

Man	Moozhchee'na
Woman	Zhen'shcheena
Boy	Mahl'cheek
Girl	Dye'vooshka
Father	Atyets'
Mother	Maht
Brother	Braht
Sister	Sestrah'
Grandfather	Dye'dooshka
Grandmother	Ba'booshka
Husband	Moozh
Wife	Zhenah'

Airport

Airplane	Samolyot'
Flight	Reys
Arrival	Prilyot'
Departure	Vylyit
Boarding	Pacad'ka
Baggage	Bagazh'
My passport	Moy pas'port
My visa	Maya' vee'za
My ticket	Moy beelyet'
Suitcase(s)	Chemodahn' (ee)
Porter	Naseel'shchik
I want to go to the airport	Ya khachoo' f aeroport'

Hotel

I want to go to the hotel	Ya khachoo' f gastee'neetsu
Where is the hotel?	Gedye' gastee'neetsa?
Where is Intourist?	Gedye' Intooreest'
Floor lady	Dezhoor'naya
Maid	Gor'nichnaya

continued

(clockwise from top) Golden Ring cathedral; summer dacha;
wooden cathedrals predate the grander ones of stone and marble

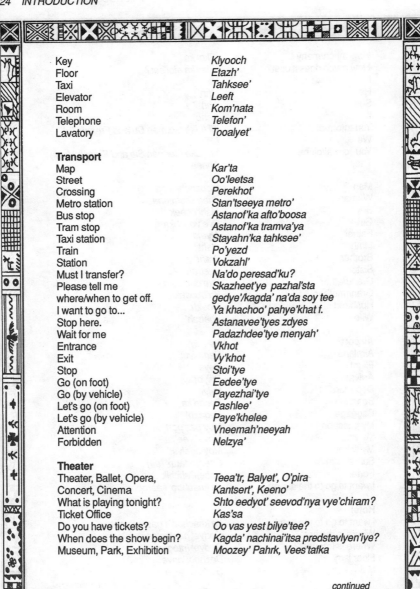

Key   *Klyooch*
Floor   *Etazh'*
Taxi   *Tahksee'*
Elevator   *Leeft*
Room   *Kom'nata*
Telephone   *Telefon'*
Lavatory   *Tooalyet'*

Transport
Map   *Kar'ta*
Street   *Oo'leetsa*
Crossing   *Perekhot'*
Metro station   *Stan'tseeya metro'*
Bus stop   *Astanof'ka afto'boosa*
Tram stop   *Astanof'ka tramva'ya*
Taxi station   *Stayahn'ka tahksee'*
Train   *Po'yezd*
Station   *Vokzahl'*
Must I transfer?   *Na'do peresad'ku?*
Please tell me   *Skazheet'ye pazhal'sta*
where/when to get off.   *gedye'/kagda' na'da soy tee*
I want to go to...   *Ya khachoo' pahye'khat f.*
Stop here.   *Astanavee'tyes zdyes*
Wait for me   *Padazhdee'tye menyah'*
Entrance   *Vkhot*
Exit   *Vy'khot*
Stop   *Stoi'tye*
Go (on foot)   *Eedee'tye*
Go (by vehicle)   *Payezhai'tye*
Let's go (on foot)   *Pashlee'*
Let's go (by vehicle)   *Paye'khelee*
Attention   *Vneemah'neeyah*
Forbidden   *Nelzya'*

Theater
Theater, Ballet, Opera,   *Teea'tr, Balyet', O'pira*
Concert, Cinema   *Kantsert', Keeno'*
What is playing tonight?   *Shto eedyot' seevod'nya vye'chiram?*
Ticket Office   *Kas'sa*
Do you have tickets?   *Oo vas yest bilye'tee?*
When does the show begin?   *Kagda' nachinai'itsa predstavlyen'iye?*
Museum, Park, Exhibition   *Moozey' Pahrk, Vees'tafka*

continued

Days of the Week

Monday	*Paneedyel'nik*
Tuesday	*Ftor'nik*
Wednesday	*Sreda'*
Thursday	*Chetvyerk'*
Friday	*Pyat'neetsa*
Saturday	*Sooboh'ta*
Sunday	*Vaskresyen'ye*

Today	*Sevod'nya*
Yesterday	*Fcherah'*
Tomorrow	*Zahf'tra*
Morning	*Oo'trom*
Day	*Dyen*
Evening	*Ve'cherom*
Night	*Noch*
Week	*Nedehl'ya*
Month	*Meh'sats*
What time is it?	*Kator'ee chahs?*

Characteristics

Good/Bad	*Kharoshaw/Plo'kha*
Big/Small	*Ballshoy'/Mal'enkee*
Open/Closed	*Atkri'to/Zakri'to*
Cold/Warm/Hot	*Kho'lodno/Zhar'ko/Gory ach'ee*
Left/Right	*Le'vo/Prah'vo*
Straight ahead	*Preeyah'mo*
(not) Beautiful	*(ne) Krahcee'vo*
(not) Interesting	*(ne) Eenteres'no*
Quick/Slow	*Bi'stra/Med'lenna*
Much(Many)/Few	*Mino'ga/Mah'lo*
Early/Late/Now	*Rah'no/Poz'no/Saychas'*
Fun/Boring	*Vesyol'ye/Skoosh'no*
(not) Delicious	*(ne) Fkoos'no*
Possible/Impossible	*Mozh'no/Nevozmozh'no*

Numbers

One	*Adeen'*
Two	*Dvah*
Three	*Tree*
Four	*Chetir'ee*
Five	*Pyaht*

continued

Six	*Shest*
Seven	*Syem*
Eight	*Vo'syem*
Nine	*Dye'vyet*
Ten	*Dyes'yat*
Eleven	*Adeen'natset*
Twelve	*Dvenaht'set*
Thirteen	*Treenaht'set*
Fourteen	*Chetir'nahtset*
Fifteen	*Pyatnaht'set*
Sixteen	*Shesnaht'set*
Seventeen	*Semnaht'set*
Eighteen	*Vasemnaht'set*
Nineteen	*Devyatnaht'set*
Twenty	*Dvaht'set*
Thirty	*Treet'set*
Forty	*So'rak*
Fifty	*Pyidesyaht'*
Sixty	*Shestdesyat'*
Seventy	*Sem'desyet*
Eighty	*Vo'semdesyet*
Ninety	*Dyevenos'ta*
One hundred	*Sto*
One thousand	*Tis'yacha*

CYRILLIC ALPHABET
WITH APPROXIMATE PRONUNCIATION

PRINTED	WRITTEN	APPROXIMATE PRONUNCIATION
Аа	*Аа*	*a* as in "father"
Бб	*Бб*	*b* as in "book"
Вв	*Вв*	*v* as in "vote"
Гг	*Гг*	*g* as in "good"
Дд	*Дд*	*d* as in "day"
Ее	*Ее*	*ye* as in "yes"
Ёё	*Ёё*	*yo* as in "yonder"
Жж	*Жж*	*s* as in "pleasure"
Зз	*Зз*	*z* as in "zone"
Ии	*Ии*	*ee* as in "meet"
Йй	*Йй*	*y* as in "boy"
Кк	*Кк*	*k* as in "kind"
Лл	*Лл*	*l*
Мм	*Мм*	*m* as in "man"
Нн	*Нн*	*n* as in "note"
Оо	*Оо*	*o* as in "pot"
Пп	*Пп*	*p* as in "pet"
Рр	*Рр*	*r*
Сс	*Сс*	*s* as in "speak"
Тт	*Тт*	*t* as in "too"
Уу	*Уу*	*oo* as in "fool"
Фф	*Фф*	*f* as in "fire"
Хх	*Хх*	*kh*
Цц	*Цц*	*tz* as in "quartz"
Чч	*Чч*	*ch* as in "chair"
Шш	*Шш*	*sh* as in "short"
Щщ	*Щщ*	*shch*
Ъъ	*Ъъ*	hard sign (silent)
Ыы	*Ыы*	no equivalent, but close to *ee*
Ьь	*Ьь*	soft sign (silent)
Ээ	*Ээ*	*e* as in "men"
Юю	*Юю*	*u* as in "university"
Яя	*Яя*	*ya* as in "yard"

RELIGION

Orthodoxy

Before Prince Vladimir introduced Byzantine Christianity to the Kievan principality in 988, Russia was a pagan state; the people of Rus worshipped numerous gods. Festivals were held according to the seasons, planting and harvest cycles, and life passages. Special offerings of eggs, wheat and honey were presented to the gods of water, soil and sun. Carved figures of mermaids and suns adorned the roofs of houses. When Prince Vladimir married the sister of the Byzantine emperor and brought in Christianity, Russia finally united under one God, and Kiev became the center of the Orthodox Church. But it took almost a century to convert the many pagan areas, especially in the north.

Churches

Earliest church architecture (11th century) was based on the Byzantine cube-shaped building with one low rounded cupola on the roof bearing an Orthodox cross facing east. The domes gradually evolved into helmet drums on tent-shaped or square, sloping roofs. These drums eventually took on the distinctive onion shape suitable for the heavy snowfalls. By the end of the 16th century, three to five domes, with one dominant central dome, were commonly installed atop Orthodox places of worship. The next two centuries brought in classical and baroque influences, and the onion domes were elaborately shaped and decorated. During a tour of the Golden Ring, try dating the churches by the shape of their domes.

The outer walls were divided into three sections by protruding vertical strips, which indicated the position of the piers inside the church. A few centuries later, the churches expanded considerably, and built from white stone or brick instead of wood. (Unfortunately, many of the wooden buildings did not survive and stone churches were built on their original site.) The main body of the church was tiered into different levels and adjoined by chapels, galleries and porches. A large tent-shaped belltower usually dominated one side.

During the two and a half centuries of Mongol occupation (beginning in the mid-13th century), Russia was cut off from any outside influence. Monasteries united the Russian people and acted as shelters and fortresses against attacks. They became the educational centers and housed the historical manuscripts, which monks wrote on birch-bark parchment. During this period, Russian church architecture developed a style all its own. Some distinctive features were the decorative *zakomara,* semi-circular arches that lined the tops of the outer walls where they joined the roof. The *trapeza* porch was built outside the western entrance of the church and other carved designs were copied from the decorations on peasant houses. Elaborate carved gables around doors, windows and archways were called *kokoshnik,* named after the large headdresses worn by young married women. Even though, through the years, the architecture took on elements of European classical, Gothic and baroque, the designs always retained a distinctive Russian flare. Each entrance of the *kremlin* had its own gate church. The most elaborate stood by the Holy Gates, the

The Orthodox churches offered both spiritual and physical shelter to Russian peasants.

main entrance to the town. Many cathedrals in the posad took years to build and twin-churches were also a common sight—one was used in winter and the other, more elaborate, for summer services and festivals.

The interior of the church was highly decorated with frescoes. Images of Christ were painted inside the central dome, surrounded by angels. Beneath the dome came the pictures of saints, apostles and prophets. Pillars held certain other saints, such as the patron saint of the church. Special religious scenes and the earthly life of Christ or the Virgin Mary were depicted on the walls and vaults. The Transfiguration was usually painted on the east wall by the altar and scenes from the Last Judgment and Old Testament were illustrated on the west wall, where the people would exit the church. The iconostasis was an elaborate tiered structure, filled with icons, that stretched behind the altar from the floor toward the ceiling. The top tiers held Christ, the middle the saints and prophets, and the lower tiers were reserved for scenes from church history. Fresco painting was a highly respected skill and many master craftsmen, such as Andrei Rublev and Daniil Chorny, produced beautiful works of art. The plaster was applied to the wall of the church, and then the artists would sketch the main outline of the fresco right on to the damp plaster. The master supervised the work and filled in the more intricate and important parts of the composition, while the apprentices added the background detail.

The building of elaborate churches and painting of exquisite icons and frescoes reached its zenith in the prosperous towns of the Golden Ring. Even cathedrals in the Moscow Kremlin were copied from church designs that originated in Rostov, Vladimir and Suzdal. Today these churches and works of art stand as monuments to an extraordinary era of Russian history.

After The Revolution

For nearly 1,000 years, the Russian Orthodox Church dominated the life of Russia and, as Tolstoy observed, for most of the Russian people, "faith was the force of life." But after the 1917 Revolution, based on Marx's proclaimation that "religion is the opiate of the people," all churches were closed to religious use and their property confiscated and redistributed by the government. Article 124 of the Soviet Constitution states that "church is separate from state" and provides "freedom of worship for all citizens." Before the Revolution, Russia had almost 100,000 churches and monasteries; today the country has fewer than 10,000 (with an increase of 3,000 in the last few years) that are open for religious activities. There are about 50 million Orthodox believers, 15% of whom are regular church attenders. Leningrad, a city of five million people, has only 18 churches.

In 1988, the Millenium of Russian Christianity was officially celebrated throughout the Soviet Union and government decrees provided a new legal status for the Orthodox Church and other religions. The Russian Orthodox Church remains headed by the Patriarch and assisted by the Holy Synod, whose seats are in Zagorsk and Moscow. But the government continues to control and dictate the moves of the Church. The topic of religion is scheduled to be discussed in future meetings of the Supreme Soviet. Positive signs of increased religious tolerance and freedom are emerging; a small number of churches, for example, have been officially given back for religious use. More people, especially the younger generation, are attending church services and being baptized. Theological seminaries are training monks and priests and church charity organizations are now permitted to help the poor, unemployed and homeless, the new paradox of Soviet society.

One well-respected Leningrad rector of the Orthodox Church and city seminary (who was recently allowed to visit Rome for a visit with the Pope) remarked that "in principle, even with *perestroika*, nothing has changed. We've been waiting for 70 years for a law, allowing the church to govern itself. But I'm an optimist. People aren't only interested in bettering themselves economically, but also morally and spiritually as well. The powers of the State cannot extend to the soul. And in these uncertain times, we would like to help the new generation find their way."

Many other religious groups are also enjoying a new period of openness. There are 1.5 million officially registered Jews (given as their nationality), four million Roman Catholics, five million Uniates (Catholics of Eastern Rite), over a million Baptists, two million Lutherans, a quarter million Pentecostalists, 50,000 each of Mennonites, Seventh-day Adventists and Jehovah's Witnesses, a half-million Buddhists, 5.5 million Moslems and about a million Old Believers, a sect resulting from the 1666 schism of the Orthodox Church.

ART

THE RUSSIAN ICON

For nearly a millenium, the Russian icon portrayed the spiritual and aesthetic ideals, as well as the historical events and lifestyles of Old Russia. Soon after Prince Vladimir introduced Christianity in A.D. 988, Byzantium's art and ideals were absorbed into Russian culture. The word icon stems from the Greek *eikon,* meaning "image"; icons portrayed the likenesses of Christ, the Virgin, saints and martyrs. Byzantium's influence dissipated during the Mongol invasions in the mid-13th century when the northern regions of Russia became greatly isolated. Between the 14th and 16th centuries, several schools of icon painting, each with its own unique style, were established. The main schools were the Novgorod, Pskov, Moscow and Central Russian. Each retained some of the original elements of color and design from early Byzantine influence.

The Colors Of Spiritual Power

The purpose of the icon was to bring spiritual power to light. The icon's own light and color mirrored the sacred qualities of the celestial world. In addition, the icon's impersonation of the divine and earthly planes was based on a hierarchy of colors: the tops were white, purple and gold, which symbolized, as in many other religions, divine light, purity, salvation and love. Blue and green, the earthy colors, represented vitality and hope, and red portrayed the Holy Spirit's flame, divine influence, and the burning fire of faith and martyrdom. Black was derived from Russia's old folk beliefs: the darkness of the underworld and the emptiness of the Non-Believer.

The Novgorod school mainly used a symmetrical design and painted in bold and simple outlines using red, white and black. The iconographers of Pskov, one of the last Russian lands to be annexed to Moscovy, developed a more dynamic style, using dramatic color schemes of gold, green, red and yellow. The Central Russian school was greatly affected by the Moscow and Novgorod styles, and used blue as its dominant color, with rich color schemes of orange, green and brown. It was located in the Golden Ring towns of Rostov, Pereslavl-Zalessky, Palekh, Yaroslavl, Vladimir and Suzdal.

Layers Of Icons

Icons were painted on panels of wood with tempera paints. Designs were initially sketched with chalk or charcoal and then filled in with colors. First glazes, and then a varnish of linseed oil, were applied to the completed work. But after about 80 years the linseed oil darkened the icon, at which time another artist usually painted over the original design. With some icons, this process was repeated many times. Today, restorers can remove the paint layer by layer to bring back many of the original portraits. These efforts have been especially concentrated in churches in Moscow and the Golden Ring area.

Icons were at the center of Old Russian art and were kept in churches, chapels and homes. Later the Iconostasis, a number of small icons layered together on wooden or stone tiers, were painted as well. This allowed Christ, the Virgin and numerous saints to be brought together as one entity.

Old Testament Trinity *by Andrei Rublev*

Andrei Rublev

By the beginning of the 15th century, Andrei Rublev had emerged as the main figure of icon art. The master painted in Moscow, establishing it as the new center of icon painting. No one is quite sure of the year of Rublev's birth, but his name became a symbol for the highest values in Old Russian art and his innovative style had a profound effect on the other schools. Rublev painted icons for the Grand-Prince of Moscovy. In his later life he became a monk, lived at the Spaso-Andronikov Monastery in Moscow, and painted frescoes in the Cathedral of Our Savior. He died there in 1430.

Lives Of Their Own

Rublev's technique was asymmetrical in form and his colorful images narrative and harmonious in tone. He meticulously individualized his portraits and gave each figure a life of its own. Instead of the simple Novgorod outline, Rublev's personages were enveloped with character and movement. Rublev also used the circle as a symbol for the unity of life, and angels and saints were portrayed in real-life scenes on Earth surrounded by rocks, trees and animals. Allegorical symbols were introduced: Christ wore purple robes; the golden chalice contained a calf's head; and angels held trumpets or swords. Dark and somber colors gave way to vibrant greens, blues and yellows. Attention was paid to background; gems and metal were even added to the setting.

Both Theophanes, Greek leader of the Novgorod school during the late 14th-century, and Rublev painted frescoes and the Iconostasis in the Cathedral of the Annunciation in the Moscow Kremlin; he and Daniil Chorny painted in the Cathedral of the Assumption in Vladimir, where the icons and frescoes are still visible today. In the Trinity-St. Sergius Monastery, Rublev portrayed the famous religious figure of Old Russia. St. Sergius blessed Dmitry Donskoi before the decisive Battle of Kulikovo, where Donskoi defeated the Mongols in 1380. For once, icons not only symbolized God, but also the events of human life. The saint's blessing (as portrayed in *The Old Testament Trinity*) symbolized the Russian's desire for freedom and unity; the Eucharist symbolized the sacrifice in battle, and the chalice hope, faith and the common bond of the Russian people.

Over 500 Years Old

Many of Rublev's works were lost through the centuries, destroyed in fires, painted over, or whitewashed. But today some of his works, such as the *Virgin of Vladimir,* can still be found in the Vladimir-Suzdal Museum; the *Archangel Michael, The Savior, Apostle Paul* and *The Old Testament Trinity* can be viewed in the Tretyakov Gallery in Moscow. Other works are exhibited at the Rublev Museum in the Andronikov Monastery. The British author Robert Byron, in viewing Rublev's icons during a trip to Moscow in the early 1930s, wrote: Rublev "has produced paintings which have no like in European art. Even in the faces [of the Old Testament Trinity] the touch of genius is apparent . . . the poetry of the country lives in his paint . . . In those grave, whiteless eyes and sad small mouth [of the Virgin of Vladimir] live the eternal sorrows, joys and the whole destiny of man. Such a picture can bring tears to the eye and peace to the soul."

The genius of Andrei Rublev can be compared to other major artists of Renaissance Europe such as Giotto and Raphael. He was so revered that a century after his death, the Church Council decreed that the style of Rublev's icons were the true standard of artistic Orthodoxy. It was Rublev's desire in life to help lead the world out of its darkness and despair and back into realms of beauty, harmony and love. By capturing the eternal goodness on a simple and timeless icon, Andrei Rublev achieved his own immortality and will always live in the hearts of those who view his work.

RUSSIAN FOLK CRAFTS

Different regions of early Russia were recognized for their special handicrafts. Towns along the Golden Ring were known for their lacquered paintings and trays, papier mâché products, embroidered shawls and clay pottery. Ceramics included hand painted plates, and jugs made for *kvas,* the national drink made from fermented black bread.

The *matryoshka* doll, a nest of colorfully painted wooden dolls, has become the traditional Russian souvenir. First appearing in Russia in the 1890s, the *matryona* doll was later called by its diminutive form, the *matryoshka.* The *matryoshkas* represented wooden peasant girls, carved and painted in traditional Russian dress, with *sarafan* jumpers,

embroidered blouses and elaborate *kokoshniki* headdresses. Later dolls were painted holding flowers, samovars or ring-shaped bread. The *matryoshka* attained popularity when it was shown abroad at the 1900 World Exhibition in Paris. Orders came in from America, Great Britain, France and Germany and the first workshops were set up in the Golden Ring town of Sergeiyev Posad, now called Zagorsk. The dolls were carved from dried linden or birch wood. Up to 24 smaller dolls could be found within the largest, which also included Russian lads, *boyar* families or fairy-tale characters. One of the earliest *matryoshka* dolls ever made is preserved at the Museum of Toys in Zagorsk. Today, in keeping with tradition, *matryoshka* dolls, painted with their traditional costumes, are still being made in Zagorsk.

Craftsmen in villages surrounding Zagorsk had for centuries carved furniture, chests and boxes. In the 15th and 16th centuries, the towns of Zagorsk and Bogorodskoye were famous for their wooden toys; the Trinity-St. Sergius Monastery had its own special carving school. The founder of this monastery, Sergius Rodonezhsky, used to present carved horses, bears and troikas to the children of the town. Later, more comical and movable toys were carved depicting monks and merchants. By 1900, over 150 different types of dolls were being carved.

Icons And Boxes

The Golden Ring town of Palekh was famous for its hand-painted lacquered boxes. Before the Revolution, Palekh was an icon-painting center, whose artists painted and restored icons and took care of the churches in the Moscow Kremlin, Novgorod and St. Petersburg. After the 1917 uprising, icons were no longer allowed to be painted. Instead the artists began painting lacquered boxes, reproducing copies of famous Russian paintings and scenes from Russian fairy tales.

One of the most famous Russian box painters was Ivan Golikov, who lived from 1886-1937. Golikov attended the St. Petersburg Arts Academy and painted frescoes in the churches. After the Revolution, Golikov worked as a theater decorator. During this time, he began a long friendship with the writer Maxim Gorky, who often asked Golikov to illustrate his texts. Eventually Golikov re-

a hand-painted box (see detail next page)

turned to his native Palekh to take up box painting. Gorky himself said that "the masters of Palekh carry on the icon painting traditions through their boxes . . . and with these beautiful achievements, win the admiration of all who see them."

The box was fashioned from linden or birch wood and usually varnished black on the outside with a red interior. The top of the box was dusted with a special powder and the outline of the painting sketched on with white paint. A series of coats of special translucent paint was applied over the finished design, allowing the painting to shine with an unusual brightness. The top was varnished again and decorated with gold, silver and mother-of-pearl. A wolf's tooth was used to finely polish the gold and silver. The artists did all their own priming, used special tempera paints and made fine brushes from squirrel tails.

The Palekh box was almost always black, but sometimes came in red, brown or white. A lot of gold was interwoven into the painting's design, but blue skies were never painted. Golikov loved dramatic movement and painted scenes from Russian battles, hunts and fairy tales. *Troikas* were painted with very decorative horses in red and gold and battle scenes appeared like flowers from a distance. Golikov, who also lined his boxes with poetry, could paint up to five boxes a day. The boxes of Golikov are now displayed at the Museum of Palekh Art; the modest timber house, where he lived and painted, is now open to the public. Today the Russian Box Factory in Palekh carries on the tradition with over 250 artists. It takes a day for a simple box to be painted and up to a week or more for a more decorative painting.

Classical art and folklore are still popular in the Soviet Union. You can find *matryoshkas* and other wooden toys, trays, samovars, pottery, glassware and the beautiful hand-painted boxes in the Beriozka stores. They make superb presents, and a *matryoshka* doll or lacquer box at home will always remind you of your visit to the Soviet Union.

ILYA REPIN

During Russia's Golden Age in the 19th century, as the arts began to portray the realistic aspects of Russian life, the painter Ilya Repin greatly influenced the artistic development of this period. Russian art grew beyond portraying a simple spiritual significance, depicted in the icon, to encompass the whole world of the "common man" with all his hopes, sufferings and desires for change. It strove to portray the social phenomena of the times, including the struggle against oppression and the desire for liberation.

The Wanderer

Ilya Yefimovich Repin was born in a small Ukrainian town in 1844, where his father served in the army of Czar Nicholas I. At 19, Ilya moved to St. Petersburg to study at the Academy of Arts. His arrival there in 1863 coincided with one of the most significant events of St. Petersburg artistic life: a small number of prominent art students, led by Ivan Kramskoi, rebelled against the strict academic standards and demanded to choose the subject of their own graduation thesis. The students resigned after the Academy denied their request. In 1870, this group of artists began its own movement called the Society for Travelling Exhibitions, or as they became known, The Wanderers or Peredvizhniki.

Later, Repin joined their circle and furthered the realistic trend in Russian art. During Repin's last year at the Petersburg Academy in 1871, he painted *The Barge Haulers on the Volga,* which brought him both Russian and European recognition as an artist; *Barge Haulers* characterized the heavy burdens borne by the Russian people. Repin believed that the intelligentsia's responsibility was to bring these social realities to light. He later wrote that "the pictures of those days made the viewer blush, shiver and look carefully into himself. . . . They upset the public and directed it on the path of humaneness."

After living abroad for three years and studying the works of the European impressionists, Repin moved to Moscow in 1877, where he frequented the salon of Pavel Tretyakov and the Abramtsevo Estate of Savva Mamontov, both well-known patrons of the arts. The Mamontov circle became the center of Moscow cultural life, and included such other great Russian painters as Serov, Korovin and Vrubel. Their circle combined the romantic world with the realistic portrayal of human existence.

Painting The Issues

In 1881, Repin witnessed the public execution of five people, who had taken part in the assassination of Czar Alexander II. The following year, he moved back to St. Petersburg, where he began to explore revolutionary ideas. Like his literary contemporaries Turgenev, Dostoevsky and Tolstoy, Repin strove to capture the moral and philosophical issues of the time. His paintings *Arrest of a Propangandist, They Did Not Expect Him* (concerning the unexpected return of a political exile to his home), and *Ivan the Terrible and his Son —16 November 1581* (the date Ivan the Terrible killed his son in a fit of rage) can now be seen along with many of his other works in the Moscow Tretyakov Gallery. In Leningrad, some of his paintings can be viewed in the Russian Museum and the Repin Institute of Painting, Sculpture and Architecture is one of the largest art schools in the world.

Repin also drew portraits of the writer Maxim Gorky and Modest Mussorgsky, and dedicated other canvasses to Pushkin and Gogol. He had a 30-year friendship with Leo Tolstoy and frequently stayed with Tolstoy on his estate outside Moscow at Yasnaya Polyana. During these years, Repin produced a large body of paintings and drawings of Tolstoy at home and at work. In 1899, Repin bought an estate outside of St. Petersburg. He named his estate The Penates, after the Roman gods who protected the home and family. Repin lived and continued to paint here right up to his death in 1930 at the age of 86. Today the estate, Repino, can easily be visited from Leningrad. Repin's home and studio are fully restored and a museum houses many of his works. He is buried in the park on the Penates Estate.

Ilya Repin, self-portrait

RUSSIAN MUSIC

Fall And Rise Of Folk Music

The origins of Russian music can be traced back to pagan times, long before the introduction of Christianity. Slavonic music was based on pagan traditions and folk mythologies, played mainly during wedding celebrations and harvest festivals. Simple wind or string instruments were carved out of wood.

When Prince Vladimir converted the Kievan States to Christianity in A.D. 988, Byzantine chants and church hymns were mixed in with ancient folk traditions. Music played a role in both church and secular life. Musical jesters provided entertainment at court functions, and wandering minstrels known as *skomorokhi* played at fairs and festivals.

When Moscow was declared the Third Rome during the reigns of Ivans III and IV, the Orthodox Church consolidated its power within the state. The Metropolitan of Moscow declared all music outside the Church an evil influence and forbade the folk music performances of the *skomorokhi*. Later, at the turn of the 18th century, Peter the Great took Russia out of her long isolation and weakened the supremacy of the Orthodox Church. It was Peter who introduced Western music into Russian culture. The Emperor of All Russia invited Western musicians to play at his court and it soon became fashionable for German and Italian musicians to perform in the homes of the aristocracy. Western music continued to be performed during the reign of Catherine the Great, who built many opera and concert halls in St. Petersburg. This period also saw a strong revival of folk traditions, and the balalaika and the accordian were introduced into musical ballads.

Golden Age

As with the development of literature, Russian music didn't generate its own unique style until the beginning of the 19th century. As Alexander Pushkin is called the Father of Russian Literature, Mikhail Glinka (1804-57) is looked upon as sparking the Golden Age in Russian music. Glinka was the first Russian composer to mix Slavic folk traditions with European classical music. He also in-

troduced romantic and exotic elements into his compositions. Glinka is also heralded as the Father of Russian Opera. His two most famous operas are *Ruslan and Ludmilla* and *Ivan Susanin* (also known as *A Life For The Czar*). *Susanin* premiered at the Bolshoi in Moscow on 7 Sept.1842.

Following Glinka, a group of Russian musicians known as "The Mighty Handful," Borodin, Cui, Balakirev, Mussorgsky and Rimsky-Korsakov, composed some of Russia's finest music. Much of it was based on Russian history, Pushkin's poetry, folk traditions, and the exoticism of Russia's far eastern lands. These include Borodin's *Prince Igor,* Tchaikovsky's *Yevgeny Onegin,* Rimsky-Korsakov's *The Snow Maiden* and *Shéhérazade,* and Mussorgsky's *Boris Godunov,* which premiered at the Bolshoi Theater in Moscow on 7 Sept. 1842; the role of Godunov was often sung by the great opera singer, Fyodor Chaliapin.

Real Realism

Modest Mussorgsky (1839-81) shifted classical traditions to a more realistic style. He once exclaimed, "How rich a treasure awaits the composer in the speech of the people!" His well-known composition *Pictures at an Exhibition* was based on a series of watercolor paintings by his artist friend Victor Hartmann, composed as a special tribute upon his death.

Russian composers frequently included church bell chimes in their works. Slavic bell chiming had a tradition all its own; the church belfry in the Golden Ring town of Rostov with its 15 bells was famous around the world. The bell ringer didn't ring the bell itself, but manipulated the tongue or clapper with ropes in such a way as to soften the bell sounds. Glinka was the first to weave the sounds of bells into his works, which can be heard in the "Glory Chorus" of *Ivan Susanin.* Other bell sequences can be heard in Mussorgsky's *Boris Godunov* during his coronation in the Moscow Kremlin and in *Pictures at an Exhibition* in the segment "The Great Gate of Kiev."

Pyotr Tchaikovsky (1840-93), probably the most loved of Russian composers, wrote the music for many ballets, operas and symphonies, including

Swan Lake, Sleeping Beauty and the *1812 Overture.*

Socialist Realism

The Bolshevik Revolution in 1917 put a serious damper on experimentation in Russian music. Many Russian composers such as Stravinsky, Rachmaninoff and Prokofiev fled the country for the West; only Prokofiev later returned to Russia. Igor Stravinsky gained a measure of fame in the West, scoring Walt Disney's brilliant animated film *Fantasia* in 1940.

Under the new regime, the Soviet Union heard new Socialist Realism works by Myakovsky and Shostakovich. Uplifting melodies were song by the Red Army Chorus and patriotic works were composed by Kabelevsky and Khachaturian *(Spartacus).* Today, about 2,000 composers are registered in the official Union of Composers.

Music Schools, Halls, And Stores

The first institute of higher musical learning in Russia, the Petersburg Conservatory, was founded in 1862 by Anton Rubenstein; one of its first graduates was Tchaikovsky. Today in Leningrad it's known as the Rimsky-Korsakov Conservatory, named after the composer who taught here for 37 years. It has an opera studio and music school. The Conservatory is located on Glinka Street and Theater Square, where monuments to Glinka and Rimsky-Korsakov also stand. In the Tikhvinskoye Cemetery at Alexander Nevsky Monastery in Leningrad are the graves of Rubenstein, Glinka, Borodin, Mussorgsky and Rimsky-Korsakov.

The Tchaikovsky Conservatory in Moscow, where the composer himself was once a professor, is the largest music school in the Soviet Union. The annual international Tchaikovsky piano competitions, begun in 1958, are held here every four years. The USSR State Symphony Orchestra performs regularly in Moscow's Tchaikovsky Concert Hall. The Glinka Museum, in Moscow as well, exhibits the personal collections of many of Russia's famous composers. Tchaikovsky lived and composed many of his works in the small town of Klin, not far from Moscow. His estate here has been made into a museum.

Today both Soviet and foreign visitors alike enjoy performances by these and other contemporary composers at the Bolshoi and Kirov and in

Pyotr Tchaikovsky (1840-93) by Ilya Repin, 1888. Russian Museum, Leningrad

other Philharmonic halls in Moscow and Leningrad. Musical recordings of compositions can be found in Beriozka shops and in record stores under the Russian Melodiya label. In the spring of 1990, the renowned Soviet cellist and conductor, Mstislav Rostropovich and his opera singer wife, Galina Vishnyevskaya, were allowed to visit the Soviet Union after 16 years of exile; the Soviet government even restored their citizenship. The international organization UNESCO named 1989 the year of the Russian composer Modest Mussorgsky, to commemorate his music, which is enjoyed by people around the world.

BALLET

The first form of ballet-dance to appear in Russia was staged in 1672 by a German ensemble in Moscow for Czar Alexcei. The theatrical performance, lasting 10 hours, was based on the Bible's "Book of Esther." Alexcei's daughter, Sophia (the future Regent), was very fond of dancing, and composed comedy ballets, such as *Russalk* ("The Mermaids"). Sophia's half-brother, Peter the Great, encouraged Western dance and brought in German, French, English and Polish companies to put on lavish productions in his new capital.

Ballet grew in popularity under Empress Anna who, in 1734, hired the Frenchman Jean-Baptiste Landé to open up a ballet school for aristocratic children; she founded the Petersburg Imperial Ballet School (in the Winter Palace) in 1738. The first theatrical ballet school began in Moscow in 1763; the Petrovsky Theater (later renamed the Bolshoi) opened in 1780. During the reigns of Elizabeth and Catherine the Great, many French and Italian ballet masters took up residence in St. Petersburg and Moscow as ballet became a much more respected form of entertainment in Russia than in the West.

Didelot And Petipa
One of the most influential characters of early Russian ballet was Charles Didelot, a Frenchman who arrived in Russia in 1801. He taught at the Petersburg Imperial Ballet School for more than 25 years and wove French classical and Russian folk themes through the new romantic style of the times. Didelot also introduced the *pas de deux* and *pointes* on the tips of the female ballet shoes. Under his direction, the ballet was made into a *grand spectacle,* incorporating the entire corps de ballet, costumes, scenery, and even special effects—dancers were fitted with mobile wings and live pigeons flew across the stage. One Russian writer wrote that "there was more poetry to be found in Didelot's work than in the whole of French literature."

Another of St. Petersburg's best-known dancers was the Frenchman Marius Petipa, who came to Russia in 1847. Petipa later choreographed over 60 ballets for the Imperial Ballet, highlighting the solo within a performance; he worked 56 years on the Russian stage. In the early 1890s, this grand master teamed almost exclusively with Tchaikovsky, choreographing *Sleeping Beauty, The Nutcracker,* and *Swan Lake,* performed at the Mariinsky Theater (named after Maria, wife of Alexander II), later known as

the Kirov. Many of these ballets were danced by his favorite ballerina, Matilda Kschessinska (who was the mistress of Nicholas II before he married).

Glushkovsky And Gorsky
Around the same time in Moscow, the ballet master, Glushkovsky, a former student of Didelot, was introducing mythological and romantic ballets to the Bolshoi. In 1821, he staged Pushkin's *Ruslan and Ludmilla.* The first Muscovite to dance the part of Giselle was the famous ballerina Yekaterina Sankovskaya. One of the Bolshoi's later directors, Alexander Gorsky, brought the art of realism (influenced by Stanislavsky's method in theater) to his choreography. After witnessing a performance in Russia by the American dancer Isadora Duncan, he added more artistic design and free-flowing, dramatic action to Bolshoi ballets. In 1900, Gorsky premiered in Moscow the ballet *Don Quixote.*

Ballets Russes
A Petersburg artistic entrepreneur, Sergei Diaghilev (1872-1929), formulated the individual and innovative style of the Russian ballet into the Ballets Russes and The World of Art Society. Diaghilev brought dancers, choreographers, musicians and artists together to create some of the most stunning spectacles that the ballet world had ever known. His dancers were Pavlova, Karsavina and Nijinsky (graduates of the Petersburg Imperial Ballet School); his choreographers Fokine, Massine, Nijinskaya (Nijinsky's sister) and later Balanchine; musicians Tchaikovsky, Chopin, Stravinsky and Rimsky-Korsakov; and artists Benois, Bakst, Goncharova and even Picasso. During the first season abroad in Paris in 1909, the repertoire of the Ballets Russes consisted of Borodin's *Polovtsian Dances from Prince Igor,* Chopin's *Les Sylphides* (danced by Anna Pavlova, Karsavina and Nijinsky), and *The Banquet,* with music by Tchaikovsky, Mussorgsky and Rimsky-Korsakov. The programs were done by the French writer Jean Cocteau, and posters painted by Moscow artist Valentin Serov. Parisian audiences were swept off their feet; as one critic remarked, "Like a great gust of fresh wind . . . dance has come back to us from the north."

Diaghilev returned to France over the next decade; in addition, the company held performances throughout the world, including England and America. One Frenchman who saw their ballets each season in Paris wrote: "The Ballets Russes are one of the great epochs of my life. I mean the early Ballets Russes, the great unforgettable days of 1909-12. The Russians, how can we explain their powers of enchantment? The Ballets were an incident, a surprise, a shock, and then a miracle. *Schéhérazade, Le Pavillon d'Armide, L'Oiseau de Feu, Cleopatra,* and *Le Spectre de la Rose.* In a way I can say without exaggeration that my life is made up of two periods, before and after the Ballets Russes. Our ideas, our whole outlook was altered." The designer Alexander Benois later reminisced that "not Borodin or Rimsky-Korsakov or Diaghilev triumphed in Paris, but all Russian culture . . . the inimitable features of Russian art, its freshness and spontaneity, its wild force and, at the same time, its extraordinary refinement." With the Ballets Russes, Diaghilev heralded in a new artistic era that brought world recognition to ballet.

Post Revolution

After the Revolution, Diaghilev and other prominent ballet personalities left Russia. Even though stifled, Soviet ballet continued with Glière's *The Bronze Horseman,* Shostakovich's *The Golden Age* and Prokofiev's *Cinderella* and *Romeo and Juliet,* danced by Galina Ulanova. Later, under Stalin, ballet was considerably repressed and was staged only in order to promote uplifting Soviet Realism. But out of this period came *The Red Poppy, Icarus* and *Spartacus,* choreographed by the Bolshoi's Yuri Grigorovich, with music by Aram Khachaturian. The composer Rodion Shchedrin wrote the *Carmen Suite* and *Anna Karenina* for his wife, the great dancer Maya Plisetskaya.

Schools And Companies

Agrippina Vagonova (a graduate of the Petersburg Imperial Ballet School) opened up her dance school in Petrograd after the Revolution. Today in Leningrad, the Vagonova Dance School on Rossi Street is one of the most highly respected dance schools in the world. Three Vagonova-trained dancers, Nureyev, Makarova and Baryshnikov, later went on to world recognition when they extended their careers in the West. The Kirov and Vagonova have their own museums, the latter displaying everything from the costumes of Nijinsky and shoes of Pavlova to albums and display cases filled with the history of the Russian ballet. A museum dedicated to the famed designer Benois is located on the grounds of Peter the Great's Summer Palace, Petrodvorets, outside of Leningrad.

Today many of the classical favorites, along with other contemporary ballets, can be seen on stage at the Bolshoi, Kirov and Maly theaters, whose companies often tour abroad. New Moscow ballet companies perform at the Moscow Ballet and the Stanislavsky-Danchenko Theaters. In Leningrad, the choreographic Miniatures Company has staged the jazz ballet *Three Musketeers,* and the Chamber Ballet offered the rock ballet *Boomerang.* Dancers Altyna Asylmuratova and Konstantin Zalinsky dazzle audiences at the Kirov, and performed the Kirov's first Balanchine ballet, *Theme and Variations.*

Tickets for ballet or opera performances can be ordered through your hotel's Intourist Desk.

THE GOLDEN AGE OF RUSSIAN LITERATURE

A virtual explosion of national self-awareness occurred in Russia toward the end of the reign of Catherine the Great. The population was not only rising up against political and social oppression, but also searching for a new inner, spiritual freedom following the Age of Reason. After the French Revolution in 1789, the European and Russian intelligentsia established new trends, especially in art and literature. The classicist ideals gave way to romanticism and realism. After the War of 1812 with Napoleon, a surge of patriotic feeling and pride boosted the emancipatory feelings conceived by Russian progressives in the late 18th century.

For many years Russia translated and circulated the works of European writers and philosophers because she had few known works of her own. The first significant Russian book was written and published by Alexander Radishchev in 1790, entitled *A Journey from St. Petersburg to Moscow;* this book described the terrible conditions of serfdom and rewarded Radishchev with exile to Siberia.

On 14 Dec. 1825, the first revolutionaries from among the Russian nobility led an insurrection against the St. Petersburg court. The Decembrist revolt failed because the noblemen didn't have the support of the common people. Thereafter, Russian writers took up where the Decembrists left off. Literature would now communicate the urgency of change, the truths behind the class struggle and the intense feelings of backwardness and alienation felt by the Russian people. In a letter about literary ideals, Anton Chekhov wrote, "The best writers are realistic and portray life the way it is; because each line is permeated with their awareness of this goal, you feel not just life the way it is, but the way it ought to be." With the advent of Alexander Pushkin, Russian literature blossomed into a period of prolific poetry and prose that not only opened the eyes of Russia, but the rest of the world as well.

Pushkin

Alexander Sergeyevich Pushkin was born in Moscow in 1799. Pushkin's father was from the Russian gentry, and his mother was the granddaughter of Peter the Great's Abyssinian General, Gannibal; the poet was proud of his nobility and African blood. In 1811, Pushkin was sent off to school at the Lyceum at Czarskoe Selo just outside of St. Petersburg, where he began writing poetry. After graduation, he worked both as a clerk in St. Petersburg and on a long romantic poem, which contained Russian folklore and described the conditions of the time. When this poem was published in 1820, *Ruslan and Ludmila* caused such an immediate stir in the younger generation that it was censored by Czar Alexander I, and Pushkin was immediately ordered out of St. Petersburg. He lived in the Caucasus and began work on *Yevgeny Onegin,* considered the most brilliant of all his works. *Onegin* describes the life and journeys of a young St. Petersburg nobleman taken from Pushkin's own experiences. The epic poem's publication in 1825 marked the beginning of the Golden Age in Russian literature.

In 1824, while living in Odessa, a letter of Pushkin's, which hinted at a positive attitude toward atheism, was intercepted and read. He was promptly expelled from his job in the civil service and sent to live on his mother's estate at Mikhailovskoye outside of St. Petersburg in the province of Pskov. This turned out to be a stroke of luck for him. The period of exile forced him to miss the Decembrist revolt. The Emperor overlooked his probable connections and ordered the poet to Moscow.

In 1831 he married young Nathalie Goncharova, at the same time his verse drama *Boris Godunov* was allowed to be published. His famous novel *Queen of Spades* was out in 1833; the gambler Hermann symbolized the secret craving of the people to take a hand in the gamble of winning freedom during an opportunistic age. The same year Pushkin also wrote one of his last great narrative poems, *The Bronze Horseman*.

When the Czar later forbade him any travel abroad, Pushkin had to reconcile himself to leading a stifled and censored life in St. Petersburg. In fact, Nicholas I, known as the "Iron Czar," declared himself Pushkin's personal censor. When the French Baron George-Charles D'Anthès began flirting with his wife Nathalie (and she returning his advances), Pushkin challenged him to a duel. Alexander Pushkin, the greatest poet that Russia had ever known, was seriously wounded in this duel on 27 Jan. 1837. Two days later, he died in his study in St. Petersburg. Today, the Pushkin Museum in Leningrad occupies the house where Pushkin lived and wrote. He's buried on the Mikhailovskoye Estate outside of Leningrad.

Classics

Pushkin was the fountainhead of modern Russian literature. In the decades following his death, Russia produced some of the greatest classics in world literature: Gogol's *Dead Souls;* Turgenev's *Fathers and Sons;* Chekhov's *The Cherry Orchard;* Dostoyevsky's *Crime and Punishment* and Tolstoy's *War and Peace* and *Anna Karenina* to name a few.

Tolstoy died in 1910, just seven years before Lenin would break the bonds of czarist rule. By the end of the 19th century, the Golden Age of Russian literature had come to its end. The struggles within the new Soviet society were later expressed by Blok, Mandelstam, Mayakovsky and Akhmatova. Pasternak would later write about the troubled Revolutionary period in his legendary novel, *Dr. Zhivago*.

YOUTH AND CULTURE

For the first time in our lives, we are experiencing a revolution in consciousness. We are what we think. We're not only Soviets, but global citizens and must not only practice humanism, but vitalism as well.

—Young citizen of Leningrad

Me Is In

Perestroika is heralded as the catalyst of what many are calling the new Soviet Renaissance. A time in Soviet openness that was once termed the "Khrushchev Thaw" is now being hailed as the "Spring Flood Glasnost" under Gorbachev. Since Gorbachev came to power in 1985, there has been a virtual explosion of Soviet culture. Today's youth are experiencing more freedom and openness than in the entire history of post-revolutionary Russia.

Perestroika and *glasnost* are the symbols of a new generation; they epitomize a spirit of newfound individuality. Nowadays, with the Pepsi Generation, "Me is in and masses are out!" In a capital that once had no memorable nightlife to speak of, there's now not enough time in a day to attend all the cultural happenings, theater and film premiers, art exhibits, poetry readings and musical concerts.

Over 200 experimental theaters have sprung up in Moscow alone. Spellbinding and witty plays come out of Moscow's avant-garde Theater Ta-

ganka, where Yuri Lyubimov once again directs after being exiled for controversiality in 1984. After a play, many flock to the bar down the street named after the legendary folk singer Vladimir Vysotsky, who now receives far more recognition for his folk ballads about everyday life than when he was alive.

Astonishing Range Of Material

The Moscow Sovremennik (Contemporary) Theater staged *Journey into the Whirlwind,* an emotional play based upon the memoirs of an innocent Gulag victim during the Stalinist purges. Other cultural centers and theaters host readings from Anna Akhmatova's long banned poem *Requiem* and plays like *Stars in the Morning Sky* about the clean-up campaign that swept drunks, prostitutes and derelicts off the streets before the 1980 Olympics. From Dostoevsky's *Notes from the Underground,* Bulgakov's *Master and Margarita* and Chekhov's *Ward Six* to flamboyant men in drag in the psychological drama, *The Maids,* and the revived *Letuchaya Mysh* ("The Bat"), a cabaret composed of satirical skits, the range of material is astonishing in a society that was once only permitted to portray uplifting and censored Social Realism.

The popular *glasnost* comic Mikhail Zhvanetsky openly jokes about all the food in American

Russian youths face the same clash with older generations as their Western counterparts.

supermarkets, while scantily clad females put on dance and variety shows at restaurant co-ops like the Skazka (Fairytale) in Moscow and Fantanka 77 in Leningrad. The first McDonald's opened in Moscow on 31 Jan. 1990, selling the Bolshoi Mac! The largest McDonald's in the world, it seats 700 people. Over 20,000 Muscovites applied for 630 jobs serving 35,000 people daily! McDonald's plans to open another 19 restaurants in Moscow.

T-shirts, emblazened with the Cyrillic letters of *perestroika, glasnost* and *demokratizatsiya*, are for sale everywhere. More than 10,000 spectators crowded into Moscow's Luzhniki Stadium to watch the contest for the very first Soviet beauty pageant. After thousands of girls competed in such categories as Aerobic Dancing and Miss Harmony, the judges elected Masha Kalinina the first Miss Moscow. Later, Yulia Sukhanova captured the title in the first Miss USSR contest.

In *The Suicide,* a play banned by Stalin since 1930, the hero, unhappy with his life and work, contemplates suicide. He comes to the simple conclusion that "if we could just say how bad things are, we'd already feel better." This line can be especially appreciated in the context of decades of paranoia and censorship. But today, people are discovering the small joy of what it's like to openly voice their opinions.

Media

Even Soviet prime-time television has blossomed from its war musicals and stifled news shows.

(One show still running is "Come on Girls," in which young women compete against each other in the domestic chores of cooking, cleaning and vacuuming.) Now, programming includes informative and probing shows like "Problems, Searches and Decisions," "Good Evening, Moscow," "Vzglyad (Glance)," "World and Youth," "The 12th Floor" (with live satellite links to other cities) and "600 Seconds." On the show "120 Minutes," clairvoyants Alan Chumak and Yuri Kashpirovsky, whose aims are "to help people muster their psychological energy to restore harmony of the spiritual and physical world," guide their audience through meditations. Viewers have claimed to be healed of aches, pains and more serious illnesses. Chumak had such a strong following that the Ministry of Health recently took him off the air, stating that he was turning into a "cult phenomenon." People are reading newspapers and magazines again, full of current news and blunt social criticisms as in *Ogonyek, Novy Mir* and *Krokodil.* Interesting pieces can even be found in the English-language version of *Moscow News.*

Books And Canvas

In literature, Pasternak's *Dr. Zhivago* and Bulgakov's *The Heart of a Dog* have gone back to print, along with stories and poetry by Nabokov, Solzhenitsyn and Brodsky. Anatoly Rybakov's *Children of the Arbat,* a moving tale about what it was like in Moscow's Arbat section during Stalin, has already been translated into other languages and is available in Western bookstores.

In fact, the Arbat in Moscow, an old pedestrian thoroughfare where once you could mostly buy posters of Lenin, samovars and *blini* dinners, is now beautifully restored and filled with musicians, poets, political cartoonists, portrait sketchers, demonstrators, mimes, break dancers and even hippie look-alikes selling pictures of "Jesus Christ, Superstar." The same goes for Nevsky Prospekt in Leningrad. On Sundays in Moscow painters exhibit everything from icon reproductions to futuristic canvasses in Izmailovo Park.

The art scene is booming. In a country where an artist once had to be officially registered in the Artist Union to work full-time as an artist (and painting only Soviet Realism), unofficial artists are now exhibiting and even traveling abroad with their works. The first unofficial Artist Co-op, Tovarishchestvo (Association for Experimental Art), is based in Leningrad and has over 200 members. Other co-ops such as Octrov (Island) now exhibit in halls right next to official artists. Many hope to reform a 1932 Soviet law stating that creative works can only be determined by the Party, thereby making it possible for every professional artist to contribute to national and world culture without being censored. In the past few years alone, over 300,000 people from around the world have viewed Tovarishchestvo exhibits. Since work and viewing space is still hard to come by (up to 60% of city populations still live in communal housing), AEA has opened up the first co-op exhibiting space in Leningrad, known as the Gallery. In 1988, Sotheby's held the first auction of Soviet art in Moscow with some paintings selling for over $400,000, such as *A Fundamental Lexicon* by the Moscow artist Grigory Bruskin. The Polyanka in Moscow, a 17th-century Orthodox Church on Polyanka Street, houses artists' collections for Western dealers to view.

Ceremonies, Seminars And Singles

A new atmosphere of spirituality is manifesting with a resurgence in religion. There are church restorations, baptisms, Orthodox weddings and even seminars in Alcoholics Anonymous, yoga, meditation, ESP and UFOs. The first Soviet-American matchmaking and dating service was inaugurated in the summer of 1990.

Film

Even after the Revolution, Russia put forth some of the world's most memorable cinema classics: Pudovkin's *Mother*, Vertov's *Man With A Movie Camera* and Dovzhenko's *Earth* were at the core of the silent cinema. One of the greatest filmmakers of all time was Sergei Eisenstein. His films *Strike, October* and *Battleship Potemkin* were produced in Leningrad and Moscow. With the advent of sound, Eisenstein directed *Ivan the Terrible* and *Alexander Nevsky.*

The first motion picture in Russia was shown in St. Petersburg on 4 May 1896 at the Aquarium Theater (now Lenfilm Studios). And the first sound-film theater was opened in Leningrad on 5 Oct. 1929 at no. 72 Nevsky Prospekt (now the Znaniye Cinema). On the average, Soviets go to the movies five times more often than people in the West (almost 20 times per year); and at any one time, over 100 features play in Moscow for the nine million inhabitants. Time-Warner plans to open American-style, multiple-screen movie theaters in Moscow and Leningrad—and introduce popcorn to the Soviets! Long-banned films have been released to packed houses, including Tengiz Abuladze's *Repentance* (about Stalinist horrors and now released abroad), Alexander Askoldov's *The Commissar* (set during the Civil War and made in 1967), Alexcei German's *My Friend Ivan Lapshin,* Alexander Sodurov's *The Solitary Voice of a Man* and Gleb Panfilov's *Tema,* whose hero (a censored writer forced to work as a gravedigger to earn a living) has the memorable line, "Death is living in a country where one cannot practice the craft that gives one life."

The Soviet film industry has had a history of repression. Goskino, the Film Censor Board in Moscow, decided what films could be made and distributed. Now, says a young popular filmmaker at Lenfilm Studios in Leningrad, "If a director has an idea and a good script, almost anything goes. There's a prevailing atmosphere of openness and experimentation. But no one knows where it's all heading. . . . We can only hope that it will continue." For the first time in Soviet film history, an actual filmmaker and not an *apparatchik* (bureaucrat) is making cinematic decisions; Elem Klimov now heads the Union of Cinematographers.

And out they come as Soviet-style mixtures of Warhol, Buñuel, Woody Allen and Truffaut. Juris Podniek's *Is It Easy To Be Young?,* probably the most widely viewed documentary in Soviet history, openly portrays the life of young people today—from punks to Afghanistan war vets. Other popular and poignant favorites include *Confession: Chronicle Alienation* (observing a drug addict), *The Black Square* (the experiences of nonconformist artists), *Intergirl* (problems of Soviet prostitution), *Solovki Power* (about the notorious Siberian prison island under Stalin) and *Lonely Woman Searching For a Life Companion*. Yet another, Stanislav Govorukhin's *This Is No Way To Live*, graphically documents the tragedies of Communist rule and the humiliations of Soviet life. The film was a sensation when it opened in Moscow. Gorbachev surprisingly remarked that the film was "wonderful" after a private screening.

One of the most popular films to come out of the Soviet Union since *Moscow Doesn't Believe in Tears* is Vasily Pichul's *Little Vera,* a candid portrayal of the young Vera and her family in a small industrial Soviet town. The films's star, Natalya Negoda, was the first Soviet woman to appear in *Playboy* magazine (with official permission)!

Rock

During the Brezhnev regime, rock music was carefully controlled and censored by the State Concert Agency and the Ministry of Culture, which decided what bands could record albums and officially play in public places. Many musicians worked as furnace stokers and night watchmen to have time for their music. If termed "official," a band member (even if performing before a crowd of 20,000) would still earn about $35 a performance. Only official bands had access to State musical equipment; without guitars or keyboards, the State thought it could squelch undesirables. The KGB arrested unofficial rockers for strange attire and hairstyles as they tried to play to underground audiences. Rock music was viewed as a dangerous social phenomenon and unofficial recordings were secretly made in basements. The *magizdat* movement, like the underground *samizdat* press, secretly made and distributed tapes.

Today the Soviet Union is being bombarded by pop and rock culture. Now even unofficial bands are touring the USSR and the West and are able to earn a better percentage of the profits. Some claim that the USSR is now going through its own Woodstock era. What's been coined as the "Russian Woodstock" took place in Moscow at the 75,000-seat Lenin Stadium with Western groups performing, such as Bon Jovi, Ozzy Osbourne and Mötley Crue, along with popular Soviet bands. At another concert in Moscow's Gorky Park, the crowd hummed such tunes as "We Shall Overcome" and the Beatles' "Revolution"; to entice an encore, they burned *Pravda* and held up cigarette lighters. Stas Namin of the Stas Namin Rock Group opened the Soviet version of the Hard Rock Cafe (no affiliation to the Western clubs) in Gorky Park. Devoted Elvis Presley fans formed the All-Union Association of Rock and Roll in Moscow to popularize Elvis's music.

One of the hottest bands from Moscow is Brigade S, a cross between the big-band sounds

Rock 'n' Roll is alive and well in the Soviet Union.

of the Andrews Sisters and Glenn Miller and hard rock. The lead singer, Igor Sukachev, who was arrested countless times in the past, now earns up to the equivalent of $5000 (15 times the Soviet average) per month doing concerts. The Proletarian Jazz Group has a few albums out and occasionaly tours in the West.

The Leningrad band Pop Mechanics is headed by avant-garde jazz musician, Sergei Kuryokhin, who was expelled from the Conservatory of Music for "non-conformity." Now the band, with 10 to 200 people on stage, uses everything from Red Army choruses and balalaika ensembles to goats. Since Kuryokhin loves the elements of "spontaneity and surprise," he never rehearses until a few days before the actual concert.

"Russia is a Godsend. You need oppression to sing the blues," once said Boris Grebenschikov, the lead singer of the Leningrad band Aquarium. Fans from all over Russia came to his Leningrad apartment to write graffiti on his stairwell. Until 1987, his underground cult band never played an offical concert. Now Aquarium has albums out on the Soviet Melodiya label. A write-up in *Rolling Stone* magazine reported on their American and European tour. A recent album, Radio Silence, was recorded in the United States on CBS Records, with the help of British rockers David Stewart and Annie Lennox. The popular singer Alla Pugachova frequently tours Europe and even sang at Carnegie Hall in New York.

The music of four underground bands from the USSR was released in the West on the Red Wave Album (Big Time Records), which includes the Leningrad pop band Kino. Other Moscow and Leningrad bands, which appear in such places as the Rok Club and Saigon in Leningrad and Klub Vytyazi (Warrior Club) in Moscow, are Zvuki Mu, Alisa, Strange Games, New Composers, DDT, Time Machine, Grand Prix (with hit single "Gorbachev"), Zoo and Televisor.

Top jazz groups, such as Avia, perform in Moscow's Bluebird Cafe. If, as Bluebird's manager Vartan Tonayan says, "Jazz is the language of democracy," then rock is the symbol of the newfound individuality as expressed in Televisor's hit song "Get Out Of Control":

Get out of control
And sing what you want
And not just what is allowed
We have a right to yell.

The group Alisa sings for the new generation:

A wave is coming
So listen to the sound
Until the new calm is here
A wave is coming
A wave is coming.

The Red Wave has hit like never before.

HOLIDAYS AND FESTIVALS

The Soviet Union has only a few of the traditional holidays celebrated in the West. Most of the national holidays are connected with Lenin and the Revolution. Still, holidays are holidays: a big cause for celebration, especially May Day (International Labor Day) and the Anniversary of the October Revolution.

SOVIET HOLIDAYS

January 1: **New Year.** The last week in December is quite festive, culminating with New Year's Eve. Presents are given on New Year's Day.

March 8: **International Women's Day.** Established after the Second International Conference of Socialist Women in Copenhagen in 1910, women receive gifts and usually don't have to work!

May 1-2: **International Workers Solidarity Day.** This holiday, better known as May Day, has massive parades and demonstrations, especially in Moscow's Red Square and Leningrad's Palace Square. All the leaders come out to watch the pageant and sport displays.

May 9: **Victory Day.** Parades are held at war memorials such as the Piskaryovskoye Cemetery in Leningrad to celebrate V-E Day at the end of World War II in Europe.

October 7: **Constitution Day.** Commemorates the adoption of the 1977 Constitution.

November 7-8: **Anniversary of the October 1917 Revolution.** So called because the Revolution on the old calendar took place on October 25, which differs from the Gregorian calendar by 13 days. These celebrations are the most festive of the year, with colorful parades and marches of everything from bands to workers. Firework displays go on at night, the streets are lit up and people are out late into the evening. In Leningrad, the Baltic fleet sails up the Neva and drops anchor by the Winter Palace; torches are lit atop the Rostral columns and Peter and Paul Fortress.

(Be aware that hotels must be booked far in advance during May and Revolution days.)

FESTIVALS

February 23: **Soviet Army Day**

April 22: **Lenin's Birthday**

Each **spring** there's a music festival in Leningrad. Many gather on the Strelka to watch the breaking ice floes on the Neva.

May 5 to 13: **Festival of Moscow Stars**

June 6: **Pushkin's Birthday.** Poetry readings by Pushkin monuments.

A WW II veteran proudly displays war medals, Minsk.

The last Sunday in July is **Navy Day** In Leningrad. The Soviet fleet, including ships, submarines and sailors are displayed around the city.

June 21 to July 11: **Leningrad White Nights Festival.** While the sun doesn't set, many musical concerts, theatrical performances, outdoor street events and celebrations take place througout the city. From June 21-29, there's the **Festival of the Arts,** which includes ballet and theater performances outside in front of the fountains of Petrodvorets, Peter the Great's summer palace. (In August, the **Festival of Fountains** is here too.) On some evenings during the summer, the Neva River is turned into a giant theatrical stage—hundreds of boats fill the river, cannons fire, fireworks flare and fountains soar into the air. Every night people gather to watch the bridges of the city open at 2 a.m. Additional performances and celebrations are on the Kirov Islands in the Gulf of Finland. Similar white night festivals are held in Vladimir, Suzdal and Novgorod.

September 8: **Seige of Leningrad Day.** This day marks the end of the 900-day seige of Leningrad, and includes special ceremonies at the Piskarovskoye Cemetery.

September 19: **Moscow Day.** A day for merry-making in the city.

December 25 to January 5: **Russian Winter Festival.** Events are held to celebrate the coming new year especially in Moscow, Leningrad, Novgorod, Vladimir and Suzdal. In Leningrad's Kirov Central Park of Culture and Rest, *troika* rides, along with other traditional Russian folk customs, take place.

OTHER EVENTS

Many church holidays are celebrated by the Russian Orthodox Church, such as Easter, the Orthodox New Year (usually in January) and church name days.

A few Saturdays each year, especially the Saturday before Lenin's birthday on 22 April Soviets practice the **Subbotnik,** voluntary and non-paid work on a day off. (*Subbota* means Saturday.) The first Subbotnik was held on 1 May 1920, when citizens of Moscow and Leningrad planted trees and worked together to clean up their city, neighborhoods, schools and work places.

Moscow and Leningrad have many other art, music and sports festivals during the year. Every odd year in summer, Moscow hosts the **Moscow International Film Festival.** Every August, the **Moscow International Marathon** is run through the city.

PLANNING YOUR TRIP

Compared to most other countries of the world, traveling to the USSR requires much more careful advance planning. It's advised to begin preparing long ahead of time, particularly if it's your first trip. Read some literature on the cities you plan to visit and talk to people who've been there. Locate travel agents or other special organizations that deal with travel to the USSR.

Intourist

Most travelers organize their stay in the USSR through Intourist, the official Soviet company for foreign travel. An Intourist branch is located in each of the approximately 150 cities that are officially open to tourists. Under most circumstances, visitors stay in Intourist hotels, which have an Intourist service desk. All hotel reservations must be prepaid before entering the country. Visas won't be issued by a Soviet embassy or consulate without a confirmed reservation. It often takes up to one month for reservations and itineraries to be confirmed.

Group Tours Vs. Going Solo

You have a multitude of packaged and special-interest group tours from which to chose. The advantage of a group tour (especially if it's your first trip and you don't speak the language) is that everything is set up for you. Travel agencies handling USSR excursions have a list of packaged tours available. Most group tours have preset departures and a fixed length of stay, and usually visit Moscow and Leningrad. The group rate includes roundtrip airfare, visa-processing fees, first-class Intourist accommodations, up to three meals a day, all transportation within the USSR, sightseeing excursions and a bilingual Intourist guide. Special-interest groups offer trips that include some sightseeing, but focus more on specific issues such as sports, ecology, the arts, citizen diplomacy, religion or world peace.

Independent travelers can also organize a stay through Intourist, even though it takes a bit more work on their part. Since one cannot just hop a flight over and freely roam through the country, a lot of spontaneity is taken out of traveling. But once there, the traveler can set out and discover each city on his own. You must plan the cities to be visited and the exact length of stay, and devise a preset route. Reservations can be made through a travel agency that has connections with Intourist. Any slight change made in the itinerary can delay the process by weeks. A cancellation after payment can take up to six months to be refunded by Intourist.

Visas

All travelers to the Soviet Union must have a visa. There are three types of visas: Tourist, Business and Visitor. The travel agency working with the packaged tour or individual supplies each person with a Tourist visa application (or it can be picked up at a Soviet embassy or consulate). A processing fee may be charged. Four passport-size photos and a xerox of the informational page of your passport are also required. The host agency telexes Intourist, requesting your intinerary. Once a confirmation is received, your visa is issued. Independent travelers are advised to book at least six to eight weeks in advance to guarantee space and the best rates in hotels. Once the bookings are confirmed, all hotel costs and internal transfers must be prepaid. The individual may also apply directly to the Soviet embassy or consulate for a visa, but must show a letter from a travel agency confirming Intourist reservations before a visa will be granted.

The travel agency then issues an Intourist voucher—a prepaid confirmation booklet for hotel and transfers. Show this at check-in. Once in the USSR, you can lengthen your stay or visit another city by making arrangements with the Intourist desk at your hotel. If you're sponsored by a Soviet organization, relative or friend, you can enter the Soviet Union on a Visitor's visa. You must fill out a visa application in duplicate (not a xerox copy) and send it to them. The host must then take it to their own travelers' organization, OVIR, from which a Visitor's visa is issued after several months. The traveler is only allowed to travel to the cities and stay with the persons designated on the visa.

When To Go
The season of travel affects itineraries and hotel prices of many of the tour programs. Peak season is from May to September. Alternatives are to go in the spring (1 April-15 May) or fall (1 Sept.-31 Oct.) when prices are lower and the cities less crowded. Consider your own personal preference. Summer in Moscow can be humid and dusty; at the same time, the White Nights in Leningrad are spectacular. Indian summer in the fall is quite pleasant. If you don't mind the cold and snow, the winter season is cheapest, and accommodations most readily available. The rainiest months for both cities are July and August.

Time Zones
The Soviet Union has 11 time zones. Moscow and Leningrad are in the same time zone. Many train and plane schedules are listed throughout the country as Moscow time. Always check to see what time is actually meant by the listing. It's an 11-hour time difference from the U.S. West Coast, eight hours from the East Coast, and three hours from London. Most other European cities are two hours. Helsinki is one.

WHAT TO TAKE

Packing
For your own convenience, travel as light as possible. Most airlines allow up to two pieces of luggage and one carry-on. Baggage allowance is very strict when exiting the USSR. Often, all bags are weighed, including your carry-on. Anything over 20 kilos (coach) and 30 kilos (first and business class) gets charged per each additional kilo! This is usually the procedure for internal flights as well.

Documents
Keep your passport, visa, important papers, tickets, vouchers, money, etc., in your hand luggage at all times. Also carry a xerox of your passport and visa, and an extra set of luggage lock keys, in case of loss. Keep in mind that you'll need to show some ID to get into certain places, like your embassy. Serious photographers with a lot of film should have it inspected separately—Soviet X rays aren't always guaranteed film-safe.

Clothes
Aside from personal tastes, the season of the year is the major factor in deciding what to bring. Summers are warm, humid and dusty, with frequent thunderstorms, especially in Moscow. Bring a rain parka or an umbrella. Summer evenings with the White Nights are delightful in Leningrad, but you'll occasionally need a sweater or light jacket. Winters are cold and damp, with temperatures well below freezing. It can snow from November until April, when, especially in Leningrad, the cold Arctic winds deepen the chill. Be prepared with your warmest clothes —waterproof boots, gloves and long underwear. Interiors are usually well heated, so dress in layers. It's best to bring everything along that you'll need, since there's rarely any Soviet clothing of high quality—except for the Russian fur hats (shapki) found in the Beriozkas, the foreign-currency shops. Bring slightly dress-up attire for ballets and banquets. A must is a good pair of walking shoes that you won't mind getting dirty. Wearing shorts or sleeveless shirts may prevent you from entering a church during services.

Medicines
Take a good supply of regular medicines, prescription drugs, and remedies for flu and minor illnesses. Recommended: aspirin or Tylenol, throat lozenges, cold formulas, a course of antibiotics against a very bad cold or infection, vitamins (especially C), laxatives, lip salve, travel sickness pills, water-purifying tablets, and contact-lens cleaners. For an upset stomach: indigestion tablets, Alka-Seltzer, Pepto Bismol. If diarrhea strikes, cut out heavy foods, drink plenty of fluids and ask for rice

in the restaurants. Take Lomotil, if necessary. Each hotel has a resident nurse or doctor and a small apothecary stand with a few medications on hand for sale.

Personal Articles
Remember that the Soviet Union lacks many supplies that we take for granted. Bring cosmetics, lotions, shampoo, conditioner, razors, shaving cream, toothpaste, lavatory paper, Kleenex, feminine products, a water bottle for long trips, soap, Woolite or washing powder, flat bathtub stopper, pantyhose, sewing kit, Scotch and strong wrapping tape, pens, an extra pair of glasses or contact lenses, sun glasses, and extra small screws for glasses.

Food
The Soviet diet is quite heavy. Snacks. except for sweets, can't be found quickly. Consider bringing dried fruits, nuts, granola bars, powdered milk and instant coffee, Cup-a-Soup, a few small cans of fruit juice, tuna fish, peanut butter, Lifesavers. If you're a vegetarian or require a special diet, definitely bring what you need. Cigarettes (but not pipe tobacco) and some brands of alcohol can be found in Beriozkas. Buy what you like in duty-free shops at the airport before entering the country.

Film
Film is expensive and hard to find. Bring whatever you plan to use. Since flash is prohibited in many museums and churches, have high-speed film on hand. New photo-developing centers are opening up, as on the third floor of Moscow's Mezhdunarodnaya Hotel and the Pribaltiickaya in Leningrad. You must pay in foreign currency. If you can wait, it's advised to have your film, especially slides, processed at home.

Gadgets
Voltage varies from 220 to 127. Sometimes hotels have plugs for 220/110. Pack an adaptor/transformer. New hair dryers, travel irons and electrical shavers are now made with safety ends that don't fit into many adaptors—check before you go. A dual voltage coil is good to have for boiling water and brewing tea and coffee in hotel rooms. Use with *extreme caution*. It's nice to have a Walkman along. Bring plenty of batteries. Also check to see what batteries your camera, alarm clock and watch take. Also handy is a penknife with a bottle opener and corkscrew.

For Sightseeing
A Russian phrasebook and dictionary are necessary. Try to master the Cyrillic alphabet before you leave in order to read the letters. It'll be especially helpful in places like the Metro. Bring reading material and travel literature. (The Soviet government is the largest book publisher in the world, though most are in Russian.) Check in the Beriozka or kiosks in your hotel for books or maps printed in English. Giftgiving is a part of Russian *gostyepriimstvo* (hospitality). Buy a small supply of gifts for your Intourist guide and new friends: paperbacks, travel picture books, fashion magazines, T-shirts, music cassettes, cosmetics, colognes. Cigarettes and scotch can be found in Beriozkas. Small souvenir items such as disposable lighters, pantyhose, boxes of herbal teas, perfumed soaps, bubble bath, and felt pens are great gifts for taxi drivers and maids. Bubble gum, baseball cards, etc., are terrific for children, who'll trade *znachki* (pins).

GETTING THERE

International Flights

Most major airlines fly to Moscow (Airport Sheremetyevo II) and Leningrad (Pulkovo II). Moscow is connected with 121 cities in Europe and 70 countries around the world. Inquire at travel agencies and call around to the different airlines. The advance-purchase (APEX) fares give the best rate. A **Pan Am** (in the U.S., tel. 800-221-1111) nonstop flight to Moscow from New York and Washington, D.C. (and other U.S. cities with a stop in Frankfurt) with a 14-day advance-purchase starts at roundtrip $885. The Soviet airline, **Aeroflot,** also flies from most major cities to Moscow. **British Air** (U.S. tel. 800-247-9297; London tel. 897-4000) offers a fare with a 28-day advance-purchase roundtrip London-Moscow (twice weekly to Leningrad) for £270/$430. Flights from Hong Kong to Moscow are provided by Lufthansa, Cathay Pacific and Aeroflot.

Aeroflot is the largest airline in the world, carrying 100 million passengers each year. You can fly to and from destinations in Asia and Europe on Aeroflot with stopovers in Moscow (a Transit visa and hotel confirmation are required). Since flying, especially from points outside of Europe, involves large time differences, consider a stay in a European city for a day or two. Stopovers are sometimes included or provided for a minimal extra charge in the fare.

Another pleasant way to travel is to take a train from a European city to Moscow or Leningrad. For example, **Finnair** (U.S. tel. 800-950-5000; London tel. 408-1222) flies daily from New York to Helsinki (21-day advance-purchase is from $745 roundtrip)

and on Thursdays and Saturdays nonstop from Los Angeles (from $965 roundtrip). After a few relaxing days in Helsinki, take the train to Leningrad or Moscow. (Finnair also flies daily from Helsinki to Moscow or Leningrad.)

Connecting Trains

The train leaves daily from Helsinki at 1 p.m., arriving the same day in Leningrad at 8:45 p.m. (one hour time change). The Moscow train leaves each day at 5 p.m. and arrives the next morning at 9 a.m. (you cross the border the day you depart), costing $110 ($160 first class) each way. You can even book and pay for the train through your travel agency. Return trains leave Moscow at 11:20 a.m. and arrive in Helsinki at 12:30 p.m. the next day (cross border the following day). Trains from Leningrad depart at 11:45 a.m. and arrive in Helsinki at 5 p.m. the same day.

Customs

Visitors arriving by air pass through a passport checkpoint in the airport terminal. Those arriving by train do this at the border. Uniformed border guards check passports and stamp visas. (A passport is never stamped. One page of the visa is taken upon arrival. The rest of the visa is turned in upon exiting the country.) Soviet customs declarations are issued during your flight or train ride, or one can be picked up from stands, written in numerous languages, located near the baggage claim area in the airport. Fill in exactly how much foreign currency you're bringing into the country (there's no limit unless it's ridiculously high). De-

INTERNATIONAL TRAINS FROM MOSCOW/LENINGRAD

FROM MOSCOW TO	TRAIN NO.	DEP.	ARR.	DAY OF DEP.	DURATION HRS	MIN	FARE IN US$ SOFT	HARD
Athens	9	1635	0840	1, 3, 6,	65	5	570	354
Berlin	13	1806	2016	daily	28		164	106
	15	2017	2204	daily	27	47	164	106
	125	1238	1608	daily	29	30	164	106
Brussels	15	2017	1130	daily	41	13	696	452
Bern	13	1806	1309	3, 4, 6	45	3	750	484
Budapest	15	2310	0743	daily	34	33	152	98
	69	2140	0503	daily	33	59	152	98
Copenhagen	15	2017	0850	1, 3, 5	38	33	600	384
Frankfurt/Main	13	1806	0709	3, 4, 6	40	3	624	404
Hamburg	15	2017	0640	7	36	23	616	396
Hannover	15	2017	0364	daily	33	23	576	370
Helsinki	32	2200	1230	daily	15	30	156	92
Holland	15	2017	0942	daily	39	25	696	452
Istanbul	13	2201	1010	3	65	34	378	240
Kars	55	2359	1632	2,6	65	34	–	84
Koln	15	2017	0724	daily	36	10	–	348
London	15	2017	1906	daily	47	39	812	540
Oslo via Brest	13	1806	2150	1	53	44	732	468
Ostende	15	2017	1250	daily	42	33	732	474
Paris	15	2017	1250	daily	42	54	764	492
Rome via Chop	15	2359	1755	except 2 (S)	67	57	636	418
	15	2359	1755	except 2, 7 (W)	67	57	636	418
Rotterdam West	15	2017	0920	daily	39	3	696	492
Stockholm	13	1806	1749	2	49	43	696	444
Tereran	93	2135	1130	6	82	25	264	164
Turku	32	2200	2040	daily	25	40	–	106
Vienna via Brest	21	2347	0720	daily	33	33	476	304
Vienna via Chop	51	1740	1210	daily	44	30	236	132
Warsaw	9	1637	0806	daily	17	43	120	84
	125	1238	0606	daily	19	27	120	84
FROM LENINGRAD TO								
Berlin	25	2345	0720	daily	33	17	156	106
Bucharest	189	1120	1100	daily	46	40	–	108
Budapest	189	1120	0703	daily	45	43	–	96
Helsinki	33	1100	1700	daily	7		104	68
Koln	25	2345	1550	2, 6	42	5	656	424
Prague	189	1120	1223	daily	51	3	–	120
Sofia	189	1120	2227	daily	60	7	–	140
Warsaw	109	1530	1800	2, 4, 6	28	30	114	78
	25	2345	2105	daily	23	20	114	78

(S = Summer, W = Winter)

clare your valuables (gold, silver, jewelry, etc.). An inspector will look at or through your luggage in varying degrees and stamp your declaration. Do not misplace it. You need it to exchange money and exit the country. Your valuables could be confiscated if you can't otherwise prove that you brought them into the country. When you exit the country, another declaration (same format) must be filled out, which is compared to your original. Make sure you aren't exiting the country with more foreign currency than you declared upon arrival. Even though Soviet customs has become considerably easier and faster than in years past, your bags may be thoroughly searched when you leave. Do not overwrap items, which may be picked for inspection.

It's forbidden to bring in what's considered anti-Soviet material and pornography. You may be asked to show all your printed matter. Drugs, other than medicinal, are highly illegal. Any video or small-film camera, VCR, personal computer, or typewriter should be written onto the customs form. You must exit with these items (unless you have official permission to leave them) or else pay a huge duty up to the full worth of the items in question. In addition, any exposed movie film or pre-recorded cassettes may be confiscated upon arrival and held a few days for review. You cannot leave with antiques, icons, or expensive works of art, unless you have permission from the Ministry of Culture. A law states that any Soviet book printed before 1975 can't be taken out of the country. This is not strigently upheld, but books have been confiscated; don't pack such printed matter right at the top of your suitcase.

GETTING AROUND

When arriving in Moscow or Leningrad, group travelers are automatically taken by bus to their hotel. Individual travelers should hold a transportation voucher issued at home before departure. Report to the Intourist desk at the airport or train station upon arrival. The respective airports are about 45 minutes from the centers of the two cities; the train stations are more centrally located. For those without transportation, inquire at the Intourist desk. Or bargain with drivers of taxis or individual cars for a ride into town. Remember to reconfirm your departure flight sometime during your stay. This can be done through the Intourist desk at your hotel or by phoning the airlines directly. Reconfirm internal flights as well, for they tend to be overbooked.

Inter-city Movement
Most of your bookings have been taken care of before your arrival. Report any changes in plans to Intourist. If you'd like to extend your visa, visit another city that isn't on your visa or make train or plane reservations, check at the hotel's Intourist desk. Always do this as soon as you can.

By Air
The airports used for internal flights are much more crowded and chaotic than the international airports. Special preference is usually given to foreign groups at check-in, and Intourist waiting areas are provided. Passports and visas are required at check-in. Boarding passes are issued, either with open seating or with seat numbers, and rows are written in Cyrillic. Groups are usually seated first on the plane. Remember that the locals are quite assertive and will push vigorously to get on the plane, especially with open seating. On internal flights, there's one class and no nonsmoking sections. Sometimes the only meal consists of seltzer water, bread and cucumbers! Bring along some snacks. There's no airport departure tax.

By Train
Trains are much more fun than flying. The *Red Arrow* trains between Moscow and Leningrad are a wonderful way to travel. Board the sleeper at night and arrive the next morning for a full day of sightseeing. Since there are several train stations in each city, make sure you know which one you're departing from. In Moscow, trains for Leningrad leave from the *Leningradski Vokzal,* the Leningrad station. In Leningrad, they leave from the *Moskovski Vokzal,* the Moscow station. (*Vokzal* is taken from the English word, Vauxhall.) The trains always leave on time with a broadcasted five-minute warning before departure—and that's

all! So don't miss the train! First class has two berths to a compartment and second class has four. It's an excellent way to meet Russians. A personal car attendant will bring tea (brewed in the car's samovar) and biscuits, and wake you up in the morning. Remember to turn off the radio at night or the national anthem will blast you awake at 6 a.m. The compartments aren't segregated. If you have a problem, the attendent can usually arrange a swap. Foreigners cannot buy train or plane tickets at stations or ticket counters. Tickets must be bought through Intourist, and each city you visit must be listed on your visa.

By Bus And Coach

Group tourists are shown around Moscow and Leningrad by coach. Many times the buses aren't air conditioned, but all are heated in winter. Individual travelers can sign up through Intourist for city sightseeing excursions; check at Intourist for a listing. Comfortable coach excursions are offered to areas in the Golden Ring as well. Always remember the number of your bus; parking lots tend to fill up quickly.

Local Buses, Trams And Trolleys

Local transportation runs throughout the cities from 6 a.m. to 1 a.m. and is charged by distance. A short hop is five kopeks. Rides run by the honor system. Either you put five kopeks into a machine and roll out a ticket by hand or you must pre-purchase tickets at a special kiosk. These get stamped with a device on the wall. Sometimes there are control checks. If you're caught without a ticket (fine: three rubles), plead in your native tongue—you may not be fined! You may find someone muttering *"peredaitye pazhalsta"* ("please pass this on"), and thrusting a few kopeks into your hand! This is meant to be passed back to the ticket machine where a ticket, in turn, will find its way back to the donor. Even if you don't speak Russian, people will help to direct you to the proper bus or stop. Never be afraid to ask, even if in sign language! Many do understand a little English, German or French.

Metro

The Metro is the quickest and least expensive way to get around Moscow and Leningrad. At five kopeks to any destination, it's the travel bargain of the century. More than eight million people ride the Moscow Metro daily. They run every 50 seconds during rush hour. Central stations are beautifully decorated with chandeliers and mosaics. Metro stations are easy to spot; entrances on the street are marked with a large M. Even the long escalator rides are great entertainment. Metro maps can be purchased in the hotels and are posted inside each station. Automatic machines change 20-, 15- and 10-kopek coins to five-kopek coins. Deposit a five-kopek coin in the turnstile. Wait for the green light—the doors do close, with a ghastly thrust, if nothing has registered. All stations and transfer areas are clearly marked in Russian. If you don't read Cyrillic, have someone write down the name of your destination in Russian. People are always most helpful and will point you in the proper direction. It's time to be adventurous!

Taxi

Taxi service desks are located in the lobbies of most hotels. Here you can order a taxi—but at least one to two hours in advance, if not the night before! A service fee of one ruble is charged. If the desk says *nyet,* no taxis available, simply walk to the front of the hotel. Many times a taxi or private car can be found. Payment is made directly to the driver in rubles; each taxi should have a meter. Hailing taxis on the street can be a problem and some will request some other form of payment, like Marlboro cigarettes (try to carry a few packs at all times). It's illegal to pay in foreign currency, but some travelers do so in order to get a ride. Use your own judgment. Another way to get where you're going is to simply stick your hand out. Hitching is quite common, since everyone has problems getting a ride, and private cars are eager to earn a few extra rubles by picking up paying passengers.

Hired Car Or Rent-a-car

Many hotels offer car service with a driver. A guide can also be hired for the day. This must be paid in foreign currency. Outside the hotel, you'll usually find many cars and off-duty taxi drivers lolling around, who'll be open to a suggestion. Some can be hired for the day to take you around town. Make your own payment agreement beforehand. Moscow and Leningrad have a few rent-a-car companies. Driving in Russia is worse than

Rome! In addition, all signs are written in Russian and gas stations are hard to find (and have huge lines). It's best to hire a car or use public transportation. It's also possible to drive your own car in from Europe. This requires advance planning and permissions, since a few borders are crossed and special insurance is necessary.

THE TRANS-SIBERIAN RAILROAD

If you're among those intrepid souls eager to see all of the Soviet Union, then the Trans-Siberian RR might be in your travel plans. You won't exactly sip tea from a giant samovar while the frozen scenery rushes past, à la Tolstoy, but you will clatter from Moscow or Leningrad to Vladivostok, on the Sea of Japan, or to Beijing via Mongolia, or even points west such as Berlin or Paris. From Vladivostok you can take a Soviet cruise ship to Yokohama, Japan, or you can turn around and clatter back the six days to Moscow. There's no better--or cheaper--way to see interior Russia and Mongolia.

Year-round, trains go between Moscow and Beijing twice a week; the tracks to Vladivostok (Nakhadka, actually, the next town) are only open May-September. Make your reservations a minimum of two months in advance, and give yourself at least a week prior to departure to get all the visas. You'll need Russian and Mongolian visas for the trip to Beijing, a Polish visa for Berlin, and a Hungarian visa for Budapest. Contact the nearest Intourist office for local agencies that book passage on the railroad (see "Useful Addresses," p. 72).

As of August 1990, Moscow to Beijing was $350-500 per person, depending on the designation: hard class, four persons per compartment; soft class, four persons in a bigger compartment; deluxe, two persons per compartment. Regardless of your choice be sure to bring your own coffee, tea and snacks. You can eat for $1-2/day, but the food is notoriously awful. The train stops half a dozen times every day for 10-30 minutes, which is just enough time to stretch your legs and grab a more palatable meal from a vendor.

Every station has an Intourist office, coffee shop, and restaurant.

For the trip to Beijing make sure to bring both rubles and Reminbi, or Chinese foreign exchange (FEC). The Soviet dining car only takes rubles, and at the Soviet/Mongolian border the car is changed for a Chinese diner, which only takes FEC.

Beijing-Moscow
Train #3, deluxe class: $400, soft class: $355
  hard class: $270
Train #19: deluxe class: $415, soft class: N/A
  hard class: $275

Irkutsk-Moscow--train #1
Day 1 Departure: 2055
Day 4 Arrival: 1640
Soft Class: US$243; Hard Class: US$123

Moscow-Irkutsk--train #2
Day 1 Departure: 1405
Day 4 Arrival: 1455
Soft Class: US$243; Hard Class: US$123

Moscow-Leningrad--train #6
Day 1 Departure: 2310
Day 2 Arrival: 0752
Soft Class: US$68; Hard Class: US$57

Leningrad-Moscow--train #5
Day 1 Departure: 2334
Day 2 Arrival: 0740
Soft Class: US$68; Hard Class: US$57

(top) Moscow in winter; (bottom) Leningrad by night

ACCOMMODATIONS

Most group tours are provided with first-class hotel accommodations. Intourist hotels usually offer deluxe, first-class or tourist accommodations. For individual travelers, hotels are the most expensive part of the stay. To visit Russia, you must pay the fixed rate for Soviet Intourist hotels, which are expensive, costing up to $200 per person a night. (Note that in most instances it costs only a few rubles extra for a double room.) Cheap hotels, hostels or dormitories are virtually nonexistent. (One can "camp" at designated campgrounds, but this must be set up before entering the country and arranged far in advance.)

Registration

Upon arrival, hand in your passport and visa. The hotel registers you within the country and returns everything within a few days. (Notice that the hotel dates are stamped on the back of your visa. If you exit the country and haven't been stamped, you may be pulled aside for questioning. Make sure a hotel stamp appears on the back of your visa.) You will also be issued a hotel card *(propusk)* Keep this with you at all times. You need to show it to the doorman, who might block your entrance until the card is shown. This is because Soviets aren't allowed to enter the Intourist hotels unless they're registered guests.

If you have Soviet visitors, it's required that they register in the hotel, and they must leave by around 11 p.m. (You can try meeting them outside and walking in past the doorman speaking to them in English. If they go unnoticed, usually they can go "unregistered.") They could get in trouble for spending the night.

Hall Attendants

The name of the hotel is written in Russian on the hotel card, which can be shown to taxis, etc. Most hotels still have a *dezhurnaya* (hall attendent) on each floor. When you show her your hotel card, she'll give you the key. (Some "Westernized" hotels just issue the key at the front desk.) The *dezhurnaya* is also positioned to notice all that is happening in your hallway. She's very helpful and

friendly; if you have a question, she's the one to ask. Most rooms are quite adequate, but they sometimes don't match your conception of a first-class hotel, particularly those outside of Moscow and Leningrad. They have a bathroom, TV (*do* try to watch some Soviet television) and phone, but many lack room service. A laundry bag is provided in each room; dry-cleaning services aren't often available. Give your clothes to the maid or *dezhurnaya*. It's usually same-day or two-day service.

Hotel Restaurants

Hotels have a restaurant, a few cafes located on different floors, foreign currency bars and a post office. A brochure is usually provided in each room listing the facilities and phone numbers. Most Intourist hotels are accustomed to catering to groups. Sometimes it's quite impossible for an individual to get a table in a restaurant for lunch or dinner without a reservation or a group. This can get quite frustrating. Make a reservation in the morning at the service desk. Many hotels now offer the "Swedish table," a cafeteria-style restaurant. Check to see if your hotel has one. Here a quick inexpensive smorgasborg-type breakfast, lunch or dinner can be found.

Other Issues

A word of warning: Housekeepers in the USSR often lack a respect for privacy, and enter the room without knocking, or bring back your laundry at midnight. Use the chain lock! Most hotels don't have a central switchboard—which means someone calling the main number of the hotel won't be able to contact you. Each room has a phone with a corresponding seven-digit number. Only if the caller knows this number can he or she call you directly—either from another room in the hotel or the outside. A red light lit up on the nightstand doesn't mean you have messages, but that, most likely, you owe money. Each spring/summer many hydroelectrical plants shut down a few weeks for spring cleaning, and large sections of the city may be without hot water, including your hotel.

(clockwise from top) a Moscow Circus clown;
practice at the Moscow Circus; rural life near Moscow

FOOD

Russian cooking is both tasty and filling, and aside from the expected borsch and beef Stroganov, it includes many delectable dishes that originate in regions of the other 15 republics such as Uzbekistan, Georgia or the Ukraine.

History

The traditions of Russian cooking date way back to the simple recipes of the peasantry, who made full use of the abundant supply of potatoes, cabbage, cucumbers, onions and bread to fill their hungry stomachs. For the cold northern winters, they would pickle what few vegetables were available, along with preserving fruits in the form of jam. The somewhat bland diet was compensated with sour cream, parsley, dill and other dried herbs. A popular old Russian saying expressed this: *Shchi da kasha, Pishcha nasha,* "Cabbage soup and porridge are our food." The writer Nikolai Gogol painted a picture of the Russian peasant's kitchen: "In the room was the old familiar friend found in every kitchen, namely a *samovar,* and a three-cornered cupboard with cups and teapots, painted eggs hanging on red and blue ribbons in front of the icons, with flat cakes, horseradish and sour cream on the table along with bunches of dried fragrant herbs and a jug of *kvas*" (dark beer made from fermented black bread). Russians are still quite proud of these basic ingredients in their diet, which remain the staples of the Russian meal today. They'll boast that there is no better bread, *(khleb)* in the world as a freshly baked loaf of Russian black bread. Raisa Gorbachev presented Nancy Reagan with a cookbook containing hundreds of potato recipes!

Peter the Great introduced French cooking to his empire in the 18th century. While the peasantry had access only to the land's crops, the nobility hired its own French cooks, who introduced eating as an art, and often prepared up to 10 elaborate courses, filled with delicacies, just for dinner. Eventually many of the Russian writers ridiculed the monotonous and gluttonous life of the aristocracy, many of whom based their entire day around meals. Ivan Goncharov coined the term "Oblomovism" in his novel *Oblomov* (1859) to express the lazy, sluggish and stagnated life of the Russian gentry. In *Dead Souls,* Nikolai Gogol described a typical meal enjoyed by his main character in the home of an aristocrat. "On the table there appeared a white sturgeon, ordinary sturgeon, salmon, pressed caviar, fresh caviar, herrings, smoked tongues and dried sturgeon. Then there was a baked three-hundred pound sturgeon, a pie stuffed with mushrooms, fried pastries, dumplings cooked in melted butter, and fruit stewed in honey . . . After drinking glasses of vodka of a dark olive color, which one only finds in the transparent Siberian stones of which seals are carved in Russia, the guests had dessert. . . . After the champagne, they uncorked some bottles of cognac, which put still more spirit into them and made the whole party merrier than ever!"

Vodka was (and still is) the indispensable drink for any class or occasion. Neither the Russian peasant nor aristocrat ever drank vodka without doing a thorough job of it! Anton Chekhov wrote of a group of Russian peasants who, "on the Feast of the Intercession, seized the chance to drink for three days. They drank their way through fifty rubles of communal funds . . . one peasant beat his wife and then continued to drink the cap off his head and boots off his feet!" All these combina-

---

"The Russian *obyed* is a meal which starts with a fiery vodka gulp any time after noon and tails off with tea and cigarettes. The waiter puts before us little liquor glasses and another bottle of vodka. While we still gasp and blink over this, he has gotten the cold *zakuski* of black rye bread and butter, sardinka, salty beluga and cold ham, and has started us on the first course. Then comes a big pot of cabbage soup which we are to season with a swimming spoonful of thick sour cream. The chunky pieces of half-boiled meat floating in it are left high and dry by the soup's consumption. Next follows the meat and roast partridge with sugared cranberries, which we wash down with red wine from the Crimean States. For dessert, the torte (cake) and the last item, cheese. Frankly, it calls for the sauce of a prodigious appetite. But contemplating the *obyed,* as an institution so evolved as to fit into the general scheme of life, it finds merit. The Russian meal is a guide to the Russian character."

—From a foreign traveler's journal (1908)

tions of food and spirit afford us an understanding of how much the Russian meal is a guide to the Russian character.

What To Expect

Most travelers on a group tour will be provided with up to three meals a day. Breakfast *(zavtrak)* consists of coffee or tea, juice, eggs, kasha, cheese, cold meats or sausage and a plentiful supply of bread and butter. Some hotels now offer a Swedish table, providing a better selection. For those who normally don't start off a day with a heavy breakfast, bring along a bottle of instant coffee and cream, packaged oatmeal, and the like, plus an electric coil to boil water in the room. Lunch *(obyed)* consists of soup, bread, salad, and usually a choice of meat, chicken or fish with potatoes, a pickled vegetable and a sweet dessert of cakes or *morozhnoye* (ice cream). Over 170 tons of ice cream are consumed in Moscow and Leningrad each day! Don't expect a large supply of fresh vegetables or fruits. Salads or vegetables will include cucumbers, tomatoes, cabbage, beets, potatoes and onions. Sour cream *(smetana)* is a popular condiment—Russians love sour cream on everything. Some even drink a glass for breakfast! Dinner *(oozhiin)* is much the same as lunch, except vodka, wine, champagne or cognac will usually be served.

Most hotel restaurants do not offer a wide selection; on a group tour you'll be served a fixed menu each day with few alternate choices. In addition, many selections which appear on the menu do not appear in the kitchen. If the dish has no corresponding price, it's not available. Hotel and foreign currency restaurants usually have better and faster service which, on the whole, can still be quite slow. Tipping is accepted (5-10 percent), but

use your own judgment—waiters are notorious for disappearing just at the moment you have a question. If you do get discouraged with the service, the meal, or even the language problem (though many menus are written in English, German and Russian), remember always that diplomacy and patience are virtues. Find the boss or the Intourist Desk to express a complaint—or ask for the restaurant's *kniga zhalov* (complaint book).

Dining

The first point to remember when dining out is that most Soviets consider eating out an expensive and special event and enjoy turning dinner into a leisurely evening-long experience. Many restaurants provide entertainment along with a meal. Don't expect to rush in, grab a quick bite to eat, and rush out again. In the European fashion, different parties are often seated together at the same table—an excellent way to meet the locals.

If you are short of time, try to eat in your hotel. Hotels are set up to accommodate group tours. Many individual travelers experience difficulties in obtaining a simple meal in their hotel restaurant. If the hotel doesn't have a Swedish table buffet *(Shvetski Stol),* you can make a dining room reservation earlier in the day at the Intourist Service Desk. To speed up a meal you can even preorder your appetizers, so that they're on the table when you arrive. Check to see how long a dish takes to prepare—a meat dish may take 10-15 minutes, while chicken sometimes takes up to an hour!

If you're going to a restaurant in town, it's also advised to make a reservation in advance. If you have no reservaton and there's a big waiting line, talk to the *shveytsar* (doorman), who may let you in ahead of the others, as a foreigner (if you feel comfortable with that). Many times the sign, *Mect Het,* will be posted in Cyrillic, meaning No Space Available. Stick your head in the door; often, if the proprietor notices a foreigner, he will miraculously find an empty table!

Most restaurants (in Cyrillic *pectopah,* pronounced "restoran") are open from 11 a.m. to 11 p.m., and close a few hours in the afternoon. At restaurants with music and dancing, expect to spend some time, and don't expect a *quiet* time. During the music, it's hard to hear anything but! These can also be on the expensive side. Sometimes no liquor is served, but you can bring your own. Many of the newly opened co-op restaurants specialize in a regional cuisine—such as *shashlik,* shish kebab or other spicy dishes. Others may provide one choice as the "meal of the day." Even though there may not be a wide selection, the food is usually tasty and the meal served quickly in pleasant surroundings.

Food Now!
It often seems that, especially if you're an individual traveler, every time you're hungry, it's hard to find anything to eat except bread, sweets or Pepsi-Cola. Since *perestroika,* more cafes are springing up about town. Even though smaller than restaurants and with limited menus, they offer an adequate and quick meal. Look for the *zakuso-chnaya,* a snack-type bar serving hot and cold appetizers that often specialize in one dish, which reflects its name: *blinnaya* serves blini; *pelmennaya,* pelmeni; *pirozhkovnaya,* pirozhki; *shashlichnaya,* shashlik; *chainaya,* tea. Learn the letters of the Russian alphabet so you can recognize these cafes on the street. All cafes carry coffee or tea and some type of bottled soda. Recently a few Western fast-food chains have hit Moscow, such as McDonald's and even Baskin-Robbins ice cream.

Drinking
Most bars are found in all the major hotels. For *valuta* (foreign currency), they serve a selection of Soviet and Western sodas, spirits, apertifs, munchies, and sometimes a few hot dishes. At ruble bars, you'll get Russian wines, champagne and cognac, along with espresso coffee, sandwiches and pastries. These are usually open to 2 a.m. Many times a hotel will have a small bar or cafe on your floor. Drink only bottled water, though it's salty; there are many types of bottled sodas. Watch out for iced drinks, chilled fruit juices and *kompot* (fruit in sugared water), which are often made from the local water.

Food Shopping
If you're out to shop for food, grocery stores are different than we know them in the West. Usually each store sells only one type of item—a bread and pastry store, a cheese store, a milk products store. Some *gastronom* have more of a supermarket-like selection. Many of the *rinok* (markets) offer a selection of the hard-to-find fruits and vegetables, especially in summer.

Home Cooking
If invited to a Russian home, expect a large welcome. The Russians love hospitality and usually go all-out to prepare a spread. If you can, bring along a bottle of champagne or vodka—since they're harder for Russians to buy. A toast is usually followed by swigging down the entire shot of vodka —and then another toast! Be aware that vodka adds up after an entire evening of toasts— you may want to consider sipping a few (to the

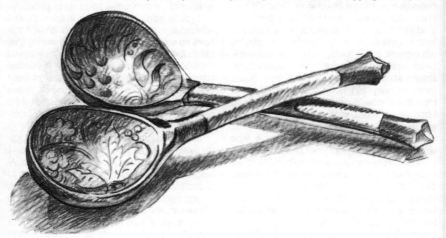

chagrin of your host). Unless you have the stomach stamina of Rambo, you'll more likely feel like Godzilla in the morning! Some popular toasts are: *Za Mir I Druzhba* (To Peace and Friendship), *Do Dnya* (Bottoms Up), and the most popular, *Na Zdoroviye* (To Your Health!).

ON THE MENU

The menu is divided into four sections: *zakuski* (appetizers), *pervoye* (first course), *vtoroye* (second course), and *sladkoe* (dessert). The ordering is done all at once, from appetizer to dessert. *Zakuski* are Russian-style hors d'oeuvres that include fish, cold meats, salads and marinated vegetables.

Ikra is caviar: *krasnaya* (red from salmon) and *chornaya* (black from sturgeon). The best is *zernistaya,* the fresh unpressed variety. The most expensive is the black *beluga*; another is *sevruga*. Caviar is usually available at Intourist restaurants and can be bought in the beriozkas.

Many varieties of Russian soup are served, more often at lunch than dinner. *Borshch* is the traditional red beet soup made with beef and served with a spoonful of sour cream. *Solyanka* is a tomato-based soup with chunks of fish or meat and topped with diced olives and lemon. *Shchi* is a tasty cabbage soup. A soup made from pickled vegetables is *rasolnik*. *Okroshka* is a cold soup made from a *kvas* base.

Meals consist of meat *(mya'so),* chicken *(kur'iitsa),* or fish *(rii'ba)*. *Bifshtek* is a small fried steak with onions and potatoes. Beef Stroganov is cooked in sour cream, and served with fried potatoes. *kutlyeta po Kiyevski* is chicken Kiev, stuffed with melted butter (cut slowly!); *kutlyeta po pajarski* is a chicken cutlet; *tabak* is a slightly seasoned fried or grilled chicken. The fish served is usually salmon, sturgeon, herring or halibut.

Other dishes include *blini,* small pancakes stuffed with different fillings; *pelmeni,* boiled dumplings filled with meat and served with sour cream; and *pirozhki,* fried rolls with a meat filling.

Dessert includes such sweets as *vareniki,* sweet dumplings filled with fruit and topped with sugar; torte, cake; *ponchiki,* sugared donuts; or *morozhnoye,* ice cream.

Liquid Refreshment

Chai (tea) comes with every meal. Many times it is presugared; ask for *biz sak'hera,* if you go without sugar. Many Russians stir in a spoonful of jam instead of sugar. Coffee is not served as often. Alcoholic drinks consist of *pivo* (beer); *kvas* (like near-beer); *shampanskoye* (champagne); *vino* (wine) and vodka. Alcoholic drinks are ordered in grams; a small glass is 100 grams and a normal bottle consists of 750 grams or three-quarters of a liter. The best wine comes from Georgia and the Crimea. There are both *krasnoye* (red) and *beloye* (white). The champagne is generally on the sweet side. The best brandy comes from Armenia—*Armyanski konyak. Nalivka* is a fruit liqueur.

Vodka is by far the favorite drink and comes in a number of varieties other than Stolichnaya, Moskovskaya or Russkaya. There is *limonnaya* (lemon vodka), *persovka* (with hot peppers), *zubrovka* (flavored with a special grass), *ryabinovka* (made from ash berries), *tminaya* (caraway flavor), *starka* (a smooth dark vodka), *ahotnichaya vodka* (hunter's vodka), and *zveroboy* (animal killer!). One of the strongest and most expensive is *Zolotoye Koltso,* the Golden Ring. Vodka can be most easily found in the beriozkas, along with beer, champagne, wine and Western alcohols, such as scotch and whiskey. For a listing of restaurants and cafes see the "Practicallities" section for each city.

MENU VOCABULARY

Zakus'ki	**Appetizers**
gribi' so smetan'oi	mushrooms in sour cream sauce
ikra'	caviar
lososin'a	salmon
maslin'i	black olives
sardin'i	sardines
seld	herring
salat'	salad
salat kra'bi pod	crab salad in mayonnaise
salat iz ogurtsov'	cucumber salad
salat iz pomidor'	tomato salad
stolich'ni Salat	salad made with potatoes, mayo, small chunks of meat, pickles

Sup	**Soup**
borshch	borsch
bulyon	bouillon
pokhlyob'ka	meat and potato soup
shchi	cabbage soup
solyan'ka-riibni or *myac'ni*	fish or meat soup

Mya'so	**Meat**
bara'nina	mutton
bifshteks'	steak
bitoch'ki	meatballs
file	filet
govya'dina	beef
gulyash	goulash
kolbasa'	sausage
kotle'ti	meat patties
lyul'ya kebab	lamp patties/kebab-style
shashliik"	shish kebab
shnit'sel	schnitzel
sosis'ki	wieners
svini'na	pork
telya'tina	veal
vetchi'na	ham
yaziik'	tongue

Ptiitsa	**Fowl**
kur'iitsa	chicken
ut'ka	duck

MENU VOCABULARY (CONTINUED)

Riiba	Fish
kra'bi	crab
kambala'	flounder
karp	carp
krevet'ki	shrimp
lososi'na	salmon
o'kun	perch
osetri'na	sturgeon
sudak'	pike
treska'	cod

Other Dishes	**Other Dishes**
blin'chiki	blintzes
blini'	pancakes with fillings
chebur'eki	fried meat pastries
kash'a	hot cereal
pelmen'i	boiled meat dumplings
pirogi	baked dough with fillings
pirozhki	small hot pastries with fillings
ris	rice
siir'niki	cheese pancakes
varen'iki	fruit or cheese dumplings
vatrush'ki	cold cheese tarts

Khleb (chorni/belii)	**Bread (black/white)**
bulochki	rolls
dzhem	jam
varen'ye	preserves

Molochniye Blyuda	**Dairy Products**
kefir'	thick buttermilk-like yoghurt
mas'lo	butter
prostok'vasha	yoghurt
sliv'ki	cream
smetan'a	sour cream
siir	cheese
tvorog'	cottage cheese
yait'so	egg

Ovoshchi	**Vegetables**
goroshek'	peas
griibi'	mushrooms
kapus'ta	cabbage
kartofel/kartoshka	potatoes

MENU VOCABULARY (CONTINUED)

luk	onions
morkov'	carrots
ogurtsi'	cucumbers
pomidor'i	tomatoes
svyok'la	beets

Frukti — **Fruit**

apelsi'ni	oranges
arbuz'	watermelon
dii'nya	melon
grush'i	pears
klubnika'	strawberries
limon'	lemon
malin'a	raspberries
per'siki	peaches
vinograd'	grapes
vish'nia	cherries
yab'loki	apples

Preprava — **Condiments**

chesnok'	garlic
garchee'tsa	mustard
ketsup	ketchup
myod	honey
per'ets	pepper
sak'har	sugar
sol	salt

Sladkoye — **Dessert**

konfeti	candy
orozh'noye	ice cream
orek'hi	nuts
pirozh'noye	small cake/cookie
plombir'	ice cream with fruit topping
shokolad'	chocolate
sukhari'	pretzels
tort	cake

Napitki — **Beverages**

chai	tea
kofe	coffee
kvas	near-beer
limonad	seltzered soda

MENU VOCABULARY (CONTINUED)

pivo	beer
vino	wine
vodka	vodka
voda	water
mineralnaya	mineral
gaziro'vannaya	seltzered
sok	juice
apelsinovi	orange
tomatni	tomato
vinogradni	grape
yablochni	apple

Termen	**Terms**
goryach'ee	hot
kho'lodno	cold
slish'kom	too
slad'kee	sweet
sukhoi'	dry
svezh'ee	fresh
he svezhee	not fresh

vkus'no	tasty
eto o'chen vkusno	it's very good/delicious
ne vkus'no	not tasty
s sak'harom	with sugar
biz sah'kara	without sugar
s molokom'	with milk
biz moloka'	without milk

s krov'yu	rare (meat)
sred'ne	medium
prozhar'enye	well done

restoran'	restaurant
samaapsloo'zhevaneye	self-service
otkri'to	open
zakri'to	closed
(obyed) pereriv'	(lunch) break
oo'zhin	dinner
zaf'trak	breakfast
mest nyet	no space available

MENU VOCABULARY (CONTINUED)

tarel'ka	plate
salfet'ka	napkin
chash'ka	cup
stakan'	glass
nozh	knife
vil'ka	fork
lozh'ka	spoon
stol	table
stul	chair
ceegare'tee	cigarettes
speech'kee	matches
ofit'siant/ka	waiter/waitress
Ya khachu'	I want
Ya khachu' chai	I want tea
menyoo	menu
schot	bill
preenesee'te bootil'koo	bring me a bottle of
veena'/pee'va	wine/beer
dai'te menye'	give me
peredai'tye menye	pass me
pozhal'sta	please
spasee'bo	thank you

SHOPPING

Most group travelers to the Soviet Union don't have much time, in between excursions, to spend on leisurely shopping. Besides, unlike other countries in the world, the Soviet Union is not a shopper's paradise. Stores don't brim over with specialty goods, and many items are always in short supply. Most goods are set at a fixed (state) price, sales are rare, and bargaining is not widely practiced.

The *Beriozka*

The best, quickest and most convenient way to shop is at the *beriozka*, the foreign currency store, which is usually located right in your hotel. These range from a few counters to large two-story emporiums that resemble a Western department store. *Beriozkas only* accept foreign currency (cash, travelers checks, credit cards). Bring a supply of small bills and change—the clerk gives change in whatever currency is left in the cash register.

The *beriozkas* have the best selection of Soviet goods at the most reasonable prices. Many times the same product is more expensive (in rubles) in local stores, if it can be found at all. Probably the most popular Russian souvenir is the *matryoshka,* the painted set of nested dolls. *Khokhloma* lacquerware comes in the form of trays, cups, spoons, bowls and vases. There are also miniature painted lacquer boxes and brooches from the Golden Ring villages of Palekh and Fedoskino. Other good buys are handicrafts, woodcarvings, amber, fur hats, embroidered shawls and linens, lace, filigree jewelry, ceramics, samovars, balalaikas, painted eggs, caviar, tea and tea sets, vodka, books, records and *znachki* (small pins used for trading). These stores also have a small supply of food, snacks, sodas, liquor and cigarettes. It's good to pick up a few items for late-night munchies.

Most *beriozkas* are open from 9 a.m. to 8 p.m. daily and close an hour for lunch sometime between noon and 3 p.m. In Moscow, the largest *beriozkas* are in the Rossiya, Mezhdunarodnaya and Ukrainia hotels. Your hotel also has small kiosks and post offices that sell foreign newspapers, magazines and books, postcards, stamps and pins.

The Local Store

If there's time, try to visit a few of the local stores about town. This gives a much better feel for the shopping life of the average Soviet citizen. These stores accept only rubles, no traveler's checks or credit cards. Some of the shopping stores are: the *univermag*, the large department store; *kommissioniye*, commission or second-hand stores, *co-op*, cooperatives; *rinoks*, the farmers market (both government and private—there's even a pet *rinok*); and kiosks, small booths. Most stores are open daily (except Sundays) from about 10 a.m. to 8 p.m., and close for an hour for lunch.

A Few Soviet Shopping Tips

Usually the procedure for purchasing an item in a local store involves several steps. First, locate the desired item and find out its price. Second, go to the *kassa* (cashier's booth) and pay. Third, bring the receipt back to the salesgirl, who will wrap and hand over your purchase. Prices are usually posted, especially in food stores. If things get too mathematical for you to fathom (one kilo of chocolate is three rubles and one kilo of candy is two rubles and you want a quarter kilo of each), ask a salesgirl to give you the total. Most stores still use an abacus to tally. Know your exact bill; if you are even one kopek off, you must return to the cashier to pay the discrepency! Sometimes you'll have to muscle your way toward the counter. If you have to stand in a long line (a way of life for most of the population), take the opportunity to practice your Russian. If you have any questions, don't be afraid to ask—many even know a few words of English and would be glad to help. If you see something you like, buy it! Most likely, it won't be there when you go back. Always bring along a small shopping bag; the stores and markets don't provide any (or you will end up with two kilos of strawberries in your pocket or purse!).

Some of the interesting stores in Moscow are **Gum** Department Store in Red Square, **Detsky Mir** (Children's World) and **Dom Knigi** (House of Books). Popular shopping districts are along the Arbat, Kuznetsky Most, Gorky, Petrovka and Stoleshnikov streets. Many Western companies are coming to Moscow; Christian Dior and Estee Lauder opened shops on Gorky Street. For a more complete listing of *beriozkas,* and local stores and their locations, see the "Practicalities" section for each city.

TERMS FOR LOCAL STORES

**Learn the Russian alphabet,
so you can sound out these store signs on the street.**

aptyeka	pharmacy
bukinist	second-hand bookstore
bulochnaya	bakery
chasy	watches and watch repair
galanteriya	clothing, fabrics and lingerie

TERMS FOR LOCAL STORES (CONTINUED)

gastronom	food store
khozyaistvenny magazin	hardware and kitchen supplies
khudozhestvenny	art gallery
kiosk	small stand
kino	movie cinema
knizhny (knigi) magazin	bookstore
kommissiony magazin	second-hand store
konditerskaya	confectionery—sweets and tea
kulinariya	small take-out delicatessens
magazin	store
mekha	fur shop
moloko	dairy products
morozhenoye	ice cream
myaso-Riiba	meat-fish
oboof	shoe store
odezhda	clothing store
ovoshchi-Frukti	vegetables and fruit
podarki	gifts
produkti	produce
remont	repair shop
rinok	farmer's market
shkolnik	school and office supplies
tabak	cigarettes and tobacco
tkani	sewing, fabrics, perfumes
tsvyeti	flowers
univermag	department store
viictavka	exhibit
yarmarka	string of small outdoor kiosks
Gedye' magazeen'?	Where is the shop?
Pakazhee'te	I would like to see
Oo vas yest?	Do you have?
Droogoi' raz'mair?	Another size?
Deshe'vlye/daro'zhe	Cheaper-more expensive
Droogo'va tsvet'a?	Another color?
Skol'ka e'to stoi'yeet?	How much does it cost?
Mozh'na primyer'eet	Can I try it on?
Menye' e'to (ne) nrav'eetsa	I (don't) like it.
Ya e'to kooplyoo'	I'll buy it.

CLOTHING AND SHOE SIZE CONVERSION

Women's Dress Sizes

USSR	44	46	48	50
US	6	8	10	12
European	34	36	38	40

Women's Shoes

USSR	34	35	36	37
US	4	5	6	7

Men's Suits

USSR	48	50	52	54	56
US	37-8	39-40	41-42	43-44	45-46

Men's Shoes

USSR	38	39	40	42	44
US	6 1/2-7	7 1/2-8	8 1/2-9	9 1/2-10	10 1/2-ll

HEALTH

Immunizations aren't required, unless you're coming from an affected area. The Soviet Union doesn't have many health risks, except for the cold and food! Some people may have trouble adjusting to Russian cuisine, which includes heavy breads, thick greasy soups, smoked fish and sour cream. Vegetables and fruit are in low supply. Bring digestive or stomach-disorder remedies. If you're a vegetarian or require a special diet, bring along what you need, even if it's instant, freeze-dried mixes or nutritional supplements. In the wintertime, be prepared for a possible cold. Do not drink the water, especially in Leningrad, where it's highly polluted. The parasite *Giardia lamblia* can cause severe illness. Drink bottled or boiled water. The bottled water does have an enormously high salt content; you may prefer soda or tea. Juices or flavored sugar waters cannot always be trusted, and watch out for iced drinks. In case of any illness, medical care in the Soviet Union is free of charge. Each hotel usually has its own resident physician. For a serious illness, contact your embassy or consulate and consider leaving the country for proper care. If you have a health ailment, consider purchasing some type of travel medical insurance before the trip. Do note that even though some areas of the USSR are experiencing unrest, it's considered safe to walk around Moscow and Leningrad any time during the day or evening. As in any big city, just take care of your valuables.

MONEY AND MEASUREMENTS

Currency Exchange

It's illegal to bring in or take out Soviet currency. (Small change is exempted as a souvenir.) Officially, foreign currency can only be converted into rubles at exchange offices at fixed rates. You can convert some currency to rubles at the airport or in your hotel. The customs declaration form must be presented when money is exchanged. The date and amount converted is noted on the form. You can re-exchange your unused rubles at the end of your trip (not before) at the airport or border. Remember when exiting that you cannot convert more rubles than you officially exchanged. It's illegal to change foreign currency on the black market. If the opportunity presents itself, be discreet, and be forewarned that you can be arrested. An interesting note is that the Soviet government, in a major move on 1 Nov. 1989, devalued the ruble by 90%. The ruble, for many years, was worth about $1.60; now it's worth about 16 cents. This was to bring the ruble closer to its actual value and to discourage the huge black-market exchanges. It also provided a further step in bringing the ruble closer to an open exchange on the world market.

Rubles

Soviet currency is the *ruble*. It comes in note denominations of 1, 3, 5, 10, 25, 50 and 100. The ruble is divided into 100 *kopeks*. There are 1, 2, 3, 5, 10, 15, 20, and 50 kopek coins, and a one-ruble coin.

Traveler's Checks And Credit Cards

Travelers checks and cash are accepted at banks and *beriozkas,* the foreign currency stores. It's advised to bring cash, especially small notes and change. Very often the beriozkas will not have your currency and will give a mixture of every other country's change. Also, foreign-currency bars and restaurants found in hotels don't often take traveler's checks. And it's very difficult to exchange traveler's checks into foreign cash. Major credit cards are accepted at Intourist hotels, beriozkas and some hotel restaurants. You should have rubles for regular stores and local transportation.

Valuables

Hotels usually have safety-deposit boxes by the front desk. It's advised to lock up your valuables, money, passport and airline tickets, even if it's with a lock on your suitcase. There have been reports of thefts from hotel rooms. In case of loss or theft, notify the Service Bureau at your hotel.

Times And Holidays

Most local stores open between 8 and 10 a.m. and close between 5 and 8 p.m. They close for an hour sometime between noon and 3 p.m. for lunch. Restaurants and cafes also close for a few hours during the day. If you're on a tight schedule, try to check operating hours first. *Beriozkas* are open from 9 a.m. to 8-11 p.m. Some also close an hour for lunch. Check the "Holiday and Festival" sections for each city for dates when stores are usually closed.

THE METRIC SYSTEM

1 inch = 2.54 centimeters (cm)
1 foot = .304 meters (m)
1 mile = 1.6093 kilometers (km)
1 km = .6214 miles
1 fathom = 1.8288 m
1 chain = 20.1168 m
1 furlong = 201.168
1 acre = .4047 hectares (ha)
1 sq km = 100 ha
1 sq mile = 59 sq km
1 ounce = 28.35 grams
1 pound = .4536 kilograms (kg)
1 short ton = .90718 metric ton
1 short ton = 2000 pounds
1 long ton = 1.016 metric tons
1 long ton = 2240 pounds
1 metric ton = 1000 kg
1 quart = .94635 liters
1 US gallon = 3.7854 liters
1 Imperial gallon = 4.5459 liters
1 nautical mile = 1.852 km

To compute centigrade temperatures, subtract 32 from Fahrenheit and divide by 1.8. To go the other way, multiply centigrade by 1.8 and add 32.

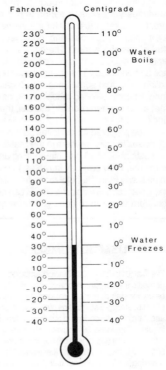

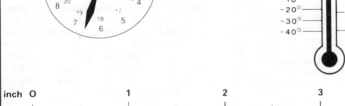

COMMUNICATIONS AND CONDUCT

The Telephone

Communication can be a *bolshoi* problem in the Soviet Union! Be patient—take deep breaths and/or recite your mantra. Calls to the States can take days, but those to Europe go through faster. You can order a call for a specific time at the Service Bureau in your hotel. Your call may come through immediatly (put through to your room); sometimes your waiting period is two days or more. (Try to reserve a call for the evening. This way, if it's late, you'll be in the room sleeping, instead of missing a tour.) There's also a central number in each city that you can dial directly to place a phone order. The operator usually speaks English. Note that sometimes the operators disconnect if an answering machine comes on. Try to get across, when ordering the call, that a machine is just fine!

Also, be prepared for overseas calls to be quite expensive. To call anywhere in the States at anytime costs about $10 per minute. England is $5 per minute. (You can pay in rubles.) Local calls can be made from the hotel room, free of charge. Long-distance calls within the USSR can be made (right from your room) once you know the area code. For example, Moscow is 095 and Leningrad is 812. To call Moscow from Leningrad dial 8 (to get a long-distance line), then 095 and the seven-digit number. To make a local call from the street: pay phones take two kopeks. Use either a two-kopek piece or two one-kopek pieces. A 10-kopek coin also works.

Long Distance

Special "long-distance" phones can also be used for calling other cities within the Soviet Union. Here you must use 15-kopek coins only. Deposit the coins and remember to push the black button at the bottom when the call goes through. If you don't, the connection is broken. You can also go to the city's long-distance telephone center *(peregovorny punkt)*. You must preorder and pay for the number of minutes of your call. There's usually a waiting line. It's announced by loudspeaker what number booth you're assigned to. Some hotels have telex and fax facilities.

Mail

The post office sends telegrams and packages. Do not wrap the package; the contents must be inspected before shipping. Mail is slow and erratic. Many travelers arrive home before their postcards! Any mail sent to the USSR takes several weeks to a month. If you're staying for a length of time, mail to each city can be addressed to either "Post Restante" or care of Intourist. The Moscow address is Hotel Intourist (Poste Restante), 3/5 Gorky St., K-600 Moscow, USSR. In Leningrad: Poste Restante, C-400/6 Nevsky Prospekt, Leningrad. If you know what hotel you'll be staying in, have mail addressed to you in care of that hotel. Mail won't be delivered to you in your room, nor will you be contacted. You must check at the lobby service counter, which gives you the whole guest-mail stack to sift through.

USEFUL NUMBERS

Fire Dial (01); Police (02); Medical Ambulance (03) (If medical emergency contact your hotel or embassy for staff doctor); Local long-distance asst. (07); Local long-distance line dial 8—wait for tone and then dial city code and number); information inquiries (business 09) (private 00); correct time (Moscow 100) (Leningrad 08) (Leningrad weather 001); taxi (Moscow 2250000) (Leningrad 3120022; ordering an international call (Moscow 8-194) (Leningrad 3144747)—or order through your Intourist Hotel Service Desk.

City Area Codes

Moscow 095; Leningrad 812; Yaroslavl 0852; Kostroma 09422; Ivanovo 09322; Vladimir 09222; Novgorod 816; Pskov 81122.

Etiquette

Russians on the surface appear very restrained, formal, even somewhat glum. But there is a dichotomy between public and private appearance. In private and informal situations or after friendship is established, their character is suddenly charged with emotional warmth, care and humor. They're intensely loyal and willing to help. Arriving in or leaving the country will merit great displays of affection, usually with flowers, bear hugs, kisses and tears. If invited to someone's home for dinner, expect large preparations. The Russians are some of the most hospitable people in the world. If you can't handle alcohol, watch out for the endless number of toasts!

The formal use of the patronymic (where the father's first name becomes the children's middle names) has been used for centuries. For example, if Ivan named his son Alexander, his patronymic is Ivanovich. Especially in formal or business dealings, try to remember the person's patronymic: Alexander Ivanovich, or Mariya Pavlona (her father's name is Pavel or Paul). As with Western names, where Robert is shortened to Bob, the same is done with Russian first names, once you've established a friendship. Call your friend Alexander "Sasha," Mikhail "Misha," and Mariya "Masha," or even by the further diminutive form, "Mashenka."

Complaints

Each restaurant and cafe has a service book *(kniga zhalov),* where you can register complaints. Hotel complaints can be reported to the service desk. Remember that rules, regulations and bureaucracy play a large role in Soviet life—with many uniformed people enforcing them. People here aren't always presumed innocent until proven guilty. When dealing with police or other officials, it's best to be courteous while explaining a situation. For example, police in the streets will randomly pull over vehicles to spot-check the registration. If you're pulled over, it doesn't mean you did anything wrong. If you're kept waiting long, as in restaurants for service, remember that everyone else is waiting too. Be patient and reminded that you are in someone else's country. Don't lose your temper (humor often works better), mock or laugh when not appropriate.

A few commonly used words are *nyet* and *nelzya,* which mean "no" and "it's forbidden." The Russian language uses many negations. If someone tells you that it's forbidden, it may mean that they simply don't know or don't want to take responsibility for something. Ask elsewhere. The *babushki* (elderly women) are a hearty breed and love to take on the voice of authority!

Photography Restrictions

You may photograph anything you wish except for the following: military installations, border areas, airports and from airplanes inside the country, railway stations, bridges, tunnels, power and radar stations, telephone and telegraph centers, and industrial enterprises. If you aren't sure, inquire before you shoot. Ask permission at factories, state institutions and farms—and of individuals, who may not want their picture taken. Many times people love to take on authority and will demand the film or assert that it's forbidden (when it's actually not). Understand that Soviets are sometimes sensitive about foreigners photographing what they perceive as being backward or in a poor state of affairs. Always remain courteous.

Travel Restrictions

One cannot venture more than 35 km outside of each city. Only the cities specified on your visa can be visited. Unless the visa is extended, one must exit the country on the date that is shown on the visa.

Speculators

Especially in the big cities, you'll most likely be approached by people asking, "Do you speak English?" and trying to sell everything from lacquer boxes and caviar to army watches. Some may even want to buy your clothes. The government is trying to discourage speculation, since most want to sell their wares for foreign currency. Dealing in foreign currency is illegal. Work out your own bargain, but be discreet. Many will ask to change money; it's best to stay away. One added note: These days, any male may be approached by an attractive lady in the hotel bar or even in an elevator. Prostitution is becoming a large problem in Moscow and Leningrad. Paying for more than a drink can lead to an arrest. Plainclothes police often patrol the hotels.

USEFUL ADDRESSES AND PHONE NUMBERS

IN THE U.S.

Soviet Embassies And Consulates
Soviet Embassy: 1115-1125 16th St. NW, Washington, D.C. 20036, tel. (202) 628-7551/7554.
Visa Consular Office: 1825 Phelps Place NW, Washington, D.C. 20009, tel. (202) 332-1513.
Soviet Consulate General in New York: 9 E. 91st St., New York, NY 10020, tel. (212) 348-6772.
Soviet Consulate General in San Francisco: 2790 Green St., San Francisco, CA 94123, tel. (415) 922-6642.

Airlines
Finnair: tel. (800) 950-5000.
Pan Am: tel. (800) 221-1111.
British Air: tel. (800) 247-9297.
Aeroflot: 630 Fifth Ave. Suite 241, New York, NY 10111 tel. (212) 397-1660.

Travel Organizations:
Pan Am Tours to USSR: Call (800) 843-8687 and press 2.
Intourist: 630 Fifth Ave. Suite 868, New York, NY 10111 tel. (212) 757-3884/5.
American Express Travel Services: World Financial Center, 200 Vesey St., New York, NY 10285-0320, tel. (212) 640-2000.
Council on International Exchange (CIEE): 205 E 42nd St., New York, NY 10017, tel. (212) 661-1414.
Tour Designs, Inc.: 510 H St. SW, Washington, D.C. 20024, tel. (800) 432-8687/(202) 554-5820.
Vega International Travel Service, Inc.: 201 N Wells St. Suite 430, Chicago, IL 60606, tel. (312) 332-7211.

Beverly International Travel, Inc.: 9465 Wilshire Blvd. Suite 432, Beverly Hills, CA 90212, tel. (213) 271-4116/272-3011.
Center for US-USSR Initiatives: 3268 Sacramento St., San Francisco, CA 94115, tel. (415) 346-1875 (Exec. Dir. Sharon Tennison). For more information on the work of citizen diplomacy and trips to the USSR, you may write to the above address.

IN THE U.K.

Soviet Embassies And Consulates
Soviet Embassy: 18 Kensington Place Gardens, London W8 4QP tel (01) 229-6412/727-6888.
Soviet Visa Consulate: 5 Kensington Place Gardens, tel. (01) 229-3215/16.

Airlines In London
British Air: tel. (01) 897-4000.
Finnair: tel. (01) 408-1222.
Pan Am: tel. (01) 409-0688.
Aeroflot: 69-72 Piccadilly W1, tel. (01) 493-7436/492-1756.

Travel Organizations
Intourist: 292 Regent St., London W1R, tel. (01) 580-1221/631-1252.
Barry Martin Travel, Ltd.: 342/346 Linen Hall, 162/168 Regent St., London W1X 1RA, tel. (01) 439-1271.
Progressive Tours, Ltd.: 12 Porchester Pl., Connaught Square, London W2 2BS, tel. (01) 262-1676.

MOSCOW

Embassies
U.S.: 19/23 Chaikovsky St., tel. 252-2451-59.
U.K.: 14 Morisa Toreza Emb., tel. 231-8511/12.

Airlines

Finnair: 5 Proyezd Khudozhestvennovo Teatra, tel. 292-8788. Open Mon.-Fri. 9 a.m. to 5 p.m..

Pan Am: Hotel Mezhdunarodnaya II, Krasnopresnenskaya 12, Rm. 1102, tel. 253-2658/59. Open Mon.-Fri. 9 a.m. to 6 p.m..

British Air: Hotel Mezhdunarodnaya II, Krasnopresnenskaya 12 Rm. 1905, tel. 253-2482.

Aeroflot: Head Office Frunzenskaya Emb. 4 tel. 241-9947

Airports

Sheremetyevo: Leningradskoe Shosse (Sheremetyevo II is the International Airport about 20 miles/32 km outside the city); **Vnukovo** and **Domodedovo** (both local airports). Domodedovo is the largest airport in the Soviet Union.

Train Stations

Byelorussky: Byelorussky Square, tel. 253-4908 (trains to and from Berlin, Warsaw, London, Paris, Vilnius, Minsk, Smolensk and Brest).

Kazansky: Komsomolsky Square, tel. 266-2542 (trains to and from Siberia and Central Asian Republics).

Kievsky: Kievsky Square, tel. 240-7622 (trains to and from the Ukraine and Eastern Europe).

Kursky: 29 Chkalov St., tel. 266-5652 (trains to and from Armenia, Azerbaijan, the Crimea and the Caucasus).

Leningradsky: 1 Komsomolsky Square, tel. 262-4281 (trains to and from Leningrad, Finland, Novgorod, Pskov and Tallinn, Estonia).

Paveletsky: Leninsky Square, tel. 235-4673 (trains to and from the Volgograd region).

Rizhsky: Rizhsky Square, tel. 266-1176 (trains to and from the Baltic).

Savyolovsky: Butyrskoi Zastavy Square, tel. 285-9000 (trains to Uglich).

Yaroslavsky: Komsomolsky Square, tel. 266-0595 (trains to and from the Far East. The Trans-Siberian departs daily at 10 a.m.).

Travel Agencies

Intourist: Moscow Main Office, 16 Prospekt Marxa, tel. 203-6962, telex 411211. At Airport Sheremetyevo II 156-9435 (Each Intourist hotel has an Intourist Service Desk.).

American Express Co.: Moscow, 21-A Sadovo-Kudrinskaya St., tel. 254-0671. Open Mon.-Fri. 9 a.m. to 5:30 p.m. Note: American Express now changes traveler's checks into dollars.

Barry Martin Travel: Moscow, Hotel Mezhdunarodnaya II, Krasnopresnenskaya Emb. 12 Rm. 940, tel. 253-2940.

LENINGRAD

Airports
Pulkovo: (Pulkovo II is International).

Airlines
Finnair: 19 Gogol St., tel. 315-9736/312-8987.

Pan Am: 36 Herzen St. (in Aeroflot office), tel. 311-5819.

Train Stations

Baltiisky: 120 Obvodnov Kanal (trains to and from Petrodvorets and Lomonosov).

Finlandsky: 6 Lenin Square (trains to and from Repino and Finland).

Moskovsky: 2 Vosstaniya (Uprising) Square (trains to and from Moscow and points south).

Varshavsky: Izmailovsky Prospekt (trains to and from Warsaw, Eastern Europe and Berlin).

Vitebsk: 52 Zagorodny Prospekt (trains to and from Pushkin and Pavlovsk).

Embassies
U.S. Consulate: 15 Petra Lavrova St., tel. 274-8235.

*"Moscow
Fervent and mighty
The heart of my native land
No invader could ever make you fall
Of my country
Moscow—Moskva' Moya'
Is my favorite place of all!*—Ti sam'aya lubi'maya.

—popular Muscovite song

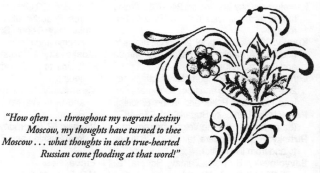

*"How often . . . throughout my vagrant destiny
Moscow, my thoughts have turned to thee
Moscow . . . what thoughts in each true-hearted
Russian come flooding at that word!"*

—Alexander Pushkin

MOSCOW

INTRODUCTION

History

Moscow *(Moskva)* has, for centuries, been inseparably linked with the life of all Russia. Moscow's history dates back more than 800 years to 1147, when Prince Yuri Dolgoruky established the first small outpost on the banks of the Moscow River. The settlement grew into a large and prosperous town, which eventually became the capital of the principality of Moscovy. By the 15th century, Moscow was Russia's political, cultural and trade center, and during the reign of Ivan the Great, it became the capital of the Russian Empire as well. Ivan summoned the greatest Russian and European architects to create a capital so wondrous that "reality embodied fantasy on an unearthly scale," and soon the city was hailed as the "New Constantinople." In the next century, Ivan the Terrible was crowned the first czar of all Russia inside the Kremlin's magnificent Uspensky Cathedral. The words of an old Russian proverb signified the power within the Kremlin: "There is only God and the center of government, the Kremlin." People from all over the world flocked to witness the splendors in the capital of the largest empire on earth. By the 18th century, a foreign traveler wrote that Moscow, "so irregular, so uncommon, so extraordinary, and so contrasted, had never before claimed such astonishment!"

In 1712, after Peter the Great transferred the capital to St. Petersburg, Moscow remained a symbol of national pride and continued to play a major role in the course of Russian history. Many eminent writers, scientists, artists and musicians, such as Pushkin, Tolstoy, Lomonosov, Repin and Tchaikovsky, lived and worked in Moscow, which never relinquished its political significance, artistic merit and nostalgic charm. Even when Napolean invaded in 1812, he wrote "I had no real conception of the grandeur of the city. It possessed fifty palaces of equal beauty to the Palais d'Elysee, furnished in French style with incredible luxuries." After a terrible fire destroyed Moscow during Napoleon's hasty retreat, Tolstoy wrote that "it would be difficult to explain what caused the Rus-

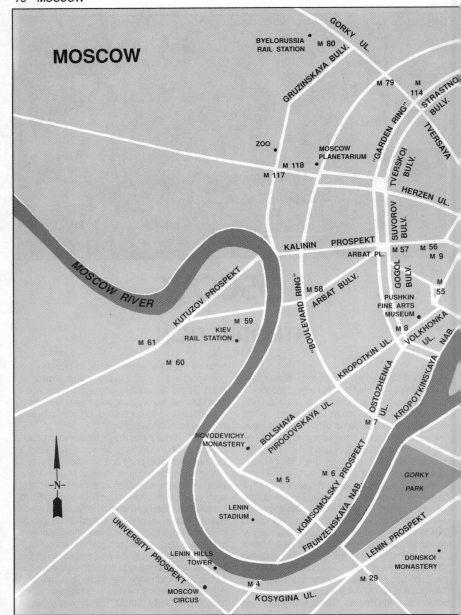

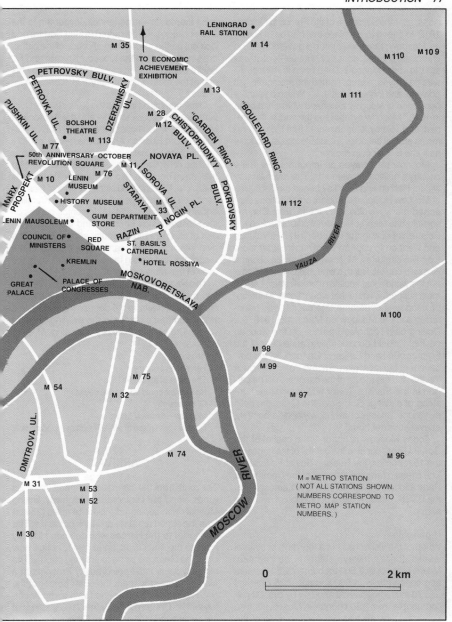

sians, after the departure of the French in October 1812, to throng to the place that had been known as Moscow; there was left no government, no churches, shrines, riches or houses—yet, it was still the same Moscow it had been in August. All was destroyed, except something intangible, yet powerful and indestructible. . . . Within a year the population of Moscow exceeded what it had been in 1812!" Moscow symbolized the soul of the empire, and Tolstoy later observed that Moscow remains eternal because "Russians look at Moscow as if she is their own mother."

Moscow also played an important role in the country's political movements. The revolutionary writers Herzen and Belinksy began their activities at Moscow University. Student organizations supported many revolutionary ideas, from Chernyshevsky's to Marx's. Moscow workers backed the Bolsheviks during the October 1917 Revolution and went on to capture the Kremlin. After more than two centuries, Moscow once again became Russia's capital. But this time, the city would govern the world's first socialist state. Trotsky, Lenin's main supporter, wrote that when "finally all the opposition was overcome, the capital was transferred back to Moscow on March 12, 1918. . . . Driving past Nicholas's palace on the wooden paving, I would occasionally glance over at the Emperor Bell and Emperor Cannon. All the barbarism of Moscow glared at me from the hole in the bell and the mouth of the cannon. . . . The carillon in the Savior's Tower was now altered. Instead of playing `God Save the Czar,' the bells played the `Internationale,' slowly and deliberately, at every quarter hour."

Today Moscow is not only the capital of the Soviet Union, but also the capital of the largest of the 15 republics, the Russian Soviet Federation. The Kremlin remains the seat of the Communist Party and the Soviet government. Largest city in the USSR, Moscow has a population of over nine million.

Highlights

Whether the visitor has but a few days or several weeks, there's always plenty to do and see. Moscow has over 2,500 monuments, 50 theaters and concert halls, 4,500 libraries, 125 cinemas and 70 museums, visited annually by over 20 million people from 150 countries. Moscow is also rich in history, art and architecture. One of the

most memorable experiences of your trip to the Soviet Union will be to stand in Red Square and look out on the golden magnificence of the cathedrals and towers of the Moscow Kremlin and St. Basil's Cathedral. One traveler noted the view "as one of the most beautiful fairy-tale scenes imaginable."

Other attractions include the Novodevichy Convent that dates back to 1514 and the Andronikov Monastery, which houses the Andrei Rublev Museum of Old Russian Art and the famed iconist's masterpieces. Moscow's museums and galleries host the collections of brilliant Russian and foreign masters. There are also all the cozy side streets to explore, little changed since the time of Ivan the Terrible. The nighttime reflections of the Kremlin's ancient clock tower and golden onion domes on the Moscow River bring to mind the lyrics from one of Russia's most popular songs: "Lazily the river like a silvery stream; ripples gently in the moonlight; and a song fades as in a dream, in the spell of this Moscow night."

There's an eternal enchantment about Moscow that makes the city unforgettable. It's felt in the early light of dawn, in the deepening twilight, in a warm summer's day or in the swirling snow of winter. The people of the city often sing, *Moskva Maiskaya,*

"Moscow
Fervent and mighty
The heart of my native land
No invader could ever make you fall
Of my country
Moscow—*Moskva' Moya'*
Is my favorite place of all!—*Ti sam'aya lubi'maya."*

ARRIVAL

The route from the international airport into town winds along the Leningradsky Highway, linking Moscow with Leningrad. About 14 miles (23 km) from the airport are large anti-tank obstacles, **The Memorial to the Heroes** who defended the city against the Nazi invasion in 1941; notice how close the Germans came to entering the city. The highway turns into Leningradsky Prospekt at a place that used to mark the outer border of the city. Here the street was lined with summer cottages. The **Church of All Saints** (1683) stands at the beginning of the prospekt. Other sights along the route are Peter the Great's Moorish-Gothic style **Petrovsky Palace,** built in 1775, and the 60,000-seat Dynamo Stadium. At no. 33 is the **Palace of Newlyweds,** where marriage ceremonies are performed. As you approach the center of Moscow, the Byelorussky Railway Station is on your right. Trains run to destinations in Western and Eastern Europe. This station marks the beginning of one of Moscow's main thoroughfares, Ulitsa Gorgovo (Gorky Street).

Before setting out on your first tour, take a minute and study a map of Moscow. Notice that it is made up of a system of rings. The Kremlin and Red Square lie at the center. A series of thoroughfares jut out from the square. Five concentric rings circle Red Square, each historically marking an old boundary of the city. Like a cross section of a tree, they tell us the age.

Each ring, centuries ago, was fortified by stone, wooden or earthen ramparts, which one could only enter through a special gate. The area around the Kremlin, once known as Kitai-gorod, formed the original border of the city in the 15th and 16th centuries. Many of the streets and squares in this area carry their original names: Petrovskaya Vorota (Peter's Gate), Kitaisky Proyezd (Kitai Passage), Razina Ulitsa (Razin Street), and Valovaya Ulitsa (Rampart Street).

The second ring is known as Bulvarnoye Koltso (Boulevard Ring). The city's suburbs were placed beyond this ring in the 17th century. The Sadovoye Koltso (Garden Ring) is the third ring that runs for 10 miles (16 km) around the city. In the 18th century, Moscow was surrounded here by an earthen rampart. This is also connected by the Koltso Metro line that stops at various points around this ring. The remains of the fourth ring that stretched 25 miles (40 km) around the city was known as the Kamer-Kollezhsky Rampart; it served as a customs boundary in the 18th and 19th centuries. The fifth ring is the Moscow Circular Road, which marks the present boundary of Moscow. The area past this ring is known as the Green Belt, a protected forested area where many Moscovites have country and summer houses, known as *dacha.*

METRO

One of the quickest and easiest ways of getting around Moscow is by Metro. It's also the most

popular method of transportation—over 10 million people use the metro daily. Construction began in 1931, under Stalin. Many Soviet and foreign architects and engineers spent four years building the deep stations, which served as bomb shelters during WW II. The first line was opened on 15 May 1935. Today, 10 lines and over 100 stations connect all points of the city. The Metro (with over 125 miles/200 km of track) operates daily from 6 a.m. to 1 a.m. and the trains are frequent, arriving every 50 seconds during rush hour. Many of the older stations are beautifully decorated with mosaics, marble, stained glass, statues and chandeliers, and are absolutely immaculate. Some of the more interesting ones are: Prospekt Marxa, Mayakovskaya, Byelorusskaya, Komsomolskaya, Kievskaya and Ploshchad Sverdlova.

The Metro is easy to use. By looking at a map, all the color-coded lines branch out from a central point, and are intersected by the brown Koltso (Circle) line. Entrances above ground are marked by a large "M." Take the escalator down to the station, quite an interesting experience, for many are long and fast. Maps are located before the turnstiles. It costs five kopeks to any destination. If you don't have a five-kopek coin, automatic machines give change in each station. (Change for ruble notes or a 10-day and monthly pass can be purchased at the cashier window.) Since station names are written only in Russian, have someone write down the name of your destination. If you have trouble finding your way, show it to the atten-

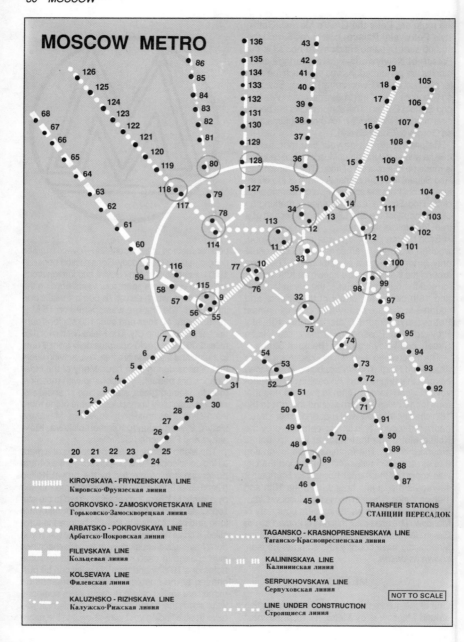

dant, who usually stands at the entrance—or ask, people are very helpful to strangers and many understand some English. At times, the trains can be crowded and commuters push to get where they're going. Stand near a door as your stop approaches. The names of stops are announced in each car. As the train leaves each station, you'll hear *"Ostorozh'no, d'veri zakriva'yutsya—slye'du-yushaya stan'tsiya. . . ."* "Be careful, the doors are closing. The next stop is. . . ." Maps of the route are also posted inside each train car (in Russian). Metro tours can be booked through Intourist.

MOSCOW METRO

1. Yugo-Zapadnaya
2. Prospekt Vernadskovo
3. Universitet
4. Leninskiye Gory
5. Sportivnaya
6. Frunszenkaya
7. Park Kultury
8. Kropotkinskaya
9. Biblioteka imeni Lenina
10. Prospekt Marksa
11. Dzerzhinskaya
12. Kirovskaya
13. Krasniye Vorota
14. Komsomolskaya
15. Krasnoselskaya
16. Sokolniki
17. Preobrazhenskaya Ploshchad
18. Chepkizovskaya
19. Podbelskovo
20. Butsyevsky Park
21. Yacehyevo
22. Teply Stan
23. Konkovo
24. Belyayevo
25. Kaluzhskaya
26. Noviye Cheryomushki
27. Profsoyuznaya
28. Akademicheskaya
29. Leninsky Prospekt
30. Shabolovskaya
31. Oktyabrskaya
32. Tretyakovskaya
33. Ploshchad Nogina
34. Turgenevskaya
35. Kolkhoznaya
36. Prospekt Mira
37. Rizhskaya
38. Shcherbakovskaya
39. VDNKh
40. Botanichesky Sad
41. Sviblovo
42. Babushkinskaya
43. Medvedkovo
44. Prazhskaya
45. Yuzhnaya

46. Chertanovskaya
47. Sevastopolskaya
48. Nakhimovsky Prospekt
49. Nagornaya
50. Nagatinskaya
51. Tulskaya
52. Serpukhovskaya
53. Dobryninskaya
54. Polyanka
55. Borovitskaya
56. Kalininskaya
57. Arbatskaya
58. Smolenskaya
59. Kievskaya
60. Studencheskaya
61. Kutuzovskaya
62. Fili
63. Bagrationovskaya
64. Filevsky Park
65. Pionerskaya
66. Kuntsevskaya
67. Molodyozhnaya
68. Krilatskoye
69. Kakhovskaya
70. Varshavskaya
71. Kashirskaya
72. Kolomenskaya
73. Avtozavodskaya
74. Paveletskaya
75. Novokuznetskaya
76. Ploshchad Revolutsii
77. Ploshchad Sverdlova
78. Gorkovskaya
79. Mayakovskaya
80. Belorusskaya
81. Dinamo
82. Aeroport
83. Sokol
84. Voikovskaya
85. Vodny Stadion
86. Rechnoi Vokzal
87. Krasnogvardeiskaya
88. Domodedovskaya
89. Orekhovo
90. Lenino
91. Kantemirovskaya

92. Vikhino
93. Ryazansky Prospekt
94. Kuzminki
95. Textilshchiki
96. Volgogradsky Prospekt
97. Proletarskaya
98. Taganskaya
99. Marksistskaya
100. Ploshchad Ilicha
101. Aviamotornaya
102. Shosse Entuziastov
103. Perovo
104. Novogireyevo
105. Shchelkovskaya
106. Pervomaiskaya
107. Izmailovskaya
108. Izmailovsky Park
109. Semyonovskaya
110. Electrozavodskaya
111. Baumanskaya
112. Kurskaya
113. Kuznetsky Most
114. Pushkinskaya
115. Arbatskaya
116. Smolenskaya
117. Krasnopresnenskaya
118. Barrikadnaya
119. Ulitsa 1905 Goda
120. Begovaya
121. Polezhayevskaya
122. Oktyabrskoye Pole
123. Shchukinskaya
124. Tushinskaya
125. Skhodnenskaya
126. Planernaya
127. Tzvetnio Boolvar
128. Novoslobodskaya
129. Meholeleevskaya
130. Saveloskaya
131. Dmitrovskaya
132. Timiryazevskaya
133. Petrovsko-Rozymovskaya
134. Vladvikhino
135. Otradnoye

SIGHTS

RED SQUARE

Most visitors begin their acquaintance with Moscow at Red Square, Krasnaya Ploshchad, the heart of the city. It was first mentioned in 15th-century chronicles as the Torg, the Great Marketplace and main trading center of the town. Starting during the time of Ivan the Great, the square was used as a huge gathering place for public events, markets, fairs and festivals. Many religious processions came through the square led by the czar and patriarch of the Orthodox Church. It was also the scene of many political demonstrations and revolts, and the site of public executions. The square received its present name in the 17th century from the old Russian word, *krasny,* meaning both red and beautiful, though the red has been used only since the Revolution.

Red Square, encompassing an area of over 70,000 square meters, is definitely one of the world's most beautiful. The square is bounded by the **Kremlin** walls, **St. Basil's Cathedral, Lenin Mausoleum,** the **Historical Museum** and **GUM Department Store.**

Today, national celebrations are held in the square; on holidays such as May Day and Revolution Day (November 7), huge parades and festivities fill Red Square. The closest Metro stop to Red Square is Prospekt Marxa.

St. Basil's Cathedral

The square's most famous and eye-catching structure is St. Basil's Cathedral. This extraordinary creation was erected by Ivan IV (the Terrible) in 1555-61, to commemorate the annexation to Russia of the Mongol states of Kazan and Astrakhan. Since this occurred on the festival of the Intercession of the Virgin, Ivan the Terrible named it the Cathedral of the Intercession. The names of the architects weren't known until 1896, when old manuscripts were found that mentioned its construction. According to tales, Ivan the Terrible had the two architects, Posnik and Barma, blinded so they could never again create such a beautiful church. But in 1588, a quarter century after the

cathedral's completion, records also indicate that Posnik and Barma built the chapel at the northeast corner of the cathedral, where the holy prophet, Basil (Vasily), was buried. Canonized after his death, Basil the Blessed died the same year (1552) that many of the Mongol Khanates were captured. Basil opposed the cruelties of Ivan the Terrible; since most of the population also despised the czar, the cathedral took on the name of St. Basil's after Ivan's death.

The cathedral is built of brick in traditional Russian style with colorful, asymmetrical, tent-shaped, helmut and onion domes situated over nine chapels. The interior is filled with 16th- and 17th-century icons and frescoes, and the gallery contains bright wall and ceiling paintings filled with red, turquoise and yellow flower patterns. Locals often refer to the cathedral as the "stone flower in Red Square." The French stabled their horses here in 1812 and Napoleon wanted to blow up the place. Luckily, his order was never carried out.

St. Basil's Cathedral

The interior, now open to the public, has undergone much restoration. Inside is a branch of the Historical Museum that traces the history of the cathedral and Ivan IV's campaigns. Under the belltower (added in the 17th century), an exhibition room traces the architectural history of St. Basil's with old sketches and plans. The museum is open daily from 9:30 to 5:30 except Tuesday and the first Monday of each month.

In front of the cathedral stands the bronze **Monument to Minin and Pozharsky,** the first patriotic monument in Moscow built from public funding; it originally stood in the middle of the square. Sculpted by Ivan Martos in 1818, the monument depicts Kozma Minin and Prince Dmitri Pozharsky, whose leadership drove the Polish invaders out of Moscow in 1612. The pedestal inscription reads "To Citizen Minin and Prince Pozharsky from a grateful Russia 1818."

Near the monument is Lobnoye Mesto, the "Place of Skulls." A platform of white stone stood here for more than four centuries, around which public executions (beheadings and hangings) were carried out. Church clergymen blessed the crowds and the czar's orders and edicts were also announced from this spot.

The Lenin Mausoleum

By the Kremlin wall on the southwest side of the square is the Lenin Mausoleum. Inside in a glass sarcophagus lies Vladimir Ilyich Lenin, who died on 21 Jan.1924. Three days after his death, a wooden structure was erected on this spot. Four months later, it was rebuilt and then replaced in 1930 by the granite, marble and black-labradorite mausoleum, designed by Alexei Shchusev. "Lenin" is inscribed in red porphyry. For more than 65 years, Soviets and foreigners have stood in the line that stretches from the end of Red Square to the Mausoleum to view the idolized revolutionary leader and "Father of the Soviet Union." Two guards man the entrance, and at every hour on the hour, as the Kremlin clock chimes, the ceremonial changing of the guard takes place. Exactly two minutes and 45 seconds before the hour, two armed sentries march toward the entrance of the mausoleum to relieve the stationed guards.

Photography is prohibited and cameras should be placed out of sight in a bag. Even the slightest impolite gesture, such as placing hands in pockets, will draw a reprimand from the security guards. Once inside, visitors are not allowed to pause and hold up the line. If you are with a group, the tour will usually be brought to the front of the line. If you aren't with a tour group, foreign tourists can wait at the corner of the Historical Museum (facing 50th Anniversary of October Square), where officers organize a separate, much shorter line and lead you right in on Tues., Wed., Thurs., and Sat. from noon to 1 p.m. and on Sundays from 1 to 2 p.m. Otherwise the mausoleum is open in summer on the same days as above from 9 a.m. to 1 p.m. (in winter 11 a.m. to 2 p.m.) and on Sundays from 9 a.m. to 2 p.m. (in winter from 11 a.m. to 4 p.m.).

Marble viewing stands on both sides of the mausoleum hold up to 10,000 spectators during national holidays. Atop the mausoleum is a tribune, where the heads of the Soviet government and Communist Party stand on May and Revolution days.

Behind the mausoleum, separated by a row of silver fir trees, are the remains of many of the country's most honored figures in politics, culture and science, whose ashes lie in urns within the Kremlin wall. Some include Lenin's sister, his wife Nadezhda Krupskaya, Sergei Kirov, Maxim Gorky, A.V. Lunacharsky, the physicist Sergei Korolyov and the cosmonaut Yuri Gagarin. Foreigners include John Reed and William Hayword (USA), Arthur McManus (England), Clara Zetkin and Fritz Heckert (Germany) and Sen Katayama (Japan). There are also the tombstones of previous leaders of the Communist Party: Sverdlov, Dzerzhinsky, Frunze, Kalinin, Voroshilov, Suslov and Stalin, who was once buried next to Lenin in the mausoleum. Nearby are the granite-framed common graves of 500 people who died during the October 1917 Revolution.

The Historical Museum

At the opposite end of the square from St. Basil's is a red-brick building, decorated with numerous spires and *kokoshnik* gables that houses the Historical Museum. This building was constructed by Vladimir Sherwood between 1878 and 1883 on the original site where Moscow University was founded in 1755 by the Russian scientist, Mikhail Lomonosov. When opened in 1883, the museum had over 300,000 objects and was supported by private donations. Today, the government museum contains over four million items in 48 halls that house the country's largest archaeological collection, along with manuscripts, books, coins, ornaments and works of art from the Stone Age to the present day. These include birch-bark letters, clothing of Ivan the Terrible, Peter the Great's sleigh, Napoleon's sabre and the "Decree on Peace," written by Lenin. The museum is open Wed. 11 a.m. to 7 p.m., other days 10 a.m. to 6 p.m. It's closed on Tuesday and the last day of each month.

GUM

Next to the Historical Museum, stretching across the entire northeast side of Red Square, is the three-story State Universal Store, known as GUM ("goom"), largest shopping center in the Soviet Union, with a total length of 1.5 miles (2.5 km). It was designed by Alexander Pomerantsev in 1895, when it was known as the Upper Trading Stalls and contained 200 shops. In 1953, the building was reconstructed and now handles almost a half-million shoppers a day! It's definitely worth a visit to see the interior of old Russian shops, ornate bridges, ornamental stucco designs and the large glass roof. Souvenir shops are on the ground floor. It's open daily 8 a.m. to 9 p.m. and closed on Sunday.

The Alexandrov Gardens

The entrance to the lovely gardens lies across from the Historical Museum at the Kremlin's wrought-iron Corner Arsenal Gate. The gardens were laid-out by Osip Bovet in 1819-22 for Alexander I on the banks of the Neglinnaya River, which was diverted by a system of pipes to flow beneath them. An eternal flame burns before the Tomb of the Unknown Soldier, who died for his country during WW II. It was unveiled on 8 May 1967, on the eve of Victory Day. It's a tradition for newlyweds on their wedding day to lay flowers on the tombstone, on which is inscribed, "Your name is unknown, your feat immortal. To the fallen 1941-45." Along the alley, in front of the tomb, are blocks of red porphyry that hold earth from "Hero Cities," that include Moscow and Leningrad, designated after WW II. Also in the gardens are a memorial to the War of 1812 and a granite obelisk with the names of the world's great revolutionaries and thinkers. The monument was originally erected in 1913 to commemorate the 300th anniversary of the Romanov Dynasty. On Lenin's orders in 1918,

the double-headed eagle was replaced by the obelisk.

The central alley of the Alexandrov Gardens leads to the Troitsky Bridge that approaches an entrance of the Kremlin.

THE KREMLIN

"The earth as we all know, begins at the Kremlin. It is the central point."'

—Vladimir Mayakovsky

The Moscow Kremlin, an outstanding monument of Russian history, winds around a steep slope high above the Moskva River, enclosing an area of over 70 acres next to Red Square. The Russian word *kreml* (that now represents the seat of Soviet government) was once used to describe a fortified stronghold that encased a small town. A Russian town was usually built on a high embankment, surrounded by a river and moat, to protect against invasions. The word *kreml* may originate from the Greek *kremnos*, meaning "steep escarpment." The medieval kremlin acted as a fortress around a town filled with palaces, churches, monasteries, wooden peasant houses and markets. The Moscow Kremlin was built between the Moskva River and Neglinnaya River, which now flows underground. It's about a half mile (one km) long and up to 62 feet (19 meters) high and 21 feet (6.5 meters) thick. Twenty towers and gates and over 10 churches and palaces lie inside its walls. The Moscow Kremlin has a fascinating eight-century history. The closest Metro stops are Prospekt Marxa and Biblioteka Imena Lenina.

History

The Kremlin is the oldest historical and architectural feature of Moscow. The first written account of Moscow comes to us from an old chronicle that describes Prince Yuri Dolgoruky of Suzdal receiving Prince Svyatoslav on Borovitsky (now Kremlin) Hill, in 1147. Nine years later, Dolgoruky ordered a fort built on this same hill, which later became his residence. In 1238 the invading Mongols burned the fortress to the ground. By 1326 the Kremlin was encased by thick oak walls, and Grand-Prince Ivan I added two stone churches to the existing wooden ones. During this time, the metropolitan of Kiev moved the seat of the Orthdox Church from Vladimir to Moscow. In 1367, Prince Dmitri Donskoi replaced the wooden walls with limestone to fortify them against cannon attack. Moscow was referred to as Beli Gorod, the "White Town." The Mongols invaded once again in 1382; they razed everything and killed half the population. Within 15 years, the Kremlin walls were rebuilt and the iconists Theophanes the Greek and Andrei Rublev painted the interior frescoes of the new Cathedral of the Annunication.

Ivan III (1460-1505) and his son, Vasily III, were responsible for shaping the Kremlin into its present appearance. After the Mongols no longer posed a threat to the city, the leaders concentrated more on aesthetic than defensive designs. Ivan the Great commissioned well-known Russian and Italian architects to create a magnificent city to reflect the beauty of the "Third Rome" and the power of the grand-prince and metropolitan. The white stone of the Kremlin was replaced by red-brick walls and towers, and the Assumption and Annunciation cathedrals were rebuilt on a grander scale. During the reign of Ivan IV, the architecture took on more fanciful elements and asymmetrical designs with colorful onion domes and tall pyramidal tent roofs, as embodied in St. Basil's—a style now termed "Old Russian." The Patriarch Nikon barred all tent roofs and ornamental decorations from churches when he took office in 1652, terming the external frills sacrilegious. By 1660, though, the reforms of Nikon had created such schisms in the church that he was forced to step down. Immediately, the old decorative details were again applied to architecture.

Catherine the Great drew up plans to redesign the Kremlin in the new neoclassicism, but they were never carried out. During the War of 1812, Napoleon quartered his troops inside the Kremlin for 35 days. Retreating, he tried to blow it up, but townspeople extinguished the burning fuses, though three towers were destroyed. In the mid-1800s, the Kremlin Palace and Armory were built. In 1918, the Soviet government moved the capital back to Moscow and made the Kremlin its permanent seat. Lenin signed a decree to protect the works of art and historical monuments and ordered the buildings restored and turned into museums.

View From Red Square

Red-ruby stars were mounted on the five tallest towers in 1937, replacing the double-headed eagle. The towers of the Kremlin were named

the Kremlin clock tower, Moscow

after the icons that used to hang above their gates. The most recognizable tower, the **Spasskaya (Savior) Clock Tower**, stands to the right of St. Basil's. It is 201 feet (67 meters) high and served as the official entrance for the czars, who had to cross a moat over an arched stone bridge to get to the gate. It's now the main entrance used by goverment officials, who pull up in black limousines. The Savior Icon once hung above the Spasskaya gate. Inscriptions in Latin and Old Russian name the Italian Solario as the builder in 1491. Later, the Scottish architect Christopher Galloway mounted a clock on its face in the mid-17th century, which was replaced in 1918. It plays the anthem "Internationale," and like Big Ben in London, the chimes of the Spasskaya Tower are broadcast over the radio to mark the hour.

The tower behind Lenin's Mausoleum is known as the Senate Tower; it stands in front of the Senate building. To the right of the mausoleum stands the Nikolskaya Tower, where the Icon of St.

Nicholas was kept. In 1492, Solario built a corner tower next to a courtyard used by the Sobakin *boyars*. The Sobakin Tower is now called the Corner Arsenal Tower, where munitions were stored.

Entering The Kremlin

The two main entrances into the Kremlin are through the Kutafya or Borovitskaya towers. All group tours are taken through the latter gate on the west side, which is closest to the Kremlin Armory. If you're near the Alexandrov Gardens, go through the Kutafya Tower (which runs through the middle of the gardens) from Revolution Square and turn right next to the Metro stop Biblioteka Imeni Lenina. The Kutafya watchtower, built in the early 16th century, was approached by a drawbridge that spread over a moat. The tower was connected by a stone bridge, under which the Neglinnaya River once ran, to the Troitskaya (Trinity) Tower. Built in 1495, it was named after the Trinity-Sergius Monastery. It is the tallest tower (240 feet/80 meters), where ammunition used to be stored. Clergy and military officers entered through the Trinity Gate.

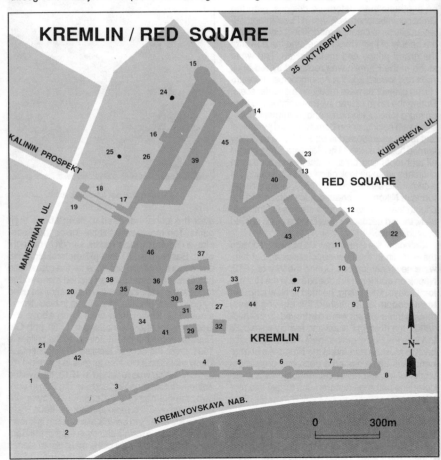

KREMLIN / RED SQUARE

KREMLIN/RED SQUARE

1. Borovitskaya Tower
2. Vodovzodnaya Tower
3. Annunciation Tower
4. Tainitskaya Tower
5. 1st Nameless Tower
6. 2nd Nameless Tower
7. Peter Tower
8. Beklemishev Tower
9. Konstantin-Yelena Tower
10. Alarm Tower
11. Tsar Tower
12. Saviour Tower
13. Senate Tower
14. Nikolaskaya Tower
15. Corner Arsenal Tower
16. Middle Arsenal Tower
17. Trinity Tower
18. Trinity Bridge
19. Kutafya Tower
20. Commandement Tower
21. Armoury Tower
22. St. Basil's Cathedral
23. Lenin Mausoleum
24. Tomb of the Unknown Soldier
25. Obelisk to Revolutionary Thinkers
26. Grotto in Alexander Gardens
27. Cathedral Square
28. Cathedral of the Dormition
29. Cathedral of the Annunciation
30. Church of the Deposition of the Robe
31. Faceted Palace
32. Cathedral of the Archangel Michael
33. Ivan the Great Bell Tower
34. Terem Palace
35. St. Lazarus Church
36. Upper Saviour Cathedral
37. Church of the Twelve Apostles and
    Patriarch's Palace
38. Poteshny Palace
39. arsenal
40. Council of Ministers
41. Great Palace
42. Armoury Palace
43. Presidium of the Supreme Soviet
44. Tsar Bell
45. captured cannon
46. Palace of Congresses
47. Monument to Lenin

Palace Of Congresses

As you enter the Kremlin through the Kutafya/Trinity Towers, the modern Palace of Congresses is on your right. Khrushchev approved the plans for this large steel, glass and marble structure. Built by Mikhail Posokhin, it was completed in 1961 for the 22nd Congress of the Communist Party. When no state congresses or international meetings are in session, the palace is used for ballet and opera performances. Sunk 45 feet (15 meters) into the ground so as not to tower over the Kremlin, the Palace contains 800 rooms and the auditorium seats 6,000.

The Arsenal

The yellow two-story building to the left of the entrance tower was once used as the arsenal. Peter the Great ordered it built in 1702 (completed in 1736), but later turned it into a trophy museum. Along the front of the arsenal are 875 cannons and other trophies captured from Napoleon's armies in 1812. Plaques on the wall list the names of men killed defending the arsenal during the Revolution and WW II.

Council Of Ministers Building

As you walk through the square, the three-story triangular building of the former Senate is directly in front. Catherine the Great had it built in classical style by Matvei Kazakov in 1787. It's now used by the Soviet Council of Ministers. The large green dome is topped by the national flag. The front wall plaque is marked by Lenin's portrait and the inscription, "Lenin lived and worked in this building from March 1918 to May 1923." The Central Committee of the Communist Party meets in **Sverdlov Hall.** The hall's 18 Corinthian columns are decorated with copies (originals in the Armory) of bas-reliefs portraying czars and princes; the ideals of Catherine the Great line the bottom. Lenin's study and flat are in the east wing. Special objects stand atop his desk, such as the Monkey Statue presented to him by Armand Hammer in 1921. The study leads to a small four-room apartment that Lenin shared with his wife and younger sister. Across from the Council of Ministers, near the Spasskaya Tower, is the Presidium of the Supreme Soviet and the Kremlin Theater, which was built between 1932 and 1934. The theater seats 1,200. These buildings can only be visited with special permission.

Patriarch's Palace

Opposite the former Senate is the four-story Patriarch's Palace and his private chapel, the Church of the Twelve Apostles, which now house the **Museum of 17th-Century Life and Applied Art,** with over 1,000 exhibits. Patriarch Nikon commissioned the palace for himself in 1635. After Nikon banned the usage of elaborate decorations on church buildings, he had the architects Konstantinov and Okhlebinin design the structure in simple white Byzantine fashion. The palace was placed near the main cathedral and the Trinity Gate, where clergy formally entered the Kremlin. The vaulted Krestovskaya Chamber (Hall of the Cross), built without a single support beam, was used as a formal reception hall. Every three years, the chamber was used for making consecrated oil for the Russian churches. In 1721, Peter the Great gave the palace to the Church Council of the Holy Synod. The museum has an interesting collection of rare manuscripts, coins, jewelry, furniture, fabrics, embroidery and even table games. Books include an ABC primer written for the son of Peter the Great. Two of the halls are decorated to look like a 17th-century house. Some of the displays in the Church of the Twelve Apostles are wine coffers and ladles, on which Bacchus is carved. These objects belonged to the society of the "Highest and Most Jolly and Drunken Council," founded by Peter the Great to make fun of all the (non-progressive) church rituals. The museum is closed on Thursday.

Emperor Cannon

Right next to the Palace is the 40-ton Emperor Cannon. The 890mm-caliber makes it the largest cannon in the world. It was cast in 1586 by Andrei Shchokhov and never fired. A likeness of Fedor I is on the barrel. The decorative iron cannon balls (weighing one ton each) were cast in the 19th century.

Right across from the cannon lie the Tainitsky (Secret) Gardens in the southeast corner of the Kremlin. Winter fairs are held here for children during New Year celebrations. A statue of Lenin rests on the highest spot, known as Kremlin Hill. To the left of the statue is the Cosmos Oak, which cosmonaut Yuri Gagarin planted on 14 April 1961. This vantage point affords a good view of the Kremlin and Spasskaya Tower. The Czar's Tower stands to the right of it, which is decorated with

The Emperor Cannon, testimony to Russia's love for sheer size, has never been fired.

white-stone designs and a weathervane. A wooden deck was on top of the tower, from which Ivan the Terrible supposedly watched executions on Red Square. The tower directly behind Lenin is the Nabatnaya (Alarm); the bell that used to hang here is on display in the Armory Museum. Farther to the right is the Konstantino-Yeleninskaya Tower, which honors St. Constantine and St. Helen. The corner tower is called Moskvoretskaya, built in 1487 by Marco Ruffo. It was known as Beklemischevskaya, named after Ivan Beklemisch, whose home stood next to the tower in the 16th century; his spirit is said to have haunted it. The Mongols broke through this tower to enter the Kremlin in the 17th century.

Emperor Bell

The largest bell in the world stands atop a stone pedestal by the Secret Gardens. The bell, 18 feet (six meters) high, weighs 210 tons. The surface bears portraits of czars and icons. It was first designed in 1733 by Ivan Matorin and his son Mikhail and took two years to cast. The 11.5-ton fragment broke off during the fire of 1737, when water was thrown on it. After the fire, the bell was returned to its casting pit, where it lay for a century. The architect Montferrand raised the bell in 1836.

The square between the Spasskaya Tower and the bell was known as **Ivan's Square,** along which government offices were located. Officials read the czar's new decrees and criminals were flogged here.

Bell Tower

Behind the Emperor Bell stands the three-tiered **Bell Tower of Ivan the Great.** Built from 1505 to 1508, the tower contains 21 bells that hang in the arches of each section, the largest of which is the Uspensky (Assumption) Bell, weighing 70 tons. The Old Slavonic inscription around the gilded dome notes that it was added to the belfry in 1600 by Boris Godunov. This was once the tallest structure (243 feet/81 meters) in Moscow and was used as a belfry, church and watchtower. When the enemy was sighted, the bells signaled a warning. A small exhibition hall is on the ground floor of the belfry.

Cathedral Of The Assumption

In front of the bell tower stands the Kremlin's main church, the Assumption Cathedral or Uspensky Sobor. It faces the center of Cathedral Square, the oldest square in Moscow. Built in the early 14th century as the main square, here processions gathered and foreign ambassadors were received. In 1475, Ivan the Great selected the Italian architect Aristotile Fioravante to design the church, who modeled it after the Cathedral of the Assumption in Vladimir. This church, also known as the Cathedral of the Dormition of the Virgin, was built on the site of a stone church by the same name, first constructed by Ivan I. For two centuries, this national shrine stood as a model for all Russian church architecture. Within its walls, czars were coronated and patriarchs crowned. It also served as the burial place for Moscow metropolitans and patriarchs.

Combining Italian Renaissance and Byzantine traditions, the cathedral is built from white limestone and brick with *zakomara* rounded arches, narrow-windowed drums and five gilded onion domes. The ornamental doorways are covered with frescos painted on sheet copper; the southern entrance is especially interesting, decorated with 20 biblical scenes in gold and black lacquer.

The spacious interior, lit by 12 chandeliers, is covered with exquisite frescoes and icons that date back to 1481. The artists, Dionysius, Timofei, Yarets and Kon, wove together the themes of heaven and the unity of Russia's principalities, symbolizing the "Third Rome." Some of these can still be seen over the altar screen. The northern and southern walls depict the life of the Blessed Virgin. In 1642, more than 100 masters spent a year repainting the church, following the designs of the older wall paintings. These 17th-century frescoes were restored after the Revolution. The elaborate iconostasis dates from 1652. Its upper rows were painted by monks from the Trinity-Sergius Monastery in Zagorsk in the late 1600s. The silver frames were added in 1881. To the right of the royal gates, are two 12th-century icons from Novgorod, *St. George* and the *Savior Enthroned.* A 15th-century copy of the country's protectress, the *Virgin of Vladimir,* also lies to the left. The original (in the Tretyakov Gallery) was brought to Moscow from Vladimir in 1395 by Vasily I. The icons,*Savior of the Fiery Eye, The Trinity* and *Dormition of the Virgin,* were specially commissioned for the cathedral in the 14th and 15th centuries. Napoleon's armies used some of the icons as firewood and tried to carry off tons of gold and silver. Most of it was recovered, and the central chandelier, Harvest, was cast from silver recaptured from the retreating troops.

The Metropolitan Peter (co-founder of the cathedral) and his successor are buried in the southern chapel. The 15th-century fresco *Forty Martyrs of Sebaste* separates the chapel from the main altar. Other metropolitans and patriarchs are buried along the northern and southern walls and in underground crypts. Metropolitan Iov is buried in a special mausoleum, above which hangs the icon of *Metropolitan Peter,* the first Moscow metropolitan. The gilded sarcophagus of Patriarch Hermogenes (1606-12) stands in the southwest corner covered by a small canopy. During the Polish invasion, when imprisoned by the Poles, he starved to death. After Patriarch Adrian, Peter the Great did away with the position and established the Holy Synod. The patriarch seat remained vacant until 1917.

Ivan the Terrible's carved wooden throne stands to the left of the southern entrance. Made in 1551, it's known as the Throne of the Monomakhs. It is filled with elaborately carved decorations representing the transfer of imperial power from the Byzantine Emperor Monomakus to the Grand-Prince Vladimir Monomakh (1113-25), who married the emperor's sister. The patriarch's throne can be found by the southeast pier; the clergy sat upon the elevated stone that is decorated with carved flowers. The Last Judgment is painted over the western portal. Traditionally, the congregation exited through the church's western door. The last theme portrayed was the Last Judgment—a reminder for the people to work on salvation in the outside world. Closed Thursday.

Church Of The Deposition Of The Robe
Right next to the Assumption Cathedral is the smaller single-domed Church of the Deposition of the Virgin's Robe, built by Pskov craftsmen in 1484-85. It once served as the private chapel of the patriarchs and was linked by a small bridge to the palace. It later became a court chapel in 1653. The iconostasis was done by Nazari Istomin in 1627. The interior wall paintings are devoted to the Blessed Virgin. The northern gallery displays an exhibit of wooden handicrafts. Closed Thursday.

Terem Palace
In the small courtyard next to the church is the Terem Palace and the Golden Palace of the Czarina, which served as the reception place for czarinas in the 16th century. The Terem Palace resembles a fairy-tale creation with its checkerboard roof and 11 golden turrets. The Terem housed the children and female relatives of noblewomen. The Terem Palace was built for Czar Mikhail Romanov, whose private chambers on the fourth floor were later occupied by his son, Alexei. Many state functions took place here and in the Hall of the Cross. The czar received petitions from the population in the Golden Throne Room. Only the czar's wife, personal confessor and blind storytellers were allowed into the private chapel and royal bedchamber, which looks like a scene out of the *Arabian Nights*. All the chapels of the Terem were united under one roof in 1681, which included the Churches of the Resurrection, Crucifixion, Savior and St. Catherine. The adjoining Golden Palace of the Czarina was built in 1526 by Boris Godunov

for his sister Irina, who was married to Czar Fedor I. This was her own private reception hall. When Fedor died, Irina refused the throne (the last son of Ivan the Terrible had died earlier during an epileptic attack); her brother, Boris Godunov, became the first elected czar. Admission to the Terem requires special permission.

Palace Of Facets
Facing the bell tower is the two-story Renaissance-style Palace of Facets, one of Moscow's oldest civil buildings, constructed by Ruffo and Solario between 1487 and 1491. It took its name from the fancy stone facets decorating the exterior. State assemblies and receptions were held here—Ivan the Terrible celebrated the victory over Kazan in 1532 in this palace, and Peter the Great celebrated his triumph over the Swedes in Poltava in 1709. After Ivan III, all wives, including the crowned czarinas, were barred from attending state ceremonies and receptions in the Hall of

journalist and adventurer John Reed (1887-1920), the only American citizen buried in the Kremlin

Facets; a small lookout room was built above the western wall, from which the women could secretly watch the proceedings. Today the hall is used for state occasions. Entrance to the Palace of Facets is by special permission only.

Cathedral Of The Annunciation

This white-stone cathedral, with its nine gilded domes, stands next to the palace and was built from 1485 to 1489 by Pskov craftsmen as the private chapel of the czars. After a fire in 1547, Ivan the Terrible rebuilt the cathedral with four additional chapels. Inside, frescoes that date back to 1508 were painted by Theodosius; many were restored in the 1960s. The iconostasis contains icons by Andrei Rublev, Theophanes the Greek and Prokhor of Gorodets, painted in 1405. Portraits of princes and Greek philosophers and poets, like Plato, Aristotle and Virgil, can be found on the pillars and in the galleries. Closed Thursday.

Archangel Cathedral

The third main cathedral of the Kremlin is the five-domed Cathedral of the Archangel (1505-08), which served as the burial place of the czars. It stands directly across from the Annunciation Cathedral. Ivan the Great commissioned the Italian architect Alevisio Novi to rebuild the church. He combined the styles of Old Russian and Italian Renaissance; notice the traits of a Venetian palazzo. The surviving frescoes date back to 1652 and depict aspects of Russian life. A large iconostasis (1680) is filled with 15th- to 17th-century icons, including the *Archangel Michael*, by Rublev. Nearly 50 sarcophagi line the walls of the cathedral, containing grand-princes and czars and some of their sons. White tombstones give the names of each in Old Slavonic script. The first grand-prince to be buried here was Ivan I in 1341, who built the original church. After Peter the Great moved the capital to St. Petersburg, the czars were buried in the Peter and Paul Fortress, except for Peter II, who died in Moscow. Closed Thursday.

Behind the cathedral stands Peter's Tower, named after the first Moscow metropolitan. The fourth unadorned tower from the corner is the Tainitskaya (Secret) Tower, which had an underground passage to the Moskva River. The next one over is the Annunciation Tower, which contained the Annunciation icon. The corner round tower is called the Vodovzvodnaya or Water-Drawing Tower, which once raised water from the river to an aqueduct that led to the gardens.

Grand Kremlin Palace

The Grand Palace, behind the Archangel Cathedral, was the Moscow residence of the Imperial family. Nicholas I had Konstantin Thon erect it on the site of the Grand-Prince Palace in 1838-49. There are 700 rooms and five elaborate reception halls; two of these, along the southern wall overlooking the river, were combined to form the Meeting Hall of the Supreme Soviet and Russian Federation. The long gold and white St. George Hall has 18 columns, holding statues of Victory. The walls are lined with marble plaques with the names of heroes awarded the Order of St. George (begun by Catherine the Great) for service and courage. The six bronze chandeliers hold over 3,000 light bulbs. This hall is now used for special state receptions and ceremonies; cosmonaut Yuri Gagarin received the Golden Star Hero Award in 1961. The Hall of St. Catherine served as the Empress Throne Room. The Hall of Vladimir connected the Palace of Facets, Golden Palace of the Czarina and Terem Palace. The ground-floor rooms used to contain the imperial family's bedchambers. Entrance is gained only by special permission.

Amusement Palace

The Poteshny (Amusement) Palace, situated right behind the Grand Palace and the Commandment's Tower, was built in 1652 by Czar Alexis as the residence for his father-in-law. After he died, Alexis turned the palace into a theater.

Armory Palace

The Oruzheinaya Palata (Armory Palace) is the oldest museum in the Soviet Union. In 1485, Grand-Prince Vasily III, son of Ivan the Great, constructed a special stone building on the edge of the Kremlin grounds to house the growing collection of the royal family's valuables. It also contained the czar's workshops and a place where armor and weapons were stored. In the late 1600s, Peter the Great converted the whole place into a museum to house the art treasures of the Kremlin. The present building, designed in 1651 by Konstantin Thon, has nine exhibit halls that trace the history of the Kremlin and the Russian state. It also houses a magnificent collection of

Western European decorative and applied art from the 12th to 19th centuries.

Hall I (Halls I-IV are on the first floor) exhibits armor and weaponry from the 13th to 18th centuries. Hall II has displays of gold and silver from the 12th to 17th centuries, including jewelry, chalices (one belonging to Yuri Dolgoruky), bowls and watches. Hall III contains gold and silver jewelry from the 18th to 20th centuries, that includes snuff boxes and the fabulous Fabergé eggs. Hall IV has a collection of vestments and robes, including a robe of the first Metropolitan Peter, Peter the Great, and a coronation robe of Catherine the Great. One robe presented to the metropolitan by Catherine contains over 150,000 semiprecious stones. Hall V (V-IX are on the ground floor) exhibits many of the foreign gifts of silver and gold from the 13th to 19th centuries from England, France, Sweden, Amsterdam and Poland to the czars. Hall VI is known as the Throne and Crown Room. The oldest throne belonged to Ivan the Terrible. A Persian shah presented Boris Godunov with a throne encrusted with 2,000 precious stones in 1604. The throne of Czar Alexei Romanov contains over 1,000 diamonds. The most interesting is the Double Throne used by Peter the Great and his half-brother Ivan, when they were proclaimed joint-czars. Peter's older half-sister, Sophia, acted as regent and used to sit in a secret compartment in the throne behind Peter to advise him. The Crown of Monomakh (first worn by Grand-Prince Vladimir Monomakh in 1113) was used by all grand-princes and czars until Peter the Great. The room also contains gowns and jewelry. Halls VII and VIII contain saddles, bridles and sleigh covers. Hall IX is the Carriage Room, with the world's largest collection of carriages, dating back to Boris Godunov. The most elaborate is the coronation coach made for the Empress Elizabeth. The Diamond Fund Exhibit is a collection of the crown jewels and precious gems. These include the Orlov Diamond (189 carats) that Count Orlov bought for his mistress Catherine the Great. Catherine the Great's coronation crown is covered with pearls and 4,936 diamonds. (This section is opened with special permission.) A new section of the Armory displays gifts to the USSR from foreign countries.

The State Armory is one of the most interesting museums in Moscow and should definitely be visited. If it's not included in your visit, an Intourist service desk can book a tour. Only group tours are allowed in. These are usually conducted daily, except Friday, at 9:30 and 11:30 a.m., 2:30 and 4:30 p.m. in English.

The Armory Tower is behind the Armory Palace. One can exit through the Borovitskaya Tower (1490). Kremlin Hill was originally called Borovitskaya. Bor in old Russian means a "thick forest." This gate used to serve as the service entrance to the Kremlin.

OLD MOSCOW

The area to the east of the Kremlin was once known as Kitai-gorod. Kitai is derived from either the Mongolian word for "central" or the Old Russian kiti, meaning "palisade." Gorod is the Russian word for town. (In modern Russian, Kitai means China. Foreign settlements were later established in this area.) In the 14th century, the central town was surrounded by a protective earthen rampart and served as the central market and trade area, where merchants and townspeople lived. Beyond the rampart lay the forest. Later Ivan the Terrible constructed a larger fortified wall. The original area of Kitai-gorod stretched from the History Museum on Red Square, along the back of GUM Department Store, and east down to what is now the Hotel Rossiya and the banks of the Moskva River. On each side of GUM are the small streets of 25th October and Kuibyshev. The Rossiya Hotel (behind St. Basil's) is bordered by Razin Street and Kitaisky Prospekt.

25th October Street

This street begins at the northeast corner of Red Square and runs along the left side of GUM Department Store. Its former name was Nikolskaya, after the nearby Nikolsky Monastery. It now commemorates the first day of the 1917 Revolution. In the 17th century, the area was nicknamed the "Street of Enlightenment"; Moscow's first learning academy, printing yard and bookshops lined the passage.

The first corner building, as you leave the square, was the Governor's Office, where the writer Alexander Radishchev was held before his exile to Siberia (by Catherine the Great) in 1790. His book, A Journey from St. Petersburg to Moscow, described the terrible conditions of serfdom.

The Old Royal Mint stands inside the small courtyard. An inscription on the gates shows that Peter the Great built the mint in 1697. When he later moved it to St. Petersburg, the vice-governor had his office here.

Across the street by House no. 7 are several buildings that remain from the Zaikonospassky Monastery, founded by Boris Godunov in the early 1600s. The name means "Icon of our Savior"; the monastery used to make and sell icons, and had the nickname of the "Savior Monastery Behind Icon-Trading Stalls." The red and white **Savior's Church** was built in 1661. The church and adjoining buildings housed the Slavic-Greek-Latin Academy, Moscow's first and largest academy for higher education, which operated from 1687 to 1814. Among the first students were the poet Kantemir, the architect Bazhenov and Mikhail Lomonsov (1711-65), who became a renowned poet, historian and educator. Known as the "Father of Russian Science," he established Moscow University under Empress Elizabeth in 1755.

At no. 15 was the first printing yard, now the **History and Archives Institute.** Ivan the Terrible brought the first printing press to Russia in 1553. On the green building still hang the emblems of the old printing yard, a lion and unicorn, along with a sundial, mounted in 1814. The thick black gates lead to the colorfully tiled building of the Old Proofreader, where Ivan Fedorov spent a year printing Russia's first book. Ivan the Terrible visited Fedorov daily until *The Acts of the Apostles* was completed on 1 March 1564. (It's now in the Lenin Library.) Issues of the first Russian newspaper, *Vedomosti,* were printed here in 1703. The present building went up in 1814 and was used as the printing center for the Holy Synod, the council established by Peter the Great that regulated church affairs.

At no. 19 is the **Slavyansky Bazaar,** one of Moscow's oldest, and still most popular, restaurants. When it opened in the 1870s, it became a popular meeting spot for Moscow merchants who negotiated deals over the delicious *blini* pancakes. On 21 June 1877, stage directors Konstantin Stanislavsky and Vladimir Nemirovich-Danchenko worked out the details for the formation of the Moscow Art Theater, over an 18-hour lunch.

Opposite the Printing House is the former Chizhov Coach Exchange. The Chizhov family hired out taxis of horse-drawn carriages and carts.

The Coach Exchange was popular year-round, when Moscow streets were either muddy or frozen. In winter, one could hire a Chizhov *troika* (sled). Next door is the one-domed Church of the Dormition.

The small passage known as Tretyakov Proezd links 25th October Street with Prospekt Marxa. The wealthy merchant Sergei Tretyakov knocked a passage through the Kitai-gorod wall in 1871 to gain quick access to the banks along Prospekt Marxa.

25th October Street leads to Dzerzhinsky Square where it turns into Kirov Street, which runs east to the Leningradsky and Yaroslavky train stations and Sokolniki Park.

Halfway down 25th October Street, make a right on Kuibyshev Proyezd. Near the corner stands the red baroque 17th-century **Cathedral of Bogoyavlensky** (Epiphany), once part of a monastery established in the 13th century by Prince Daniil. The cathedral was created over the site of Moscow's first stone church, built by Ivan I. Many of the sculptures that were in the church are now on display in the Donskoi Monastery. The wealthy *boyar* Golitsyn family had their burial vaults here until the mid-18th century; they were switched to the Donskoi Monastery outside of town when a cholera epidemic precluded burial in the city's center.

The Pharmacy Shop at no. 21 is over a century old. The first pharmacy was set up in the Kremlin by Ivan the Terrible in 1581. Beginning in the 1600s, pharmacy shops sold medicinal herbs in Moscow. The herbs were grown in the area of what is now the Alexandrov Gardens near the Kremlin.

In the small park stands the **Monument to Ivan Fedorov** (1510-83), the first Russian printer. The passage is still lined with small bookshops; a popular one is Knizhnaya Nakhodka.

Kuibyshev Street

Kuibyshev Passage leads into this street, which begins off the Square and continues past the right side of GUM. It was once the main thoroughfare of Kitai-gorod. In 1497, Ivan the Great gave a parcel of land on this street to 500 Novgorod merchant families to establish the Moscow-Novgorod Trade Exchange, at a time when Novgorod was still independent of Muscovy. The wealthy merchants erected St. Ilyia Church, recognized by its single dome and *zakomara* gabled arches. Up to 1935 (after which the street was named after a popular revolutionary figure), this passage was known as Ilyinka Street, once the busy thoroughfare of Moscow's bank and financial district. The classical building of the **Moscow Stock Exchange** (1875), with its large Ionic columns, now houses the Chamber of Commerce.

The wealthy merchant Pavel Riabushinsky had Fedor Shekhtel build the Riabushinsky Bank in 1904. Shekhtel also designed the nearby Moscow Merchants Building in 1909. Riabushinsky was a well-respected spokesman for the merchant class and chairman of the Moscow Stock Exchange.

As Kuibyshev Passage continues past the street of the same name, it turns into Ribny Pereulok (Fish Lane), where many food stalls were set up. Later, in 1805, the Italian architect Quarenghi built the **Old Merchant Arcade** that occupied an entire block. The white structure with its Corinthian columns, once filled with boutiques, is now an office building.

Razin Street

Ribny Pereulok leads into Ulitsa Razina, which starts near St. Basil's and continues on past the Rossiya Hotel. Near the hotel are the remains of the 16th-century brick rampart walls that surrounded Kitai-gorod; this wall was over 2,500 meters long and six meters high. The street, once known as Varvara, was renamed after Stenka Razin, a popular cossack rebel who was executed in Red Square in 1671.

The immense structure behind St. Basil's is the **Rossiya Hotel,** completed in 1967 by the architect Chechulin. The hotel is the largest in the world, with rooms for 6,000 people and a superb view of the Kremlin. One of Moscow's largest *beriozka* shops is located at the back of the hotel. It also has many cafes and restaurants, the large Central Concert Hall and the Zariadi Cinema. In old Russian, *zariadi* meant "beyond the trading stalls." This area used to lie beyond the old marketplace on the outer fringes of Red Square.

The salmon and white **Church of St. Varvara** (Barbara) stands at the beginning of the street, once named after this saint. This passage once stretched from the Kremlin, along the old trade route, to the town of Vladimir. Prince Dmitri Donskoi used this route on his way to fight the Mongols in the Battle of Kulikovo in 1380.

The small cube-shaped and five-domed **Church of St. Maximus** stands nearby. Built in 1698 by Novgorod merchants, it held the remains of St. Maximus, an ascetic prophet who died in 1433. It now houses a branch of the Society for Environmental Protection.

Between the two, at no. 4 Razin, is the **Old English Inn,** a whitewashed house with tiny irregularly placed windows. It originally belonged to a wealthy Russian merchant until, in 1556, Ivan the Terrible presented it to Sir Richard Chancellor, an English merchant who began trade relationships with Russia. Ivan even proposed marriage to Queen Elizabeth, but she declined and instead offered Ivan asylum in England whenever he might need it. Later the inn was used by English merchants for their stores and living quarters, and English diplomats also stayed here. It has recently been restored and houses findings from local archaeological digs.

Next to the Inn is the **House of Boyars Romanov,** now a branch of the State History Museum that has displays of life from 17th-century boyardom. The rich boyar, Nikita Romanov, had his home in the center of Kitai-gorod. Nikita's sister, Anatasia, was married to Ivan the Terrible. Nikita's grandson, Mikhail, who was born in the house, was later elected to the throne in 1613 and began the reign of the Romanov Dynasty. The house was restored in the 19th century and is furnished to look like an early noble household. Open on Wed. 11 a.m. to 7 p.m. and other days 10 a.m. to 6 p.m. Closed Tuesdays and the first Monday of the month.

At the back of the hotel is the **Church of St. George on Pskov Hill.** The colorful church, with red walls and a blue belfry (1818), was erected by Pskov merchants in 1657.

On the other side of the Rossiya Hotel, on Kitaisky Proezd by the Moskva River, is the **Church of the Conception of St. Anne in the Corner.** The church stood at the corner of the Kitai-gorod wall and was named after the Virgin's mother, St. Anne. The barren wife of Prince Vasily III, Solomonia (whom he later divorced), often prayed here.

Nogin Square

Razin Street leads north into Ploshchad Nogina (with a Metro stop), both named after the revolutionary, Viktor Nogin. On Nogin Square stands the **Church of All Saints on Kulishki.** After Prince

Dmitri Donskoi defeated the Mongols at Kulikovo in 1380, he erected a wooden church on the *kulishki* (marshy land). It was replaced by a stone church in the 16th century, which has since been restored.

To the left of the church are the gray buildings of the **Delovoy Dvor**, the business chambers. Built in 1913, they were used for the business operations of the city.

Near the square are the **Ilyinsky Gardens**, with a monument to the Russian grenadiers who died in the Battle of Plevna against Turkey in 1877. Along the small side street called Staraya (Old) Prospekt, are the buildings of the Central Committee of the Communist Party. A few-minute's walk away is a "jewel of merchant architecture," the five-domed **Church of the Holy Trinity in Nikitniki**. In 1620, Mikhail Romanov hired a wealthy merchant from Yaroslavl, Grigory Nikinikov, to work in the financial administration. Nikinikov named his street after himself and later built this church on the site of the wooden Church of St. Nikita (his family saint), which burned down. The oldest icon is St. Nikita, which Nikinikov supposedly rescued from the burning church. The icon of the Trinity can be found on the iconostasis, carved in 1640. The burial chapel of the Nikinikovs lies to the right of the altar.

To the left, Staraya Prospekt turns into Novaya (New) Prospekt. In the other direction, Staraya Prospekt turns into Solyanka Street. *Sol,* in Russian, means salt, and the old saltyards were along this street in the 17th century. Farther up the street is the **Church of St. Vladimir in the Old Gardens**. At the time, this area was considered the countryside of Moscow; Ivan the Great had a summer palace near the Convent of St. John.

Solyanka intersects with Arkhipov Street, named after the artist, who lived here in 1900. Many middle-class artisans lived in this part of the city. On this street, at no. 8, is the Moscow Synagogue.

MARX PROSPEKT

Prospekt Marxa, the city's busiest avenue, sweeps through the center of town, stretching northeast along the Kremlin wall to Sverdlov and Dzerzhinsky squares.

Dzerzhinsky Square

Marx Prospekt begins at this square with a bronze Statue of Feliz Dzerzhinsky (1877-1926), a prominent revolutionary leader, marking its center. The Metro station Dzerzhinskaya lets out right onto the square. The large department store on one corner is **Detsky Mir** (Children's World), largest children's store in the USSR. More than a half-million shoppers visit daily. Behind it is the Savoy Hotel, and in front, KGB Headquarters.

Three interesting museums are also along the square. The **Mayakovsky Museum** is on the corner of Kirov Street and Serov Passage. The poet lived here for over a decade; many of his works and personal items are on display. The museum is open Mon. and Thurs. 12-8 p.m. and other days 10 a.m. to 6 p.m.; closed Wednesday. On Novaya (New) Square Street is the **Museum of the History and Reconstruction of Moscow,** open Wed. and Fri. 12-8 p.m., other days 10 a.m. to 6 p.m., closed Mon. and the last day of the month. Next to it is the **Polytechnical Museum;** opened in 1872, it houses more than 30,000 items that trace the history of Russian science and technology. The library has over three million volumes. It's open Tues. and Thurs. 12-8 p.m., other days 10 a.m.to 6 p.m., closed same as above. The statue of Ivan Fyodorov, the first Russian printer, stands a few minutes walk down the prospekt.

Sverdlov Square

The next section of Prospekt Marxa opens on Ploshchad Sverdlova, named after the first president of Soviet Russia, Yakov Sverdlov (1885-1919). The statue of Karl Marx, inscribed with the words, "Workers of All Countries Unite!", marks its center. The Metro stop is Ploshchad Sverdlova Revolutsii.

On one corner is the Metropole Hotel, built in 1903 and recently renovated. The mosaic panels on the front were designed by the Russian artist, Mikhail Vrubel. Entrance plaques commemorate events of the Revolution. Facing the hotel to the right are walls of the 16th-century Kitai-gorod.

Up until 1919, the area was known as Theater Square, for two of Moscow's most prominent theaters were built here, the Bolshoi (Big) and the Maly (Small). One of the world's most famous theaters, the **Bolshoi** was built in 1824 by Osip Bovet and Alexander Mikhailov to stage performances of ballet and opera. After a fire in 1856, it was rebuilt by Albert Kavos. The stately building, with the large fountain in front, is crowned by the famous four bronze horses pulling the chariot of Apollo, patron of the arts. This is the work of sculptor Pyotr Klodt. The gorgeous interior consists of five tiers of gilded boxes, whose chairs are covered with plush red velvet. The chandelier is made from 13,000 pieces of cut glass. The theater premiered compositions by Tchaikovsky, Glinka, Mussorgsky and Rimsky-Korsakov. The Intourist service bureau at your hotel sells tickets for Bolshoi performances.

Across from the Bolshoi is the light yellow building of the **Maly Drama Theater.** At its entrance stands the Statue of Alexander Ostrovsky (1823-86), the outstanding Russian playwright. The theater is nicknamed the "Ostrovsky House." Many classic Russian plays are staged here. On the other side of the Bolshoi is the Central Children's Theater.

The other end of the square is flanked by the three-story ornamented brick building of the **Central Lenin Museum** (closed Mondays and last Tuesday of each month) that marks the entrance to Revolution Square. This building, erected in 1892, once housed the Duma (City Hall) of Moscow. In 1937, its 34 halls were converted into the country's largest Lenin museum. Across from the museum is the Moskva Hotel. Before continuing down the avenue to Revolution Square, some old and interesting side streets off Sverdlov Square merit a few minutes of exploration.

Petrovka Street

Ulitsa Petrovka is a small side street that begins in front of the Maly Theater. Three centuries ago, the passage was named after the Petrovsky (St. Peter) Monastery, which also served as a protective stronghold and entrance to the town. The

monastery was built by Prince Dmitri Donskoi to honor the Mongol defeat in the Battle of Kulikovo in 1380. Much of this monastery has been restored. The **Museum of Literature** (open Wed. and Fri. 2-9 p.m., other days 11 a.m. to 6 p.m., closed Mondays and the last day of the month), now located at no. 28, traces the history of Russian literature. This neighborhood was the residence of Moscow's coachmakers. The area was nicknamed Karetny Ryad (Carriage Row).

For a long time, the street has been a popular shopping district with stores selling *podarki* (gifts), *bukinisti* (second-hand books) and *almazi* (diamonds). Next to the Maly is the large central department store, TsUM. The Russikiye Uzory sells handicrafts, and at no. 8 is Chasy, one of Moscow's best watch stores. The Society of World Art had its first exhibition at no. 15, displaying the work of Alexander Benois. Anton Chekhov lived for many years at no. 19. The Hermitage Gardens have been here for over a century.

Kuznetsky Most

The poet Vladimir Mayakovsky wrote, "I love Kuznetsky Most . . . and then Petrovka." Petrovka Street leads to Kuznetsky Most, a small lane branching to the right. As far back as the 15th century, the area was the popular residence of Moscow's blacksmiths, who lived along the banks of the Neglinnaya River, which, at the time, flowed through here. (In the 19th century, the river was diverted to an underground aqueduct.) *Kuznetsky Most,* in Russian, means "Blacksmith's Bridge."

Almost every building along this passage has a fascinating story behind it. The steep passage became a highly respected shopping district in the 19th century; items were stamped with "Bought in Kuznetsky Most." At no. 9 was a restaurant called Yar, which Pushkin and Tolstoy mention in their writings. The Artist Unions have their exhibition halls at no. 11. Tolstoy listened to one of the world's first phonographs in the musical shop that was at no. 12, and he wrote of Anna Karenina shopping at Gautier's, at no. 20. The House of Fashion and many airline agencies are also located along the narrow street. At the end is Metro stop Kuznetsky Most.

Neglinnaya Street

Kuznetsky Most connects to Ulitsa Neglinnaya, which runs from Marx Prospekt to Trubnaya

Square on the Boulevard Ring. This street also sprang up alongside the banks of the Neglinnaya River, where many popular shops were located. The revolutionary Nikolai Schmit had his furniture store at the corner of Kuznetsky Most. The Moorish-style building of the **Sandunovsky Baths** at no. 14 was frequented by Chekhov. This is still a popular *banya*. The building was bought by the actor Sila Sandunov, who turned them into sauna-baths in the 18th century. On the street is also Moscow's oldest sheet music shop and the State Bank of the USSR. At no. 29 is the popular Uzbekistan Restaurant.

The continuation of Marx Prospekt from Sverdlov Square leads to Revolution Square (50th Anniversary of the October Revolution Square). This area was once known as Okhotny Ryad (Hunter's Lane). The main markets of Moscow were spread from here to Red Square. Across from the Moskva Hotel is Dom Soyuzov (House of Trade Unions) on the corner of Pushkin and Tverskaya streets. Built in 1784 by Matvei Kazakov, it used to be the Noble's Club.

Crossing the prospekt via the underpass brings you out in front of the National Hotel. Built in 1903, it's still one of Moscow's finest hotels. Lenin stayed in Suite 107, marked by a plaque. One down is the Intourist Board of Foreign Tourism. Next comes one of the oldest buildings of Moscow Univeristy, built between 1786 and 1793 by Kazakov. In the courtyard are two statues of graduates, Nikolai Ogarev and Alexander Herzen.

In the center of the avenue in Manezhnaya Square, stands the Central Exhibition Hall, which used to be the Manège, the czar's riding school. It was built in classical style in 1817 by Augustin Betancourt. Moscow's largest art exhibitions are now shown here. At no. 21 is the **Kalinin Museum**, tracing the life of the party leader Mikhail Kalinin. It's open 10 to 6, 12 to 8 Tues. and Wed., closed Monday. Prospekt Marxa ends a few-minutes' walk farther down by the Lenin Library and Ulitsa Volkhonka. The closest Metro stop is Biblioteka 1. Lenina.

Kropotkin Street

Volkhanka Street begins at the Kremlin's Borovuitsky Tower and turns into Kropotkin Street. The **Pushkin Museum of Fine Arts** is at no. 12. The Greek-style building was constructed in 1898 by Roman Klein to house a collection of fine arts that had over 20,000 items on display at the 1912 opening. Today, the museum boasts one of the world's largest collections of ancient classical, Oriental and Western European art, with over a half million works. It is open daily 10 a.m. to 8 p.m., Sun. till 6. Directly behind the Pushkin is the **Marx and Engels Museum** at no. 5 Marx and Engels Street, open Tues., Wed. and Fri., 12 to 7 p.m., other days 11 a.m. to 6 p.m. Both are closed Monday and the last day of each month.

Across from Metro stop Kropotkinskaya, is the heated **Moskva Open-Air Swimming Pool,** open year-round. Tickets are bought at the small *kassa* desk next to the main building. Bathing suits, caps and towels can also be rented. One enters the heated pool through a passage from inside the complex.

Ulitsa Kropotkinskaya was named after the revolutionary scholar, Pyotr Kropotkin (1842-1921). For centuries, the street was known as Prechistenka (Holy), after the Icon of the Holy Virgin kept in a nearby monastery. Many aristocratic families built their residences along this street. At no. 10 lived Count Orlov, a friend of Pushkin's. The mansion now houses the Soviet Peace Commission. The writer Turgenev and the poet Zhukovsky also lived on the street. The mansion at no. 12 was built by Afanasy Grigorev. It now houses the **Alexander Pushkin Museum,** with over 80,000 items connected with the poet. It's open Sat. and Sun. from 10 a.m. to 6 p.m., other days 12 to 8 p.m., closed Mon. and the last Friday of each month. Across the street at no. 11 is the **Leo Tolstoy Museum.** This museum is open from 12 to 7 p.m. and closed Mon. and the last Friday of month. The poet Denis Davydov lived at no. 17, and Prince Dolgorukov (related to Prince Dolgoruky) once lived at no. 21. The Palace of Fine Arts, at no. 21, hosts art shows. Kropotkin Street ends at the Garden Ring by a statue of Tolstoy.

Across the river at no. 10 Lavrushinsky (near Metro Novokuznetskaya) is the **Tretyakov Art Gallery.** In 1856, the brothers Sergei and Pavel Tretyakov, avid art patrons, began to collect the works of Russian artists. In 1892, they founded the museum and donated their collection to the city. Today the gallery houses one of the world's largest Russian and Soviet art collections from the 10th to the 20th centuries. It's open daily 10 a.m. to 7 p.m. and closed Monday, but check first; the museum is closed now and then for restoration. A new

(clockwise from top) Golden Ring cathedral; summer dacha; wooden cathedrals predate the grander ones of stone and marble

branch of the Tretyakov (also closed Monday) has opened at no. 10 Krymsky Val. This is across from Tverskaya Park near Metro stop Oktyabrskaya.

TVERSKAYA OR GORKY STREET

In the 18th century, Ulitsa Gorkovo was the main street of the city; today, it's still one of the busiest in Moscow. The long thoroughfare stretches from Red Square past Pushkin and Mayakovsky squares to Belorusskaya Train Station, where it turns into Leningradsky Prospekt.

The passage was once known as Tverskaya, since it led to the old Russian town of Tver (now Kalinin) 160 miles (256 km) north, and on to St. Petersburg. In prerevolutionary days, the street, once twisting and narrow, was known for its fashionable shops, luxurious hotels and grandiose aristocratic mansions. Installed here were the city's first electric lamps. The first trams ran along the street, and the first movie theater opened here. In 1932, the street was renamed after the Russian writer Maxim Gorky, a favorite of Lenin and Stalin. At this time, it was also reshaped and widened and now retains little of its former appearance. The street continued to be known as Gorky up until 1990, when the Moscow City Council voted to restore the street's old name of Tverskaya.

It takes about an hour and a half to stroll up Tverskaya Street. One can also ride the Metro to various stops along Tverskaya—Pushkinskaya, Mayakovskaya and Belorusskaya—to cut short the time.

Tverskaya Street begins in front of Red Square at the **50th Anniversary of the October Revolution Square,** known as Manezhnaya before 1967. The Metro stop Prospekt Marxa is right at the beginning of the street. On the corner is the elegant old National Hotel with a splendid view of Red Square. A small *beriozka* shop is inside to the left. The 22-story structure next door is the modern Intourist Hotel, opened in 1971. Inside, toward the back, are slot machines, *beriozkas* and a hard-currency cafe. Stop in the cafeteria for a quick lunch. Next to the hotel is also a cooperative restaurant. In between the two hotels is an Intourist booking office and a foreign-currency Exchange Bank. Across the street are a number of shops, including the souvenir Podarki (Gifts).

Continuing up the street leads past the Yermolova Drama Theater, named after a famous actress, to the Central Telegraph Building, with its globe and digital clock, on the corner of Ogareva Street. The building, designed by Ilya Rerberg in 1927, is open round-the-clock. Telegrams and long-distance calls can be made here.

Across the street at no. 3 Proyezd Khudozhestvennovo Teatra, (Arts Passage Street) is the **Moscow Arts Theater,** established by Stanislavsky and Nemirovich-Danchenko in 1896. Here Stanislavsky practiced his "method-acting" and staged many plays by Tverskaya and Chekhov. After *The Seagull,* the bird became the emblem on the outside of the theater. The new building of the Moscow Arts Theater is at no. 22 Tsverkoi Boulevard, off Tverskaya.

The Aragvi Restaurant stands on the next corner of Stoleshnikov Lane (a right off Tverskaya), which specializes in Georgian cuisine. This lane has been here for over 300 years. Craftsmen embroidered tablecloths for the czar's court. *Stoleshnik*, in old Russian, meant tablecloth. The Stoleshnik Cafe, at no. 6, is decorated in old-Russian style. At no. 11, the pastry shop still uses old-fashioned ovens built into the walls, and has some of the best cakes in the city. The Russian writer Vladimir Giliarovsky, who wrote *Moscow and Moscovites,* lived at no. 9 for over a half century. The lane leads to Petrovka Street, a popular shopping area.

The side street to the left, Nezhdanovoi, leads to the Church of the Resurrection, founded by Czar Mikhail Romanov. It's filled with many beautiful 17th-century icons and is open daily for worship.

Sovietskaya Square

Sovietskaya Square is marked by the equestrian Statue of Yuri Dolgoruky, founder of Moscow. It was erected in 1954 to mark the 800th anniversary of the city. The building behind the square, in the small garden, holds the Party Archives of the Marxism-Leninism Institute, built in 1927. The archives contain more than 6,000 documents of Marx and Engels and over 30,000 of Lenin. In front is a granite statue of Lenin by Sergei Merkurov.

Directly across the street stands the large red-brick and white-columned Moscow Soviet of People's Deputies, the Mos-Soviet or City Council.

The architect Matvei Kazakov designed the building as the residence for the first governor-general, appointed by Catherine the Great, in 1782. Two of Moscow's governors were Prince Dmitri Golitsyn (1820-44), who paved the streets and installed water pipes, and Vladimir Dolgorukov, a descendant of Yuri Dolgoruky. In 1946, the building was moved back 42 feet (14 meters) and two more stories were added.

A Stretch With Good Food

Farther up Tverskaya is the Tsentralnaya Hotel at no. 10. In the same building is the most famous bakery in Moscow, formerly known as Filippov's. Next door is the old **Gastronom no. 1,** another popular food store. Beautiful white sculptures and garlands line the shop's face, and the gilded interior is filled with stained glass and colorful displays. It's still known as Yeliseyev's, after the original owner, who also had a popular gourmet store by the same name in St. Petersburg on Nevsky Prospekt (which is also still there). The merchant bought the mansion from a princess in 1898 and opened the store in 1901. Even though delicacies are lacking, it's worth a visit to see the interior.

At no. 14 Tverskaya is the **Memorial Museum of Nikolai Ostrovsky** (1904-36) who wrote, *How the Steel Was Tempered.* His house is now a museum with documents and photographs of this Soviet author. It's open 10 to 6, Wed. and Fri. noon to 8, closed Mon. and the last day of the month. Next to the museum is the Central Actors Club and the All-Russia Theatrical Society.

Down the side street, at no. 6 Stanislavsky, is the **Stanislavsky Memorial House-Museum.** It's open on Wed. and Fri. 2 to 9 p.m. and others days 11 a.m. to 6 p.m. Closed on Monday and Tuesday.

At Tverskaya and no. 12 Shchukin St. is the **Sergei Konenkov Studio Museum,** displaying marble and wooden statues of this famous sculptor (1874-1971). Open on weekends 10 a.m. to 5 p.m. and other days 12 to 7 p.m. Closed Monday and Tuesday. Nearby is the store Armenia, specializing in food from this republic.

Pushkin Square

As Tverskaya crosses the Boulevard Ring, it opens onto Pushkin Square. In the 16th century, the stone walls of the Beli-gorod (White-town) stretched around what is now the Boulevard Ring.

Alexander Pushkin (1799-1837)

They were torn down in the 18th century. The Strastnoi Convent used to stand on what is now Pushkin Square—the square was named Strastnaya, after the Convent of the Passion of Our Lord. The convent was demolished in the 1930s. In the center of the square stands the **Statue of Alexander Pushkin,** by sculptor Alexander Opekulin. It was erected in 1880 from funds donated by the public. Pushkin lived over a third of his life in Moscow, where he predicted, "word of me shall spread across the Russian land." Dostoevsky laid a wreath on the statue at its unveiling; today it's still always covered with flowers and a popular spot for open-air readings.

Behind the square is the 3,000-seat Rossiya Cinema, built in 1961 for the 2nd International Moscow Film Festival. This area is also Moscow's major publishing center. Here are the newspaper offices of *Izvestia, Trud, Novosti (APN)* and *Moscow News.*

A quick walk down Chekhov Street (behind *Izvestia*) leads to the tent-shaped Church of the Nativity, built in 1649-52. Legend had that a noblewoman gave birth in her carriage as she passed this spot and later commissioned a church to honor the Nativity. When it burnt down, Czar

Alexei Romanov donated money to have it rebuilt, along with a chapel dedicated to the icon that prevented fires, Our Lady of the Burning Bush, which is in the chapel.

Central Museum Of The Revolution

This museum is at no. 21 Tverskaya Street. This mansion was built for Count Razumovsky in 1780 by the architect Manelas. In 1832, when it was rebuilt after a fire by Adam Menelaws, the mansion was bought by the Angliisky (English) Club, formed in 1772 by a group of foreigners residing in Moscow. The club's members (all men) were made up of Russian aristocratic intellectuals and included the best minds in politics, science, art and literature. Tolstoy once lost 1,000 rubles in a card game in the "infernal" room. Pushkin wrote of the club in his long poem *Evgeny Onegin.* When Tatiana arrived in Moscow, Evgeny described "the two frivolous looking lions" at the gates. The last *bolshoi* gala at the club was a banquet thrown for Nicholas II to celebrate the 300th anniversary of the Romanov Dynasty in 1913. The museum, opened in 1924, exhibits over a million items from the Revolution. The gun outside was used to shell the White Guards in 1917. It's open 10 a.m. to 6 p.m., 11 a.m. to 7 p.m. Wed. and Fri., closed Monday.

Next to the museum, at no. 23, is the Stanislavky Drama Theater. Behind it, is the Young Spectator's Theater for children. The Baku Restaurant, at no. 24, serves delicious Azerbaijani food.

To The End Of Tverskaya

Passing the Minsk Hotel, whose restaurant specializes in Byelorussian cuisine, and a few other shops brings you to the corner of Tverskaya and Sadovoye Koltso (Garden Ring). On the corner stands a large building with 10 columns, the Tchaikovsky Concert Hall, where orchestras and dance ensembles perform. The Mayakovsky Metro station is in front. Directly behind the Hall, at no. 18, is the circular-domed building of the Satire Theater. The Aquarium gardens are next with the Mossoviet Theater, at no. 16 Bolshaya Sadovaya Street. Also nearby is the Sovremennik Theater, staging contemporary plays. Across the street is the Peking Hotel, with a Chinese-food restaurant.

A statue of the poet Vladimir Mayakovsky (1893-1930) stands in Mayakovsky Square. On the other side of the square is the Sofia Restau-

rant, with Bulgarian food. To the right is the Moskva Cinema. At no. 43 Tverskaya is the House of Children's Books, and at no. 46 is the Exhibition Hall of Artist Unions.

Tverskaya Street ends at Byelorusskaya Square. At the center of the square is a monument to Maxim Tverskaya (1868-1935), erected in 1951. The Byelorusskaya Railway Station, over 100 years old, has trains coming and going to points west, including Warsaw, Berlin, Paris and London. The Metro station Byelorusskaya is out front. At the station, Tverskaya Street turns into Leningradsky Prospekt, which runs all the way to the international airport, Sheremetyevo.

On the next side street are the offices of the newspaper *Pravda,* with a daily distribution of 10 million. The Race Course is down Begovaya Street. A little farther up, at no. 25 Leningradsky, is the Hotel Sovetskaya with the Romany Gypsy Theater.

From here, head back into the center of town on the metro or continue by bus along Leningradsky Prospekt.

KALININ PROSPEKT

Another main Moscow street, Prospekt Kalinina, begins across from the Kremlin Trinity and Kutufya Towers (by the Alexandrov Gardens) and runs westward toward the Moskva River. Here it turns into Kutuzovsky Prospekt and later the Minsk Highway.

The old route was known as Novodvizhenskaya, and stretched from the Kremlin to the outer walls of the city. A new thoroughfare was built along the old passage; in 1963, it was renamed Kalinin, after a leader of the Communist Party, Mikhail Kalinin. The old section of the prospekt runs from the Kremlin to the Boulevard Ring, where the more modern part begins.

The road starts by a large gray building off Prospekt Marxa, the **Lenin State Library.** The library opened in the 1800s, when the book collector, Nikolai Rumyantsev, moved his collection from St. Petersburg into a Moscow mansion across from the Kremlin. A new building was constructed on the site in 1940, and now houses the largest collection of books in the USSR, over 36 million.

The first part of the prospekt still contains a few 18th-century buildings. At no. 7 is the former Monastery of the Holy Cross. The house at no. 9

belonged to Tolstoy's grandfather, on whom he based a character in *War and Peace.*

At the corner of Granovsky is an early 18th-century mansion that belonged to the wealthy Count Sheremetev. Across the street, at no. 5, is another old mansion, built by Kazakov. It now houses the **Alexei Shchusev Museum of Architecture,** which features the history of Russian and Soviet architecture. It's open 11 a.m. to 7 p.m. and closed Monday and Friday. The nearest metro stop is Kalininskaya.

At no. 16 is the white medieval former mansion of the merchant Morozov, who hired the designer Marizin in the 19th century to model his residence after a Spanish castle. In 1959, it was turned over to the House of Friendship, where delegations of foreign friendship societies meet.

Near the Metro stop Arbatskaya, on the side street Suvorov, is the Journalist Club. Across from the club is a monument to Gogol, standing in front of the house where the writer lived. On this corner is the large Dom Svyazi (House of Communications) with a post office, telephone center and video-phone links to a few other Russian cities.

The Arbat

The Prague Restaurant, on the other corner, marks the entrance to one of the city's oldest sections, the Arbat. Long ago, the Arbat Gates led into Moscow. *Arbad* is an old eastern-Russian word meaning "beyond the town walls." The area was first mentioned in 15th-century chronicles. It lay along the Smolensk Road, making it a busy trade center. Many court artisans lived here in the 16th century; in the 19th century, many wealthy and educated residents chose to live in the Arbat. Today the old Arbat (along Arbat St.) is a cobbled pedestrian passage and one of the most popular meeting and shopping spots in Moscow. Along with shops, cafes, art galleries, concert and theater halls and a museum tracing the history of the area are groups of painters on the sidewalks that sketch portraits, performance artists and even demonstrators. It's also a frequent site for festivals and carnivals.

All the colorful buildings along the pedestrian mall and side streets have a rich and romantic history. Many poems, songs and novels, such as Anatoly Rybakov's *Children of the Arbat,* have been written about the Arbat. The czar's stablemen once lived along Starokonivshenny (Old-Sta-

ble Lane). An old church stood on the corner of Spasopekovsky Lane. Other small streets have the names Serebryany (Silversmith), Plotnikov (Carpenter) and Kalachny (Pastrycook). Pushkin rented a house at no. 53 Arbat in 1831, and lived here with his new bride, Natalia Goncharova. The house is now the **Pushkin Museum.** It's open 12 to 6 p.m. and Sat. and Sun. 11 a.m. to 5 p.m.; closed Mon. and Tuesday. The poet Lermontov, the writer Herzen, the composer Scriabin and the sculptress Golubkina lived in the Arbat neighborhood. Their residences are also museums (see museum listings for locations).

After a leisurely stroll down the Arbat to Smolensky Square, you'll better understand the lyrics to a popular song: "Oy, Arbat, a whole lifetime is not enough to travel through your length!"

New Arbat

The area along Kalinin Prospekt from Arbat Square on the Boulevard Ring to the Kalinin Bridge is better known as the New Arbat. This area consists of shops and flats built during Khrushchev's regime in the 1960s. Across the street from the Prague Restaurant (one of the oldest in Moscow) is the Church of Simon Stylites, now an exhibition hall. Down the side street, behind the church, at no. 2 Malaya Molchanovka, is the **House-Museum of Lermontov.** It's open 11 a.m. to 6 p.m. and on Wednesday and Friday 2 to 9 p.m.; closed Monday and Tuesday.

Next to the church, on Kalinin, is **Dom Knigi** (House of Books), the city's largest bookstore. The Malachite Casket Jewelry Shop is also in this building. On the same side is the Melodia Record Shop and the 3,000-seat Oktyabr Cinema.

A series of shops and cafes line the left side of Kalinin. The block begins with the Valdai Cafe and the New Arbat Supermarket. Other shops include the Moskvichka (Miss Moscow) fashion shop, Sintetika Department Store, Metelitsa (Snowball) ice-cream cafe, Charodeika (Sorceress) Beauty Shop, Jazz Cafe Pechora and the Podarki (Gift) shop. The block ends at the 2,000-seat Arbat Restaurant with a large globe on its roof.

The prospekt crosses the Garden Ring at Tchaikovsky Street and ends at the river. Before Kalinin Bridge, on the right, stands the 30-story CMEA/COMECON building, headquarters for the East European economic trade community. The Hotel Mir is behind it. Farther down, on the same side of the river, is the Sovincenter and Mezh-dunarodny (International) Hotel, built with the help of Armand Hammer and used by foreign firms. Nearby is also the building of the Soviet Federal Republic's Council of Ministers.

Kutuzovsky Prospekt

After crossing the Kalinin Bridge, Kalinin St. turns into Kutuzovsky Prospekt, named after the Russian General, Mikhail Kutuzov (1745-1813), who fought against Napoleon. The building on the right, with the star-spire, is the Hotel Ukrainia, which has a *beriozka* and Ukrainian restaurant. A statue to the Ukrainian poet Taras Shevchenko stands in front. Nearby is the House of Toys. Across the street, at no. 6, is the Central Art Fund, selling local handicrafts and artwork. At the next corner is the Hero City of Moscow Obelisk. Troops left from here to fight the Germans in 1941. At no. 26, a plaque marks the 30-year residence of Leonid Brezhnev.

The obelisk stands at the entrance of Bolshaya Dorogomilovskaya St., along which are the Kievskaya Railway Station (with a Metro stop), and a foreign-currency food *beriozka*.

The prospekt ends at the **Triumphal Arch** in Victory Square, designed by Osip Bovet in 1829-34 to honor Russia's victory in the War of 1812. It originally stood in front of the Byelorusskaya Train Station, and was moved to this spot in 1968, when Tverskaya Street was widened. Here on Poklonnaya Hill, Napoleon waited for Moscow's citizens to relinquish the keys to the city. *Poklon* in Russian means "bow." It was once the custom for people entering or leaving Moscow to stop and bow to the city. From the hill is a magnificent view of Moscow; Anton Chekhov once said "those who want to understand Russia should look at Moscow from Poklonnaya."

In between the Metro station Kutuzovskaya and the arch is the statue of Mikhail Kutuzov, by Nikolas Tomsky, and the obelisk that marks the common graves of 300 men who died in the War of 1812.

The large circular building at no. 3 is the **Battle of Borodino Panorama Museum.** The 68 cannon in front were captured from Napoleon. In 1912, to commemorate the 100th Anniversary of the war, Franz Rouband was commissioned to paint scenes of the Battle of Borodino, which occurred on 12 Aug. 1812. The building that holds the large murals was constructed in 1962 to honor the 150th anniversary. Behind the museum is the **Kutuzov Hut.** Here on 1 Sept. 1812, as the French invaded Moscow, Kutuzov and the Military Council decided to abandon the city. The museum and hut are open 10:30 a.m. to 4 p.m. and closed Friday.

From here, Kutuzovsky Prospekt turns into Mozhaiskoye Chausee (Minsk Highway), along which is the Mozhaisky Hotel and campgrounds.

THE BOULEVARD RING

Ulitsa Gerzena (Herzen Street), named after revolutionary writer Alexander Herzen, runs out from the Kremlin's Manezhnaya Square (in between Gorky and Kalinin streets) to the Boulevard Ring. In the 15th century, this was the passage to the town of Novgorod. At no. 13 is the Moscow Conservatory Grand Hall, built in 1901. The conservatory was founded in 1866 by Rubenstein. A statue of Tchaikovsky stands in front. Count Menschikov once lived in the palace at no. 12. Pushkin was married in the nearby Church of the Ascension. At no. 19 is the Mayakovsky Theater, and at no. 6 the **Zoological Museum.** It's open 10 a.m. to 5 p.m. and on Wednesday and Friday 12 to 8 p.m.; closed on Monday.

During the 16th and 17th centuries, the stone walls of the Beli-gorod (White-town) stretched around the area now known as the Boulevard Ring. During the Time of Troubles at the end of the 17th century, Boris Godunov fortified the walls and built 28 towers and gates. By 1800, the walls were taken down and the area was planted with trees and gardens, made up of a number of small connected boulevards. Ten *bulvari* (boulevards) make up the Bulvarnoye Koltso, the Boulevard Ring, a horseshoe shape that begins in the southwest off Kropotkinskaya Street and circles around to the back of the Rossiya Hotel on the other side of the Kremlin. Frequent buses run around the ring, stopping off at each intersecting boulevard.

Gogol

The first bears the name of the writer, Nikolai Gogol. Gogolevsky Bulvar stretches from the Moskva open-air swimming pool to Arbat Square. It was once known as the Immaculate Virgin Boulevard. At no. 14 is the Central Chess Club.

Suvorovsky Boulevard extends from Kalinin Street to Herzen Street. It was named after the famous Russian army commander Alexander Suvorov, who lived at the end of it. Gogol lived at no. 7; increasingly despondent in his later years, he burned the second volume of his novel *Dead Souls* in this house, and died here in 1852. A monument to Nikolai Gogol stands in front, on which characters from his books are depicted. Built in Russian Empire style by Gilliardi in 1823, the Lunin House is at no. 12. It's now the **Museum of Oriental Art,** open 11 a.m. to 8 p.m., closed Monday. The Nikitskiye Gates used to stand at the junction of the boulevard and Herzen Street, which is named Nikitskaya Square after a monastery that was in the area.

Tverskoi

Tverskoi Boulevard begins with the monument to Kliment Timiryazev, a prominent Russian botanist. Built in 1796, it's the oldest boulevard on the ring, and was once a very fashionable promenade. Pushkin, Turgenev, Tolstoy, all mentioned the Tverskoi in their writings. The house, where the great Russian actress Yermolova lived (no. 11), is now the **Maria Yermolova Museum.** It's open 1 to 8 p.m., Sat. and Sun. 12 to 7 p.m.; closed on Mon. and Tuesday. At no. 23 is the Pushkin Drama Theater, and at no. 25 the Gorky Literature Institute. Across the street is the Theater of Friendship of the Peoples of the USSR.

Continuing Around The Ring

The Strastnoi (Passion) Monastery used to be in the area of the Strastnoi Boulevard, which begins at Pushkin Square with a statue of Pushkin. On Pushkin's birthday, 6 June, many people crowd the square to honor the poet. Pushkin and Chekhov streets branch out from the center. The hospital at no. 15 was the Palace of the Gagarin Princes, also the English Club from 1802 to 1812.

The Petrovskiye Gates used to stand at what is now the beginning of Petrovsky Boulevard, which runs from Petrovsky Street to Trubnaya Square. A few buildings still remain from the 14th-century Vysoko-Petrovsky Monastery that once stood on the banks of the Neglinnaya River (now underground). Many of the old mansions on this boulevard were converted into hospitals and schools after the Revolution. At no. 13 Tsvetnoi Bulvar is the **Old Circus.**

Rozhdestvensky (Nativity) Boulevard ends at Sretenka Street, a popular shopping area. On the right are 14th-century walls from the Convent of the Nativity of God. An exhibit of the Soviet fleet is now in the 15th-century Church of the Assumption.

The statue to Nadezhda Krupskaya (1869-1939), Lenin's wife, marks the beginning of Sretensky Boulevard. It ends on Turgenevskaya Square with a Metro stop. In 1885, Moscow named its first public library, located here, after the writer Ivan Turgenev. The Central Post Office is on Kirov Street. To the right, one can make out the tower of the Church of the Archangel Gabriel. Prince Alexander Menschikov ordered it built on his estate in 1707; he wanted it to be taller than the Kremlin's Ivan the Great Belltower. In 1723, the archangel at the top was struck by lightning; so, for a time, the tower was the second largest structure in Moscow. Today it's known as the **Menschikov Tower.**

A statue of Griboyedov (1795-1829), the writer, marks the beginning of Christoprudny Boulevard. The name "Clear Pond" comes from the artificial pond at its center, with boating and ice skating in winter. The Sovremennik Theater is at no. 19.

Pokrovsky (Intercession) Boulevard begins at Chernyshevsky Street. The czars often took this route to their estate in Izmailovo, now a popular 3,000-acre park with a theater, amusement park and summer tent-circus. It can be reached from Metro stop Izmailovo Park. The buildings on the left used to serve the Pokrovsky barracks. A highly decorative rococo-style house built in 1766 was known as the "Chest of Drawers."

The last section of the Boulevard Ring is intersected by Yauzsky Boulevard. This ends by the Yauza River, where it joins the Moskva River. A few 18th-century mansions remain in this area. Continuing along the banks of the Moskva, past another one of Stalin's Gothic skyscrapers, brings you around the back side of the Kremlin. One of the best views of the Kremlin is from the **Bolshoi Kammeni Most** (Large Stone Bridge).

THE GARDEN RING

After much of Moscow burned in the great fire of 1812 (over 7,000 buildings were destroyed), it was decided to tear down all the old earthen ramparts and in their place build a circular road around the city. Anyone who had a house along the ring was required to plant a *sad* (garden); thus the passage was named Sadovaya Koltso (Garden Ring). The ring, Moscow's widest avenue, stretches for 10 miles (16 km) around the city, with the Kremlin's bell tower at midpoint. It is less than a mile (two km) from the Boulevard Ring. The 16 squares and streets that make up this ring each have a garden in their name, such as Big Garden and Sloping Garden. Buses, trolleys and the Koltso Metro circle the route. Along the way, modern buildings are sprinkled with 18th- and 19th-century mansions and old manor homes.

Beginning by the river, near Metro stop Park Kultury, is Krymskaya (Crimean) Square, surrounded by old classically designed provisional warehouses, built by Stasov in 1832-35. Nearby is the Olympic Press Center, Novosti Press Agency and Progress Publishers, publishing books in foreign languages.

At Zubovsky Square, Bolshaya Pirogovskaya (named after Nikolai Pirogov, a renown surgeon) leads to Novodevichy Monastery. Many of Moscow's clinics and research institutes are located here. The street begins at Devichye Park (Maiden's Field), where many carnivals were held; maidens would dance to Russian folk tunes. To the right, Kropotkinskaya Street leads down to the Kremlin. The area between the Boulevard and Garden rings was once an aristocratic residential district; many old mansions are still in the area. At no. 18 is the former estate of the wealthy merchant Morozov.

At Smolenskaya (formerly called Sennaya, the Haymarket) is the tall Ministry of Foreign Affairs. Nearby is Belgrade Hotel. The square turns into Tchaikovsky Street. In 1940, Novinsky Street was renamed after the composer who lived here. The poet Alexander Griboyedov grew up at no. 17. The great singer Fyodor Chaliapin (1873-1938) lived at no. 25 for over a decade. The American Embassy is at no. 19-32 Tchaikovsky.

Vosstaniya Square

The next square, Vosstaniya (Uprising), was named after the heavy fighting that took place here during the revolutions of 1905 and 1917. It was once called Kudrinskaya, after the local village of Kudrino. The side street off the square is still known as Kudrinskaya. The square is sur-

Anton Pavlovitch Chekhov (1860-1904)

rounded by large apartment complexes, except for the 18th-century Widow's House, the residence of widows and orphans of czarist officers killed in battle. Once the home of writer Alexander Kuprin, it's now a medical institute.

Before the square, off to the right, is Vorovsky Street, once one of the most fashionable areas of the city. Centuries ago, when the czar's servants and cooks lived in this area, the street was known as Povarskaya (Cook). Other side streets were Khlebny (Bread), Nozhevoy (Knife), and Chashechny (Cup). The two lanes Skaterny (Tablecloth) and Stolovoy (Table) still branch off the street. In *War and Peace,* Tolstoy described the Rostov's estate at no. 52 Povarskaya St., where there's now a statue of Tolstoy. Next door is the Writer's Club, named after the Soviet writer Alexander Fadeyev. The **Maxim Gorky Museum** at no. 25, recognizable by the statue of Gorky out front, tells about the life of the Russian writer. It's open from 10 a.m. to 6 p.m. and on Wed. and Fri. 12 to 8 p.m.; closed Mon. and Tuesday. Gorky also spent his last years in a house on the neighboring street of Kachalov no. 6, which is also a museum, open the same times as the museum on Vorovsky.

On the other side of Vosstaniya Square is Barrikadnaya St., with a Metro stop by the same name. The planetarium and zoo are in the area. This street leads into Krasnaya Presnaya, once a working-class district and the scene of many revolutionary battles. On the nearby side street of Bolshevistskaya, at no. 4, the **Krasnaya Presnya Historical Revolutionary Museum** traces the history of the area. It's open 11 a.m. to 6 p.m., closed Monday. 1905 Street leads to the International Trade Center, along the Krasnopresnenskaya Embankment. It was built with the cooperation of the American firms Occidental Petroleum and Welton-Becket to promote cultural relations and international exhibits. Anton Chekhov lived in the small red house at no. 6 Sadovaya Kudrinskaya, now the Chekhov House-Museum. It's open 11 a.m. to 6 p.m., and on Wed. and Fri. 2 to 8:30 p.m.; closed Monday.

Squares On The Ring

Bolshaya Sadovaya (Great Garden) Street once had a triumphal arch through which troops returned to Moscow. Past Mayakovsky Square (with a Metro stop of the same name) is the **All Russia Museum of Decorative, Applied and Folk Art** at no. 3 Delegatsky Street. It's open 10 a.m.to 6 p.m., Tues. and Thurs. 12:30 to 8 p.m., closed Monday. Along the next street at no. 3 Sadovaya Samotechnaya is the **Central Puppet Theater,** better known as the Obraztsov, its founder. The puppet clock on the front of the building has 12 little houses with a tiny rooster on top; every hour, one house opens. At noon, all the boxes open, each with an animal puppet dancing to an old Russian folk song. Tsvetnoi (Flower) Boulevard, branching off the square, has the Old Circus and popular Tsentralny Rinok (Central Market). Nearby is the Soviet Army Museum and Theater.

The next square, Kolkhoznaya (Collective Farm), used to be called Sukharevskaya, after Sukhorov, a popular commander of the czar's *streltsy* guards, quartered here. Peter the Great opened Russia's first navigational school in the center of the square where the Sukharov Tower had stood. Prospekt Mira leads to the Exhibition Park of Economic Achievements. At no. 28 are the oldest botanical gardens in the city, known in Peter the Great's time as the Apothecary; the Metro stop is Botanichesky Sad. At no. 94, near the Rizhskaya (Riga) Railway Station (with a Metro stop of the same name) is the popular Rizhsky marketplace. The **Museum of Cosmonautics** is on the Alley of Cosmonauts. It's open 12 to 8 p.m., Fri.-Sun. 11 a.m. to 5:30 p.m.; closed Monday. Prospekt Mira led to the old towns of Rostov and Suzdal; it now turns into the Yaroslavl Highway, which runs to Yaroslavl in the Golden Ring.

The next square, Lermontovskaya, is named after the Russian poet Lermontov, who was born in a house near the square on 3 Oct. 1814; a plaque on a building marks where the house stood. The plaque is inscribed with Lermontov's words: "Moscow, Moscow, I love you deeply as a son, passionately and tenderly." The square was known as Krasniye Vorota (Red Gate), as red gates once marked the entrance to the square. The Metro station was given this name. The czar's kitchen gardens were in this area. Nearby is the Academy of Agriculture, housed in a 17th-century mansion once owned by Count Yusupov, a descendant of a Mongol khan.

Chakalov is the longest street on the ring, named after the pilot, Valeri Chakalov, who made the first nonstop flight over the North Pole from the USSR to America in 1936. At no. 14-16 lived the poet Marshak, the composer Prokofiev and the violinist Oistrach. Tchaikovsky once lived at no. 47. Behind the Kursky Railway Station is an 18th-century stone mansion, the Naidyonov Estate. Gilliardi and Grigorev built the estate, whose gardens stretch down to the Yauza River; it's now a sanatorium. After crossing the Yauza River, the ring becomes Taganskaya Square (with a Metro stop of the same name), where the popular avant-garde theater **Taganka** is located.

The Bolshaya Krasnokholmsky Bridge crosses the Moskva River off of Zetsepsky Street. Near the Pavletskaya Metro stop is Bakhrushina Street. At no. 31 is the Bakhrushkin Theatrical Museum (closed Tuesday) with collections on the history of Russian theater. It was named after the merchant Alexei Bakhruskin, who opened the museum in 1894.

Dobryninskaya Square was named after the revolutionary Dobrynin, killed in the 1917 Revolution. The next square, Oktyabrskaya, leads to the entrance of **Gorky Park,** with two large Ferris wheels. The Hotel Warsaw is also nearby. Across from the park is the State Art Gallery (a branch of the Tretyakov, closed Monday) and the Park of

Arts. Krimsky Val (Crimean Rampart) is the last section of the ring. It crosses the Moskva River by way of the Krymsky suspension bridge that brings us back to Park Kultury.

THE LENIN HILLS

The Lenin Hills, in the southwest, are the highest point in Moscow and provide one of the best views of the city. Group tours usually include a stop on the hills, or they can easily be reached by taking the Metro to the stop Leninskiye Gory (Lenin Hills). The Metro here rides above ground and crosses the Moskva River, and pedestrian walkways are on each side of the bridge.

Viewpoint
A short walk from the Metro is a glass-enclosed escalator to the top of the hill. The avenue to the right leads to an observation platform, about a 15-minute walk away. The platform provides a spectacular view of the city; in good weather the golden domes of the Kremlin can be recognized. If you turn, with the Moskva River in back, you can see a massive 36-story building. This is Lomonosov University, more widely known as **Moscow University,** founded in 1755 by Russian scientist Mikhail Lomonosov. This new university building was put up in 1949-53 by Stalin, who had six other similar Gothic-style structures built throughout the city. The top of the university's main tower is crowned by a golden star in the shape of ears of corn. It's the largest university in the Soviet Union, with students from over 100 countries. The campus consists of 40 buildings, including sports centers, an observatory, botanical gardens and a park. The Gorky Library has over six million volumes. Gorbachev graduated from Moscow University with a degree in law; his wife Raisa with a degree in Leninist philosophy. Lomonosov Prospekt stretches behind the university, and Universitetsky Prospekt lies in front.

Circuses
A few blocks to the left, in between the two prospekts, is the circular building of the Novi Tsirk (New Circus) situated right on Vernadsky Prospekt. The circus is one of the most popular forms of entertainment in the Soviet Union and the Moscow Circus is famous throughout the world.

This circus building, opened in 1971, seats 3,400. Its ring has four interchangeable floors that can be switched in less than five minutes. One is the regular ring, another a special ring for magicians, and the others are a pool for the aquatic circus and a rink for the ice ballet. The Universitet Metro station is right behind the circus.

The other main circus of Moscow is the Stari Tsirk (Old Circus) at no. 13 Tsvetnoi Boulevard. The Old Circus was the first circus built in Moscow. When it closed down, the New Circus took its place. But recently a circus was built on the site of the Old Circus to match the original building. The new Old Circus was reopened in 1989 and directed by the famous (now retired) clown, Yuri Nikulin. In summer, tent circuses operate in Gorky and Izmailovo Parks. Tickets can be booked for the circus through the Intourist service Desk at your hotel.

Right in front of the New Circus is the Moscow Palace of Young Pioneers, referred to as Pioneerland. This is a large club and recreational center for the children who belong to the Communist Youth Organization known as the Young Pioneers. Older members belong to the Young Komsomol League. Over 25 million members in the Soviet Union belong to the Young Pioneers, and over 39 million to the Komsomol. The Young Pioneers are similar in structure to Western scouting organizations. The 400 rooms in the palace include clubs, laboratories and workshops. It also has its own concert hall, sports stadium, gardens, and even an artificial lake for learning how to row and sail. There are over 35 other branch Pioneer Houses in Moscow. The entrance to the palace is marked by the statue of Malchish-Kibalchish, a character from a popular children's book. On the corner is the Children's Musical Theater.

Stadium
The Lenin Hill Ski Jump is on your left. The hills are a favorite picnic spot in summer, and in winter there's skiing and tobogganing. Across the river are the white buildings of the **Lenin Central Stadium** in the wide meadow area known as Luzhniki. *Lug* in Russian means "meadow." The complex consists of the Lenin Stadium (seating 100,000), the Palace of Sport, Swimming and Tennis Stadiums, Friendship Hall and Museum of Physical Culture. Many events of the Moscow 1980

Olympics were held here. The Olympic Village was built behind the University on Lomonosov Prospekt. Glancing to the left of the stadium, you can make out the golden domes of the Novodevichy Convent. To the right of the stadium, on Komsomolky Prospekt, is the Church of St. Nicholas at Khamovniki, built in 1682. Weavers lived in this area of town centuries ago. The old Russian word for weavers is *khamovniki*. A side street off the prospekt near the Garden Ring is **Leo Tolstoy Street,** where the Russian writer lived for 19 years. Some of the works that he wrote while living in the house at no. 21 were *Power of Darkness* and *Resurrection*. The museum is open 10 a.m. to 5 p.m., closed Monday.

Novodevichy Convent
Ride the Metro one stop from the Lenin Hills back across the river to *Sportivnaya*, and get off in front of the Lenin Stadium. Walking a few blocks down Fruzensky Street leads to one of the oldest religious complexes in the city, the Novodevichy Convent, a baroque-style complex of 15 buildings and 16 gilded domes from the 16th and 17th centuries. Grand-Prince Vasily III founded the convent in 1514 to commemorate the capture of Smolensk from Lithuania, which had controlled the area for over a century. The convent was also one in the group of fortified monasteries that surrounded Moscow. Novodevichy served mainly as a religious retreat for Russian noblewomen. Peter the Great banished his half-sister Sophia and first wife Evdokia to the convent and forced them to wear the veil. Napoleon tried to blow up the convent before he fled the city, but a nun pulled out the fuses. The convent was converted into a museum in 1922.

The five-domed Smolensky Cathedral was the first stone building and lies at the center of the convent. It was dedicated to the Virgin of Smolensk, a much revered icon, and modeled after the Kremlin's Uspensky Cathedral. Many 16th-century interior frescoes portray the life of Vasily III (the father of Ivan the Terrible). A copy of the *Icon of Our Lady of Smolenskaya* hangs over the altar. The beautiful five-tiered iconostasis (1683-86) was presented by Sophia. Ivan the Terrible's daughter, Anna, is one of the noblewomen in the burial vault. There are two Gate Churches: the Transfiguration Gate Church at the northern entrance and the

Church of Pokrov at the southern. Other structures include the Refectory Church (1685-87), Bell Tower (1690) and four nun's residences. The Miloslavsky Chambers are named after Sophia's sister, Maria Miloslavskaya, who lived here until her death. Sofia's Chamber Prison is where Peter the Great imprisoned his half-sister when he deposed her as Regent and took the throne. Irina Godunova had her chamber here. She was the sister of Boris Godunov and was married to Czar Fedor. When Fedor died, Irina refused the throne and her brother Boris was elected Czar. Peter the Great's first wife, Evdokia Lopukhina, lived in the Lopukhina Chamber. The Convent (with a large *beriozka* next door) is open daily 10 a.m. to 5:30 p.m., closed Tuesday.

Many notable Russian personalities are buried in the Novodevichy Cemetery. These include Chekhov, Gogol, Scriabin, Stalin's first wife and Nikita Khrushchev. This part of the convent is currently under restoration and closed to the public.

Gorky Park
Gorky Park lies a few-minutes' walk over the Moskva River from the Metro station Park Kultury in the Frunze district. It can also be reached from the other side of the river at Metro stop Oktyabrskaya, on the Square of the October Revolution, which has a bronze statue of Lenin. A large archway marks the entrance to the park. This large park has amusement rides, boat rentals and the Zelyoni (Green) open-air theater. In summer, the park is packed with strollers, along with performance artists and circus performers of the tent circuses. In winter, the popular Gorky Park ice skating rink is operating. The park is open daily 9 a.m. to midnight.

Also part of the park are the Neskuchny Sadi (Not-Boring Gardens), originally part of the Alexandrov Estate and now used by the Academy of Sciences. The estate is part of the main Botanical Gardens (with a collection of over 16,000 varieties of roses) that stretch all the way to the river.

Donskoi Monastery
Not far from Gorky Park near the Metro stop Shabolovskaya is the Donskoi Monastery. This monastery and seven churches were founded by Czar Fedor and Boris Godunov in 1591 on the

spot of the Russian army's defense line against the invading Mongols. Legend claims the protection of the city came from the Donskaya Virgin Icon, the icon that Prince Donskoi took for protection into battle against the Tatars in 1380.

In the 16th century, six fortified monasteries formed a defensive ring to protect the city from the Mongols. The monasteries were connected by an earthen rampart, the Garden Ring today. The Donskoi Monastery houses a branch of the Shchusev Museum of Architecture, opened in 1934; it has exhibits of prerevolutionary Russian architecture. The Old Cathedral of the Donskaya Virgin was the first building of the monastery. The cube roof and onion domes are topped with golden half-moon crosses that symbolize the Christian victory over Islam. A copy of the *Donskaya Virgin Icon* is on the eight-tiered iconostasis. (The original is in the Tretyakov Gallery.) Patriarch Tikhon, who was appointed the head of the Orthodox Church on the eve of the October 1917 Revolution, is buried in a marble tomb at the southern wall.

The Naryshkin-baroque style New Cathedral of the Donskaya Virgin was commissioned a century later by the Regent Sophia, Peter the Great's half-sister. The interior frescoes were painted by the Italian artist Antonio Claudio between 1782 and 1785. At the southwest corner of the monastery is the classical Church of the Archangel Michael, built in 1806-09. The Church served as a memorial chapel for the Golitsyn family. Mikhail Golitsyn (1681-1764) was Peter the Great's star general who began his career as a service drummer. Fourteen Golitsyns are buried here, including Dmitri and his wife Natalia, who is the subject of Pushkin's novel *Queen of Spades*. The church is now the Museum of Monumental Sculpture. Some pieces include the *Sitting Christ* by Antokolsky and two lions from the old English Club. Some of the people buried in the cemetery are Turgenev, the architect Bovet and a few of Tolstoy's relatives. Other buildings include the Tikhvin Gate Church, the Abbot's residence, a belltower and the 20th-century Church of St. Seraphim, now a crematorium. Outside the gates is the Church of Rizpolozhenie, whose priests also conduct mass in the Old Cathedral on Sundays and holidays.

At no. 56 Donskaya Street is the Moscow-baroque Church of the Deposition of the Lord's Robe, built in 1701. The Church is filled with interesting cherubs and contains a copy of the *Icon of the Deposition of the Lord's Robe* under a gilded canopy. In 1625, an envoy of a Persian shah presented Czar Mikhail Romanov and the Patriarch Filaret with a fragment of Jesus' robe. Filaret had an icon painted and declared a new church holiday. The icon shows Romanov and Filaret placing the gold box, containing the piece of cloth, on the altar of the Kremlin's Uspensky Cathedral. The original icon is now in the Tretyakov Gallery.

The Danilovksy Monastery

This old monastery lies south of the Donskoi (Metro stop Danilovskaya) and was founded in 1276 by Prince Daniil (later canonized), who's buried in a golden coffin in the Cathedral of the Holy Fathers of the Seven Ecumenical Councils. This Church was built by Ivan the Terrible in 1565 on the original site of St. Daniil's Church. The fresco of St. Daniil is the oldest in the church. In 1983, the Soviet government returned the monastery to the Orthodox Church. It's now the residency of the Moscow Patriarchy and in the process of being restored.

Leninsky Prospekt runs in front of the Donskoi Monastery along the river and leads into Moscow's modern southwest district, which consists mostly of residential housing. It winds past the Soviet Academy of Sciences, formerly Neskuchny (Not-Boring) Castle, and Gagarin Square with its 40-m- high monument, cast from titanium, of Yuri Gagarin, the first Soviet man in space. At the base of the monument is a replica of the space capsule Vostok (East), in which Gagarin traveled on 12 April 1961. (Gagarin died in a plane crash in 1968.) This square used to mark the city limits in the 1950s. The prospekt continues past many department stores to the Lumumba People's Friendship University, with 6,000 students from around the world. It eventually turns into the Kievsky Highway and ends at the Vnukovo local airport.

Spaso-Andronikov Monastery

This monastery is situated along the River Yauza, a tributary of the Moskva, in the southeast part of the city, near the Metro station Ploshchad Ilicha. It was founded in 1359 by the Metropolitan Alexei during the reign of Prince Donskoi and has quite an interesting history. After Alexei was confirmed by the Byzantine Patriarch in Constaninople, a heavy storm occurred at sea during his return journey. Alexei promised God, if he should live, to build a monastery dedicated to the saint, whose feast day was celebrated on the day of his safe arrival in Moscow. Alexei returned on 16 August, the "Savior Day" or "Vernicle." When the Mongol khan suddenly summoned Alexei to help his ailing wife in the south, the metropolitan appointed Andronik, a monk at Zagorsk's Trinity-Sergius Monastery, to oversee the operation in his absence. His monastery was called the Spaso-Andronikov, after the Savior and the first abbot of the monastery; it later became the stronghold for the Old Believers. The white Cathedral of the Savior was built in 1420-27; the iconist Andrei Rublev, who also trained as a monk at the Trinity-St. Sergius Monastery in Zagorsk, painted the interior frescoes. The baroque Church of the Archangel Michael was commissioned by Ustinia Lopukhina in 1694 to celebrate the birth of her grandson Alexei, son of Peter the Great and her daughter Evdokia. Peter later banished Evdokia to Novodevichy Monastery (a form of divorce in those days) and the Lopukhinas to Siberia. The church is now an icon restoration studio.

The **Andrei Rublev Museum of Religious Art** is housed in three separate buildings. The former Seminary Building contains many 15th- and early 16th-century icons by Rublev and his students. Some of the icons include St. Sergius, St. George, John the Baptist and the Savior. Many of the icons found in the Monks Quarters (behind the Savior Cathedral) were painted in Novgorod in the 17th century. Nearby is a new Exhibition Hall of mainly 17th- and 18th-century icons that include Our Lady of Tikhvin. The museum is open daily 11 a.m. to 6 p.m. and closed Wednesday.

EXHIBITION OF ECONOMIC ACHIEVEMENTS

Known in Russian as Vy'stavka Dostizhen'ii Narod'novo Khozyai'stva (VDNKh), the exhibition (opened in 1959) should be visited if you have the time; most group tours make a stop. The park is situated right across the street from the Kosmos Hotel at the end of Prospekt Mira, near the Metro station VDNKh. Nearly 100,000 objects are exhibited in 300 buildings and 80 pavilions which cover 545 acres, representing the latest achievements in science, industry, transport, building and culture. The first monuments that come into view are the 96-meter-high **Sputnik Rocket** (1964) that appears to shoot into space, and the **Monument to the Worker and Collective Farm Girl**, a piece of 1937 Soviet-realist architecture. Pavilions include the Atomic Energy, Agriculture and Culture. The most interesting, located at the end of the park, is the **Kosmos Pavilion**. In front stands a replica of the Vostok rocket that carried Yuri Gagarin into space in 1961. Inside are displays of rockets and space capsules, including the first Sputnik, Lunnik, Soyuz rockets and Salyut space stations. Pictures of Yuri Gagarin, Valentin Tereshkova (the first woman into space), Alexi Leonov (who pioneered the first space walk), and the first dogs in space (Laika, Belka and Strelka) line the walls. One exhibit tells of the first joint US-USSR space mission, Soyuz-Apollo, undertaken in July 1975. Other buildings include an open-air theater, small zoo, amusement park, shopping center, the Circorama (standing-only) circular movie theater and restaurants. You can hire boats and go fishing in the ponds; fishing gear can be rented from booths along the bank. In the winter, especially during the Winter Festival, there's plenty of entertainment, including ice-skating and troika rides.

The park is open daily 10 a.m. to 10 p.m. and 10 a.m. to 11 p.m. on weekends; the pavilions are open 10 a.m. to 7 p.m. A half-hour tour of the park can be taken on electric trams.

Ostankino

Not far from Metro stop VDNKh near the Exhibtion Park is the **Ostankino Palace**. At the close of the 18th century, Nikolai Sheremetev built a palace on the grounds of his family's Ostankino estate. The Palace (1792-97) was built of wood, but painted to resemble bricks and stone. Interesting rooms are the Blue Room, Egyptian Ballroom, Italian Reception Room, and the Picture Gallery and Theater, which had over 200 serf actors, dancers and musicians. The palace also houses the **Museum of Serf Art**. The beautiful serf-actress Prashkovya Kovalyova-Zhemchugova later became the count's wife. One of the streets in Ostankino bears her name. The Trinity Church adjoins the palace. The museum is open daily 10 a.m. to 5 p.m. (winter 10 a.m. to 3 p.m.) and closed on Tues. and Wednesday. A short walk away is the **Ostankino TV Tower,** 160 feet (40 meters) high. The tower has an observation deck and the rotating restaurant, Sedmoye Nebo (Seventh Heaven).

DOWN THE MOSKVA RIVER

The Moskva River winds through the city for about 30 miles (48 km). If your tour doesn't include a trip on the river, the best **boat cruises** leave from Kievsky Railway Station and run eastward to Novospassky Bridge (May to October). To get there, take the Metro to Kievskaya, not far from Hotel Ukrainia. The boat pier is located on the Berezhkovskaya Embankment, at one end of Borodinsky Bridge. Some sites along the way are the Novodevichy Monastery, Lenin Hills and Stadium, Gorky Park, Strelka Rowing Club, Moscow Open-Air Pool, Kremlin, Hotel Rossiya, and many estates, palaces and churches. The tour lasts about 80 minutes and ends at the Novopassky Monastery, founded in the 15th century.

A second boat also leaves from the same pier and runs westward to Kuntsevo-Krylatskoye in Fili-Kuntsevo Park, which has a river beach. This trip lasts about an hour.

The Moskva River

PRACTICALITIES

HOTELS

Most foreigners are required to stay in Intourist hotels (prebooked before you enter the USSR), which have restaurants, cafes, *beriozkas,* post offices, and usually nightly entertainment. "Unofficial bed and breakfasts" have sprung up in Moscow (and other major cities), and you might be approached by a Muscovite, offering to put you up in their own home for as little as $4 per night.

Moscow Intourist Hotels

Belgrade: 5 Smolensky St., tel. 248-6692, nearest Metro station Smolenskaya. First-class hotel near the Arbat and Kalinin Prospekt.

Kosmos: 150 Prospekt Mira (across from Park of Economic Achievements), tel. 217-0785, nearest Metro station VDNKh). Deluxe hotel, with bowling alley, sauna and pool; built by French. Far from center, but close to Metro.

Leningradskaya: 21 Kalanchovsky St., tel. 975-3008. One of the Stalinist wedding-cake buildings, this hotel has traditional rooms and restaurant. About 15 minutes from city center.

Intourist: 3 Gorky St., tel. 203-4008, nearest Metro Prospekt Marxa. First-class hotel; centrally located right on Gorky Street and a few-minutes' walk to Red Square.

Metropole: 1 Prospekt Marxa (near Bolshoi Ballet), tel. 225-6673, nearest Metro Prospekt Marxa. First-class prerevolutionary hotel; recently renovated. Short walk to Red Square.

Mozhaiskaya: 165 Mozhaisky St., tel. 447-3434. Standard hotel, less expensive, away from downtown; also has camping facilities available in summer (must prebook before arrival in country).

Mezhdunarodnaya: Kracnopresnensky Emb., tel. 253-7708/2378. The "International Hotel" or Mezh, as it's nicknamed, is part of the Sovincenter, known as the Armand Hammer Center. Used mainly for businessmen and delegations. Has every modern convenience, an expensive Japanese restaurant and Baskin-Robbins ice cream. It's a bit outside of town near the Moskva River.

National: 14 Prospekt Marxa, tel. 203-6539, nearest Metro Prospekt Marxa. Old charming deluxe hotel right across the street from Red Square; Lenin lived here after the Revolution.

Rossiya: 6 Razin St., tel. 298-5530/5437, nearest Metro Ploshchad Revolutsii. The world's largest hotel, accommodates 6,000 people. First-class; overlooks St. Basil's and Kremlin.

Savoy: 3 Zhdanov St., tel. 928-9169 or 230-2625, nearest Metro Smolenskaya. Deluxe hotel, remodeled by the Finns (used to be Hotel Berlin). Even has 24-hour CNN cable channel. Bookings can be made through Finnair.

Sevastopol: 1-A Bolshaya Yushunskaya St., tel. 110-4659/318-2827. First-class/standard hotel; less expensive, since not centrally located, but near Metro.

Ukraine: 2 Kutuzovsky Prospekt, tel. 243-3030. Modern first-class hotel on the Moskva River. A close hop to the center by Metro (nearest stop Kievskaya).

FOOD

A boom in co-operative restaurants over the last several years has increased the number of eating establishments in Moscow to well over 9,000. Every Intourist hotel has several restaurants (that usually offer nightly entertainment), cafes and bars. It's advised to reserve a place in the restaurant in advance through the hotel service desk. The restaurants are usually open for lunch and dinner from 11 a.m. to midnight, with a few-hours' break in the late afternoon. Two types of bars, ruble and *valutni* (hard-currency only), are usually open till midnight or 2 a.m. More and more hotels are now offering the Svetsky Stol, Swedish table. This smorgasbord-style cafeteria is open for

breakfast, lunch and dinner and is an excellent way to get a quick, filling meal, in contrast to the slow service found in many restaurants. Remember that Russians expect to spend a full evening when dining out in a good establishment (an expensive luxury). Many times the service is slow (to stretch out the night), the music can be loud, and other people may be seated at your table. Anticipate a dinner with entertainment to last all evening.

Try a few of the restaurants and cafes outside of the hotel. Even though the menu is in Russian and the waiters speak only Russian, be up for an adventure and some fun. Bring your phrasebook and a good time will be had by all! (If you want chicken, try pantomine too—act like one!) Many of the co-operatives have delicious regional food, fast service, and some offer floor shows, folk music or dance bands. For the more popular ones, advance reservations are recommended.

Restaurants

Abkhazia: 28 Novocheremushkinsky St., tel. 128-8040. Northern Georgian food, such as chicken *abkhaz* and *hachapuri* bread and cottage cheese dish. Nightly music and dancing. Moderate.

Alma-Alta: 13 Shvernika St., tel. 127-3283. Kazakh Asian food. Music and dancing in evening. Moderate.

Aragvi: 6 Gorky St., tel. 229-3762. The most popular Georgian restaurant in town. (Winston Churchill once ate here.) Among the specialties are *lavash* (bread) with hot *sulguni* (cheese), *kharcho* spicy meat soup, *satsivi* chicken in walnut and coriander sauce, *shashlik* and tasty Georgian wines. Music, dancing in evenings. Expensive. Reservations essential.

Arbat: 29 Kalinin Prospekt, tel. 291-1403. One of Moscow's largest restaurants. Lively music, dancing. Expensive. Reservations necessary.

Baku: 24 Gorky St., tel. 299-8506. Azerbaijani food, wine and music. Try *piti* (lamb and potato soup in a clay pot), *narkurma* (roast lamb with pomegranates), chicken, lamb or beef *pilau*. Expensive. Make a reservation.

Bega: 22 Begovava (in Hippodrome "Race" Track), tel. 259-9947. One of oldest restaurants in Moscow, specializing in Tatar food, such as *tebe* lamb and *kalzha* spicy meat. Music nightly, except Wednesday. Moderate.

Belgrade: 8 Smolensky Square (in Belgrade Hotel), tel. 248-2696. Yugoslavian dishes and nightly entertainment. Expensive.

Bombay: 61 Rublyobsky Hwy., tel. 141-5502. Indian food and decor. Music and dancing. Moderate.

Bucharest: 1 Balchug St., tel. 223-7854. Romanian and Transylvanian cooking. Moderate.

Budapest: 2/18 Petrovsky Linii, tel. 221-4044. Hungarian cuisine and nightly entertainment; dance orchestra. Moderate.

Bukhara: 2/34 Sadovo-Sukharevsky, tel. 221-5259. Great Uzbek food. No music. Moderate.

Delhi: 23b Krasnaya Presnensky St., tel. 252-1766. Indian food.

Dubrava: 150 Prospekt Mira (Hotel Cosmos), tel. 217-0495. A lively night spot with dancing. Specialty is chicken Kiev. Expensive.

Havana: 88 Leninsky Prospekt, tel. 138-0091. Cuban food and decor. Rock 'n' roll music and dancing. Moderate.

Hanoy: 60 Prospekt Let Oktyabr 20, tel. 124-

Moscow in winter

4884. Vietnamese food. Music and dancing (except Wed.). Moderate.

Izba Rybaka: 48 Baumansky St., tel. 261-5685. The "Fisherman's Hut" serves seafood only. Inexpensive.

Jaltarang: 12 Chistoprudny Blvd. Indian food. Reasonable.

Labirint: 29 Kalinin Prospekt, tel. 291-1172. Nightly dancing and dining under Arbat nightclub. Moderate.

Kropotkinskaya 36: 36 Kropotkinsky St., tel. 201-7500. Popular co-op with Russian and European cuisine. Reservations recommended.

McDonald's: off Gorky St., and Pushkin Square. Usually long lines. Now there's even a black market for Big Macs!

Mercury: in Mezhdunarodnaya Hotel. tel. 255-7792. Very plush restaurant and night club, featuring jazz and Las Vegas-type floor shows. Music and dancing. Very expensive. Reserve table.

Metelitsa: 27 Kalinin Prospekt, tel. 291-1130. The "Snowball" is a popular disco. Light snacks. Inexpensive.

Minsk: 22 Gorky St., tel. 299-1248. Byelorussian cuisine.

Moldavia: 6 Bol. Cherkizovsky St., tel. 161-1051. Moldavian cooking. Reasonable.

National: 1 Gorky St. (National Hotel), tel. 203-5590. Elegant 19th-century decor restaurant with nice views of Red Square, serving classic Russian cooking. Folk music and dance bands. Expensive. Popular foreign-currency bar is on the second floor.

Okhotnichi: 17/3 Selskohozyaistvenny St., tel. 181-0190. "Hunters" specializes in Russian game and fowl. Shows, music and dancing. Moderate.

Pekin: 1/7 Bolshaya Sadovaya, tel. 209-1865. Chinese food.

Pitsunda: 3 Krzhizhanovsky St., tel. 125-6128. Quiet Georgian restaurant. Try the trout in nut sauce and *chihirtma*, spicy chicken soup. Moderate.

Polonais: 9 Marksistsky, tel. 270-6666. Polish food, music and dancing. Inexpensive.

Praga: 2 Arbat, tel. 290-6171. Old-fashioned atmosphere with Czech and Russian cuisine. Advertizes the "best chicken Kiev in Moscow." Nightly music and dancing. Expensive. Make reservations.

Russkaya Izba: Naberezhnaya 1 (40-minute drive to Ilyinskoye Village outside Moscow), tel. 561-4244. Built to look like traditional Russian *izba* (wooden cottage). Serves authentic old Russian cuisine, such as *pokhlyobka* mushrooms and wild berries. Tea served from samovar. Music by a balalaika band. Expensive. Reserve a day in advance.

Russkiye Pelmeni: 50 Arbat St., tel. 241-8304. Delicious dumplings. Music. Moderate.

Russky Zal: 3 Gorky St., tel. 203-0150. The "Russian Hall" has decor of red velvet and offers Russian food with musical ensembles. Expensive.

Sakhura: 12 Krasnopresnenskaya Emb. (Mezhdunarodnaya Hotel), tel. 253-2894. Excellent Japanese food, prepared by Japanese cooks. Very expensive. Reservations necessary.

Savoy Hotel Restaurant: tel. 929-8600. Delicious food, even has a Sunday brunch 11 to 3.

Sedmoye Nyebo: in Ostankino TV Tower, tel. 282-2293. The revolving "Seventh Heaven" Restaurant has a great panoramic view of the city. Order a day in advance. Bring your passport.

Slavyansky Bazaar: 25 Oktyabr St. 13, tel. 221-1872. A favorite for artists in the 19th-century restaurant. Here dined Chekhov, Tchaikovsky and Tolstoy. In 1898 Stanislavsky and Nemirovich-Danchenko discussed the formation of the Moscow Art Theater. Try the *rasstegai* meat pie and *medok* honey drink. Music and dancing in the evenings. Expensive.

Sofia: 32 Gorky St., tel. 251-4950. Bulgarian food and wine. Dance bands in the evening. Moderate.

Sinyaya Ptitsa: 23 Chekhov St., tel. 299-8702. The "Blue Bird" is a popular jazz club with dancing. Good food. Moderate.

Tbilisi: 1 Generala Tyuleneva, tel. 337-0000. Decorated as a Georgian *patsha* peasant hut. Georgian food and music. Moderate.

Terek: 25 Obruchev St., tel. 331-5388. Popular place with Russian cuisine; orchestra and dancing. Dishes include lamb and baked piglets. Moderate.

Tsentralny: 10 Gorky St. (in Tsentralny Hotel), tel. 229-0241. Founded in 1865, the decor is elegant and ornate. Delicious Russian cuisine, for moderate prices. Quartet plays baroque music in the evenings.

Turkmenia: 34 Perovsky St., tel. 306-7940. Central Asian Turkmenian food. Music and dancing. Moderate.

Ukrainia: 2 Kutozovsky Prospekt (in Hotel Ukrainia). Ukrainian food, wine and music. Try the *vareniki* (meat-filled dumplings). Moderate.

Uzbekistan: 29 Neglinnaya St., tel. 221-3833. Uzbek food and music. Try the *lagman* (meat and noodle soup), *manty* (spicy lamb dumplings) and *plovi* (pilafs); even offers camel meat. Nightly music and dancing. Expensive.

Varshava: 2 Oktyabrsky Square (in Warsaw Hotel), tel. 238-1847. Polish food and music, dancing. Try *zrazy* (Polish meat rolls). Moderate.

Vilnius: 12 Butlerov St., tel. 336-1502. Some Lithuanian food. Music. Moderate.

Vitosha: 35/2 Khoroshcusky Hwy., tel. 195-4084. Bulgarian food. Reasonable.

Yakor: 49 Gorky Street. The "Anchor" is a fish restaurant.

Zakarpatskiye Uzori: 2 Nizhegorodsky St., tel. 279-4580. Ukrainian restaurant, music and dancing. Reservations advised.

Cafes

Adriatica: 19/3 Ryleyev St., in the Arbat, tel. 201-7302.

Aelita: Exhibition Park of Economic Acheivements, Pavilion 76. French breads and pastries, drinks.

Aist: "Stork" 33a Leningradsky Pr., tel. 255-8676.

Angara: 27 Kalininsky Prospekt, tel. 291-2209. Popular dancing spot.

Artisticheskoye: Proyezd Khudozhestvennovo Teatra (across from Moscow Art Theater off Gorky), tel. 292-0673. Popular meeting place before and after theater.

Atrium: 44 Leninsky Prospekt, tel. 137-3008. Russian-European food.

Baskin-Robbins ice cream in the Rossiya Hotel for foreign currency. Also, for rubles, at 31 Gorky Street.

Bely Lyebyed: The "White Swan" at 3/18 Sivtsev Vrazhek in the Arbat, tel. 203-1283. Russian and Armenian food. Inexpensive.

Bely Medved: 116 Prospekt Mira. "Polar Bear" has ice cream.

Bistro 1: 49 Arbat (next to Prague Restaurant), tel. 241-7054. Appetizers, drinks and *shashlik.*

Bistro 3: 4 Chekhov St., tel. 299-3073.

Bistro-Nedelya: 18 Oktyabr St., tel. 288-9398. Open 24 hours. Serves recipes from the Caucasus. Moderate.

Buratino: 31 Arbat, tel. 241-0886. "Pinocchio" cafe is popular with children. Some live animals, games and toys.

Chaihana: 40 Kropotkinsky St., Azerbaizhani tea room.

Gumista: 29 Kalyayevsky St., tel. 258-1315. Reasonable.

Gzhel: 21 Shukhova St., tel. 237-1020. Inexpensive food, music and dancing.

Hard Rock Café: at Gorky Park in the basement of Green theater, owned by rock star/producer Stas Namin. Russian-Armenian food, popular hangout of musicians. Open till after midnight; bring your own alcohol.

Ivushka: 28 Kalininsky Prospekt, tel. 925-4383. Blues music. Inexpensive.

Khrustalnoye: 17 Kutuzovsky Prospekt, tel. 243-4576. Popular dance spot, pizza served. Inexpensive.

Lasagne: 40 Pyatnitsky St., tel. 231-1085. Italian cuisine.

Lira: 19 Gorky St., tel. 299-8632. Popular dance spot. Good band music. Reasonable.

Margarita: 28 Mahlaya Bronnaya, tel. 299-6534. Tea room with pastries. Hot breakfasts in the morning from 8-11.

Mars: 7 Gorky Street. Quick-food co-op next to Intourist Hotel.

Myikhooa: 2/1 Rusakovsky St., Sokolniki. tel. 264-9574. Chinese food. Inexpensive.

Ogni Arbata: 12 Arbat, tel. 291-4359. "Arbat's Lights" serves lamb *lyula kebab,* bifsteak and beverages.

Okhotnik: 40 Gorky St., tel. 251-4268. "Hunter's" cafe.

Ooh Kameena: 32 Chernyshevsky, tel. 297-0840. The "Fireside" has European food like pot roasts. Inexpensive.

Ooh Yuzefa: 11/17 Doobinsky, tel. 238-4646. "At Yoseph's" offers European food, a band.

Perekop: 33 Kalanchovsky St., tel. 280-4033. Band music, dancing. Reasonable.

Pokrovka: 4 Chernyshevsky St., Byelorussian food. Reasonable.

Razgooliay: 11 Spartakovsky St., tel. 267-7613. Russian food.

Rioni: 43 Arbat Street. Central Asian grilled dishes, such as *shashlik.* Inexpensive.

Rooslan: 32 Vorontsovsky, tel. 272-0632. Russian and Oriental food.

Ryleyeva 9: 9/5 Ryleyeva in the Arbat, tel. 291-6063. European and Oriental food.

Sayat-Nova: 17 Yasnogorsky St., tel. 426-8511. Tbilisi food; music and poetry recitals.

Sever: 17 Gorky Street. Ice cream parlor.

Sorok-Chetiri: 44 Leningradskoe Hwy., tel. 159-9951.

Sibir: 25 Bolshaya Dorogomilovsky, tel. 240-1440. Specializes in Siberian *pelmeni* and other dumplings.

Stanislavskovo II: 2 Stanislavsky St., tel. 291-8689. Intimate club atmosphere. Russian and Greek dishes.

Staroye Foto: 40 Arbat, tel. 241-2202. Quaint cafe in the old Arbat.

Stoleshniki Cafe: 8 Stoleshniki Perevlok, tel. 229-2050. Tavern, set meal and champagne by the glass.

U Nikitskih Vorot: Herzen St. and Suvorovsky Blvd., tel. 290-4883. "At Nikita's Gate" is a popular cafe with recorded music.

Uyoot: 1/2 Dmitrovsky Hwy., tel. 216-7096. Serves eggplant, veal, fish, *shashlik* dishes.

Valdai: 19 Kalininsky Prospekt, tel. 291-1034. Specializes in *pirozhki.*

Viktoria: 78 Prospekt Mira, tel. 971-0721.

Vremena Goda: Gorky Park, tel. 237-0827. Popular disco of young crowd. Inexpensive.

Yakimanka: 2/10 Bolshaya Polyanka, tel. 238-8888. Uzbek food with a band.

Zamoskvorechie: 54 Bolshaya Polyanka, tel. 230-7333. Russian food, variety shows, band and bar. Serves lunch and dinner.

Groceries

Gastronom no. 1 is at 14 Gorky Street. The pre-revolutionary store was known as Yeliseyev's; today, even though the food is lacking, it still has an ornate interior. Armenia is at 17 Gorky St. and Georgian food is at 27 Gorky. Other stores on Gorky are at 10 (bread), 12 (waters) and 14 (groceries). Novoarbatsky Gastronom is at 21 Kalinin Prospekt. Russky Pryanik (Russian Gingerbread) is at 40 Leninsky Prospekt. The Kulinaria at the Prague Restaurant on the Arbat sells delicious pastries.

Farmers' Market (*Rii'nok*)

The following farmers' markets sell fresh vegetables, fruits, flowers and other wares and produce. Bring a few bags; otherwise the loose strawberries or nuts go into your handbag or pocket! Markets are open from 7 a.m. to about 6 p.m, but a better selection is found in the morning.

Babushkinsky (Grandmothers) is at 30 Menzhinsky Street.

Baumansky is at Baumansky St. 47.

Krestovsky is at 1 Krestovsky Val.

Leningradsky is at Chasovaya St. 11

Rizhsky is by the Metro stop (same name) at 94 Pr. Mira and the **Yaroslavsky** is at 122.

Tsentralny is on Tsvetnoi Blvd. 15 (near the Old Circus).

Zhandovsky 12 Lyublinsky Street.

Katitnikovsky is the pet market and a sight to see! It's held on weekends at 42a Kalitnikovsky Street. Here is also the **Ptichi Rinok**, the Bird Market. Many animals on sale are dogs, cats, rabbits and an assortment of birds and fish. Try to get there in the morning (opens at 8 a.m. to about 2 p.m.).

SHOPPING

The easiest and quickest way to purchase souvenirs of your trip to Moscow is to make a stop at a *beriozka,* the foreign-currency store. Here one may purchase Soviet goods that are usually cheaper than in ordinary street shops. Each city has large department stores, *univermag,* an arcade of shops that sell a variety of products for rubles. Specialty shops sell items such as books and records. If you have time, take a walk through a shopping district, such as GUM and Gorky Street. This also gives you an idea of how the locals shop and what is available to them.

In most Soviet stores, one must first pay a cashier at the *kassa,* then show the receipt to the salesperson, who then wraps and hands over the purchase. If something catches your eye outside of a *beriozka,* buy it; it may not be there tomorrow. Many goods are not available in large quantities; people stand in long lines to quickly purchase whatever is available. Soviet stores sell items only for rubles and do not accept foreign currency. If shopping in town, make sure you have some rubles. Most stores are open from 10 a.m. to around 7 or 8 p.m. and close for an hour in the afternoon. In purchasing antiques or rugs, official permission is required; many times a duty is levied. Check before buying; the items could be confiscated.

The main shopping areas of Moscow are located along Gorky St., Kalinin Prospekt, the Arbat and the small side streets (like Stoleshnikov, Petrovka and Kuznetsky Most) behind GUM Department Store on Red Square.

Beriozkas

The largest are found at the Rossiya (in the back) and Ukraine hotels. Others are located in the National, Intourist, Kosmos and Mezhdunarodny. (All Intourist hotels have a *beriozka*.) Two *beriozkas* are opposite the Novodevichy Monastery and at No. 9 Kutuzovsky Prospekt (near the Ukraine Hotel). A book *beriozka* is at 31 Kropotkinsky Street. At No. 60 Dorogomilovsky Street is a food (*gastronom*) *beriozka*. The Vneshtorgbank Gold Shop (gold, silver, coins and precious stones) is at 9 Pushkin Street.

Department Stores

GUM, Gosudarstvenny Universalny Magazine (Government Universal Store) ison Red Square. Built in the 1880s, GUM is the largest shopping center in Moscow. Merchants once rented out the long rows of small shopping alcoves now filled with Soviet-made products. Don't let the crowds and lines stop you from strolling inside. **TsUM**, Central Department Store, at 2 Petrovka St., is the next largest store of this type in the city. **Moskva** Department Store is at 54 Leninsky Prospekt.

Antique Shops

China and crystal can be found at 46 Gorky St., 32 Arbat, 56 Dimitrov St. and 99 Prospekt Mira.

Arts And Crafts

46b Gorky St., 12-16 Petrovka, 9 and 24 Kutuzovsky Prospekt, 54 Dimitrov St., 24 Leningradsky Prospekt, 8 25 Oktyabr St., 10/4 Krymsky Emb. (across from Gorky Park), and at 5 Smolensky Embankment.

Bookstores

Dom Knigi (House of Books) at 26 Kalinin Prospekt is the largest bookstore; it also sells foreign publications, posters and postcards; a must to visit. **Druzhba** (Friendship) has books from socialist countries at 15 Gorky Street. **Inostrannaya Kniga** (Foreign Books), at 16 Kachalov St., sells foreign books and old engravings. **Knigi-Podarki** (Books-Gifts), at 16 Stoleshnikov Pereulok, has gift books. Next door, at No. 14, is a *bukinist* (second-hand bookstore), selling used and rare books. At 6 Kirov St. is **Knizhny Mir** (Book World) with books, prints, posters and postcards. **Moskva** sells books, maps and postcards at 8 Gorky Street. **Planeta** at 8 Vesnin St. and **Progress** at 17 Zubovsky Blvd. both sell books in foreign languages.

Food stores in the Soviet Union commonly sell only one item.

GUM Department Store

Children's Stores
Detski Mir (Children's World), at 2 Prospekt Marxa, is the largest toy store in Moscow. **Dom Igrushki** (House of Toys) is at 8 Kutuzovsky Prospekt. **Mashenka,** 10 Smolensky St., sells girls' clothing.

Cosmetics And Cologne
Christian Dior and Estée Lauder have shops on Gorky Street. Some others are at 6 Gorky, 12 Petrovka and 44 Kalinin Prospekt.

Commissioni (Second-hand Stores)
Samovars, crystal and china are sold at 32 Arbat, 46 Gorky, 54 Dimitrov, 8 Izmailovsky and 99 Prospekt Mira. Furniture and clocks are at 5 Smolensky and 54 Frunzensky Embankments. Old musical instruments and electronic gear are at 31 Oktyabr St. and 7 Sadovo-Kudrinsky. The **Izumrud** (Emerald) at 23 Lomonosovsky Prospket has jewelry and stones.

Crystal, China And Glass
Dom Farfora (House of China) is at 36 Leninsky Prospekt. Others are at 15 Gorky St., 8 Kirov St. and 19 Komsomolsky Prospekt.

Furs
Fur coats and hats can be found at No. 13 Stoleshnikov Pereulok. Down the street at No. 5 is a used fur store. A *mekha* (fur) shop is also at 13 Pyatnitsky Street.

Gifts And Souvenirs
Podarki (Gifts) is at 4 and 37 Gorky Street. **Suveniri** (Souvenirs) at No. 12 and 45 Gorky, **Azerbaijani** souvenirs at No. 24, **Olimpiisky** at 37 and **Tadjikistan** products at No. 52. Other souvenir shops are at 24 and 29 Kalinin Prospekt, 9 Kutuzovsky Prospekt, 12 and 16 Petrovka St. and 3 and 39 Leninsky Prospekt.

Jewelry
Yantar (Amber) is at 13 Stoleshnikov Pereulok, 14 Presnensky Val and 14 Gruzinsky Val. **Almaz** (Diamond) is at 14 Stoleshnikov. The **Biryuza** (Torquoise) Store is at 21 Sadovaya Spasskaya. **Zemchug** (Pearl) is at 22 Olimpiisky Prospekt and **Malakhitovaya Shkatulka** (Malachite Box) is located at 24 Kalinin Prospekt. **Agat** (Agate) is found at 16 Bolshaya Kolkhoznaya and **Rubin** (Ruby) at 78 Leningradsky Propsekt. **Samotsveti** (Semi-Precious Stones) is at 35 and 11 Arbat. Other shops are on Gorky at nos. 12 and 32. The **Jewelery Salon** is on Grokholsky Pereulok 30.

Maps
Kuznetsky Most nos. 9 and 20 (also sells stamps).

Records
Melodiya at 40 Prospekt Kalinin is one of the largest record stores. Others are at 24 Herzen St. and 6 Arbat.

Rugs

Rug stores are located at 9 Gorky St., 11 Stoleshnikov, 4 Gruzinsky Pereulok and 99 Prospekt Mira.

THEATERS

Bolshoi Opera and Ballet Theater: 1 Sverdlov Square.

Central Children's Theater: 2 Sverdlov Square.

Chamber Musical Theater: 71 Leningradsky Prospekt.

Chamber Yiddish Musical Theater: 12 Tagansky Square.

Children's Musical Theater: 5 Vernadsky Prospekt

Durov Animal Theater: 4 Durov Street.

Gogol Drama Theater: 8a Kazakov Street.

Kremlin Palace of Congresses: the Kremlin (entrance through the Borovitsky Gate).

Lenin Komsomol Theater: 6 Chekhov Street.

Malaya Bronnaya Drama Theater: 4 Malaya Bronnaya Street.

Maly Theater: 1/6 Sverdlov Square.

Maly Theater Branch: 69 Bolshaya Ordynka

Mayakovsky Theater: 19 Herzen Street.

Mime Theater: 39/4 Izmailovsky Blvd.

Miniature Theater: 3 Karetny Ryad Street. (Hermitage Garden)

Moscow Academic Art Theater: 22 Tverskoi Blvd. (new building); 3 Proyezd Khudozhestvennovo Teatra (old building)

Moscow Puppet Theater: 26 Spartakovsky Street.

Moscow Regional Drama Theater: 9 25th October Street

Mossoviet Theater: 16 Bolshaya Sadovaya Street.

Novy Drama Theater: 2 Prokhodchikov Street.

Obraztsov Puppet Theater: 3 Sadovo Samotechnaya (with the puppet clock on building).

Poezia Hall: 12 Gorky Street.

Pushkin Drama Theater: 23 Tverskoi Blvd.

Regional Puppet Theatre: 24 Bolshaya Kommunisticheskaya Street.

Romany Gypsy Theater: 32 Leningradsky Prospekt (in Hotel Sovetskaya).

Satire Theater: 2 Mayakovsky Square/18 Bolshaya Sadovaya Street.

Satiricon Theater: 8 Sheremetyevksky Street.

Soviet Army Theater: 2 Commune Square.

Sovremennik Theater: 19 Chistoprudny Blvd.

Stanislavsky Drama Theater: 23 Gorky Street.

Stanislavsky and Nemirovich-Danchencko Musical Theater: 17 Pushkinskaya Street.

Taganka Drama and Comedy Theater: 76 Chkalov Street.

Theater of Friendship of the Peoples of the USSR: 22 Tverskoi Blvd.

Variety Theater: 20/2 Bersenevsky Embankment. Also known as the Estrada.

Yermolova Drama Theater: 5 Gorky Street.

Yevgeny Vakhtangov Drama Theater: 26 Arbat Street.

MOVIE THEATERS

Kosmos: 109 Prospekt Mira.

Mir: 11 Tsvetnoi Blvd.

Moskva: 2/2 Mayakovsky Square.

Oktyabr: 42 Kalinin Prospekt.

Tsircorama: At Exhibition of Economic Achievement complex.

Zaryadye: Rossiya Hotel.

Zvezdny: 14 Vernadsky Prospekt.

CONCERT HALLS

Andrei Rublev Museum of Early Russian Art: 10 Pryamikov Square.

Cathedral of the Sign: 8 Razin Street.

Central Concert Hall: in the Hotel Rossiya.

Church of the Intercession in Fili: 6 Novozavodsky Street.

Church of St. Vlasii: 20 Ryleyev Street.

Conservatory Grand Hall: 13 Herzen Street.

Glinka Concert Hall: 4 Fadeyev Street.

Gnesin Institute Concert Hall: 30/36 Vorovsky Street.

October Hall of the House of Trade Unions: 1 Pushkinsky Street. Also known as the Hall of Columns.

Olympic Village Concert Hall: 1 Pelshe Street.

Operetta Theater: 6 Pushkin Street.

Ostankino Palace-Museum of Serf Art: 5 lst Ostankinsky.

Rachmaninov Hall: Herzen Street.

Tchaikovsky Concert Hall: 20 Gorky Street, Mayakovsky Square.

CIRCUSES

New Circus: 7 Vernadsky Prospekt.
Old Moscow Circus: 13 Tsvetnoi Blvd.
Durova Zoo Circus: 4 Durov Street.
Tent Circus: Gorky and Izmailovo parks (summer only).
During the year are performances of the Moscow Ice Ballet and the Circus on Ice.

SPORTS FACILITIES

The Aquatic Sports Palace: 27 Mironovsky Street.
The Central Chess Club: 14 Gogolevsky Blvd.
The Central Lenin Stadium: At Luzhniki.
The Chaika Swimming Pool: 1/3 Turchaninov Lane.
The Chaika Sports Complex: 3/5 Kropotkinsky Emb. (across from Moskva Pool), tel. 202-0474

Soviet circuses draw and delight millions every year.

or 246-3521. Has fully equipped gym, sauna, pool, tennis courts, massage, restaurant, bar. Hard currency only. Open 7 a.m. to midnight.
The Dynamo Stadium: 36 Leningradsky Prospekt.
Horseback Riding: 35 Leningradsky Prospekt, tel. 135-8255. Riding co-op, ride or take lessons for $10 an hour.
Hippodrome Race Course: 22 Begovaya Street.
Krylatskoye Sports Complex: 10 Pyataya Krylatskaya.
The Moskva Open Air Swimming Pool: 37 Kropotkinskaya Emb. (open year-round).
The Olympic Sports Complex: 16 Olympisky Prospekt.
The Sokolniki Sports Palace: 1 Sokkolnichesky Val.
The Spartak Sports Palace: 23 Maly Oleny Lane.
The Sports and Tennis Palace: 39 Leningradsky Prospekt.
The Young Pioneers Stadium: 31 Leningradsky Prospekt.
Sandunovskiye Banya: 1st Neglinni Perevlok 1A, tel. 295-4631.
Tsentralniye Banya: 4 Prospekt Marxa, tel. 925-0888.

PARKS AND GARDENS

Botanical Garden of the Academy of Sciences: 4 Ostankino-Botanicheskaya Street.
Druzhba Forest Park: 90 Leningradsky Highway.
Gorky Central Recreation Park: 9 Krymsky Val.
Hermitage Garden: 3 Karetny Ryad Street.
Izmailovo Recreaton Park: 17 Narodny Prospekt (Metro Izmailovo Park).
Kuskovo Forest Park: 40 3rd Muzeiny Street.
Moscow University Botanical Gardens: Lenin Hills.
Old Botanical Gardens: 28 Prospekt Mira.
Sokolniki Park: 62 Rusakovsky Street (Metro Sokolniki).

VICINITY OF MOSCOW

The priviliged classes of Russia used to build their summer residences in the countryside around Moscow. Many of these palaces and parks have been preserved and turned into museums easily reached by Metro, bus or car. Excursions can also be booked through the Intourist service bureau at your hotel, which include transportation and a tour of the sights.

ABRAMTSEVO

The **Abramtsevo Estate Museum** is located along the Yaroslavsky Highway near the town of Zagorsk, 37 miles (60 km) north of Moscow. In 1843, Russian writer Sergei Aksakov bought the country estate (built in the 1770s); over the next 15 years, it was frequented by many prominent writers, such as Gogol, Tyutchev and Turgenev. Here Gogol gave a reading of the first chapter from his second volume of *Dead Souls,* which he later burned at his home in Moscow. In 1870, art patron Savva Mamontov bought the estate and turned it into a popular meeting spot and artists' colony. There were art, theater, writing and pottery workshops; Serov, Vrubel, Repin, Chaliapin and Stanislavsky all lived and worked here. The 12th-century-style Orthodox church in the park

was designed by Victor Vasnetsov and painted by Polenov and Repin. Vasnetsov also built the park's "Hut on Chick Legs," based on a popular fairy tale. Abramtsevo, now a museum, displays rooms as they were used by Aksakov and Mamontov. Paintings and artwork done on the estate, including many of Vrubel's, are on display in the art studio. The museum is open 11 a.m. to 5 p.m., closed Mon., Tues., and the last day of each month.

ARKHANGELSKOYE ESTATE MUSEUM

This museum lies in the village of Arkhangelskoye, 10 miles (16 km) west of Moscow. Take the Volokolamskoye Highway and then the left road toward Petrovo-Dalniye. The closest Metro station is Tushinskaya; then proceed with bus no. 549. The estate, situated along the banks of the Moskva River, took 40 years to complete. Prince Golitsyn originally founded the estate at the end of the 18th century. The mansion and park were designed in French style by the architect Chevalier de Huerne and built by serf craftsmen. In 1810, the estate passed into the hands of the wealthy landowner, Prince Yusupov (a descen-

*fording a stream
near Moscow*

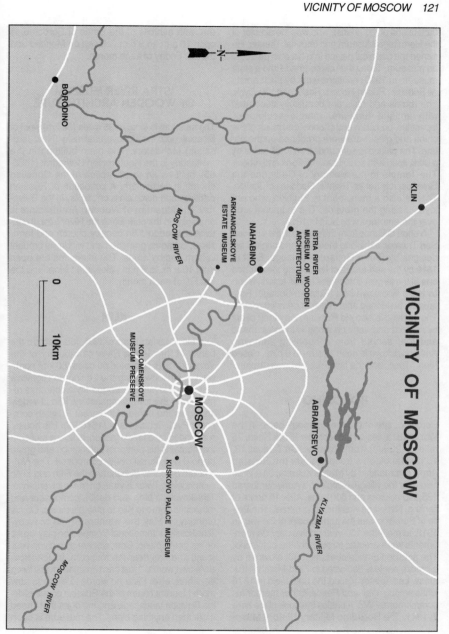

VICINITY OF MOSCOW

dant of one of the khans), who was the director of the Hermitage Museum and Imperial Theater. He turned the classical palace into his own personal art museum. Today the palace (made into a state museum in 1919) contains work by such artists as Boucher, Hubert Robert, Roslin and Van Dyck. The rooms and halls are beautifully decorated with antique furniture, marble sculptures, tapestries, porcelain and chandeliers; much of the china and glassware were produced on the estate. The palace is surrounded on three sides by a park, lined with sculptures, pavilions and arbors. The Temple to the Memory of Catherine the Great depicts her as Themis, Goddess of Justice. There's also a monument to Pushkin, who enjoyed visiting the grounds. The triumphal arch over the entrance was built in 1817.

A short distance from the palace is the wooden Serf Theater, exhibiting theatrical and original set designs by Pietro Gottardo Gonzaga. Built in 1819 by the serf-architect Ivanov, the theater had one of the largest companies of serf actors. Nearby is the Russkaya Izba (Russian Cottage) Restaurant, fashioned after Russian peasant rooms. The cooking is also old Russian; the menu offers bear meat and venison along with *kvas*, mead and tea, served from a bubbling samovar. Arkhangelskoye is open 11 a.m. to 6 p.m., closed Mon., Tues. and the last Friday of each month.

BORODINO

Borodino, site of the most famous battle in the War of 1812, lies on the Moscow-Minsk Road, 75 miles (120 km) from Moscow. On August 26, 1812, Napoleon's troops fought the Russian Army, commanded by Mikhail Kutuzov, on a large field near the village. Napoleon's Army numbered 135,000 soldiers and 600 guns. After 15 hours of fighting, Napoleon was forced to retreat. The Battle of Borodino was the turning point of the war. In 1912, to mark the 100-year anniversary, 34 monuments were erected throughout the battlefield. The polished granite obelisk (1966) crowned by a bronze eagle is dedicated to Field-Marshall Kutuzov. Leo Tolstoy visited the battlefield in 1876 while writing *War and Peace*. Other memorials commemorate WW II battles that took place here in 1941. The **Borodino Military History Muse-**

um, with exhibits of the Battle of Borodino, is open 10 a.m. to 6 p.m., closed on Monday and the last Friday of each month.

ISTRA RIVER MUSEUM OF WOODEN ARCHITECTURE

The museum is located 35 miles (56 km) west of Moscow near the Novoyerusalimsky (New Jerusalem) Monastery. The main building in the monastery is the Resurrecton Cathedral (1656-85), built as an exact replica of the Christian church in Jerusalem. A collection of Russian paintings and porcelain is on display in the Refectory. The **Museum of Wooden Architecture** is on display in the park along the River Istra. It contains a wooden 17th-century church and farmstead, cottages, granaries and windmills brought in from nearby areas. The museums are open from 10 a.m. to 6 p.m., closed on Mon. and the last Fri. of each month.

KLIN

The old Russian town of Klin, founded on the banks of the Sestra River (a tributary of the Volga) in 1318, is located 50 miles (80 km) northwest of Moscow along the Leningrad Highway. Only two Naryshkin baroque-style churches remain from the town's monastery. Klin is widely known as the home of the great Russian composer Pyotr Tchaikovsky (1840-93). His house, surrounded by a lovely garden, is now a museum that contains his personal belongings and grand piano. Here Tchaikovsky composed *The Nutcracker, Sleeping Beauty,* and the Fifth and Sixth symphonies. Twice a year, on the anniversary of Tchaikovsky's birth and death, composers and musicians come to Klin to play his music. On his birthday, 7 May the winners of the Moscow Tchaikovsky International Competition play works on his grand piano. Concerts are also given year round in a hall near the museum. In Tchaikovsky's own words, "I just can't imagine myself living anywhere else. I find no words to express how much I feel the charm of the Russian countryside, the Russian landscape and the quiet that I need more than anything else." The museum is open

10 a.m. to 6 p.m., closed Wed., Thurs. and the last Mon. of each month.

KOLOMENSKOYE MUSEUM PRESERVE

This preserve is on the southern side of Moscow on the banks of the Moskva River and can be reached from the Metro station Proletarsky Prospekt. Kolomenskoye was once the estate of numerous Russian princes and czars, including Ivan the Terrible and Peter the Great. It's now an open-air museum of 16th- and 17th-century style architecture. The tent-shaped Church of the Ascension, decorated with *kokoshnik* gables, was the highest structure in Moscow (189 feet/63 meters) when it was built in 1532. Other structures of interest are the Dyakovskaya and Kazanskaya churches (open for services), the water and clock towers, a Siberian watchtower (1631), and a cottage used by Peter the Great (built in 1702), which was brought from Archangel. These buildings now exhibit 16th- to 19th-century Russian applied and decorative art that include collections of paintings, ceramics, woodcarvings and clocks. The museum is open September through April from 11 a.m. to 5 p.m., May through August 1-8 p.m. on Wed. and Thurs. and other days 11 a.m. to 5 p.m., closed Mon. and Tuesday.

KUSKOVO PALACE MUSEUM

This museum is located within the city limits and can be reached easily from Metro station Zhdanovskaya. The Kuskovo Estate was in the Sheremetev family since the 16th century. In the early 18th century, Count Pyotr Sheremetev, who had over 200,000 serfs, transformed Kuskovo into his summer residence. His wooden mansion (1769-75), designed by Karl Blank and the serf-architect Alexei Mironov, is faced with white stone and decorated with parquet floors, antique furniture and crystal chandeliers; it also houses an excellent collection of 18th-century Russian art. Other buildings of special interest in the gardens are the Hermitage (1767), the Dutch Cottage (1750), Italian Cottage (1755), the Grotto Pavilion (1771), and the Greenhouse. The **Ceramics Museum** exhibits a fine collection of Russian and European porcelain, faience and glass. The museum is open 11 a.m. to 7 p.m. or 10 a.m. to 4 p.m. depending on time of year, and closed on Mon. and Tues., and the last Wed. of each month.

NAHABINO

Located about 18 miles (28 km) northwest of Moscow, Nahabino is the Soviet Union's first golf course. It's designed by Robert Trent Jones II who, along with Dr. Armand Hammer, spent nearly 15 years negotiating the permissions. Nahabino is an 18-hole, 7,000-plus-yard (6,735-meter) par-72 championship course, with an adjoining sport and hotel complex. It's scheduled to open in 1991.

PEREDELKINO

A few stops from Moscow's Kievsky Railway Station is Peredelkino. Here you can visit the estate and grave of the great Russian writer Boris Pasternak, who received the Nobel Prize for Literature for his novel *Dr. Zhivago*.

YASNAYA POLYANA

This town lies south of Moscow along the Simferopolskoye Highway. The great Russian writer Leo Tolstoy was born in Yasnaya Polyana and lived and worked here for over 60 years. Everything on the estate has been preserved as he left it—his study, library and parlor, where his wife Sofia Andreyevna meticulously copied his manuscripts. Here he wrote *Anna Karenina, War and Peace* and chapters of *The Resurrection*. Peasants would gather under the "Tree of the Poor" to ask his advice. Nearby, Tolstoy opened a school for peasant children. He's buried on the estate grounds. The museum is open 10 a.m. to 5:30 p.m. and closed on Mon. and Tuesday.

Count Leo Tolstoy *by Ilya Repin, 1892.*

THE GOLDEN RING

INTRODUCTION

The ancient towns of the Golden Ring, built between the 11th and 17th centuries, were the cradle of Russian culture. During Russia's early history, the two most important cities were Kiev in the south and Novgorod in the north. Both, situated in what is now western Russia, lay along important commerce routes to the Black and Baltic seas. The settlements that sprang up along the trade routes between these two cities prospered and grew into large towns of major political and religious importance. From the 11th to 15th centuries, the towns of Rostov, Yaroslavl, Vladimir and Suzdal became capitals of the northern principalities, and Zagorsk served as the center of Russian Orthodoxy. In the 12th century, Moscow was established as a small protective outpost of the Rostov-Suzdal principality. By the 16th century, Moscow had so grown in size and affluence that it was named the capital of the Russian Empire. At the turn of the 18th century, St. Peters-

burg became the center of Russian power. The prominent towns that lay in a circular formation between Moscow and Leningrad became known as the Golden Ring.

THE RUSSIAN TOWN

Up to the end of the 18th century, a typical Russian town consisted of a *kremlin*, a protective fortress surrounding the area. Watchtowers were built in strategic points along the *kremlin* wall and contained vaulted carriageways, which served as the gates to the city. The "timber town" within the *kremlin* contained the governmental and administrative offices. The *boyars* (noble class) had homes here too that were used only in time of war—otherwise they lived outside the town on their own country estates, where the peasants or serfs worked the land. The *posad* (earth town)

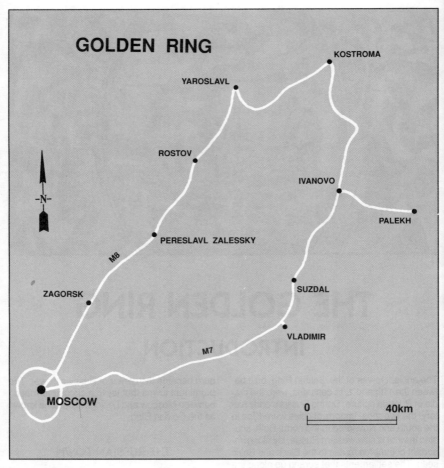

was the settlement of traders and craftsmen. The *posad* also contained the *rinoks*—the markets and bazaars, as well as the storagehouses for the town. The merchants and *boyars* used their wealth to help build the churches and commissioned artists to paint elaborate frescoes and icons. The number of churches and monasteries mirrored the prosperity of the town. The rest of the townspeople lived in settlements around the *kremlin* known as the *slobody*. The historical nucleus and heart of the town was known as the *strelka*. The regions were separated into principal-ities with their own governing princes. The ruler of the united principalites was known as the grand-prince, and later, czar. The head of the Orthodox Church was called the metropolitan or patriarch.

The Golden Ring area provides an excellent opportunity to view typical old Russian towns, which are still surrounded by ancient *kremlins*, churches and monasteries. The towns of Rostov, Vladimir, Suzdal and Pereslavl-Zelessky retain much of their original layouts. Outside of Zagorsk and Kostroma are open-air architectural muse-ums—entire wooden villages built to typify old

Russian life. All the towns of the Golden Ring have been well restored, and many of the buildings are now museums that trace the history of the area that was the center of the Golden Age of Rus for more than four centuries.

GETTING THERE

Many travel organizations offer package tours specifically to the Golden Ring area that include stops in Moscow and Leningrad; most tour the Golden Ring by bus—an excellent way to also see the Russian countryside. Intourist can also help book excursions to cities along the Golden Ring route from Moscow or Leningrad once you're already in the USSR—they also add the towns to your visa. Some places, such as Zagorsk, can be done in a day from Moscow. Others you may

overnight in, as long as you've prebooked the hotel through Intourist. You can travel quite comfortably to the areas via bus, train or car. There are restaurants along the way, but bring some food and drink for the bus rides.

The towns of the Golden Ring are a majestic mirror to all of Russia's past grandeur. The churches and monasteries are beautifully preserved and their frescoes and icons have been painstakingly restored. Many of the churches still hold religious services, which you're welcome to attend, as long as you're not wearing shorts or sleeveless shirts. Other religious buildings have been converted into museums that house the art and history of the regions. A splendid skyline of golden-domed churches, tent-shaped towers, ornamental belfries, picturesque old wooden buildings and rolling countryside sprinkled with birch greets you—as it did the visitor more than seven centuries ago.

ZAGORSK

A 45-mile (70 km) ride north of Moscow on the Yaroslavskoye Highway leads to Zagorsk, the most popular town on the Golden Ring route. As soon as the road leaves Moscow, it winds back in time through dense forests of spruce and birch, past old wooden *dacha* (country homes) and collective farms, and eventually opens onto a magical view, upon which fairy tales are based. Once upon a time on a hilltop in a large white fortress surrounded by the rivers Koshura and Glimitza and filled with star-studded golden onion domes, sparkling in the sunlight and dusted lightly with glistening snow, an obscure monk, who was destined to become a saint, founded the small settlement of Sergiev Posad and a monastery that was to be the center of Russian Orthodoxy for centuries to come. Zagorsk, the jewel among jewels of old Russian towns, gives the visitor a marvelous glimpse into the Russian life of six centuries ago.

History

In order to unify the Russian territories during the Mongol invasions (beginning in the 13th century), Sergius and his pupils founded 23 monasteries across Russia that also acted as regional strongholds. Moscow princes, czars and rich *boyars* contributed heavily to the Troitse Lavra until the

monastery became not only the wealthiest in all Russia, but also the most revered pilgrimage shrine in Moscovy. For centuries, it was the center of the Church and today stills seats the patriarch of the Orthodox faith.

Grand-Prince Dmitri Donskoi defeated the Khan Mamai's horde in 1380. At the monastery, one of St. Sergius's pupils, the famous iconist Andrei Rublev, painted the *Old Testament Trinity* (now in Moscow's Tretyakov Gallery) to commemorate this famous battle at Kulikovo on the Don. The town's original name of Sergiyev Posad (Settlement of Sergius) was changed in 1930 to Zagorsk, after the revolutionary Vladimir Zagorsk. It has a population of over 100,000.

The art of carving wooden toys has long been a tradition in Zagorsk; the first toys were made and distributed by St. Sergius to the children of the town. Many painters, sculptors and folk artists trace their heritage back to the 17th century, when the first toy and craft workshops were set up in the town. The *beriozka*, to the left as you pass through the main gates, sells many locally made wooden toys.

The thick *kremlin* walls were built around the monastery in 1540 during the reign of Ivan the Terrible to protect it from attack. A half-century later, the *lavra* (as large monasteries were called in Russia) withstood a 16-month seige by Polish forces. The monastery complex was such an important center for the Russian people that its fall would have meant the end of Rus. The monastery remained an important fortress that defended Moscow well into the 17th century. Eleven octagonal towers were built into the walls as key defense points. The most famous, the northeast tower, is known as the Utichya (Duck) Tower; the duck atop its spire symbolizes Peter the Great's hunting expeditions in Zagorsk.

SIGHTS

The parking square, near the main gates of the monastery complex, looks out over many ancient settlements that dot the landscape, and the large *kremlin* citadel that houses priceless relics of old Russian architecture. Enter the main gates at the eastern entrance through the Pilgrim Tower; paintings of the Holy Pilgrims depict the life of Sergius Radonezhsky (from the town of Radonezh), the 14th-century monk who established the Troitse-

Sergiyev Lavra—the Trinity Monastery of St. Sergius, lying beyond the gates. The small **Church of St. John the Baptist,** built in 1693 by the Stroganov family (a wealthy, titled family), stands over the main or Holy Gates.

Assumption Cathedral

The first large structure that catches the eye is the monastery's main Assumption Cathedral. This blue and gold-starred, five-domed church, with elegant sloping *zakomara* archways and consecrated in 1585, honored Ivan the Terrible's defeat of the Mongols in the Asian territory of Astrakhan. Yaroslavl artists, whose names are inscribed on the west wall, painted the interior frescoes in 1684. The burial chambers of the Godunov family (Boris Godunov was czar from 1598 to 1605) are located in the northwest corner.

Many of these churches are open for worship and conduct services throughout the day. Respectfully dressed visitors are welcome. Picture taking without a flash is usually permitted.

The brightly painted **Chapel-over-the-Well,** located outside by the cathedral's west wall, is built in the Naryshkin cube-shaped octagonal style. Near the riverbank stands the **Sergius Well Chapel.** It was customary for small chapels to be built over sacred wells; today pilgrims still bring bottles to fill with holy water.

Directly beyond the cathedral is the five-tiered turquoise and white baroque bell tower (1740-70) designed by Prince Ukhtomsky and Rastrelli. Topped with a dome in the form of a crown, it once held 40 bells.

Refectory

Head directly left of the cathedral to the southern end of the complex. A stroll in this direction to the refectory may lead past long-bearded monks, dressed in the traditional black robes and tall *klobuki* hats. The refectory, rebuilt in 1686, is painted in colorful checkerboard patterns of red, blue, green and yellow. It has a large open gallery with 19th-century paintings, wide staircases, and is decorated with carved columns and gables. The small chapel at the end of the hall has a carved iconostasis by the altar and a beautiful red jasper inlaid floor. Another quaint church, standing next to the refectory, is the **Church of St. Micah** (1734).

Trinity Cathedral And Monastery

Behind the Refectory, in the southwest corner, is the one-domed Trinity Cathedral, which the Abbot Nikon had erected over the site of the original Church of St. Sergius in 1422 (the year Sergius was canonized). Pilgrims still visit the remains of St. Sergius, which lie in a silver sarcophagus donated by Ivan the Terrible. An embroidered portrait of St. Sergius that covered his coffin is now preserved in the History and Art Museum, a short walk away. In 1425, Andrei Rublev and Daniil

The art of carving toys has long been a tradition in Zagorsk.

Chorny painted the icons on the cathedral's iconostasis, which include a copy of Rublev's *Holy Testament Trinity*. The cathedral contains 42 works by Rublev and is joined by the smaller **Church of St. Nikon** (1548).

Across from the cathedral is the slender **Church of the Holy Spirit** with the long bell tower under its dome. It was built in 1476 by stonemasons from Pskov.

Past the belfry, along the northwestern wall, is the softly rounded **Church of Our Lady of Smolensk** built in 1745 to house the icon of the same name. It was designed by the Russian architect, Prince Okhtomsky, and decorated in the Elizabethan baroque fashion.

Behind this church stands the **Trinity Monastery of St. Sergius**, one of the most important monuments of medieval Russia. The **Metropolitan's House**, vestry and adjoining monastery buildings now house the **Zagorsk History and Art Museum.** The museum, which displays gifts in the order they were presented to the monastery, contains one of the Soviet Union's richest collections of early religious art. The exhibits include icons from the 14th to 19th centuries, and portraits, chalices, china, crowns, furniture, jewelry and handicrafts from the 14th to 20th centuries. The museum is open daily from 10 a.m. to 5 p.m. and closed on Monday.

The monastery also served as the town's hospital and school. Next to the museum is the red brick, yellow-and-white sandstone hospital building with the adjoining all-white tent-roofed **Church of Saints Zosimus and Savvaty** (1635).

Palace And Ponds

In the opposite northeast corner, behind the Duck Tower, is the colorfully painted and tiled **Chertogi Palace,** built at the end of the 17th century for Czar Alexcei, who often came to Zagorsk with an entourage of over 500 people. One of the ceilings in the palace is covered with paintings that honor his son's (Peter the Great) victories in battle. It now houses the Theological College.

Exiting through the main gate make a right, and walk toward the **Kelarskiye Ponds,** situated beyond the southeast Pyatnitskaya Tower. There you may find artists sketching and people strolling through the old garden walls. Two churches built in 1547 stand outside the walls—the **Church of St. Parasceva Pyatnitsa** and the **Church of the Presentation of the Mother of God,** nearest the pond. The Zolotoye Koltso (Golden Ring Restaurant), is only a few minutes' walk away.

Toy Museum

The craft of woodcarving is still carried out in Zagorsk. The famous *matryoshka*, the nest of carved dolls, has its origins here. The history of toys and folk art can be viewed at the **Zagorsk Toy Museum** at 136 Krasnoi Armii Prospekt. The Zagorsk Art Workshop Collective continues to produce wooden folk art. A special souvenir section contains carved wooden dolls, boxes and jewelry.

VICINITY OF ZAGORSK

Not far outside of Zagorsk is the small town of **Alexandrov,** whose history is connected with Ivan the Terrible. The Alexandrova Sloboda was a residence of Ivan the Terrible for 17 years and one of the headquarters for his select army of *oprichniki.* The oldest buildings in the village are the (nonfunctioning) convent and **Trinity Cathedral** that women helped build in the 15th century. After Ivan's *oprichniki* sacked Novgorod, he brought the golden oak doors from the Hagia Sophia Cathedral to adorn the Trinity's entrance. The daughters of Czar Alexcei are buried in the Church of the Purification. The Church of the Intercession was Ivan the Terrible's court chapel. Next to this chapel is a bell tower and residential quarters, where Marfa, the stepsister of Peter the Great who forced her to take the veil, was exiled from 1698-1707. The future Empress Elizabeth was also banished to the Alexandrova Sloboda for nine years.

PERESLAVL-ZALESSKY

The tranquil town of Pereslavl-Zalessky is situated on a hilltop by the southeastern shores of Lake Pleshcheyevo about 35 miles (56 km) northeast of Zagorsk. Approaching Pereslavl from the road, pleasantly scented by the surrounding groves of pine and birch, you have an enchanting view of the shimmering azure waters of the lake, three old monasteries on the side of the road, and golden crosses atop painted onion domes that loom up from sprawling green fields dusted with blue and yellow wildflowers. Young boys wave at passersby as they fish in the lake with long reed poles. The River Trubezh meanders through the old earthen *kremlin* that winds around the center of town. These ramparts date back over eight centuries. One of Russia's most ancient towns,

Pereslavl Zalessky is a charming place, sprinkled with well-preserved churches and monasteries that at one time numbered over 50. After checking into your hotel and having a meal at the (Fairy Tale) Restaurant, take a pleasant walk along the dirt roads and imagine that Peter the Great may have traversed the same footpaths before you.

HISTORY

Pereslavl-Zalessky's long and fascinating history is traced back to the year 1152, when Prince Yuri Dolgoruky (who founded Moscow five years earlier) fortified the small village of Kleschchin on the banks of the Trubezh, and renamed it Pereslavl after an old Kievan town. Situated in an area on the *zalasye* (beyond the dense woods of Moscow), it became known as Pereslavl-Zalessky. The area was an important outpost of Moscow; Prince Alexander Nevsky set out from Pereslavl to win his decisive battle with the Swedes in 1240. Since the town also lay on important White Sea

trade routes, it quickly prospered; by 1302, Pereslavl had grown large enough to be annexed to the principality of Moscovy.

Ivan the Terrible later consolidated Pereslavl, along with the nearby village of Alexandrov, into a strategic military outpost to headquarter his *oprichniki* bodyguards. In 1688, the young Czar Peter I came here from Moscow to build his first *poteshny* (amusement) boats on Lake Pleshcheyevo. It was in a small shed near the lake that Peter discovered a wrecked English boat that he learned to sail against the wind. In 1692, Peter paraded these boats (forerunners of the Russian fleet) for members of the Moscow court. One of them, the *Fortuna,* can be found in the **Botik Museum,** which lies about two miles (three km) from Pereslavl (by the southern edge of the lake) near the village of Veskovo. Other relics from the Russian flotilla are also displayed here. Two large anchors mark the entrance and a monument to Peter the Great by Campioni stands nearby. It's open 10 a.m. to 4 p.m. and closed Tuesday.

SIGHTS

Cathedral Of The Transfiguration

Make your way to the central Krasnaya Square. The small grassy hills circling around you are the remains of the town's 12th-century earthen protective walls. In front of the **statue of Alexander Nevsky** is the white stone Cathedral of the Transfiguration, the oldest architectural monument in northeastern Russia. Yuri Dolgoruky himself laid the foundation of this church, which was completed by his son Andrei Bogoliubsky (God-Loving) in 1157. This refined structure with its one massive fringed dome became the burial place for the local princes. Each side of the cathedral is decorated with simple friezes. The *zakomara,* the semi-circular shape of the upper walls, distinguish the Russian-style from the original, simpler, cube-shaped byzantine design. Frescoes and icons from inside the cathedral, suc h as the 14th-century *Transfiguration* by Theophanes the Greek and Yuri Dolgoruky's silver chalice, are now in Moscow's Tretyakov Gallery and Kremlin Armory. The other frescoes were done during the cathedral's restoration in 1894. Across from the cathedral is the **Church of St. Peter the Metropolitan.** Built in 1585 (with a 19th-century bell tower), the octagonal frame is topped with a long, white, tent-shaped roof. This design in stone and brick was copied from the traditional Russian log-cabin churches of the north.

The River

Off in the distance, across the river, is the Church of St. Semion (1771). In between this church and the Lenin Monument on Svoboda Street are the early 19th-century shopping arcades, Gostiny Dvor. Religious services are held at the Church of the Intercession on Pleshcheyevskaya Street.

Take a leisurely stroll toward the river and follow it down to the lake. Scattered along the paths are brightly painted wooden *dachas* with carved windows covered by lace curtains. Children can be found playing outside with their kittens or a *babushka* (accent on first syllable) hauling water from the well. Many times the *dedushka* is picking apples and wild strawberries or carving a small toy for his grandchildren out of wood. Stop for a chat; it's amazing how far a few common words can go—before you know it, an invitation for *chai* may follow! At the point where the Trubezh flows into the lake stands the Church of the Forty Saints (1781) on Riibnaya Sloboda, the old fish quarter. With a little bargaining or a smile, get a rowboat to take out on the lake—or go out with the fishermen. On a warm day, it's a perfect place for a picnic; try taking a dip in the water!

Side Trip

On a little side trip from town are a number of monasteries and chapels that you may have glimpsed if you arrived from Zagorsk. The four monasteries lining the road into and out of Pereslavl also acted as protective strongholds, guarding the town from invasions. The one farthest away is the Convent of St. Theodore, about four miles (6.5 km) south of town on Sovetskaya Street. Ivan the Terrible built this convent and the Chapel of St. Theodore to honor his wife Anastasia, who gave birth to their first son, Fedor (Theodore), in 1557. Ivan often stopped at the shrine to pray when he visited his bodyguard army, which resided in the town.

About a mile closer to town is the memorial Church of Alexander Nevsky (1778). A few minutes' walk from this church, set in a woody rustic setting, is the Danilov Monastery. A few buildings remain from this 16th-century structure. The Trinity

Cathedral was commissioned by Grand-Prince Vasily III in 1532. The single-domed cathedral, with 17th-century frescoes by renowned Kostroma artists Nikitin and Savin, was built by Rostov architect Grigory Borisov in honor of Vasily's son, Ivan the Terrible. The Abbot Daniel, who founded the monastery in 1508, was in charge of the cathedral's construction and present at Ivan's christening. The smaller Church of All Saints was built in 1687 by Prince Bariatinsky, who later became a monk (Ephriam) at the monastery and was buried near the south wall. Other surviving structures are the two-story Refectory (1695) and the large tent-roofed bell tower (1689), whose bell is now in the Moscow Kremlin's Ivan the Great Bell Tower.

On the other side of the road, behind the Monument to Yuri Dolgoruky, is the **Goritsky Monastery,** surrounded by a large red-brick kremlin. On the high hilltop, a mass of sparkling onion domes rise up from inside the fortified walls. The monastery is now the **Museum of History and Art** (open 10 a.m. to 4 p.m., closed Tues.). The monastery, founded during the reign of Ivan I in the 14th century (rebuilt in the 18th), is a fine example of medieval architecture with its octagonal towers, large cube-shaped walls and ornamental stone entrance gates. The tiny white gate-church next to the gatekeepers' lodge was once known as the "casket studded with precious stones," for it was richly decorated with gilded carvings and colorful tiles. The large seven-domed **Cathedral of the Assumption** was built in 1757. The exquisite golden-framed and figured iconostasis, designed by Karl Blank, was carved and painted by the same team of artists who decorated the churches in the Moscow Kremlin.

The monastery, with 47 rooms filled with local treasures, is now one of the largest regional museums in the USSR. The rooms include a unique collection of ancient Russian art, sculptures and rare books. The museum also exhibits the plaster face mask of Peter the Great by Rastrelli (1719) and Falconnet's original model of the *Bronze Horseman.* The elaborately carved wooden gates from the Church of the Presentation won the Gold Medal at the 1867 Paris World Exhibition. May 2 is a town holiday, Museum Day, at the Goritsky Monastery.

Heading north outside town toward Rostov and Yaroslavl, you'll find the last monument structure of Pereslavl-Zalessky, the 12th-century **Monastery of St. Nicetas**, encased in a long white-bricked *kremlin*. In 1561, Ivan the Terrible added stone buildings and built the five-domed Cathe-dral. He intended to convert the monastery into the headquarters for his *oprichniki*, but later transferred their residence to the village of Alexandrov.

ROSTOV VELIKY

Approaching Rostov on the road from Moscow (34 miles/54 km north of Pereslavl-Zalessky), the visitor is greeted with a breathtaking view of silvery aspen domes, white stone churches and high *kremlin* towers. Rostov is one of Russia's most ancient towns and has stood along the picturesque banks of Lake Nero for more than 11 centuries. Named after Prince Rosta, a powerful governing lord, the town was mentioned in chronicles as far back as A.D. 862. Rostov's size and splendor grew to equal the two great towns of Novgorod and Kiev. By the 12th century, Rostov was named Veliky (The Great) and the capital of the Russian north. Rostov later came under the jurisdiction of Moscow and lost its importance as a trade and religious center by the end of the 18th century.

Today Rostov is the district center of the Yaroslavl region, and considered a historical preserve, heralding the glory of old Russian art and architecture. The town, with a population of about 50,000, has been restored to much of its original grandeur after a tornado destroyed many of the buildings in 1953. The oldest section of town, set by the lake, is still surrounded by low earthen walls, built around 1630. From the hotel and restaurant on Karl Marx Street, it's just a few minutes' walk to the ancient cathedrals within the *kremlin*.

HISTORY

Rostov Veliky was one of the wealthiest towns in all of Russia and the most important trade center between Kiev and the White Sea. Rostov became not only the capital of its own principality, but also the northern ecclesiastical center of early Christianity and the seat of the metropolitan, head of the Orthodox Church. In the 17th century, the Metropolitans Jonah and Ion Sisoyevich built a large number of magnificent cathedrals and church residences, decorated with the byzantine influence of icons and frescoes. The many religious shrines of a Russian town symbolized its wealth and status.

Unlike other Russian towns, the Rostov *kremlin* wasn't originally built as a protective fortress, but served as a decorative feature that surrounded the palace of the metropolitan. Also the main cathedral stood outside the *kremlin* walls and not in the town's center.

SIGHTS

In The *Kremlin*
The *kremlin* itself, built in 1670, has 11 rounded towers and encompasses an area of about five acres. At the west gate is the Church of St. John Divine (1683). The five-domed **Church of the Resurrection** (1670) at the northern gates is designed with intricate white-stone patterns and the classic Russian *zakomara*, forming the 24 slopes of the roof. The towers on either side of both churches are made from aspen and sparkle with a silken sheen. Stone iconostases (instead of traditional wooden ones) inside both churches are decorated with beautiful frescoes painted by artists Nikitin and Savin from the Golden Ring town of Kostroma. The Church of the Resurrection stands over the Holy Gates, so named because the metropolitan passed through them on the way from his residence inside the *kremlin* to the main cathedral.

The first stone of the massive **Cathedral of the Assumption** was laid by Prince Andrei Bogoliubsky (son of Yuri Dolgoruky who founded Moscow) in 1162. Bogoliubsky ruled Russia north from Rostov. The 11th-century Vladimir Virgin hangs to the left of the Holy Doors. A few of the 12th-century frescoes have survived, along with the original lion mask handles that guard the western doors. Rostov frescoes were known for their soft color combinations of turquoise, blue, yellow and white. Five large hewn-aspen onion domes and beautiful

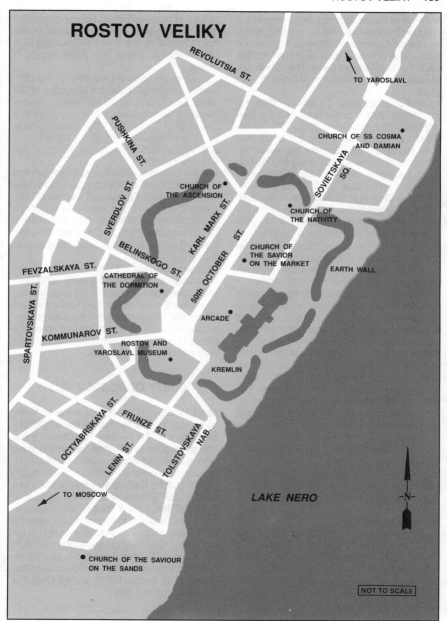

ROSTOV VELIKY

REVOLUTSIA ST.

TO YAROSLAVL

PUSHKINA ST.

SVERDLOV ST.

CHURCH OF SS COSMA
AND DAMIAN

SOVIETSKAYA SQ.

CHURCH OF
THE ASCENSION

KARL MARX ST.

CHURCH OF
THE NATIVITY

BELINSKOGO ST.

CHURCH OF
THE SAVIOR
ON THE MARKET

FEVZALSKAYA ST.

50th OCTOBER ST.

EARTH WALL

SPARTOVSKAYA ST.

CATHEDRAL OF
THE DORMITION

KOMMUNAROV ST.

ARCADE

ROSTOV AND
YAROSLAVL MUSEUM

KREMLIN

OCTYABRSKAYA ST.

FRUNZE ST.

TOLSTOVSKAYA NAB.

LENIN ST.

TO MOSCOW

LAKE NERO

-N-

CHURCH OF THE SAVIOUR
ON THE SANDS

NOT TO SCALE

white stone friezes decorate the outside of the structure. The four-tiered bell tower (1687), standing atop the Assumption Cathedral, was the most famous in all of Russia. Bells played an important role in the life of Russian towns. The 13 bells (the heaviest weighing 32 tons) can be heard 15 miles away.

Other churches inside the *kremlin* include the one-domed **Church of the Savior-on-the-Marketplace** (1690) that stands across 50th October Street; it's now the town library. In the northeast, at the end of Karl Marx Street, is the five-domed Church of St. Isodore the Blessed (1566), built during the reign of Ivan the Terrible. Right behind this church, on the other side of the earthen walls, stands the **Church of St. Nicholas-in-the-Field** (1830) on Gogol Street. This is one of the few places in town open for religious services. At the southeastern end by the water is the Church of the Nativity. Gostiny Dvor (Traders Row) marks the town's center. This long yellow arcade, marked by many carved white archways, is still the shopping and market district of Rostov.

The large main complex at the western end by the Cathedral of the Assumption is the **Metropolitan's Palace** (1680), with its highly decorated Otdatochnaya Hall; here people gathered to pay their respects to the prince and metropolitan. The White Chambers were built for the prince and later visiting czars. The Red Chambers accommodated other church and civil dignitaries. This complex of buildings now houses the **Rostov Museum Preserve of Art and Architecture.** The chambers are filled with collections of icons, woodcarvings and enamels from the 14th to 20th centuries. Rostov enamels were famous throughout Russia. Craftsmen painted miniature icons and other decorative enamels for church books and clergy robes. Today Rostov craftsmen still produce elegant enamel jewelry, ornaments and small paintings that are sold in *beriozka* stores.

Beyond The *Kremlin*

Heading west out of the *kremlin* along Lenin Street brings you to the small three-domed **Church of the Savior-on-the-Sands.** This is all that has survived from a monastery built by Princess Maria, whose husband was killed by invading Mongols in the 14th century. Princess Maria

and other noblewomen of Rostov chronicled many of the events of medieval Russia. During the 17th century, the library of Countess Irina Musina-Pushkina was one of the largest in Russia.

Down on the banks of Lake Nero are the 17th-century remains of St. Jacob's Monastery of Our Savior; the original walls are still standing. The Immaculate Conception Cathedral (1686) and Church of St. Demetrius (1800) are designed in the Russian classical style. Along the water is a park, where boats can be rented. Fishing is also a pleasant pastime.

Along the shores of the lake at the eastern end of town (at the end of Proletarskaya Street) is the Church of Saints Cosma and Damian (1775). Next to this small church stands the larger Epiphany Cathedral (1553), part of the Monastery of St. Barlaam (Abraham); this is one of the oldest surviving monasteries in Russia, dating back to the 11th century.

Outside of Rostov, in the northwestern suburbs of the village of Bogoslov, is the lovely red **Church of St. John Upon Ishnya,** one of the last wooden churches left in the region. It stands on the River Ishnya and legend has that it miraculously appeared from the lake and washed up on the shores of its present location. It's open daily for visits and closed on Wednesday.

VICINITY OF ROSTOV VELIKY

About 15 miles (24 km) outside of Rostov Veliky on the way to Yaroslavl lies the **Borisoglebsky Monastery.** Built in the early 16th century, it was later surrounded by a fortified *kremlin* during the reign of Boris Godunov to protect it from Polish invasions. The famous Rostov architect Grigory Borisov built the **Cathedral of Saints Boris and Gleb** in 1524 and decorated it with colorful tiles. Boris and Gleb, sons of Prince Vladimir (who introduced Christianity to Russia in 988), were the first saints of Russia. As political and religious turmoil swept Kiev, they passively accepted their death without fighting, believing in Christ's redemption. Borisov also built the five-domed Gate Church of St. Sergius (1545) and the Church of the Annunciation (1526).

YAROSLAVL

The English writer and adventurer Robert Byron wrote of his first visit to Yaroslavl in the early 1930s, "While Veliki Novgorod retains something of the character of early Russia before the Tatar invasion, the monuments of Yaroslavl commemorate the expansion of commerce that marked the 17th century. . . . The English built a shipyard here; Dutch, Germans, French and Spaniards followed them. Great prosperity came to the town, and found expression in a series of churches whose spacious proportions and richness of architectural decoration had no rival in Russia of their time."

Today Yaroslavl, lying 175 miles (280 km) northeast of Moscow on the M8 Highway (and via train from Moscow's Yaroslavl Station), is still an important commercial center with a population of almost a million. It occupies the land on both sides of the Volga, where the River Kotorosl flows into it. Yaroslavl, oldest city on the Volga; celebrated its 975th birthday in 1985; A monument in the city center commemorates it. This seven-ton Ice Age boulder was unearthed on the site of the Strelka; the inscription reads, "On this spot in 1010 Yaroslavl the Wise founded Yaroslavl." The oldest part of town, located at the confluence of the two rivers, contains many grandiose churches and residences, erected by the many prosperous merchants. Not far from the city is the Estate-Museum of the poet Nekrasov and the Cosmos Museum, dedicated to the first Soviet woman cosmonaut, Valentina Tereshkova.

HISTORY

The city has the symbol of a bear on its crest. In the 9th century, a small outpost arose on the right bank of the Volga River. Because the pagan inhabitants worshipped the bear as their sacred animal, the settlement was known as Bear Corner, which formed the northern border of the Rostov region. When Kievan Grand-Prince Yaroslavl the Wise visited the settlement in 1010, its name was changed to honor the grand-prince. It grew as large as Rostov; an early chronicle entry stated that in one great fire 17 churches burned to the

ground. By the 13th century, Yaroslavl had become the capital of its own principality along the Volga and remained politically independent for another 250 years.

The hordes of the Mongol Khan Batu invaded in 1238 and destroyed a great part of the city. Later, in 1463 when Prince Alexander handed over his ancestral lands to the Grand-Prince of Moscow, Ivan III, Yaroslavl was finally annexed to the Moscovy principality. For a short time, Yaroslavl regained its political importance when it was made the temporary capital during the Time of Troubles from 1598 to 1613.

The city reached the height of its prosperity in the 17th century when it became known for its handicrafts. Located along important trade routes, merchants journeyed from as far away as England and the Netherlands to purchase leather goods, silverware, woodcarvings and fabrics. The English merchants had their own residences in the *posad*. At one point, one-sixth of Russia's most prosperous merchant families lived in Yaroslavl. These families, in turn, put their wealth back into the city; by the middle of the 17th century, more than 30 new churches had been built. Yaroslavl was also Moscow's Volga port until the Moscow-Volga canal was built in 1937.

The *burlaki* (barge haulers) were a common sight, as portrayed in Repin's famous portrait, *Barge Haulers on the Volga*. In 1795, Count Musin-Pushkin discovered, in the Savior Monastery, the famous 12th-century chronicle, *The Lay of Igor's Host,* based on the fighting campaigns of Prince Igor of Novgorod who, in the words of the chronicle, "did not let loose ten falcons on a flock of swans, but laid down his own wizard fingers on living strings, which themselves throbbed out praises. . ." Later Borodin composed the opera, *Prince Igor,* based on this chronicle.

SIGHTS

A tour of Yaroslavl begins at the oldest part of town, the Strelka (arrow or spit of land), lying along the right bank of the Volga, where the Kotorosl

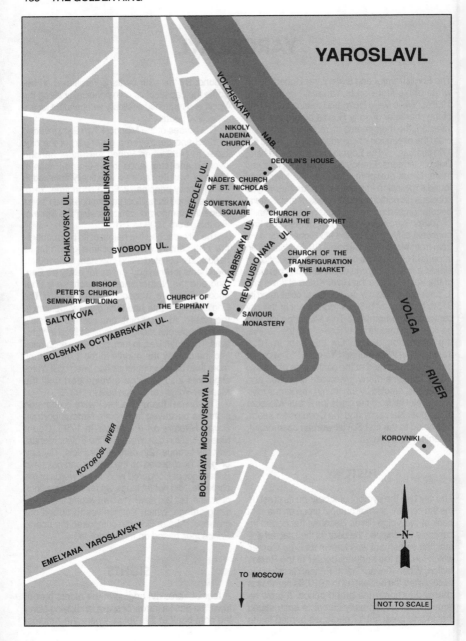

YAROSLAVL

VOLZHSKAYA NAB.

NIKOLY NADEINA CHURCH

DEDULIN'S HOUSE

NADEI'S CHURCH OF ST. NICHOLAS

TREFOLEV UL.

SOVIETSKAYA SQUARE

CHURCH OF ELIJAH THE PROPHET

CHAIKOVSKY UL.

RESPUBLINSKAYA UL.

SVOBODY UL.

OKTYABRSKAYA UL.

REVOLUSIONAYA UL.

CHURCH OF THE TRANSFIGURATION IN THE MARKET

BISHOP PETER'S CHURCH SEMINARY BUILDING

CHURCH OF THE EPIPHANY

SALTYKOVA

SAVIOUR MONASTERY

BOLSHAYA OCTYABRSKAYA UL.

KOTOROSL RIVER

BOLSHAYA MOSCOVSKAYA UL.

VOLGA RIVER

KOROVNIKI

EMELYANA YAROSLAVSKY

-N-

TO MOSCOW

NOT TO SCALE

empties into it; the Bear Ravine (now Peace Blvd) once separated the Timber Town from the Earth Town or *posad*.

Monastery

By the Kotorosl, on Podbelskov Square, is the oldest surviving structure in Yaroslavl, the **Transfiguration of our Savior Monastery,** founded at the end of the 12th century. It grew into a large feudal power; by the end of the 16th century, the monastery was one of the strongest fortresses in the northern states with a permanent garrison of its own *streltsy* (musketeer marksmen) to protect it. The *kremlin* walls were fortified to nine feet thick (three meters) in 1621. During an attack, the defenders would pour down boiling water or hot tar on their enemies.

The Holy Gates of the monastery were built at the southern entrance in 1516. The archway frescoes include details from the Apocalypse. The 16th-century bell tower stands in front of the gates; climb up to the observation platform along its upper tier for a breathtaking panorama of the city.

The monastery's gold-domed **Cathedral of the Transfiguration of the Savior** (1506) was one of the wealthiest churches in all of Russia. Frescoes cover the entire interior, the oldest wall paintings in Yaroslavl. The fresco of the Last Judgment, painted in 1564, is on the west wall; the east side contains scenes of the Transfiguration and Adoration of the Virgin. It served as the burial chamber for the Yaroslavl princes. The vestry exhibits icons and old vestments that were used during church rituals and services.

Behind the bell-clock tower are two buildings of the Refectory and the Chambers of the Father Superior and monks, which now house branches of the **Yaroslavl Museums of Art, History and Architecture.** The museums are open daily 10 to 5 and closed on Mon. and the first Wed. of each month. The refectory exhibits the history of the Yaroslavl region up to the present day. The monk cells contain collections of Old Russian art, which include icons, folk-art, manuscripts, costumes, armor and jewelry. Here is also the **Museum of The Lay of Igor's Host.** The story of this famous epic, along with ancient birch-bark documents and early printed books, are on display. Twelve years after Count Musin-Pushkin discovered the epic and other old rare manuscripts in the monastery library, the great fire of Moscow, during Napoleon's

invasion, destroyed all these originals. The Church of the Yaroslavl Miracle Workers (1827), at the south end of the cathedral, is the museum's cinema and lecture hall.

The red-brick and blue five-domed **Church of the Epiphany** (1684) stands on the square behind the monastery. The church is open from 1 May to 1 October 1 (10 to 5, closed on Tues.). It's festively decorated with *kokoshniki* and glazed colored tiles, a tradition of Yaroslavl church architecture. The interior is a rich tapestry of frescoes illustrating the life of Christ; they were painted by Yaroslavl artists in 1692. It also has an impressive gilded seven-tiered iconostasis.

Central Bazaar

Crossing the square and walking up Pervomaiskaya Street (away from the Volga) leads you to the early 19th-century Central Bazaar. Today this area is still a busy shopping district. A short walk behind the walls of the arcade brings you to the Znamenskaya (Sign) Tower of the *kremlin*. Towers in Russia were usually named after the icon that was displayed over its entranceway. This tower once held the *Sign of the Mother of God Icon.*

Ushinskov Street And Sovietskaya Square

Directly behind the tower on Ushinskov Street is the Yaroslavl Hotel. Here you can stop at the cafe and have a quick cup of *chai* or a meal in the Medvyed (Bear) Restaurant. Across from the hotel on Volkov Square is the Volkov Drama Theater, founded by Fyodor Volkov, who opened Russia's first professional theater to the general public in 1729; he formed his own drama company in 1748.

At the end of the Ushinskov Street is a statue of Lenin on Krasnaya Ploshchad (Red Square). Circle back down toward the Volga on Sovietskaya Street until it intersects with Sovietskaya Square. Dominating the town's main square is the **Church of Elijah the Prophet,** now a Branch Museum of Architecture. The church is open from 1 May to 1 Oct. (from 10 a.m. to 6 p.m., closed on Wednesday). Built, in 1647, the white stone church is decorated with ornamental tiles and surrounded by a gallery with chapels and a bell tower. The wooden iconostasis is carved in baroque fashion; the frescoes were painted in 1680 by Kostroma artists Savin and Nikitin. These murals depict

Snow is the playground for most of the year.

Christ's ascension, his life on earth, the lives of his Apostles, and the prophet Elijah. Prayer benches carved for Czar Alexcei (father of Peter the Great) and Patriarch Nikon are also found inside.

Behind this church is a **Branch Museum of Russian Art** from the 18th to 20th centuries (23 Volzhsky Emb.), housed in the former governor's residence. It's open 10 to 5 and closed on Friday. Across the street from the museum is **Nadei's Church of St. Nicholas** (1620), a gift to the city by a wealthy merchant named Nadei Sveteshnikov. This church is open from May 1 to Oct. 1 (9 to 5, closed on Thurs.). Ten churches in Yaroslavl were dedicated to St. Nicholas, the patron saint of commerce.

On The Water

The impressive **Vakhrameyev Mansion** is also right by the water, in the other direction, off Revolution Street. The house was built in the 1780s in the baroque fashion. This wealthy noble family were avid patrons of the arts in Yaroslavl. Behind the mansion (at 17 Volzhsky Emb.) is a small Branch Museum of Local History. It's open from 10 to 5:30 and closed Monday.

Walking directly along the Volga, on the Volzhsky Embankment, leads to the two-story building of the **Metropolitan's Chambers** (1690), located in the old Timber Town. It was originally built to accommodate the metropolitan of Rostov Veliky when he visited. The chambers now are a **Museum of Old Russian Art,** displaying many icons, paintings and ceramic tiles. The museum is open from 10 to 5 and closed on Friday. Of interest are the icon *The Lay of the Bloody Battle with Khan Mamai,* a portrait of Count Musin-Pushkin and a bronze sculpture of Yaroslavl the Wise.

Churches

Making your way back up toward the Savior Monastery, along the Kotorosl Embankment, leads past three distinctive churches. The first (at 8 Kotorosl) is the simple white cube-shaped Church of St. Nicholas in the Timber (1695), built by the local shipbuilders who lived in this part of the Timber Town. Next (at 10) is the **Church of the Transfiguraton in the Marketplace** (1672). It was built from funds collected by the townspeople in the old marketplace of the original Earth Town, where the local merchants and artisans lived. In the summer of 1693, 22 Yaroslavl artists helped paint the interior frescoes. The red-brick **Church of the Archangel Michael** (1658) directly across from the monastery (at 14) is filled with brightly colored frescoes painted by local Yaroslavl artists in 1730.

Outside of the Strelka in the village of Tolchkovo (in the northern part of the city) is the picturesque 15-domed **Church of St. John the Baptist** (1671), located at 69 Kotorosl Embankment on the right bank of the river. The five central green domes with the tulip-shaped middle one, gold crosses, and ornamental tiles are prime examples of the architecture of the Golden Age of Yaroslavl. The whole principality of Yaroslavl donated funds to build the church. In 1694 15 masters from around Russia painted the frescoes and icons that adorn every part of the interior. The baroque-style iconostasis was carved in 1701. The complex also includes a seven-tiered bell tower. The church is open from 10 to 6 and closed Tuesday.

Village

Also on the Kotorosl's right bank, but down along the Volga (at 2 Port Embankment), is a delightful architectural ensemble in the Village of Korovniki. The most impressive structure is the five-domed **Church of St. John Chrysostom** (1649). Its tent-shaped bell tower is known as the "Candle of Yaroslavl." The Church of Our Lady of Vladimir (1669) was used as the winter church.

Others

If you have time, take a boat ride along the Volga; cruises last about an hour. For the evenings's entertainment, book tickets at your hotel for the Yaroslavl Circus (located at 69 Svobody Street across from Truda Square). The Puppet Theater is at 25 Svobody Street.

Each summer, beginning 1 Aug. is the Yaroslavl Sunsets Music Festival, which usually opens with the overture to Borodin's *Prince Igor.*

VICINITY OF YAROSLAVL

On the Uglich Highway 15 miles (29 km) southwest of Yaroslavl is the **Cosmos Museum,** dedicated to Valentina Tereshkova, the first female cosmonaut. Valentina's flight, in 1963, lasted 70 hours and orbited the earth 48 times. The museum, near the house where she was born in the village of Nikulskoye, displays her space capsule and the history of Soviet space travel. It's open from 10 to 5 and closed on Monday. The Intourist office in your hotel can arrange excursions to these places.

About 10 miles (16 km) from Yaroslavl, along the Moscow-Yaroslavl Highway, is the **Nekrasov Estate-Museum** in the village of Karabikha. The famous Russian writer Nikolai Nekrasov stayed on the estate in the summer months; it keeps its former appearance. His poems and other works are on display. The museum is open from 10 to 5 and closed on Monday. Each summer there's a Nekrasov Poetry Festival at Karabikha.

KOSTROMA

Kostroma, 80 miles (128 km) northeast of Yaroslavl, is the only city in the Soviet Union which has retained the original layout of its city center. Constructed in the early 18th century, it's one of the country's finest examples of Old Russian classic design.

Once a bustling trade center, known as the "Flax Capital of the North," Kostroma (pronounced with last syllable accented) supplied Russia and Europe with the finest sailing cloth. The emblem of this picturesque town set along the Volga River depicts a small boat on silvery waters with sails billowing in the wind. The center mercantile square was situated right by the banks of the Volga. The Krasniye (Beautiful) and Bolshiye (Large) stalls were connected by covered galleries where fabrics and other goods were sold. Today the more modernized Arcade still houses the town's markets and stores. The Borschchov Mansion (home of a general who fought in the War of 1812), the largest of the older residential buildings, stands nearby.

Cathedral

The oldest building in Kostroma is the octagon-roofed Cathedral of the Ephiphany (1592) in the village of Krasnoye-on-the-Volga. The most beautiful structure is the **Church of the Resurrection-on-the-Debre,** situated on the outskirts of town. In 1652, the merchant Kiril Isakov built this elaborate red-brick and green-domed church from money found in a shipment of English dyes. When informed of the discovery of gold pieces, the London company told Isakov to keep the money for "charitable deeds." Some of the bas-reliefs on the outside of the church illustrate the British lion and unicorn. The towering five-domed church has a gallery running along the sides; at the northwestern end is the **Chapel of Three Bishops,** with a magnificently carved iconostasis. The gates of the church are surrounded by ornamental *kokoshniki,* and the interior is ornately decorated with frescoes and icons, dating back to the 15th century.

Monastery

The real gem of the town is the **Ipatyevsky Monastery,** founded in the 14th century by the Zernov Boyars, ancestors of the Godunovs. This large structure is enclosed by a white-brick *kremlin* and topped by green tent-shaped domes. Later, relatives of Boris Godunov built the monastery's golden-domed **Trinity Cathedral.** While Boris Godunov was czar (1598-1605), the Ipatyevsky Monastery became the country's wealthiest, containing over 100 icons. The Godunov family had its own mansion (the rose-colored building with the small windows) within the monastery, and most members were buried in the cathedral. The monastery was continually ravaged by internal strifes, blackened by Polish invasions, and captured by the second False Dmitri in 1605, who claimed the throne of the Russian Empire. Later the Romanovs, who, like the Godunovs, were powerful feudal lords in Kostroma, got the young Mikhail elected czar after the Time of Troubles. In 1613, Mikhail Romanov left the monastery to be crowned in the Moscow Kremlin. Today, the famous Ipatyevsky Chronicles are displayed here; this valuable document, found in the monastery's archives, traces the fascinating history of the area.

The **Church of St. John the Divine** (1687), which functioned as the winter church, stands nearby. From the monastery's five-tiered belltower, one has a lovely view of the countryside, and of the **Museum of Wooden Architecture,** open daily to the public. Intricately carved old wooden buildings gathered from nearby villages include the **Church of the Virgin** (1552), a typical peasant dwelling, a windmill and a bathhouse.

Others

Other churches on the right bank of the Volga are the **Church of the Transfiguration** (1685), **Church of St. Elijah-at-the-Gorodishche** (1683-85) and the lovely hilltop **Church of the Prophet Elijah.** The Kostroma Hotel, with restaurant, overlooks the Volga (request a room on the riverside with balcony). There are paths along the river and even swimming in summer.

IVANOVO

Ivanovo, an industrial and regional center 180 miles (288 km) northeast of Moscow, began as a small village on the right bank of the River Uvod. The River Talka also crosses the town; both rivers flow into the River Kliyazma, a tributary of the Moskva. The village of Voznesensk, on the left bank, was annexed by Ivanovo in 1871.

History
In 1561, a chronicle mentioned that Ivan the Terrible presented the village of Ivanovo to a powerful princely family. When, two centuries later, an Ivanovo princess married a Sheremetev, the town then passed over to this aristocratic family. In 1710, Peter the Great ordered weaving mills and printing factories built here. Soon the town grew into a major textile and commerical center, with little religious significance. Ivanovo calico was famous worldwide; by the mid-1800s, it was known as the Russian Manchester. Today almost 20% of the country's cloth is produced in this city of more than a half-million people. Ivanovo is nicknamed the "City of Brides"—since a high percentage of textile workers are women, many men come to the city looking for a catch!

Ivanovo participated actively in the revolutionary campaigns and was called the Third Proletarian Capital, after Moscow and Leningrad. Major strikes were held in the city in 1883 and 1885; in 1897, 14,000 workers held a strike against the appalling conditions in the factories. The 1905 strike, with over 80,000 participants, was headed by the famous Bolshevik leader Mikhail Frunze, who established the town's first Workers' Soviet, which provided assistance to the strikers and their families during the three-month protest.

Sights
Compared to other Golden Ring towns, Ivanovo is relatively new and modern, with only a few places of particular interest. On Lenin Prospekt, the **Ivanovo Museums of Art and History** portray the city's historical events and display collections of textiles, old printing blocks and other traditional folk arts. Off of Kuznetsov Street is the **Museum-Study of Mikhail Frunze.** On Smirnov Street is the 17th-century Shudrovskaya Chapel; on nearby Sadovaya Street stands the large red-bricked **House-Museum of the Ivanovo-Voznesensk City Soviet.** Other locations of interest in the city are the circus, puppet theater, a 17th-century wooden church and Stepanov Park, with an open-air theater, planetarium, and boat rentals. The Zarya Restaurant is on Lenin Prospekt and the Tsentralnaya Hotel on Engels Street.

PALEKH

This village lies 30 miles (48 km) east of Ivanovo and is famous for colorfully painted lacquer boxes. After the Revolution, when icon production was halted, it became popular to paint small miniatures on lacquer papier-mâché boxes, which combined the art of ancient Russian painting with the local folk crafts. Ivan Golivko (1886-1937), the master of Palekh folk art, created many beautiful lacquer scenes drawn from traditional Russian fairy tales, folk epics and songs. The **Museum of Palekh Art** displays a magnificent collection of painted boxes and other lacquer art by the folk artists of Palekh. These include works by the masters Vatagin, Bakanov, Vakurov, Butorin, Zubkov and Golivko. The **Timber House of Golivko,** where he lived and worked, is also open to the public.

The 17th-century **Cathedral of the Exaltation of the Holy Cross,** now a museum, stands in the town's center. A plaque on the outside of the west wall shows the builder to be Master Yegor Dubov. Local craftsmen carved and painted the baroque-style golden iconostasis inside the church, which is covered with almost 50 colorful icons. The highly respected Palekh artists were sent throughout Russia to paint beautiful icons and frescoes in the central Russian style. Today the artists of Palekh carry on the traditions of lacquer design and 270 craftsmen are employed at the Palekh Art Studio.

For further reading on the history and making of lacquer art, see the discussion of Russian folk crafts in the "Introduction." Painted boxes and jewelry are sold in the *beriozkas,* where Palekh lacquerware is widely displayed.

VLADIMIR

Vladimir lies 120 miles (190 km) northeast of Moscow along the M7 Highway. Trains also leave from Moscow's Kursk Station and pass through the cultivated countryside strewn with collective farms that raise corn and livestock. The same rural scenes of farmers, dressed in embroidered peasant shirts with wide leather belts and *valenki* (black felt boots), plowing the fertile land, were painted by Russian artists such as Kramskoi, Vrubel and Repin over a century ago. It's recommended to spend at least a few days in the Vladimir region. After visiting Vladimir (overnight in the Vladimir Hotel), spend the next day in the ancient town of Suzdal, only 16 miles (26 km) to the north. Between these two cities is the historic village of Bogoliubovo and the Church-of-the-Intercession on the River Nerl.

HISTORY

Even though Vladimir is now a bustling city of 325,000 and the administrative head of the region, it is still one of the best-preserved centers of 12th- and 13th-century Old Russian architecture. Eight centuries ago, Vladimir was the most powerful town of ancient Rus. Located on the banks of the Klyazma River, a small tributary of the Volga,

Vladimir was an important stop on the trade routes between Europe and Asia. Greeks from Constantinople, Varangians from the north, Bulgars from the Volga, and Central Asian merchants all journeyed through the Vladimir-Suzdal principality.

Vsevolod, the son of Kievan Grand-Prince Yaroslavl the Wise, first began to settle the area of Vladimir in northeastern Rus while Kiev was being attacked by numerous hostile tribes in the late 11th century. Many Russians, at this time, began to migrate northward; this exodus is described in one of Russia's earliest epic chronicles, *The Lay of Igor's Host*. With the death of his father, Vsevolod became the most powerful prince in all the land. Prince Vsevolod built a small fortress near the village of Suzdal on the road from Kiev. Later, a trading settlement was established around the fort by Vsevolod's son, Vladimir Monomakh, who also built the first stone church. The town was named after Vladimir Monomakh in 1108. After Monomakh's death in 1125, the Kievan states in the south began to lose their political and economic importance; under Monomakh's son, Yuri Dolgoruky, the northern territories began to flourish. Vladimir grew in such size and splendor that it became the capital of northern Rus by the middle of the 12th century.

a co-operative farm in the Golden Ring area

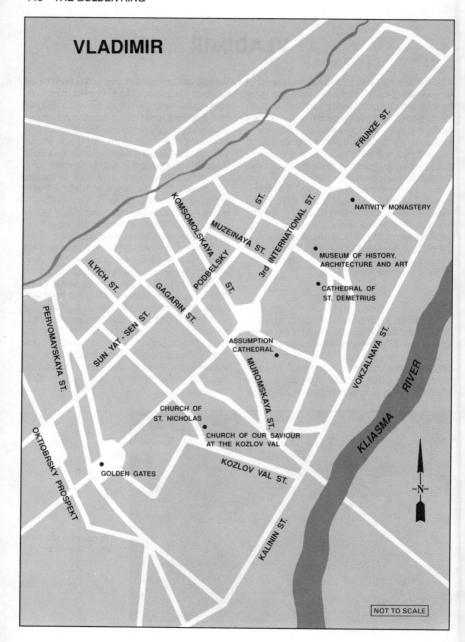

VLADIMIR

FRUNZE ST.

KOMSOMOLSKAYA

MUZEINAYA ST.

ST.

3rd INTERNATIONAL ST.

NATIVITY MONASTERY

MUSEUM OF HISTORY, ARCHITECTURE AND ART

CATHEDRAL OF ST. DEMETRIUS

ILYICH ST.

PODBELSKY ST.

GAGARIN ST.

PERVOMAYSKAYA ST.

SUN YAT - SEN ST.

ASSUMPTION CATHEDRAL

VOKZALNAYA ST.

KLIASMA RIVER

MUROMSKAYA ST.

OKTIOBRSKY PROSPEKT

CHURCH OF ST. NICHOLAS

CHURCH OF OUR SAVIOUR AT THE KOZLOV VAL

KOZLOV VAL ST.

GOLDEN GATES

KALININ ST.

-N-

NOT TO SCALE

Dolgoruky's heir, Andrei Bogoliubsky, decided to rule Russia from a more centralized and peaceful area, and transferred the throne of the grand-prince from Kiev to Vladimir in 1157, after a vision of the Blessed Virgin directed him to do so. Bogoliubsky left Kiev under the protection of a holy icon, said to have been painted by St. Luke from Constantinople, known as Our Lady of Vladimir. This revered icon became the sacred palladium of the Vladimir region; the prince even took it on his military campaigns. As the protectorate of the city, it became the symbol of divine intervention and the power of the grand-princes.

Andrei brought in master artists and craftsmen to recreate the splendors of Kiev in the new town of Vladimir. A crowned lion carrying a cross was the town's coat-of-arms. Under his brother, Vsevolod III (who ruled 1174-1212), the Vladimir-Suzdal principality, with Vladimir as its capital, reached the zenith of its political power.

When the Mongol Tatars invaded in 1238, Vladimir, like many other towns in Russia, suffered extensive damage. For a while, Vladimir retained the seat of the Church Metropolitan, and the grand-princes were still crowned in the town's Uspensky Cathedral. But eventually the princes of Moscow began governing Russia through the khans. When Vladimir was annexed to the principality of Moscovy and Moscow became the capital of the country in the 16th century, its importance slowly declined; by 1668 the population numbered only 990. After the Revolution, the city grew with industrialization and today it's a large producer of electrical machinery. The Vladimiret tractor, sold around the world, recently won a Gold Medal at a Brussels Machinery Exhibition.

SIGHTS

To enter the old part of town along the river, pass through the gates built in 1158 by Prince Bogoliubsky, who modeled them after the Golden Gates of Kiev. The oak doors of the now white gates were once covered with gilded copper; the golden-domed structure on top of the gates was the Church of the Deposition of the Robe. These gates were used as a defense fortification for the western part of town and also served as a triumphal arch—Alexander Nevsky, Dmitri Donskoi (in 1380), and troops on their way to fight Napo-

leon in the Battle of Borodino in 1812 all passed through the arch. The gates were damaged many times over the years, and were reconstructed in the 18th century. Today the Golden Gates house the local **Military Historical Museum.** Next to the gates, in the red-brick building (formerly a church) and the fire observation tower, are the **Museums of Contemporary Artists and Ancient Town Life.** The latter has many interesting old illustrations and black-and-white photographs tracing the history of the region.

Cathedrals

The oldest buildings of the city were constructed on the hills by the water, which served as a defensive wall. Walk right through the gates and a cluster of golden-domed white churches come into view. In 1158, Andrei Bogoliubsky brought in master craftsmen from all over Russia and Europe to build the triple-domed Uspensky Sobor, the Assumption Cathedral. Built to rival Kiev's St. Sophia, the cathedral was decorated with gold, silver and precious stones. It was the tallest building in all of Rus. Filled with frescoes and icons, the iconostasis was also the largest of its kind in Russia. A full tenth of the grand-prince's revenue was contributed to the upkeep of the cathedral. After much of it was destroyed by fire in 1185 (along with 33 other churches), Prince Vsevolod III had it rebuilt with five domes. Since the original walls were encased within a larger structure, the cathedral doubled in size, with an area for a congregation of 4,000 people. The Italian architect Fioravanti used it as his model for the Moscow Kremlin's own Assumption Cathedral. After more fires blackened the walls, the famous iconists, Andrei Rublev and Daniil Chorny, were sent in 1408 to restore the interior. Frescoes from the 12th and 13th centuries are still evident on the western and northern walls. Rublev's and Chorny's frescoes, including scenes from the Last Judgment, decorate two vaults beneath the choir gallery and the altar pillars. The famed icon of the Virgin of Vladimir, that once hung by the altar, was transferred in 1380 to Moscow's Assumption Cathedral; it's now in the Moscow Tretyakov Gallery.

This cathedral was one of the most revered churches in Russia; all the Vladimir and Moscow grand-princes were crowned inside it, from the son of Yuri Dolgoruky to Ivan III in the early 15th century. It was the main center of the Church metropolitan in the 14th century. The Assumption Cathedral was also the burial place of the princes of Vladimir, including Andrei Bogoliubsky and Vsevolod III. The three-story belfry was built in 1810. The cathedral has been under continuous restoration during the last century. Mass is celebrated on Saturday evenings, Sundays, and Orthodox feast days. Visitors are welcome in proper attire. Taking flash pictures is not permitted.

A short walk away to the right of the cathedral (with your back to the river) leads to one of the most splendid examples of Old Russian architecture, the **Cathedral of St. Demetrius** (1193-97). It was built by Vsevolod III as his court church; his palace once stood nearby. The cathedral, with its one large helmut drum, was named after "Big Nest," Vsevolod's patron saint (St. Demetrius of Thessaloniki) and newborn son Dmitri. (Vsevolod was nicknamed "Big Nest" for his large family of 12 children.) It's built from blocks of white limestone and decorated with intricate *kokoshniki* along the doorways and arches. Over 1,300 basreliefs cover the outer walls: decorative beasts, birds, griffins, saints, prophets, the labors of Hercules, and many elaborate floral patterns all glorify the might of Vladimir. The friezes of King David and Alexander the Great symbolize Vsevolod's cunning military exploits. At the top of the left section of the northern façade is Prince Vsevolod seated on the throne with his young son; the other sons are bowing to their father. The interior frescoes date back to the 12th century. In 1834, Nicholas I ordered the cathedral restored; it's now part of the local museum complex.

IIIrd International Street

Across from this cathedral at 64 IIIrd International Street is the **Vladimir Museum of Art and Architecture,** with displays of old religious paintings, manuscripts and architectural designs. Directly across the street is the **Museum of History.** A rich collection of artifacts, archeological materials, old fabrics and weapons, princely possessions, and the whitestone tomb of Alexander Nevsky are on display. Another branch of the museum with lacquered art, crystal and embroidery is located at the end of IIIrd International Street past the Golden Gates. The museums are open daily and closed on Thursday.

Directly behind this last branch museum is the simple white Church of the St. Nicholas and the Church of the Savior at the Kozlov Val, both built in the late 17th century. Across from them, nearer the water, is the Church of St. Nicholas-at-Galeya, with its tent-shaped bell tower. The church was built by a wealthy citizen of Vladimir in the early 18th century.

At the opposite end of IIIrd International Street toward Frunze Square is the **Nativity Monastery** (1191-96), one of Russia's most important religious complexes up until the end of the 16th century; it was closed in 1744. Alexander Nevsky was buried here in 1263; his remains were transferred to St. Petersburg by Peter the Great in 1724. The Nikolskaya Church next door is now the Planetarium.

Next to the Vladimir Hotel (across from the Planetarium on Frunze St.) is the brick and five-domed **Assumption Church** (1644), built from donations given by rich local merchants. At the end of Frunze St. is the Eternal Flame, commemorating the soldiers who lost their lives during World War II.

Shopping And Residential Districts

Right in front of the Golden Gates on Gagarin Street is the city's main shopping district, the Torgoviye Ryady. Across the street is the **Monument to the 850th Anniversary of Vladimir.**

Stroll down Gagarin Street and look out over the old section of Vladimir. In the distance are many squat old wooden houses with long sloping roofs and stone floors. Many of the town's inhabitants have lived in these homes for generations. The people enjoy a simple town life. During the day you may see residents hanging out laundry, perhaps painting the latticework around their windows a pastel blue-green, chopping wood, or gathering fruits and mushrooms. The children enjoy getting their picture taken. Bring a few souvenirs from home to trade.

Convent And Restaurant

At the end of Gagarin St. is the **Knyaginin (Princess) Convent,** founded by the wife of Vsevolod III, Maria Shvarnovna, in 1200. The grand-princesses of the court were buried in the convent's Assumption Cathedral, rebuilt in the 16th century. The cathedral's three-tiered walls are lined with fancy *zakamora* and topped with a single helmet drum. In 1648, Moscow artists painted the colorful interior frescoes. The north and south walls depict the life of the Virgin Mary, and the west wall shows scenes from the Last Judgment. Paintings of Vladimir princesses, portrayed as saints, are on the southwest side, and the pillars recount the lives of the grand-princes. The cathedral is the only remaining building of the convent complex and now houses a restoration organization. Next to the convent stands the **Church of St. Nicetas** (1762). This baroque green and white, three-tiered church was built by the merchant Semion Lazarev. The interior is divided into three separate churches on each floor. It was restored in 1970. In front of this church is a bust of the writer Gogol. Pervomaiskaya (First of May) Street leads back to the Golden Gates.

At the end of the day, your group tour may stop at the rustic hewn-log Traktir Restaurant for an enjoyable meal of the local cuisine.

VICINITY OF VLADIMIR

The quaint village of Bogoliubovo lies five miles (eight km) from Vladimir. Group tours sometimes stop; if not, a car can be hired in town. One legend says that when Prince Andrei was traveling from Kiev to Vladimir, carrying the sacred icon of Our Lady of Vladimir, his horses stopped on a large hill and would move no farther. At this junction, by the confluence of the Klyazma and Nerl rivers, Andrei decided to build a fortress and royal residence. He named the town Bogoliubovo (Loved by God) and took the name of Bogoliubsky; he was canonized by the Church in 1702. Supposedly after the Virgin appeared to him in a dream, he built the Nativity of the Virgin Church. This cathedral was still standing in the 18th century, but when one Father Superior decided to renovate it in 1722 by adding more windows, the cathedral collapsed; it was partially rebuilt in 1751. Only a few walls remain of the 12th-century palace, of which chronicles wrote, "it was hard to look at all the gold." On the staircase tower are pictures depicting the death of Andrei Bogoliubsky—assassinated by jealous nobles in this tower in 1174. The coffins of his assassins were said to have been buried in the surrounding marshes and their wailing cries heard at night. The buildings in Bogoliubovo are now museums, which are closed on Monday. About a mile southeast of Bogoliubovo on the River Nerl is the graceful **Church of the Intercession on-the-Nerl,** built during the Golden Age of Vladimir architecture. Standing all by itself in the green summer meadows or snowy winter landscape, it's reflected in the quiet waters of the river that is filled with delicate lilies. It has come down from legends that Andrei built this church in 1164 to celebrate his victory over the Volga Bulgars. The Virgin of the Intercession was thought to have protected the rulers of Vladimir. With the building of this church, Andrei proclaimed a new church holiday of the Feast of the Intercession.

SUZDAL

Suzdal is a pleasant half-hour ride from Vladimir through open fields dotted with hay stacks and mounds of the dark rich soil. Vladimir was the younger rival of Suzdal which, along with Rostov Veliky, began a full century earlier. The town was settled along the banks of the Kamenka River, which empties into the Nerl a few miles downstream. Over 100 examples of Old Russian architecture attract a half-million visitors each year to this remarkable medieval museum. Just outside Suzdal is Kideksha, a small preserved village that dates back to the beginning of the 12th century. On the left bank of the river is the lovely Suzdal Museum of Wooden Architecture, portraying the typical Russian life-style of centuries ago.

The first view of Suzdal from the road encompasses towering silhouettes of gleaming domes and pinkish walls atop Poklonnaya Hill, rising up amidst green patches of woods and gardens. Time seems to have stopped around this fantastic creation—a perfection of spacial harmony. Today Suzdal is a quiet town with no industrial enterprises. Crop and orchard farming is the main occupation of the residents who still live in the predominant *izba* wooden houses. The scenic town is a popular site for filmmaking. The American production of *Peter the Great* used Suzdal as one of its locations.

Traveling along the Golden Ring route, you may have noticed that it's much the same distance from one town to another. At the time these towns were settled, one unit of distance was measured by the amount of area covered in 24 hours by a team of horses. Most towns were laid out about one post-unit apart. So the distance between Moscow and Pereslavl-Zalessky, Pereslavl and Rostov, or Rostov and Yaroslavl could easily be covered in one day's time. Distances in medieval Russia, from Kiev to the White Sea, were measured by these units; thus, the traveler knew how many days it took to arrive at his destination—from Moscow to Suzdal took about three days.

HISTORY

The area of Suzdalia was first mentioned in chronicles in 1024, when Kievan Grand-Prince Yaroslavl the Wise came to suppress the rebellions. By 1096, a small *kremlin* had been built around the settlement, which one chronicle already described as a "town." As Suzdal grew, princes and rich nobles from Kiev settled here, bringing with them spiritual representatives from the church, who introduced Christianity to the region. The town slow-

hamming it up for the camera in the Golden Ring area

(clockwise from top) WWII veterans; the crew of the historic battleship *Aurora*; young hopefuls outside the Vagonova Ballet School

(top) *The Bronze Horseman,* depicting Peter the Great; (bottom) Palace Square, Leningrad

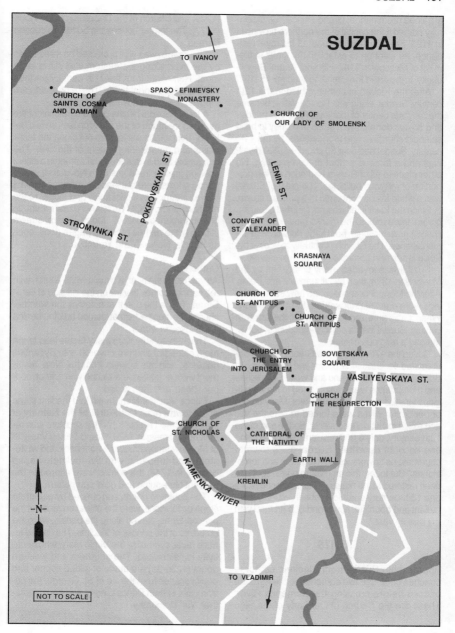

SUZDAL

TO IVANOV

CHURCH OF
SAINTS COSMA
AND DAMIAN

SPASO - EFIMIEVSKY
MONASTERY

CHURCH OF
OUR LADY OF SMOLENSK

POKROVSKAYA ST.

LENIN ST.

STROMYNKA ST.

CONVENT OF
ST. ALEXANDER

KRASNAYA
SQUARE

CHURCH OF
ST. ANTIPUS

CHURCH OF
ST. ANTIPIUS

CHURCH OF
THE ENTRY
INTO JERUSALEM

SOVIETSKAYA
SQUARE

VASLIYEVSKAYA ST.

CHURCH OF
THE RESURRECTION

CHURCH OF
ST. NICHOLAS

CATHEDRAL OF
THE NATIVITY

EARTH WALL

KAMENKA RIVER

KREMLIN

-N-

TO VLADIMIR

NOT TO SCALE

ly gained prominence; Grand-Prince Yuri Dolgoruky named it the capital of the northern provinces in 1125. From Suzdal, the seat of his royal residence, he went on to establish the small settlement of Moscow in 1147. His son, Andrei Bogoliubsky, transferred the capital to Vladimir in 1157.

After the Kievan states crumbled in the 12th century, Suzdal, along with Rostov Veliky, became the religious center of medieval Rus. The princes and *boyars* donated vast sums of money to build splendid churches and monasteries; by the 14th century, Suzdal had over 50 churches, 400 dwellings and a famous school of icon painting. No other place in all of Russia had such a high proportion of religious buildings. The crest of Suzdal was a white falcon contained in a prince's crown.

Since the town itself was not situated along important trade routes, the monks (and not the merchants) grew in wealth from large donations to the monasteries. The Church eventually took over the fertile lands and controlled the serf-peasants.

Suzdal was invaded many times, first by the Mongols in 1238, then by Lithuanians and Poles. After the Mongol occupation, no new stone buildings were erected until well into the 16th century. When it was annexed to Moscovy in the late 14th century, Suzdal lost its political importance, but remained a religious center.

During the 1700s, Peter the Great's reforms undermined ecclestiastical power and the Church in Suzdal lost much of its land and wealth. Churches and monasteries were mainly used to house religious fanatics and political prisoners. Many barren or unpopular wives were forced to take the veil and exiled to Suzdal's convents. By the end of the 19th century, only 6,000 residents remained, and one account described Suzdal as "a town of churches, belltowers, old folk legends and tombstones." But today, this enthralling poetic spot has been restored to the majesty of its former days. As one 13th-century chronicler observed, "Oi, most radiant and bountiful, how wondrous art thou with thy beauty vast."

SIGHTS

Approaching Suzdal from Vladimir, as horse coaches once did, two churches to the right are passed before crossing the Kamenka River. These are the Church of Our Lady of the Sign (1749) and Church of the Deposition of the Robe (1777). The former houses the Suzdal Excursion Bureau.

The *kremlin* was well protected on three sides by the river; along the eastern wall ran a large moat. Remnants from the 11th-century earthen walls are still evident today. These ramparts are topped with wooden walls and towers.

A tour of Suzdal begins on the right bank of the river, where much of the old architecture is clustered. Take a moment to gaze out along the fertile plains and meandering waters of the river. The rich arable land in this area first attracted settlers seeking greater freedoms from Novgorod, where pagan priests were still leading uprisings against Kievan attempts to Christianize and feudalize the northern lands. In Old Russian, *suzdal* meant "to give judgment or justice". Today, several streets still carry the names of Slavic pagan gods, such as Kupala, Netyoka and Yarunova.

Cathedral

As you cross the river, a simple white church with red outlines comes to view on the left side of Lenin Street. This is the one that acted as the summer church; the slender helmet-domed building behind it was used in winter.

The 13th-century Korsunsky Gates lead to the main cathedral and are covered with Byzantine patterns; religious scenes from the New Testament were engraved and etched with acid on copper sheets and then gilded.

Prince Vladimir Monomakh laid the first stone of the town's main **Cathedral of the Nativity** at the end of the 11th century. This structure was rebuilt many times; in 1528, Grand-Prince Vasily III of Moscow reconstructed it from brick and whitestone and topped it with five helmet-shaped domes. In 1748, the domes were altered to the present blue-onion and gold-star pattern.

The southern doors, surrounded by elaborate stone decorations, were the official entrance of the princes. Lions, carved along the portals, were the emblems of the princes of Vladimir. The carved female faces symbolize the Virgin Mary, whose nativity is celebrated. The southern and western doors (1230-33) are made of gilded copper and depict scenes from the life of St. George, the patron saint of both Prince Georgi and his grandfather, Yuri Dolgoruky.

Early 13th-century frescoes of saints and other ornamental floral patterns are still visible in the vestry. Most of the other murals and frescoes are from the 17th century. Tombs of early bishops and princes from as far back as 1023 are also found inside. The burial vaults of the early princesses are near the west wall. The octagonal bell tower was built in 1635 by order of Czar Mikhail Romanov and repaired in 1967. Old Slavonic letters correspond to numbers of the face of the clock.

Suzdal Museum

The Archbishop's Palace, now the Suzdal Museum, was built right next to the cathedral on the bank of the Kamenka between the 15th and 17th centuries. The main chamber of the palace, a large pillarless hall, held important meetings and banquets. In the 17th century, this Krestovaya (cross-vaulted) Chamber was considered one of the most elegant rooms in all Russia. The museum contains collections of ancient art and traces the evolution of architecture in the Suzdal region.

Enter the palace chamber through the western entrance. In the center stands a long wooden table, topped by a rich red cloth, once used by the archbishop and his clergy. An 18th-century tiled stove stands in one corner. The walls are decorated with many 15th-century icons. Suzdal developed its own school of icon painting in the early 13th century. Its use of lyrical flowing outlines, detailed facial qualities and soft designs in red and gold, were later adopted by the Moscow school, headed by Andrei Rublev. Both the Moscow Tretyakov Gallery and the Leningrad Russian Museum include Suzdal icons in their exhibits.

Pass through the gateway to the left of the palace to reach another art section of the museum. Here are more displays of icons, paintings, sculptures, ivory carvings, embroideries and other crafts.

In front of the palace by the river is the wooden **Church of St. Nicholas** (1766). It represents one of the oldest types of Old Russian wooden architecture and is built from logs into a square frame with a long sloping roof. The early architects used only an axe, chisel and plane to build these designs. No nails were needed; the logs were held together by wooden pegs and filled with moss. It was transferred from the village of Glotovo in

1960. Beside it, in lovely contrast, stands the red and white-trimmed Church of the Assumption (1732), with its green rounded roof and horseshoe *kokoshniki*.

Churches Along The River

Farther up along the riverbank by Sovietskaya Square (formerly Trade Square) is the yellow-white brick summer Church of the Entry into Jerusalem (1707), topped with a half-dome drum and a gilded cross. The white-washed winter Church of St. Paraskeva (1772) stands next to it.

Many of the local citizens built their own churches. Across the river are four churches constructed between the 16th and 18th centuries by money raised by the local tanners who lived and worked by the river near the marketplace. The local blacksmiths, who lived at the northern end of town, built the Churches of Saints Cosmas and Damian, the patron saint of blacksmiths.

monastery in Suzdal

Market And Lunch

The long trading stalls of the Torg (Marketplace), built in 1806, mark the center of town. During holidays, the grounds were opened to fairs and exhibitions, and were filled with jolly jesters, merry-go-rounds and craft booths. Horses were tied up along the arcade. Today, the colonnade has over 100 stores, where the townspeople congregate, especially around mid-day.

(For a lunch break, try dining at the **Trapeznaya Restaurant** , located in the Refectory of the Archbishop's Palace (closed Monday; sometimes advance reservations are needed). Sample the splendors of ancient Suzdalian monastic cooking—the local fish-soup and home-brewed mead are especially tasty. On Lenin Street are the Sokol Restaurant and a tearoom. The Suzdal Hotel and Restaurant are near the central square and the Pogrebok (Cellar) Cafe is on Kremlyovskaya Street.)

Behind the trading stalls on Lenin St. is the **Church of the Resurrection-on-the-Marketplace,** now a branch of the Suzdal Museum. Here are exhibits of architectural decorations, wooden carvings and colorful tiles used to adorn buildings in the 17th and 18th centuries.

Biggest Churches And Convents

Continuing west along Lenin St. brings you by two other sets of church complexes. Not only did the number of churches in a town symbolize the wealth, but it was also customary in medieval Russia to build twin churches; this added even more to the cluster of religious structures. These twin churches stood usually in close proximity to each other—one cool, high-vaulted and richly decorated church was used only in summer; the other, simpler and smaller, held the congregation in winter. The first set is comprised of the **Church of the Emperor Constantine** (1707), topped by five slender drum domes, a unique feature of Suzdalian architecture. The glazed green-roofed and white-bricked **Church of Our Lady of Sorrows** (1787), with the large bell tower, was for the winter. The next set is made up of the **Church of St. Antipus** (1745), recognized by its unusual multicolored octagonal red-roofed bell tower, and the **Church of St. Lazarus** (1667), topped with beautiful forged crosses on five domes.

Suzdal had the largest monasteries and convents in the region, which served as protective citadels for the citizens during time of war. These institutions, besides religious, became the educational centers for the town. Husbands could also force their wives to take the veil, a quick way to divorce. Fathers would also place daughters in a convent until they were married. In front of the twin churches, back down by the water, is the **Convent of the Deposition of the Robe,** founded by Bishop John of Rostov Veliky in 1207. The convent was rebuilt of stone in the 17th century. The white Holy Gates are topped with two red and white octagonal towers covered with glazed tile. The convent's church was built by Ivan Shigonia-Podzhogin, a rich *boyar* who served Czar Vasily III. The citizens of Suzdal erected the 72-meter bell tower in 1813 to commemorate Napoleon's defeat.

The neighboring red-brick **Convent of St. Alexander** was built in 1240 in honor of Prince Alexander Nevsky, who defeated the Swedes on the Neva River that same year. After it was burned down by the Poles in the 17th century, the mother superior had Peter the Great rebuild it. In 1682, the Ascension Cathedral was constructed from funds donated by Peter's mother, Natalya Naryshkina. The convent closed in 1764, but the church remains open to the public.

Behind this convent is a 17th-century, brick, gabled-roof tailor's house, nestled in the former *posad*. It now contains a domestic museum with displays of furniture and utensils from the 17th to 19th centuries. The rooms represent a typical peasant hut. Across from the *pechka* (stove), (upon which the eldest member of the family slept), was the *krasnaya ugol* (beautiful corner), where the family icons were kept. Usually the *gornitsa* (living area) was comprised of one or two rooms. Here were found a few beds, chairs, tables and a clothes chest. The kitchen was situated in the corner nearest to the *kamin* (fireplace) or stove. A small storagehouse was also built into the hut. This house stands next to the summer Church of Our Lady of Smolensk (1696) on Krasnaya Square.

The largest architectural complex on the right bank of the river is the **Spaso-Yevfimiev Monastery,** built in 1350 by a Suzdal prince; the monks eventually owned vast amounts of land and their monastery became the wealthiest in the region.

It's enclosed by a massive, mile-long, red *kremlin* that has 20 decorated towers. The Cathedral of the Transfiguration was built in 1594. Inside, 17th-century frescoes depict the history of the monastery. Prince Dmitry Pozharsky, hero of the 1612 Polish war and governor of Suzdal, is buried beside the altar; a monument to him, standing outside the cathedral, says "To Dmitri Mikhailovsky 1578-1642." Adjoining the cathedral is a small chapel that stands over the grave of the Abbot Yevfimy.

The Church of the Assumption, built in 1526, was decorated with *kokoshniki* and a large tent-shaped dome. The Kostroma artists Nikitin and Savin painted the frescoes on the outside southern and western walls. At one point, Catherine the Great had it converted into a prison to house those who committed crimes against the church and state. The Decembrist Shakhovskoi died in this prison. When the writer Leo Tolstoy was excommunicated by the Church, he was almost sent here too. The monk cells contain an exhibit of contemporary folk art that includes works by local painters, potters, sculptors and glass blowers.

The large complex across the river is the **Convent of the Intercession,** built by Prince Andrei in 1364. Prince Vasily III built the convent's churches in 1510. The white three-domed Cathedral of the Intercession served as the burial place for Suzdal noblewomen. Vasily used the convent to exile his wife, Solomonia Saburova. Vasily wanted to divorce his wife on the grounds that she was barren; Solomonia accused Vasily of sterility. The metropolitan granted Vasily his divorce and sent Solomonia to the Pokrovsky (Intercession) Convent to live out her life as a nun. Vasily remarried a Polish girl named Elena Glinskaya. The story continues that sometime later news reached Moscow that Solomonia had given birth to a son. Fearing for her son's life, Solomonia hid him with friends and then staged a fake burial. For centuries this tale was regarded only as legend; but in 1934 a small casket was unearthed beside the tomb of Solomonia, who died in 1594. There was no skeleton, only a stuffed silk shirt embroidered with pearls. The small white tomb and pieces of clothing are on display in the Suzdal Museum. Ivan the Terrible also sent his wife Anna to this convent in 1575. Later Peter the Great even exiled his first wife, Eudokia Lopukhina, here in 1698.

Wooden Villages

At the southern end of town on the left bank of the Kamenka is the **Suzdal Museum of Wooden Architecture.** Old wooden villages were brought in from all around the Vladimir-Suzdal region and re-assembled at this location on Dmitriyevskaya Hill, to give an idea of the way of life in a typical Russian village. This open-air museum consists of log-built churches covered with aspen-shingled roofs, residential houses, windmills, barns and bath-houses.

Change has come slowly for villages in the Golden Ring.

To The River! To The *Banya!*

At the end of the day, return to your hotel, probably at the Main Tourist Complex behind the Convent of the Intercession. Before dinner, take a walk along the river as the sun sets over the town. Young boys can be seen swimming and fishing in the warmer months or skating in winter. Many small side streets are filled with the local wooden *dachas,* covered with elaborate woodcarvings and latticework. Ask your driver to stop by the **House of Merchant Bibanov,** the most lavishly decorated house in town. If you're lucky, a pink full moon will rise above the magical display of gabled roofs and towers, to call an end to the delightful Suzdalian day! Try taking a *banya* or a dip in the hotel's indoor pool. The hotel also offers *troika* rides in winter.

VICINITY OF SUZDAL

A few miles to the north of Suzdal is the small village of **Kideksha.** According to chronicles, in 1015 the brothers Boris and Gleb, sons of the Kievan Prince Vladimir who brought Christianity to Russia, had a meeting here, where the Kamenka River empties into the Nerl. They were later assassinated by their brother, but died defending the Christian faith; they became the first Russian saints. In 1152, Prince Yuri Dolgoruky chose to build his country estate on this spot. Dolgoruky also erected the simple white-stone Church of Saints Boris and Gleb, where his son, Boris, and daughter-in-law Maria, are buried. The winter Church of St. Stephan was put up in the 18th century.

LENINGRAD

INTRODUCTION

History

St. Petersburg, Petrograd, Leningrad—each name evokes its own moments in history, differing images of a city that miraculously sprung into existence by the vision, backed up by the iron will, of a single man. Peter the Great decided to build a city along the desolate shores of the Gulf of Finland to let Russia "stand firmly on the sea." On 16 May 1703, a salute was fired to celebrate the founding of St. Petersburg, Russia's "window on the West," which became the capital of the Russian Empire only nine years later. The city was also one of the first in the world built according to preconceived plans, drawn up by the most famous Russian and European architects, as well as Peter himself, based on visits to Venice and Amsterdam. Tens of thousands of workers were brought in to dig waterways and erect palaces and fortresses on 101 islands along the Neva. Before long, St. Petersburg was compared to other great capitals of Europe and nicknamed the "Venice of the North." By the end of the 18th century, St. Petersburg had given birth to the Golden Age of Russia, and had become the center of the arts, culture and science. Petersburg was a magnet that attracted and nurtured genius from around the world. The most talented artists, poets, writers, dancers and musicians flocked to the elegant and sophisticated city. Her noble spirit was founded on beauty, innovation and progress.

> "The Neva is clad in granite,
> Bridges stand poised over her waters,
> Her islands are covered with dark green gardens
> And before the younger capital, ancient Moscow
> Has paled, like a purple clad widow
> Before a new Empress . . .
> I love you, city of Peter's creation. I love your stern
>   harmonious aspect.
> . . .the transparent twilight and moonless gleam of
>   your pensive nights."
>
> –Alexander Pushkin

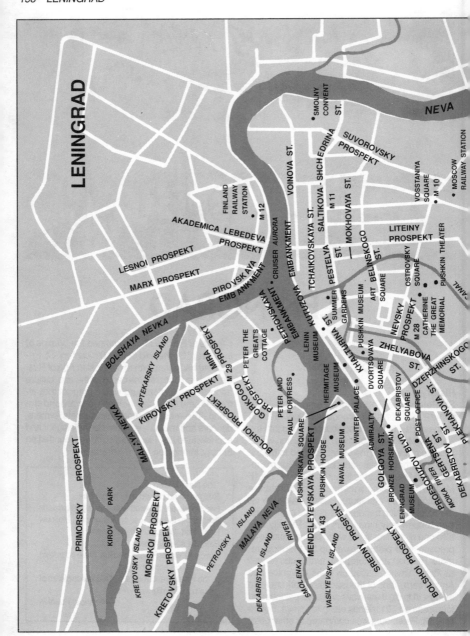

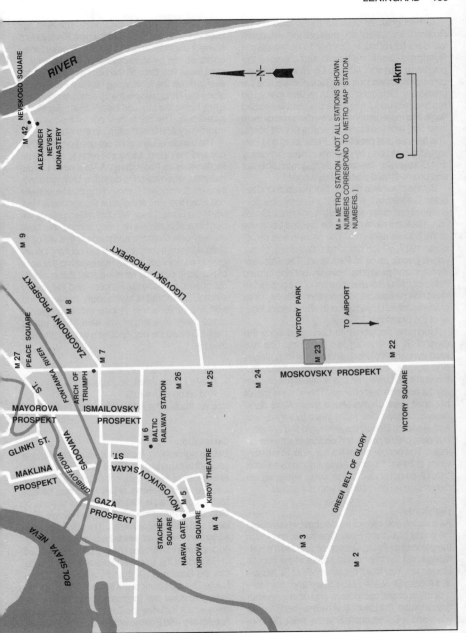

As Petrograd, the city became the "cradle of the Russian Revolution" and political and philosophical ideas flourished. In October 1917, "ten days in Petrograd shook the world" and changed the course of Russian history. Lenin and the new communist ideals took the place of czars and the aristocracy. Slogans of socialist realism rose up on red banners undulating over the double-headed eagle and royal gardens, whose monuments were inscribed with the classical words of past poets. The palaces and proletariat, Petersburg and Petrograd, existed side by side in a curious dichotomy that Dostoevsky described as "the most abstract and premeditated place in the world."

But the place was destined for yet another character. Disdaining the Orthodox Church, the government rechristened the city Leningrad. On 26 Jan. 1924, the resolution of the Second Congress of the Soviets declared, "The great events of October 1917, which decided the destiny of our country, took place in Petrograd. The first ever workers' and peasants' government was formed in this city. May this major center of the proletarian revolution be associated henceforth with the name of Vladimir Ilyich Ulyanov-Lenin, the greatest leader of the proletariat."

Much has happened to Leningrad since the days of St. Petersburg and the czars. She has lived through revolutions and repressions, sieges and purges, isolations and humiliations. But through it all, Leningrad has retained her propensity for courage and change. The white nights of her spirit have always shone through the darkness. Shut down over many years by tragedy and war, Sleeping Beauty awakened to find her glorious past, prolific poetry and dedicated subjects still intact. The people never left her side. In the very worst of times, the poet Anna Akhmatova wrote, "No, I lived not under foreign skies, sheltering under foreign wings. I stayed with my people."

Highlights

As a visitor, you cannot help but get whisked into the vortex of all three cities. One day brings you to the palaces of Peter, Catherine the Great's Hermitage and the impressive statue of the Bronze Horseman. You tour the cathedrals of St. Isaac's and Alexander Nevsky Monastery, and view monuments to czars, composers and poets. Another day recreates the Revolution before your eyes, as you stand in Decembrist's Square, inside the Winter Palace and onboard the *Aurora*. The evenings beckon you to the Kirov Ballet where Pavlova and Nijinsky once danced, or the Maly Theater for an opera written by Mussorgsky or Tchaikovsky. A stroll takes you through the back alleys of Dostoevsky, down the fascinating Nevsky Prospekt or along the Neva, where the spectacular northern lights bathe the city and canals in a magnificent pastel hue. The city is truly one of the most extraordinary and breathtaking in the world.

The people of Leningrad are quite proud of their city and their past. Many still refer to the city affectionately as Petersburg. A Vagonova-trained ballerina, when asked to describe Leningrad, answered, "Leningrad is everything that Moscow is not. Even though Leningrad is the second largest city in the Soviet Union with five million people, we don't look at ourselves as being second. We have our very own character and purpose that are often quite different from the rest of the country. Leningrad is a very special city, representing the spirit of Russia in so many ways—a spirit that is regally European, patriotically Russian and religiously eternal. Leningrad is mysterious, romantic and willfull. Everyone falls in love with Leningrad. I could never live anywhere else." One man's dream created the city. Another's words immortalized her:

"Be beautiful, city of Peter
Stay as unshakable as Russia
And let no vain wrath
Ever trouble the eternal dream of Peter."
                                    –Pushkin

Orientation

Before sightseeing, look at a map and familiarize yourself with Leningrad. Once you know the general layout of the city, it's not difficult to find your way around by walking, or taking the bus, boat or Metro. Leningrad is 400 miles (640 km) north of Moscow on the same longitude as Helsinki, Finland, and Anchorage, Alaska. The city is separated by the Neva River, which begins at Lake Ladoga and empties 46 miles (74 km) later into the Gulf of Finland. At the tip of Vasilyevsky Island, it splits into the Bolshaya (Big) and the Malaya (Little) Neva. The right bank of the Neva is known as the Petrogradskaya side (originally known as Birch Island), which includes the Zayachy, Petrogradsky, Aptekarsky and Petrovsky islands. The Kirovsky

Islands lie farther to the north. Many of the main points of interest are found on the left bank of the Neva.

Leningrad was originally spread out over 101 islands; today, because of redevelopment, there are 44 islands, connected by 620 bridges linking over 100 waterways and canals that make up one-sixth of the area of the city. Leningrad is a treasure house of activity with over 50 museums, 20 theaters and concert halls, 60 stadiums and 2,500 libraries. The whole area, a museum of architecture, has some 200 palaces and historical landmarks. As a main port, over 5,000 ships dock here annually. Residents are proud of Leningrad; each parent gets a medallion for their newborn baby with the inscribed words, "Born in Leningrad."

SIGHTS

PETER AND PAUL FORTRESS

The origins of the city are traced to the Peter and Paul Fortress, Petropavlovskaya Krepost. Peter the Great was attracted to Zayachy Ostrov (Hare Island), situated between the right bank of the Neva and the Kronverk Strait, because of its small size and strategic position in the area. On 16 May 1703, the first foundation stone of the fortress, named after the apostles Peter and Paul, was laid by Peter himself. The fortress was designed to protect the city from the invading Swedes, and was built as an elongated hexagon with six bastions that traced the contours of the island. Over 20,000 workers were commissioned and, within only six months, the earthern ramparts were set in place. Work continued on the fortress, replacing the wooden buildings with brick and stone until its completion in 1725. The new walls were over 36 feet (12 meters) thick and 300 guns were installed. Soon after its completion, the fortress lost its military significance, and over the next 200 years it served instead as a political prison. In 1922, the fortress was opened as a museum. It's open from 11 a.m. to 6 p;.m. (till 5 on Tues.), closed on Wednesday.

Ironically, the first prisoner was Peter's son, Alexcei, suspected of plotting against the czar. Peter supervised his son's torture and Alexcei died here in 1718. (Alexcei was buried by Peter beneath the staircase of the cathedral, so he would always be "trampled.") The history of the fortress is also closely connected with revolutionary movements. Catherine the Great locked up Alexander Radishchev, who criticized the autocracy and feudal system in his book *Voyages from St. Petersburg to Moscow*. Later, in 1825, the Decembrists were placed in the Alexeyevsky Bastion, a special block for important prisoners. Five were executed on July 13, 1826, and hundreds of others were sentenced to hard labor in Siberia. Members of the Petrashevsky political movement, including Dostoevsky, were sent here in 1849, and sentenced to death. Only at the last minute did Nicholas I revoke the sentence. Nikolai Chernyshevsky wrote his influential novel, *What is To Be Done?* while imprisoned here for two years in 1862. In the 1880s, many members of the Narodnaya Volya (Peoples Freedom Group) were placed in solitary-confinement cells of the Trubetskoi Bastion. In 1887, five prisoners were executed for the attempt on the life of Alexander III, including Lenin's brother, Alexander Ulyanov. The writer Maxim Gorky was incarcerated for writing revolutionary leaflets. During the October 1917 Revolution, when the fortress's last stronghold was captured by the Bolsheviks and the political prisoners set free, a red lantern was hung in the Naryshkin Bastion, signaling the battleship *Aurora* to fire the first shot of the Revolution. Every day from the Naryshkin Bastion a blank cannon shot is fired at noon. This tradition actually began in the 18th century to let the townspeople know the time. The nearest Metro stop to the fortress is Gorkovskaya.

The Cathedral

The visitor's entrance to the fortress is at St. John's Gate, on the east side of the island not far from Kirov Prospekt. After crossing St. John's Bridge, you come to **St. Peter's Gate** (1718), the main entrance and oldest unchanged structure of the fort. Hanging over the archway is a double-headed eagle, the emblem of the Russian Empire, along with bas-reliefs of the Apostle Peter. The carver, Konrad Osner, gave the Apostle the features of the czar. Beyond the gate is His

Majesty's Bastion, used as a dungeon for Peter's prisoners.

A straight path leads to **St. Peter and Paul Cathedral,** built between 1712 and 1732 in the Dutch style by the architect Trezzini. Peter the Great laid the cornerstone. The cathedral, with its long slender golden spire topped with an angel holding a cross, is the focal point of the square. The belfry used to be the tallest structure in the whole country. (Today the TV tower is the tallest structure in Leningrad.) The tower clock plays the national anthem "Internationale" four times a day and the clock chimes every quarter hour.

Inside, the gilded wooden iconostasis was carved in 1722-26 and holds 43 icons. The cathedral is the burial place for over 30 czars and princes, including every czar from Peter I to Alexander III (except for Peter II). The sarcophagi of Alexander II and his wife took 17 years to carve from Altai jasper and Ural red quartz. Peter the Great himself chose his resting place to the right of the altar.

Boat House And Mint

Outside again, with your back facing the cathedral entrance, on the right is a small pavilion with a statue of the Goddess of Navigation. The **Boat House** was built by Peter the Great in 1761 to store a small boat that he sailed as a child. Today, this "Grandfather of the Russian Fleet" is on display at the Central Naval Museum at no. 4 Pushkin Square on Vasilyevsky Island.

Directly in front of the cathedral is the yellow-white building of the **Royal Mint** (1800-06). In 1724, Peter the Great transferred the mint from Moscow to St. Petersburg. The first lever press in the world was used here in 1811. The mint still produces special coins, medals and badges. Beyond the mint are the Alexeyevsky, Zatov and Trubetskoi bastions, where many of the revolutionaries were imprisoned. The latter houses an exhibit which traces the history of prisoners who stayed in the cells.

Museums

As you leave the Cathedral, on the left side is the stone Commandant's Building, built as the commander's headquarters and the interrogation center for prisoners. It now houses the **Museum of History of Petersburg and Petrograd from**

> "The poet has long immortalized the Neva,
> The pages of Gogol are steeped in Nevsky
> Onegin was inspired by the Summer Gardens,
> Blok was enraptured by the city's islands
> But along Razyezhaya Street roamed
>   Dostoevsky."
>
>   *–Samuel Marshak*

1703 to 1917. Next door, the old Engineer's House is now the **Architectural Museum of St. Petersburg,** displaying many original drawings and drafts of the city. Both are closed on Wednesday. Behind these stands the Neva Gate, once known as the "Gate of Death," because prisoners were led through it to the execution spot. Now it leads to the beach area (with a spectacular view of the city) that is quite crowded in summer with sunbathers. The Walrus Club gathers here in winter to swim between the ice floes in the Neva!

ACROSS THE KRONVERK STRAIT

Exiting the fortress by way of St. John's Bridge takes you back to Kirov Prospect. To the right is the **Kirov Bridge,** with a splendid view of the fortress. A short walk down Kirov Prospect, to the left, leads to Metro stop, Gorkovskaya. The small path to the left of St. John's Bridge circles around the Kronverk Strait. This path leads to a monument; a small obelisk, to the Decembrist revolutionaries, standing on the spot where Nicholas I executed the five leaders of the 1825 uprising. A witness account described the execution: "The hangmen made them stand on a bench and put white canvas hoods over their heads. Then the bench was knocked from under their feet. Three men whose ropes had broken fell on the rough boards of the scaffold, bruising themselves. One broke his leg. According to custom, in such circumstances, the execution had to be canceled. But in an hour, new ropes were brought and the execution carried through."

Past the obelisk, on the right, is a large building that was once the artillery arsenal. Today it's the **Kronverk Artillery, Engineers and Signals Museum,** first formed by Peter the Great to display the history of Russian weaponry. It's open 11 a.m. to 6 p.m., closed Mon. and Tuesday.

Behind the museum is Lenin Park, stretching from the Strait to Maxim Gorky St., where the writer lived at no. 23 from 1914 to 1921. Inside the park are the zoo, with over 1,000 animals, and the planetarium. By the planetarium are the Lenin Komsomol Theater and the 3-D and first widescreen Velikan (Vulcan) cinema, opened in 1956, seating 2,000.

Sergei Kirov (1886-1934), regional head of the Leningrad Party before he was murdered, lived at no. 26 Kirov Prospect, not far from Leo Tolstoy Square. The house is now a museum, open 11 to 7, Thurs. 2-7, Sun. 10 to 5, closed Wednesday. At no. 10 Kirov is Lenfilm Studios, founded in 1918.

Revolution Square

Crossing Kirov Prospekt and walking east along the Neva (in the opposite direction of the fortress), you come to Revolution Square, formerly Trinity Square, where many of the first buildings of the city once stood. These included the Senate, Custom House and Troitsky Cathedral, where Peter was crowned emperor in 1721. Today the square is a large garden. The **Museum of the October Revolution,** located at the northern end of the square at no. 4 Kuibishev, is in a mansion (1902) that belonged to the ballerina Matilda Kshesinskaya, the mistress of Nicholas II before he married. It's open daily 10 to 6, closed Thursday.

Peter's Cottage

Continuing along Petrovskaya Embankment, you pass the two-ton granite figures of Shih-Tze, brought from Manchuria in 1907, poised on the steps by the Neva. In China, these sculptures, a cross between a lion and a frog, guarded the entrances to palaces. Behind them is the **Cottage of Peter the Great,** one of the oldest surviving buildings of the city. It was constructed in a mere three days in May 1703, out of pine logs painted to look like bricks. One room was a study and reception area and the other was used as a dining room and bedroom. The largest door was five-feet nine-inches high—Peter stood at six feet seven! From here Peter directed the building of his fortress—with no stoves or chimneys, since Peter lived in the cottage only in summer. Once his summer palace was completed, Peter stopped living here altogether. In 1784, Catherine the Great encased the tiny house in stone to protect it. The cottage is now a museum, displaying his furniture, utensils and small boat, which Peter supposedly built and used to rescue fisherman on Lake Ladoga in 1690. A bronze bust of Peter is in the garden. The cottage is open daily 10 to 6, closed Tues. and from 11 Nov. to 30 April.

The *Aurora*

The beautiful blue building of the **Nakhimov Naval School** is a short walk farther east, where young boys learn to carry on the traditions of the Russian fleet. The battleship *Aurora* is anchored in front of it. The cruiser originally fought during the Sino-Soviet War (1904-05). In October 1917, the sailors mutinied and joined in the Bolshevik Revolution. On the evening of October 24, following the orders of Lenin and the Military Revolutionary Committee, the *Aurora* sailed up the Neva and at 9:45 p.m. fired a blank shot to signal the storming of the Winter Palace. In 1948, it was moored by

the Aurora *with crew on deck*

the Navy School and later opened as a museum. Various displays include the gun that fired the legendary shot, and the radio room where Lenin announced the overthrow of the provisional government to the citizens of Petrograd. The battleship is open 10:30 to 4:30, closed Mon. and Friday. In front of the *Aurora* are a number of kiosks, one an American-Soviet joint venture that sells souvenirs and food items for foreign currency.

The **Leningrad Hotel** can be reached by crossing the bridge over the Bolshaya Neva. Here you can have a quick coffee, buffet lunch or dinner (for rubles) at the cafeteria-type restaurant on the ground floor.

KIROV ISLANDS

The northernmost islands on the Petrogradskaya side of the Neva (the right bank), the Kirov, are made up of a number of small islands: the Krestovsky, Yelagin and Workers (formerly Stone). Stone Island Bridge leads from the end of Kirov Prospekt to Workers Island, a popular summer resort area in the days of Peter. Paul I erected the beautiful yellow Stone Island Palace on the eastern part of the island. Today it's filled with holiday centers and sanitoriums. Yelagin Island was owned in the late 18th century by a wealthy aristocrat of the same name. A century later, it became the summer residence of the czars. In 1822, Carlo Rossi built the elegant Yelagin Palace for Alexander I. The Kirov Recreation Park now takes up most of the island, where festive carnivals are held during the White Nights.

The largest island in the group, Krestovsky, houses two stadiums, the Dynamo and the 80,000-seat Kirov. At the end of the island is a Buddhist temple, designed by a Tibetan monk. Nearby is the place where Alexander Pushkin fought his duel; a small obelisk marks the spot where he was mortally wounded. The main attraction is Victory Park (built in 1945 after WW II), with artificial lakes and swimming pools. Leningrad poet Anna Akhmatova wrote: "Early in the morning, the people of Leningrad went out. In huge crowds to the seashore, and each of them planted a tree up on that strip of land, marshy, deserted. In Memory of that Great Victory Day." The Metro line Moskovsko-Petrogradskaya runs out in this direction, beginning with the stop Petrogradskaya.

THE STRELKA OF VASILYEVSKY ISLAND

History

Vasilyevsky is the largest island in the Neva Delta, encompassing over 4,000 acres. At the eastern tip of the island, known as the Strelka (arrow or spit of land), the Neva is at its widest and branches into the two channels of the Bolshaya and Malaya Neva. The Palace and Workers bridges span the Bolshaya Neva to the left bank and the Malaya to the Petrogradskaya side. At first Peter chose to build his future city, modeled after Venice, on Vasilevsky Island. But when both sides of the Neva froze over in winter, the island was cut off from the rest of Russia. Even in summer, some parts of the island were very remote. By the mid-18th century, it was decided to develop the administrative and cultural centers instead on the left bank of the Neva. However, many of the original canals are still present on the island, whose streets are laid out as numbered lines (where canals were planned) and crossed by three major *prospekts*.

After Peter and Paul Fortress was completed, vessels docked along the Strelka. The Exchange Hall was the first wooden building on the Strelka, where merchants and visiting tradesmen gathered. By the end of the century, a stone building was erected to house the new Stock Exchange. Thousands of piles were driven into the riverbed to serve as the foundation for a granite embankment with steps leading to the Neva flanked on each side by two large stone globes. This area served as the main port of the city from 1733 to 1855, before it was switched to the lower left bank of the Neva. Designed by architect Thomas de Thomon, the Stock Exchange, with 44 white Doric columns and the sea-god Neptune in a chariot harnessed to sea horses over the main entrance, took five years to complete. This building, at no. 4 Pushkin Square, now serves as the **Central Navy Museum,** open 10:30 to 5, closed Mon. and Tues.). Peter originally opened this museum in the Admiralty in 1709 to store models and blueprints of Russian ships. His collection numbered over 1,500 models and the museum contains a half-million items on the history of the Russian fleet.

Pushkin Square

Pushkin Square lies in front of the Exchange. The dark red **Rostral Columns**, 96 feet (32 meters) high, stand on either side of the square. These were also built by de Thomon from 1805 to 1810. The Romans erected columns adorned with the prows of enemy ships, or *rostres,* after naval victories. These rostral columns are decorated with figures symbolizing the victories of the Russian fleet. Around the base of the columns are four allegorical figures, representing the Neva, Volga, Dnieper and Volkhov rivers. The columns also acted as a lighthouse; at dusk hemp oil was lit in the bronze bowls at the top. Nowadays, gas torches are used, but only during festivals. This area is one of the most beautiful spots in all of Leningrad, offering a large panoramic view of the city. Imagine the days when the whole area was filled with ships and sailboats. The Frenchman Alexandre Dumas was quite captivated with the area on his first visit over a century ago: "I really don't know whether there is any view in the whole world which can be compared with the panorama which unfolded before my eyes."

Two gray-green warehouses, built between 1826 and 1832, stand on either side of the Exchange. The northern warehouse is now the **Central Soil Science Museum** and the southern the **Zoological Institute and Museum** (both open 11 to 5 and closed Fri. and Sat.) which has a collection of over 40,000 animal species, including a 44,000 year-old stuffed mammoth.

The eight-columed **Customs House** (1829-32) along the embankment of the Malaya Neva is topped with mounted copper statues of Mercury (Commerce), Neptune (Navigation) and Ceres (Fertility). The cupola was used as an observation point to signal arriving trade ships. It is now the **Museum of Russian Literature,** generally known as the Pushkin House. In 1905, the museum purchased Pushkin's library. Other rooms contain exhibits devoted to famous Russian writers such as Lermontov, Gogol, Chekhov, Dostoevsky, Gorky, Blok, Turgenev and Tolstoy. Check before you visit the museum for it closes now and then for restorative work.

University Embankment

The light green and white **Kunstkammer** (1718-34), with its distinctive domed tower, is located at the beginning of Universitetskaya Naberezhnaya, the University Embankment, which extends west along the Bolshaya Neva. Nearly every building in this district is a monument of 18th-century architecture. Kunstkammer, stemming from the German words *kunst* (art) and *kammer* (chamber), was the first Russian museum open to the public. Legend has that Peter the Great, while walking along the embankment, noticed two pine trees, entwined around each other's trunks. The czar decided to cut down the trees and build a museum on the spot to house "rarities, curiosities and monsters." The tree was also in the museum. In order to attract visitors, admission was free and a glass

Peter the Great's Kunstkammer

of vodka was offered at the entrance. The building became known as the "cradle of Russian science" and was the seat of the Academy of Sciences, founded by Peter in 1724. The famed scientist, Mikhail Lomonosov, worked here from 1741 to 1765. Today the Kunstkammer is made up of the **Ethnographical Institute and Peter the Great Museum** and the **Museum of Mikhail Lomonosov.** In the museum's tower (at the top of the building), the first Russian astronomical observatory was installed. The large globe (nine feet/three meters in diameter) had a model of the heavens in its interior. Twelve people could fit inside, where a mechanism was regulated to create the motion of the night sky, a forerunner of the planetarium. Soon the Kunstkammer became too small and a new building was constructed next to it for the Academy of Sciences by the architect Giacomo Quarenghi from 1783 to 1788. A statue of Mikhail Lomonosov stands outside the Academy. The museums are open 11 to 5 and closed on Fri. and Saturday.

Peter commissioned the architect Trezzini to build the Twelve Collegiums (1722-42) next to the Kunstkammer (along Mendeleyev Street) for his future Senate and Ministries. After 1819, it became part of Petersburg University. Many prominent writers and scholars studied here; Lenin passed his bar examinations and received a degree in law. Some of the teachers were the renowned scientists Popov and Pavlov, and Dmitri Mendeleyev (Periodic Law and Tables) worked here for 25 years; the apartment where he lived is now a museum. The red and white buildings are now part of Leningrad University, which has more than 20,000 students. Higher education is free in the USSR and most students receive a state stipend.

Palace, Academy, And Pink Sphinxes
Adjacent to the University at no. 15 is the yellow baroque-style **Menshikov Palace.** Menshikov was the first governor of Petersburg. Peter the Great presented his close friend with the whole of Vasilyevsky Island in 1707. This palace of Prince Alexander Menshikov, built between 1710 and 1714, was the first stone and residential structure on the island. It was the most luxurious building in Petersburg and known as the Embassadorial Palace. After the death of Peter the Great, the building was given to the First Cadet Corps as

their Military College. The restored palace is now part of the Hermitage Museum and exhibits collections of 18th-century Russian culture. A granite obelisk, commemorating the victory of Russian troops in the Russo-Turkish War of 1768-74, stands in the garden.

The next building along the embankment, at no. 17, is the **Academy of Arts** (1764-88), adorned by the statues of Hercules and Flora and reliefs of palettes and brushes. The former Academy of the Three Most Noble Arts (painting, sculpture and architecture) was founded in 1857 and many of Russia's renowned artists and architects studied here. It's now a museum that depicts the history of Russian art and architecture; open 9:15 to 6, closed Mon. and Tuesday. The largest art school in the world is also here, the Repin Institute of Painting, Sculpture and Architecture.

In front of the Academy, two pink granite **Egyptian sphinxes** flank the stairway leading down to the water. These 3,000-year old statues were discovered in the early 19th century during an archaeological excavation on the site of ancient Thebes. A Russian diplomat had the government purchase them at an auction in Alexandria; they were sent to Petersburg in 1834. The hieroglyphics mention the Pharaoh Amenhotep III (1417-1379 B.C.), whose likeness they are thought to portray.

Beyond The Strelka
The Lieutenant Schmidt Bridge (a hero of the 1905 Revolution) separates the University Embankment from the Lieutenant Schmidt Embankment. The former Annunciation and Nikolaevsky Bridge (1842-50) was the first permanent bridge across the Neva and is the last bridge crossing the Neva before it flows into the Gulf of Finland. During the White Nights season, it's quite lovely to watch the bridges of the city open at 2 a.m. from this vantage point. The Kirov Cultural Palace is also found here. The rest of the island is largely residential and industrial. The Metro stop closest to the Strelka is Vasiloevstrovkaya.

The Pribaltiiskaya Hotel is at the western end of the island, not far from Metro stop Primorskaya (Maritime). After shopping in the large *beriozka,* watch a sunset over the Gulf from the embankment behind the hotel. A few minutes down the road from the hotel is the International Seaman's Club, near the Morskaya Vokzal (Marine Terminal), where most cruiseboats dock. The Olympia Ship, a Swedish hotel and restaurant, offers good meals for foreign currency. Marine Glory Square is in front with permanent glass pavilions that house international exhibitions. Dekabristov (Decembrist) Island lies farther to the north.

For the next 200 miles (320 km), this section of the Gulf of Finland off of Vasilyevsky Island is known as Cyclone Road. West to east-traveling cyclones create what is known as the "long wave." Originating in the Gulf during severe storms, it then rolls toward Leningrad. Propelled by high winds, it enters into the narrow banks of the Neva with the speed of a freight train. The city has experienced over 300 floods in its 300-year history. An 18-mile (29-km) barrier has been built across a section of the gulf to control the flooding. Much controversy surrounds the barrier, since many scientists believe that it's changing the ecological balance of the area.

THE PALACE SQUARE

History

Palace Square was the heart of Russia for over two centuries and is one of the most striking architectural ensembles in the world. It was not only the parade ground for the czar's Winter Palace, but a symbol of the revolutionary struggle as well. The square was, in fact, the site of three revolutions: The Decembrists first held an uprising near here in 1825. On Sunday, 9 Jan. 1905, over a 100,000 people marched to Palace Square to protest intolerable working conditions. The demonstration began peacefully as the families carried icons and pictures of the czar. But Nicholas II's troops opened fire on the crowd, and hundreds were killed in the event known as Bloody Sunday. After the massacre, massive strikes ensued. In October of the same year, the Petersburg Soviet of Workers Deputies was formed. Twelve years later, in February 1917, the Kerensky government overthrew the autocracy and in October, the Red Guards stormed through Palace Square to capture the Winter Palace from the provisional government.

In 1819, Carlo Rossi was commissioned to design the square. The government bought up all the residential houses and reconstructed the area into the Ministries of Foreign Affairs and Finance, and the General Staff Headquarters of the Russian army. These two large yellow buildings curve around the southern end of the square and are linked by the **Triumphal Arch** (actually two arches), whose themes of soldiers and armor commemorate the victories of the War of 1812. It's crowned by the 16-ton *Winged Glory* in a chariot led by six horses, which everyone believed would collapse the arch. On opening day, Rossi declared: "If it should fall, I will fall with it." He climbed to the top of the arch as the scaffolding was removed.

Alexander Column

As you enter Palace Square from Herzen Street, an unforgettable panorama unfolds of the palace and square. The Alexander Column stands in the middle of the square, symbolizing the defeat of Napoleon in 1812. Nicholas I had it erected in memory of Alexander I. The 700-ton piece of granite took three years to be extracted from the Karelian Isthmus and brought down by a system of barges to the city. Architect Auguste Montferrand supervised the polishing in 1830, and by 1834, the 143-foot-high (47.5-meter) column was erected by 2,500 men using an elaborate system of pulleys. The statue of the angel (whose face resembles Alexander I) holding a cross was carved by sculptor Boris Orlovsky. The Guard's Headquarters (to the right of the column facing the palace) was built by Bryullov (1837-43) and now serves as an administrative building.

Winter Palace

The main architectural wonder of the square is the Winter Palace, standing along the banks of the Neva. This masterpiece by Rastrelli was commissioned by the Czarina Elizabeth, daughter of Peter who, fond of the baroque style, desired a lavish palace decorated with columns, stucco and sculptures. It was built from 1754 to 1762, as Rastrelli remarked, "solely for the glory of all Russia." The palace remained the czars' official residence until the February 1917 Revolution. The magnificent palace extends over 20 acres and the total perimeter measures over a mile (two km)! There are 1,057 rooms (not one identical), 1,945 windows, 1,886 doors and 117 staircases. The royal family's staff consisted of over 1,000 servants. At 600 feet (200 meters) long and 66 feet (22 meters) high, it was the largest building in all of Petersburg. After the 1837 fire destroyed a major portion of the palace, architects Bryullov and Stasov restored the interior along the lines of Russian classicism, but preserved Rastrelli's light and graceful baroque exterior. The blue-green walls are adorned with 176 sculpted figures. The interior was finished with marble, malachite, jasper, semiprecious stones, polished woods, gilded moldings and crystal chandeliers. In 1844, Nicholas I passed a decree (in force until 1905) stating that all buildings in the city (except churches) had to be at least six feet (two meters) lower than the Winter Palace. During WW II, the Winter Palace was marked on German maps as "Bombing Objective no. 9." Today the Winter Palace houses the State Hermitage Museum.

The Hermitage Museum

Largest museum in the Soviet Union, the State Hermitage houses close to 2.8 million exhibited items, seen by more than three million people annually. It contains one of the largest and most valuable collections of art in the world, dating from antiquity to the present.

Peter the Great began the city's first art collection after visiting Europe. In 1719, Peter I purchased Rembrandt's David's *Farewell to Jonathan*, a statue of Aphrodite (Venus of Taurida), and started a museum of Russian antiquities (now on display in the Hermitage's Siberian collection).

In 1764, Catherine the Great created the Hermitage (a French word meaning "secluded spot")

in the Winter Palace for a place to house 225 Dutch and Flemish paintings she'd purchased in Berlin. Her ambassadors were often sent to European countries in search of art; in 1769, she purchased the entire collection of Count de Bruhl of Dresden for 180,000 rubles. The Hermitage numbered almost 4,000 paintings at the time of her death. Subsequent czars continued to expand the collection: Alexander I bought the entire picture gallery of Josephine, wife of Napoleon, and Nicholas I even purchased pictures from Napoleon's stepdaughter. Until 1852, the Hermitage was only open to members of the royal family and aristocratic friends. Catherine the Great wrote in a letter to one of her close friends that "all this is admired by mice and myself." A small list of rules, written by Catherine, hung by the Hermitage's entrance: "Make merry, but do not spoil, break or gnaw anything. Eat with pleasure, but drink with measure, so you will be able to find your feet when you go out the door." In 1852, Nicholas I opened the Hermitage on certain days as a public museum (but still closed to common people), and put it under the administrative direction of curators. After the 1917 Revolution, the Hermitage was opened full-time to the whole public.

The Hermitage occupies several other buildings in addition to the Winter Palace. The **Little Hermitage** housed Catherine's original collection in a small building next to the Palace; it was constructed by Vallin de la Mothe in 1764-67. Stakenschneider's Pavilion Hall is decked with white mar-

the Hermitage

ble columns, 28 chandeliers, the four "Fountains of Tears" and the Peacock Clock. The royal family would stroll in the "hanging gardens," along with peasants and peacocks, in the summer. In winter, snow mounds were built for sledding. The **Old Hermitage** (or Large Hermitage) was built right next to it to provide space for Catherine's growing collections. The **Hermitage Theater,** Catherine's private theater, is linked with the Old Hermitage by a small bridge that spreads across the Winter Ditch canal. The theater was built by Quarenghi in 1787 and modeled after the amphitheaters of Pompei. The **New Hermitage** (1839-52), located behind the Old Hermitage, houses additional works of art. Its main entrance off Khalturina Street is composed of the 10 large and powerful statues of Atlas. They were carved by Terebenyer from blocks of granite.

The Hermitage collections span a millennia of art and culture. It's said that if a visitor spent only a half minute at each exhibit, it would take nine years to view them all! A map of the layout can be purchased inside, from which you can select places of interest. Particularly impressive are the Ambassadorial Staircase (at the Neva entrance), Gallery of the War of 1812, the Royal Suites, Throne Room of Peter the Great, Golden Room, Vatican Room, Malachite Room and Hall of St. George. Where the Imperial Throne once stood in St. George Hall now hangs an enormous mosaic map of the Soviet Union covered with 45,000 semiprecious stones. Moscow is marked by a ruby star and Leningrad is written in letters of alexandrite. The 19-ton Kolyvan Vase was made from Altai jasper and took 14 years to carve. An entire wall in the Hermitage was knocked down to bring it inside.

Other exhibits delineate the history of Russian culture on the first floor; primeval art (over 400,000 objects) is covered on the ground floor; Oriental art and culture (a quarter-million pieces) from Egypt, Babylon, Byzantium, Middle East, Japan, China and India occupy the second and ground floors; antique culture and art from Greece, Italy and Rome are also on the ground floor. Over 650,000 items in the collection of the art of Western Europe are found on the first and second floors. This includes paintings by da Vinci, Raphael, Titian, El Greco, Rubens, Rembrandt, and a fine impressionist collection by Monet, Lautrec and Van Gogh along with several of Pi-

casso's works. In addition are numerous displays of sculpture, tapestries, china, jewelry, furniture, rare coins and handicrafts. A recommended book to buy at the Hermitage store is *Saved for Humanity,* tracing the history of the museum (with pictures and available in English, German and Russian). The museum is open from 10:30 a.m. to 5 p.m., Thurs. noon-8 p.m., closed Monday. Entrance tickets are sold at kiosks outside the Winter Palace. Or book a tour through the Intourist desk at your hotel.

Pushkin-House Museum

Leaving the Hermitage through Palace Square to the left and past the Guards Headquarters brings you through the Choristers Passage and across a wide bridge known as Pevchesky Most (Singers Bridge). This bridge crosses the lovely Moika Canal and leads to the former Imperial Choristers Capella (1831), now the Glinka Academy Capella. At no. 12 Moika, to the left of the Capella, is the Pushkin-House Museum, where the poet lived from October 1836 until his death in January, 1837. A statue of Pushkin stands in the courtyard. The rooms have all been preserved and contain his personal belongings and manuscripts. The study is arranged in the exact order it was left after Pushkin died on the divan from a wound he received in a duel. Even the clock is set to the moment of his death, 2:45 a.m. The next room displays the clothes worn during the duel and his death mask. Since Pushkin is still one of the most popular figures in the USSR, museum tickets are often sold out; it may be necessary to buy them a few days in advance. The museum is open 10:30 to 6:30, Thurs. noon-8, closed Tuesday.

THE AREA OF DECEMBRISTS' SQUARE

Admiralty

Walking west of the Winter Palace along the Neva, you come to another chief architectural monument of the city, the Admiralty, recognizable by its long golden spire, topped by a golden frigate, the symbol of Leningrad. The best views of the building are from its southern end. A beautiful fountain stands in the middle of Maxim Gorky Garden surrounded by busts of Glinka, Gogol and Lermontov. In 1704, Peter the Great ordered a

> "In my chamber
> I write or sit a book perusing
> Whilst, luminous, the streets lie dozing
> Beyond, great, empty blocks . . . up higher,
> Against a dark sky, the Admiralty spire is clearly etched."
>
> —Pushkin

second small outpost constructed on the left bank of the Neva and opposite the main part of town. This shipyard was later referred to as the Admiralty. Over 10,000 peasants and engineers were employed to work on the Russian naval fleet. By the end of the 18th century, the navy had its headquarters here. Whenever the Neva waters rose during a severe storm, a lantern was lit in the spire to warn of coming floods. In 1738, the main building was rebuilt by the architect Ivan Korobov, who replaced the wooden tower with a golden spire. From 1806 to 1823, the building was again redesigned by Zakharov, an architectural professor at the Petersburg Academy. The spire was heightened to 218 feet (72.5 meters) and decorated with 56 mythological figures and 350 ornamentations based on the glory of the Russian fleet. The scene over the main entrance archway depicts Neptune handing over his trident to Peter the Great, a symbol of Peter's mastery of the sea. In 1860, many of the statues were taken down when the Orthodox Church demanded the "pagan" statues removed. Today the Admiralty houses the Dzerzhinsky Naval School.

Across the street from the Admiralty at no. 6 Admiralty Avenue is the building known as the All Russia Extraordinary Commission for Struggle Against Counter-Revolution and Sabotage, the Cheka. Felix Dzerzhinsky, the first chairman of the Cheka Police Force (forerunner of the KGB) had his office here. His best-remembered words were that a member of the Cheka "must have clean hands, a warm heart and a cold head." A memorial museum, dedicated to Dzerzhinsky, has been here since 1974.

Decembrists' Square

Next to the Admiralty, situated right along the Neva, is the infamous Decembrists' Square, formerly known as Senate and Peter Square. In 1925, to mark the 100-year anniversary of the De-

cembrist uprising, the area was renamed Decembrists' Square. After the Russian victory in the "Patriotic War of 1812" and the introduction of principles from the French Enlightenment, both the nobility and peasants wanted an end to the monarchy and serfdom. An opportune moment for insurrection came on 19 Nov. 1825, when Czar Alexander I suddenly died. A secret revolutionary society, consisting mainly of noblemen, gathered over 3,000 soldiers and sailors who refused to swear allegiance to the new czar, Nicholas I. The members compiled the "Manifesto to the Russian People," which they hoped the Senate would approve. (What they didn't know was that the Senate had already proclaimed their loyalty to Nicholas.) They decided to lead an uprising of the people in Senate Square on 14 Dec. 1825 and from there to capture the Winter Palace and Peter and Paul Fortress. But Nicholas I found out about the plan and surrounded the square with armed guards. The Decembrists marched to an empty Senate and, moreover, Prince Trubetskoi, who was elected to lead the insurrection, never showed up! Tens of thousands of people joined the march and prevented the guards from advancing on the main parties. But Nicholas I then ordered his guards to open direct fire on the crowd. Hundreds were killed and mass arrests followed. Over 100 people were sentenced to serve 30 years in penal servitude. Five leaders of the rebellion were hanged in Peter and Paul Fortress. Others received such sentences as having to run a gauntlet of a thousand soldiers 12 times, amounting to 12,000 blows by rod. Even though the 1825 revolution was unsuccessful, "the roar of cannon on Senate Square awakened a whole generation," observed the revolutionary writer, Alexander Herzen.

In 1768, Catherine the Great commissioned the sculptor Étienne Falconet to build a monument to Peter the Great. For 12 years, Falconet worked "to create an alive, vibrant and passionate spirit." He successfully designed a rider on a rearing horse, crushing a serpent under its feet—just as Peter reared Petersburg. Instead of a molded pedestal, Falconet wanted to place his monument atop natural stone. A suitable rock was found about six miles (10 km) from the city. It had been split by lightning and was known as Thunder Rock. Peter the Great was said to have often climbed the rock to view his emerging city. With the help of levers, the 1,600-ton rock was raised on a platform of logs and rolled to the sea on a system of copper balls; it took a year to get it to Petersburg. The rock bears the outlines of crashing waves. Marie Collot, Falconet's pupil and future wife, sculpted the head, and the Russian sculptor Gordeyev the snake. The bronze inscription on the base, written in Russian and Latin, reads: "To Peter I from Catherine II, 1782," the date the monument was unveiled. The monument to Peter came to be known as The Bronze Horseman, after the popular poem by Pushkin.

The nearby yellow-white buildings linked by an arch were built in the 1830s by Carlo Rossi. This ensemble was used as the Senate, Supreme Court and Holy Synod before the Revolution. Today they house the State Historical Archives. Take a stroll down the small Krasnaya Ulitsa, which lies beyond the arch; this was the area of the galley shipyards. The two Ionic columns, standing at the start of the next boulevard, bear the goddesses of Glory. These monuments commemorate the valor of Russia's Horse Guards during the war against Napoleon. The building that looks like an ancient Roman temple is the Horse Guard Manège where the czar's horse guards were trained. Today it's used as an exhibit hall for the Union of Artists.

ST. ISAAC'S SQUARE

The Cathedral

The whole southern end of Decembrists' Square is framed by the grand silhouette of **St. Isaac's Cathedral**. In 1710, the first wooden church of St. Isaac was built by Peter, who was born on the day which celebrated the sainthood of Isaac of Dalmatia; it was replaced in 1729 by one of stone. At that time, the church was situated nearer to the banks of the Neva, and it eventually began to crack and sink. It was decided in 1768 to build another church farther away from the riverbank. But at its completion in 1802, the church was not deemed grand enough for the growing magnificence of the capital. After the War of 1812, Czar Alexander I announced a competition for the best design of a new St. Isaac's. The young architect Montferrand presented an elaborate album filled with 24 different variations, from Chinese to Gothic, for the czar to choose from. Montferrand was selected for the monumental task in 1818, and the czar also as-

signed the architects Stasov, Rossi and the Mikhailov brothers to help with the engineering.

The cathedral took 40 years to build. In the first year alone, 11,000 serfs drove 25,000 wooden planks into the soft soil to set a foundation. Each of the 112 polished granite columns, weighing 130 tons, had to be raised by a system of pulleys. The system was so perfected that the monolithic columns were eventually installed in a mere 45 minutes. The entire building weighs over 300,000 tons. The three domes give the cathedral a total height of 305 feet (101.5 meters). An observation deck along the upper colonnade (562 steps to climb) provides a magnificent view of the city. The state spared no expense—the cathedral cost 10 times more than the Winter Palace. Nearly 100 kilos of pure gold were used to gild the dome, which, in good weather, is visible 25 miles (40 km) away. The interior is faced with 14 different kinds of marble, and 43 other types of stone and minerals. The Foucault pendulum swings down 279 feet (93 meters) from the dome, measuring the rotation of the Earth. Inside at the western portico is a bust of Montferrand made from each type of marble. (Montferrand died one month after the completion of the cathedral. He had asked Alexander II to be buried within the walls, but the czar refused. Instead, Montferrand was buried in Paris.) The cathedral can hold 14,000 people and is filled with over 400 sculptures, paintings and mosaics by the best Russian and European masters of the 19th century. Twenty-two artists decorated the iconostasis, ceilings and walls. The altar's huge stained-glass window is surrounded by frescoes and Bryullov painted the frescoes in the ceiling of the main dome. A Petersburg newspaper wrote that the cathedral was "a pantheon of Russian art, as artists have left monuments to their genius in it." On 29 May 1858, St. Isaac's was inaugurated with much pomp and celebration as the main cathedral of St. Petersburg. In 1931, the cathedral was opened by the government as a museum. The cathedral's museum and colonnade are open daily 11 to 6, except Wednesday.

The Square

St. Isaac's Square, in front of the cathedral, was originally a marketplace in the 1830s. At its center stands the bronze statue of Nicholas I, constructed by Montferrand and Clodt in 1856-59. The czar, who loved horses and military exploits (nick-

*Griffin's Canal,
Leningrad*

named "Nicholas the Stick"), is portrayed in a cavalry uniform wearing a helmet with an eagle. His horse rests only on two points. The bas-reliefs around the pedestal depict the events of Nicholas's turbulent rule. One of them shows Nicholas I addressing his staff after the Decembrist uprising. The four figures at each corner represent Faith, Wisdom, Justice and Might, and depict the faces of Nicholas's wife and three daughters, who commissioned the statue.

The two buildings on each side of the monument were built between 1844-53 and now house the Institutes of the Lenin Academy of Agricultural Sciences. Behind the monument is the **Blue Bridge** (1818), broadest in the city. The structure, even though it appears as a continuation of the square, is actually a bridge over the Moika River. A slave market took place here before the abolition of serfdom in 1861. It's painted blue on the sides facing the water. Many of Petersburg's bridges were named after the color they were painted; up river are the Green and Red bridges. On one side of the bridge is an obelisk crowned by a trident. Five bronze bands indicate the level of the water during the city's worst floods. The Leningrad poet Vera Inber wrote of this place:

"Here in the city, on Rastrelli's marble
Or on plain brick, we see from time to time
A mark: 'The water-level reached this line'
And we can only look at it and marvel."

House With Lions

Beyond the bridge stands the former Mariinsky Palace. It was built in 1839-44 for Maria, the daughter of Nicholas I. In 1894, it was turned into the State Council of the Russian Empire. The artist Repin painted the Centennial Gala of the Council in 1901, entitled *The Solemn Meeting of the State Council;* it can be viewed at the Russian Museum. In 1917, the palace was the residence of the provisional government. It now houses the Executive Committee of the Leningrad City Soviet of People's Deputies. The red flag, with a vertical blue stripe, flies atop the building. The gray seven-story **Astoria Hotel,** on the west side of the square, was built in 1910, one of the grandest hotels in the city. Hitler even sent out engraved invitations for a banquet to be held at the Astoria on 7 Nov. 1942, as soon as he captured the city. Of course, this never took place. The hotel has recently been remodeled and is a very popular place to stay. In front of it is the Lobanov-Rostovsky Mansion. Montferrand built this for the Russian diplomat between 1817 and 1820. Pushkin mentioned the marble lions in front of the house in the *Bronze Horseman,* when the hero climbed one of them to escape the flood. The mansion is referred to as the "House with Lions."

Others

On the other side of the square stands Myatlev's House. Built in 1760 for the poet by Rinaldi, it's one of the oldest structures on the square. Behind the house is the **Museum of Musical Instruments,** with one of the largest collections (3,000) of musical instruments in the world. Some of the items on display are the grand pianos of Rimsky-Korsakov, Glinka and Rubenstein. The museum is open Wed., Fri., and Sunday.

Also in the area check out the Intourist Building, originally built in 1910 to accommodate the German Embassy. A short walk away at no. 4 Podbelsky Street is the **Popov Central Communication Museum,** which traces the history of communications in the USSR; open noon-6, closed Monday. Nearby at no. 9 Communication Union Street is the General Post Office (1782-89), with the Clock of the World mounted on its archway. Dostoyevsky lived at no. 23 Gogol Street before his imprisonment at Peter and Paul Fortress. Here he wrote *Netochka Nezvanova* and *The White Nights.*

FIELD OF MARS

Central Lenin Museum

A short walk east from the Hermitage, along Khalturin St. (once known as Millionnaya, or Millionaire's Row), brings you to the Marble Palace. In 1785, Catherine the Great commissioned Antonio Rinaldi to build a palace for her favorite (at the time) Count Grigory Orlov. But Orlov died before its completion, and it was turned over to a grand-duke. This was the only building in Petersburg faced both inside and outside with marble, 32 different kinds. In 1937, the Marble Palace opened as the Leningrad Branch of the Central Lenin Museum (open 10:30 to 6:30, closed Wednesday). Over 10,000 exhibits in 34 rooms relate to Lenin's life and work. In Leningrad alone, over 250 places are associated with Lenin. In a small garden at the main entrance stands an armored car with the inscription, "Enemy of Capital." After the February 1917 Revolution, Lenin returned to Petersburg from exile in Europe in this armored car and, upon his arrival at the Finland Station on 3 April he delivered a speech from the turret proclaiming, "Long live the Socialist Revolution!" On 22 Feb. 1924, the Central Committee declared that "All that is truly great and heroic in the proletariat—a fearless mind, a will of iron—unbending, persistent and able to surmount all obstacles, a revolutionary passion that moves mountains, boundless faith in the creative energies of the masses—all this found splendid embodiment in Lenin, whose name has become the symbol of the new world from East to West, North to South."

The Field

Right in front of the Kirov Bridge is Suvorov Square, with the statue of the Russian general Alexander Suvorov, depicted as the God of War. The square opens to one of the most beautiful places in Leningrad, the Field of Mars. Around 1710, Peter the Great drained the marshy field and held parades after military victories. The festivities ended in fireworks (known in those times as "amusement lights"), so the square was called Poteshnoye Polye (Amusement Field). By the end of the 18th century, the area was used as a routine drill field, which destroyed the grasses; for a while the field was nicknamed the "Petersburg Sahara." When, in 1801, the monument to Field Marshal Suvorov, depicted as Mars, was placed here (it was moved to its present location in Suvorov Square in 1818), the area became known as Marsovo Polye (Field of Mars). The 30-acre (12-hectare) field is bordered on the west by the barracks of the Pavlovsky Regiment, the first among the czar's armies to take the side of the people during the February 1917 Revolution. It's now the Leningrad Energy Commission. The southern side is bordered by the Moika River and Griboyedov Canal, and the eastern by the lovely narrow Lebyazhya Kanalka (Swan Canal).

The **Memorial to the Fighters of the Revolution** stands in the center. On 23 March 1917, 180 heroes of the February uprising were buried here in mass graves. The next day, the first granite stone was laid in the monument foundation, which was unveiled in 1920. On each of the eight stone blocks are words by the writer Anatoly Lunacharsky. One reads: "Not victims, but heroes, lie beneath these stones. Not grief, but envy, is aroused by your fate in the hearts of all your grateful descendents." During the 40th anniversary of the October Revolution in 1957, the eternal flame was lit, in memory of those killed during the revolutions.

Summer Garden

The eastern side of the field opens up on the lovely Letny Sad (Summer Garden). The main entrance to the garden is from the Neva-Kutuzov embankment. A beautiful black and golden grille

> "Give me roses, the gardens that are second to none,
> The finest park railings the world has ever known
> I dream in the sweet-scented shade of the limes
> Of mainmasts a-creak as in earlier times.
> And the swan slowly sails through the centuries,
> Admiring the grace of the double he sees."
>
> —Anna Akhmatova, Leningrad poet,

(1770-84 by Yuri Felten) fences it. The open railing, decorated with 36 granite columns and pinkish urns, is one of the finest examples of wrought-iron work in the world. The Summer Garden, the city's oldest, was designed by Leblond in Franco-Dutch style in 1704. Peter the Great desired to create a garden more exquisite than Versailles. On 25 acres of land, he planted trees and had hothouses, aviaries, grottos and sculptures placed within. Some of the original statues remain, such as Peace and Abundance, the busts of John Sobiesky (a Polish king), Christina (a Swedish queen), the Roman Empress Agrippina, and Cupid and Psyche. The Swan Canal dug on the western side was filled with swans and had a tiny boat for Peter's favorite dwarf jester. The garden also had many fountains, depicting characters from Aesop's Fables. The water for the fountains was drained from a river on its east side; the river was called Fontanka, from the Russian *fontan* (fountain). Pipes made from hollowed logs ran from the Fontanka to a city pool, from which a one-mile (1.6-km) pipeline brought water to the gardens. The Fontanka formed the southern border of the city in the mid-18th century. At this time, the first stone bridge was built where the Fontanka flows into the Neva. It's still known as Prachechny Most (Laundry Bridge) because it was located near the Royal Laundry. The gardens received their name from the many festivals that Peter the Great loved to hold in summer; the area became the center of social life in Petersburg.

Many of the fountains, pavilions and statues were destroyed during the 1777 and 1824 floods. The Summer Garden was open only to nobility until, in the mid-19th century, Nicholas I issued a decree stating that it would be "open for promenading to all military men and decently dressed people. Ordinary people, such as *muzhiks* [peasants] shall not be allowed to walk through the garden." After the Revolution, the Garden was opened fully to the public.

After the garden was designed, Peter had his Letny Dvorets (Summer Palace) built at the northern end by the Neva. After its completion in 1714 by Trezzini, Peter moved from his cottage into the Summer Palace. The modest stone building was decorated with 29 terra-cotta figures and a weather vane of St. George slaying the dragon. Peter lived on the ground floor and his wife, Catherine, on the second. In 1974, it was opened as a museum. The palace is open 11 to 5:30 p.m., closed Tuesday and from 11 Nov. to 30 April.

Behind the Summer Palace is an interesting bronze Monument to Ivan Krylov, the popular Russian fablist, by the sculptor Clodt, and a playground for children with subjects from Krylov's fables. Nearer to the fountain are the Chainy Domik (Tea House), built in 1827 by Ludwig Charlemagne, and Coffee House, which is known as "Rossi's Pavilion," built by Rossi in 1826; recitals are now held here. Walking south toward the Moika River, you come upon the Porphyry Vase, a gift to Nicholas I from the Swedish king, Karl Johann.

ENGINEER'S CASTLE

Crossing the Moika and continuing along the banks of the Fontanka leads to the Engineer's Castle, built in 1797-1800 by the architects Bazhenov and Brenna for Czar Paul I. Paul didn't like his mother's (Catherine the Great) residence in the Winter Palace, and fearing attempts on his life, he ordered the castle constructed as an impregnable fortress. The "Mikhailovsky Castle" (the archangel Michael was Paul's patron saint) was bordered in the north by the Moika, and the east by the Fontanka; two artificial canals, the Resurrection and Church, were dug on the other sides, creating a small island. Drawbridges, protected by cannon, were raised at 9 p.m. when the czar went to bed. In spite of all this, Paul was strangled by one of his own guards 40 days after he moved in on 11 March 1801.

In 1822, after a military engineering school was opened, the palace became known as Engineer's Castle. Dostoevsky went to school here from 1837 to 1843 (from age 16), and later lived in 17 different residences throughout the city. After the Revolution, it housed a psychiatric institute and now it's a scientific and naval library. In front of the castle's main entrance is a statue of Peter the Great, erected in 1800 and cast by Rastrelli. The inscription at its base reads: "To great-grandfather from great-grandson," ordered by Paul I.

Not far from the Engineer's Castle, along the Fontanka (no. 3) is the **Leningrad Circus**. The circular building of the Leningradsky Tsirk was constructed in 1877 by Kenel. Inside is also the **Museum of Circus History and Variety Art** (established in 1928), with over 100,000 circus-related items; closed on Sat. and Sunday.

NEVSKY PROSPECT

In the words of Nikolai Gogol, "There is nothing finer than the Nevsky Prospekt . . . In what does it not shine, this street that is the beauty of the capitol." Nevsky Prospekt, which Leningraders refer to as Nevsky, is the main thoroughfare of the city and the center of business and commerical life. A stroll down part of it, during anytime of day, is a must, for no other street like it exists anywhere in the world. It's a busy, bustling area, filled with department stores, shops, cinemas, restaurants, museums, art studios, cathedrals, mansions, theaters, libraries and cafes. The Nevsky is made even more interesting and beautiful by the stunning architectural ensembles that line the three-mile-long (4.8-km) route that stretches from the Admiralty to Alexander Nevsky Monastery. As an architectural showcase, it also brims with history; you can find the spot where Pushkin met his second on the day of his fatal duel, where Dostoevsky gave readings of his works, and where Liszt and Wagner premiered their music.

Shortly after the Admiralty was completed, a track was cut through the thick forest, linking it with the road to Novgorod and Moscow. This main stretch of the city was known as the Great Perspective Road. The road took on the name of Neva Perspectiva in 1738, when it was linked to another small road that ran to Alexander Nevsky Monastery. In 1783, the route was renamed Nevsky Prospekt, the wide, straight road from the Neva to the Nevsky. Peter the Great had elegant stone houses built along the Nevsky and ordered food sold in the streets by vendors dressed in white aprons. The first buildings went up between the Admiralty and the Fontanka Canal. The area, nicknamed "Petersburg City," was a fashionable place to live, and it became the center for banks, stores and even insurance offices. The architects desired to create a strong and imposing central district and constructed the buildings out of granite and stone brought in from Sweden.

Gogol, Tchaikovsky And Hazen
Beginning at the Admiralty (where the street is at its narrowest—75 feet/25 meters), walk along to no. 9 Nevsky. On the corner you'll find Vavelberg's House which, originally a bank, is now the Aeroflot ticket office. The large stone house was built in

view of Nevsky Prospekt

1912 by the architect Peretyatkovich to resemble the Doge's Palace in Venice and the Medici in Florence. At no. 10 across the street is the "Queen of Spades" residence, the house of the old countess on whom Pushkin based his story of the same name. Here the Nevsky is intersected by Ulitsa Gogolya (Gogol Street), where the writer lived at no. 17 from 1833 to 1836. Here Gogol wrote T*aras Bulba, The Inspector General* and the first chapters of *Dead Souls.* At no. 13 Gogol, Tchaikovsky lived up until his death in 1895.

The next intersection on the Nevsky is Ulitsa Gersena (Herzen Street); Herzen lived at no. 25 for a year in 1840. The main telephone and telegraph center is located to the left by the Triumphal Arch of the General Staff. Fabergé had its main studios at no. 24, and a *beriozka* is now at no. 26. The architect Carlo Rossi laid out the street along the "Pulkovo Meridian" (which was 0 meridian on old Russian maps) at noon, the buildings cast no shadows on the street.

Numbers 8-25

The oldest buildings are at no. 8 and no. 10 Nevsky. Built between 1760 and 1780, they're now exhibition halls for work by Leningrad artists. The house at no. 14 (built in 1939) was once a school. A pale blue rectangle plaque on the wall reads: "Citizens! In the event of artillery fire, this side of the street is the most dangerous!" The House with Columns at no. 15 was built in 1768 as a stage site for one of Russia's first professional theaters. Later a small studio, where Falconet modeled *The Bronze Horseman,* was connected to the theater. It's now the Barrikada Movie Cinema with cafes and shops. The building at no. 18 was known as Kotomin's House (1812-16), after the original owner. Pushkin often frequented the confectioner's shop that used to be in the bottom story; he lived nearby at no. 12 Moika. It was here on 27 Jan. 1837, that Pushkin met up with his second on the way to his fatal duel with George D'antès. The shop is now the **Liternaturnaya Cafe,** a popular spot to eat that offers piano and violin music. Outside the cafe, you can have your portrait drawn by one of the numerous artists.

For many years, the section on the left side of the Nevsky beyond the Moika River was reserved for churches of non-Orthodox faiths. The Dutch Church is at no. 20, built in 1837 by Jacquot. The central part functioned as a church and the wings housed the Dutch Mission. The church is now a library. Across the street at no. 17 is the baroque palace of Count Stroganov, built by Rastrelli in 1754. The Stroganov coat-of-arms is over the gateway arch and depicts two sables and a bear. The Stroganov family owned and developed vast amounts of land in Siberia.

The next intersection is at Zhelyabov Street, named after a popular revolutionary. At no. 13 Zhelyabov is the Rapsodia Music Store; no. 21 is the House of Trade, one of the largest department stories in the city; no. 25 is Chigorin Chess Club; no. 27 is the Leningrad Variety Revue Theater. Across Zhelyabov St. set back at no. 22-24 Nevsky is the Romanesque-style Peter and Paul Lutheran Church, built by Bryullov in 1838. It now belongs to a sports club.

Our Lady Of Kazan

Across the street from the church is the large, majestic, semicircular colonnade of the Cathedral of Our Lady of Kazan. The Kazanski Sobor was named after the famous icon of Our Lady of Kazan that used to be here. It's now on view at the Russian Museum. The architect Voronikhin faced two challenges in 1801. First, Czar Paul I wished the cathedral modeled after St. Peter's in Rome, and second, the Orthodox Church required that the altar face east, which would have had one side of the cathedral facing the Nevsky. Voronikhin devised 96 Corinthian columns to fan out toward the Nevsky. The bronze Doors of Paradise, which were replicas of the 15th-century baptistery doors in Florence, opened on the Nevsky side. The structure took 10 years to build and, at that time, was the third largest cathedral in the world. The brick walls are faced with statues and biblical reliefs made from Pudostsky stone, named after the village where it was quarried. The stone was so soft when dug out that it was cut with a saw. It later hardened like rock when exposed to air. In niches around the columns are statues of Alexander Nevsky, Prince Vladimir, St. John the Baptist and the Apostle Andrew. The interior was decorated by the outstanding painters Bryullov, Borovikovksy and Kiprensky. There are 56 pink granite columns and polished marble and red-stone mosaic floors. Field Marshall Mikhail Kutuzov is buried in the northern chapel. The general stopped to pray at the spot where he is now buried before going off to the War of 1812. Many trophies from this war, like banners and keys to captured fortresses, hang around his crypt. In 1837, the two statues of Kutuzov and Barclay de Tolly were put up in the front garden.

At the main entrance to the cathedral, to the right off Plekhanov Street, is a small square surrounded by a beautiful wrought-iron grille, called "Voronikhin's Railing." In 1876, the first workers' demonstration took place in front, with speeches by the Marxist Georgi Plekhanov (after whom the side street is named). A square and fountain were later added to prevent further demonstrations. But the area remains to this day a popular spot for gatherings and, since *perestroika,* political and religious demonstrations as well. Today the cathedral is the **Museum of the History of Religion and Atheism** (open 11 to 6, closed Wednesday).

Continuing East

A short walk down the Griboyedov Canal (located to the left behind the cathedral) spans the lovely footbridge of Bankovski Most (Bank Bridge), adorned with winged lion-griffins. At the time it was built in 1800, the bridge led to the National Bank; according to Greek mythology, griffins stood guard over gold. On the other side of Nevsky, also on the Griboyedov Canal, is **Dom Knigi** (House of Books). This polished granite building, topped by its distinguishing glass sphere and globe, was originally built by Susor in 1907 for the American Singer Company. The first two floors now make up one of the largest bookstores in the country. The second floor sells posters, calendars and postcards.

The Kazansky Bridge crosses the canal and was built by Illarion Kutuzov, the father of the military leader. Down the canal to the left stands the 17th-century Russian-style building (modeled on St. Basil's in Moscow) known as the Savior's Church On Spilled Blood. Spasa Na Krovi was erected on the spot where Czar Alexander II was assassinated in 1881 by a member of the revolutionary group People's Will. Alexander III ordered architect Alfred Parland to build the altar where the former czar's blood fell on the cobblestones.

The next building over the bridge at no. 30 was that of the Philharmonic Society, where Wagner, Liszt and Strauss performed. Today it is the Hall of the Glinka Maly Philharmonic. The Catholic Church of St. Catherine, built from 1763 to 1783 in baroque-classical design by Vallin de la Mothe,

is at no. 32-34 Nevsky. The former Armenian Church, built by Felten in 1780, is at no. 42.

The corner building across the street at no. 31-33 was known as Silver Rows. Built in 1784-87 by Quarenghi, it was used as an open shopping arcade, where silver merchants would set up their wooden display booths. In 1799, the structure was made into the Town Hall or City Duma, and a European Rathaus tower was installed. This served as a watchtower, and part of a "mirror telegraph" that linked the residences of the czar. A beam of light was telegraphed along other alligned towers to announce the ruler's arrival or departure.

Right across the street at no. 35 is the **Gostiny Dvor Bazaar.** Visiting merchants used to put up guest houses, *gostiniye dvori,* which served as their resident places of business. From 1761 to 1785, the architect Vallin de la Mothe built a long series of open two-tiered arcades, where merchants had their booths. Today the two-story yellow department store, containing over 200 shops, is a popular place for shopping. The small building that stands between the hall and Gostiny Dvor was built as the Portico, and now holds the Central City Theater Booking Office. The art nouveau **Evropeiskaya Hotel** is located across the street from the City Duma on the corner of Nevsky and Brodsky, named after the Soviet painter, Issak Brodsky. The popular hotel, built in the 1870s, was formerly called the Hotel de l'Europe, and has recently been renovated. Two popular cafes are on the ground floor; the Sadko Restaurant serves delicious lunches and dinners.

Across the street, on the next corner, is the Leningrad State Philharmonic Society's Great Hall, built in 1839 by Jacquot for the Club of the Nobility. The St. Petersburg Philharmonic Society was founded in 1802. The works of many Russian composers, such as Glinka, Rachmaninov, Rimsky-Korsakov and Tchaikovsky, were first heard at the Society. Wagner was the official conductor during the 1863 season. The Philharmonic Symphony Orchestra performs worldwide. The Philharmonic was named after Dmitri Shostakovich in 1976. Shostakovich lived in Leningrad during the 900-day seige of Leningrad. In July 1941, he began to write his Seventh Symphony, while a member of an air-defense unit. Hitler had boasted that Leningrad would fall by 9 Aug. 1942. On this day, the Seventh, or Leningrad Symphony, conducted by Karl Eliasberg, was played in the Philharmonic and broadcast throughout the Soviet Union and the world. Ahosta IKovich announced, "I dedicate my Seventh Symphony to our struggle with fascism, to our forthcoming victory over the enemy, and to my native city, Leningrad."

Arts Square

The square in front of the Philharmonic is called Ploshchad Iskusstv (Square of Arts). In the mid-18th century, Carlo Rossi designed the square and the areas in between the Griboyedov Canal, the Moika River and Sadovaya Ulitsa (Garden Street); Garden Street leads past the Winter Stadium and Manège Square to the Engineer's Castle and Field of Mars. The center of the square is dominated by the statue of Alexander Pushkin, sculpted by Mikhail Anikushin in 1957. To the right of the Philharmonic, along Rokov Street, is the Theater of Musical Comedy, the only theater in the city that stayed open during the seige. Next to it is the Komissarzhevskaya Drama Theater. Headed by Russian actress Vera Komissarzhevskaya from 1904 to 1906, the company staged plays (including Gorky's) around the political mood of the times.

Behind the square on Engineer's Street stands the majestic eight-columned building of the **Russian Museum**, second largest museum of art in the city. Carlo Rossi built this palace (1819-27) for Mikhail, youngest son of Paul I; it was called the Mikhailovsky Palace. A splendid wrought-iron fence (embossed by the double-headed eagle) separates the palace from the square. The courtyard allowed carriages to drive up to the front portico, where a granite staircase, lined with two bronze lions, leads to the front door. The Hall of White Columns was so admired by the czar that he ordered a wooden model made for King George IV of England. Rubenstein opened the city's first music school in the hall in 1862. The Mikhailovsky Gardens are situated behind the museum. In 1898, Alexander III set up the Russian Museum inside the palace. The 1,000-year history of Russian art is represented by over 300,000 works of art in the 130 halls of the museum (open 10 to 6, closed Tuesday). To the right of the museum is the **Museum of Ethnography of the Peoples of the USSR** (also open 10 to 6, closed Monday).

The statue of Pushkin gestures to the building in the square known as the **Maly Theater of Opera and Ballet.** Built in 1833 by Bryullov, it was known as the Mikhailovsky Theater, and housed a permanent French troupe. Today it's "the laboratory of Soviet opera and ballet," presenting 360 performances a year in a daily alternating repertory of opera and ballet. Subsidized by the government, it employs nearly 800 people, including an orchestra of 100 and a chorus of 65. It's the second most popular theater (next to the Kirov) in Leningrad. The **Brodsky Museum-Flat,** where many of the artist's paintings are displayed, is next to the Maly; open 11 a.m. to 7 p.m., closed Mon. and Tuesday.

Continuing down the Nevsky, the **Saltykov-Shchedrin Public Library** stands on the corner of Nevsky and Garden streets. Built in 1801 by Yegor Sokolov, it opened in 1814 as the Imperial Public Library. In 1832, Carlo Rossi built further additions. The statue of Minerva, Goddess of Wisdom, stands atop the building. It's one of the largest libraries in the world—over 25 million books! A reading room is inside, but no books are allowed to be checked out.

Ostrovsky Square

The library faces Ostrovsky Square, named after the playwright Alexander Ostrovsky. A **statue of Catherine the Great** graces the center; Catherine, dressed in a long flowing robe, stands on a high rounded pedestal that portrays the prominent personalities of the time: Potemkin, Suvorov, Rumyantsev and Derzhavin, to name a few. The square is surrounded by artists' booths with sketches and paintings for sale. Along the left side are two classical pavilions, designed by Rossi, in the Garden of Rest.

Behind the square is the **Pushkin Drama Theater,** a place that looks like a temple to the arts. Flanked by Corinthian columns, the niches are adorned with the Muses of Dance, Tragedy, History and Music. The chariot of Apollo, patron of the arts, stands atop the front façade. The yellow building, erected by Rossi in 1828, was known as the Alexandrinsky Theater (after Alexandra, the wife of Nicholas I), which housed Russia's first permanent theater group. Today it has a varied repertoire of classical and modern plays. Behind the theater is the State Museum of Drama and Music at no. 6 Ostrovsky Square, exhibiting the history of Russian drama and musical theater. It's open 11 to 6, Wed. 2-8, Sat., 11 to 4, closed Sun.

and Tuesday. The Lunacharsky National Library is also here, with more than 350,000 volumes.

The famous **Rossi Street** (named after the architect) stretches from Ostrovsky to Lomonosov Square. The street has perfect proportions: 68 feet (22 meters) wide, the buildings are 22 meters high and the length is 10 times the width. The world-renowned **Vagonova School of Choreography** is the first building on the left. Twelve boys and 12 girls (children of court servants) were the city's first ballet students, attending a school started by the Empress Anna in the same year, 1768, that she founded the Petersburg Imperial Ballet. The choreography school now bears the name of Agrippina Vagonova, who taught here from 1921 to 1951. Some of the Imperial Ballet and Vagonova pupils have been Pavlova, Ulanova, Petipa, Nijinsky, Fokine and Balanchine. Over 2,000 hopefuls apply to the school each year; only 90 are chosen. The school's 500 pupils hope to go on to a professional ballet company such as the Kirov. A museum inside the school to the left contains many magical displays, for example Pavlova's ballet shoes and Nijinsky's costumes. Posters and pictures trace the history of ballet from Diaghliev to Baryshnikov who, along with Natalia Makarova, attended the Vagonova School. (The museum is closed to the general public—but if you express an interest in ballet, you may get in.) A few documentary films have been done about the school, such as *The Children of Rossi Street*. The National Geographic Special, "Voices of Leningrad," available in video rental stores, includes a segment about the Vagonova.

Rev Free On Nevsky

Back on the prospekt in the corner building across the street is the impressive **Gastronom no. 1.** Once known as Yeliseyev's, it was the most luxuriant food store in Petersburg. Today, even though the food supplies have dwindled, it's well worth seeing the interior of the store. The State Puppet Theater, started in 1918, is at no. 52 Nevsky. The Comedy Theater, founded in 1929, is at no. 56. At the corner of Nevsky and the Fontanka River is the House of Friendship and Peace. A former residence, built in the 1790s, it's now a society that promotes friendship and cultural relations with over 500 organizations in 30 countries.

The area around the Fontanka River (the old southern border of the city) was first developed by an engineering team headed by Mikhail Anichkov, who built the first bridge (still named after him) here in 1715 across the Fontanka. In 1841, a stone bridge with four towers replaced the wooden structure. Peter Klodt cast the tamed-horse sculptures a century ago and today they give the bridge its distinguishing mark. During WW II, the sculptures were buried in the Palace of Young Pioneers across the street. The **Anichkov Bridge** is a popular hangout, and boats, to the left on the Fontanka, leave frequently for a city tour of the canals and waterways. A kiosk by the dock provides time departures and tickets (sold in rubles only).

The first palace built on the Nevsky was named after Anichkov. Empress Elizabeth (Peter's daughter) commissioned the architects Dmitriyev and Zemtsov to build a palace on the spot where she stayed on the eve of her coronation. In 1751, Elizabeth gave the Anichkov Palace to her favorite, Count Alexei Razumovsky. Later Catherine the Great gave it to her own favorite, Count Grigory Potemkin, who frequently held elaborate balls here. Later it was a part of his majesty's cabinet. Since 1937, it has been the Dvorets Pionerov (Palace of Young Pioneers). The Young Pioneers is a Communist organization for children from ages nine to 14, who wear distinguishing orange silk scarves to mark their membership. Nearly 15,000 children in the city voluntarily participate in some 600 youth clubs (roughly equivalent to our scouting organizations). The Communist Party Headquarters is at no. 41 Nevsky, originally a mansion built in the 1840s by the architect Stackenschneider for a prince by the name of Beloselsky-Belozersky. The Gostiny Dvor/Nevsky Prospekt Metro stop brings you right out on Nevsky Prospekt by the department store and Dom Knigi. For a list of shops along the Nevsky, see the "Practicalities" section.

Uprising Square

Following the Nevsky a bit farther (there's little of architectural interest in between), you come to Ploshchad Vosstaniya (Uprising Square), named when troops of the czar refused to shoot a group of unarmed demonstrators during the February 1917 uprising. One of the interesting buildings on the Square is Moskovsky Vokzal (Moscow Train Station). It was built by the architect Thon in 1847. The Petersburg-Moscow railway line opened on

1 Nov. 1851. A smaller version of this station in Moscow is appropriately named the Leningrad Station. The station was originally planned to contain just shops and galleries surrounded by gardens. The word *vokzal* continued to be used for a station and now Leningrad has five major train *vokzals* in the city: Moscow, Finland, Warsaw, Baltic and Vitebsky. The latter was known as "Czarskoye Selo," the station connecting Russia's first railroad line, built in 1837, to the czar's summer residence in Pavlovsk. The Hotel Oktyabrskaya dates from the 1890s. The Metro stop Ploshchad Vosstaniya/Mayakovskaya is near Uprising Square. The Mayakovskaya exit lets you out at about no. 100 Nevsky and Marata Street.

A few blocks down Marata Street from Nevsky is the Marata Banya complex; open 7 a.m. to 11, closed Mon. and Tuesday. At no. 24 Marata is the **Museum of the Arctic and Antarctic** (in the Church of St. Nicholas). It's open 10 to 6, closed Mon. and Tuesday.

Alexander Nevsky Square

The modern Moscow Hotel (with restaurants and a *beriozka)* stands at the end of Nevsky Prospect on Alexander Nevsky Square. Across the street is the **Alexander Nevsky Lavra,** the oldest monastery in Leningrad. Peter the Great founded the monastery, southeast of the city, in 1710 and dedicated it to the Holy Trinity, and military leader Alexander Nevsky, prince of Novgorod, who won a major victory on the Neva (supposedly near the spot of the monastery) against the Swedes in 1240. In Russia, the name *lavra* was applied to a large monastery. Before the Revolution, there were four prestigious *lavras* in the country. The Alexander Nevsky was in Petersburg; another was the Trinity-St. Sergius Monastery in the Golden Ring town of Zagorsk. The Blagoveshchevsky Sobor (Annunciation Church) is the oldest church in the *lavra,* built by Trezzini in 1720. It now houses the Museum of Urban Sculpture; open 11 to 6, closed Thursday.

The Troitsky Sobor (Holy Trinity Cathedral) is the main church of the complex, with a lovely interior, built by Ivan Starov in 1790. The Church of Alexander Nevsky is on the upper floor. In 1723, the remains of Alexander Nevsky himself were brought to the cathedral. The sarcophagus, cast from 1.5 tons of silver, is now at the Hermitage. Peter the Great buried his sister Natalie in the

Lazarevskoye Cemetery (to the left of the main entrance), Leningrad's oldest cemetery. To the right of the main entrance is the Tikhvinskoye Cemetery. Here are the beautifully carved gravestones of many of Russia's greatest figures such as Tchaikovsky, Glinka, Rimsky-Korsakov, Mussorgsky, Stasov, Klodt and Dostoevsky. Another entrance is right across the street from the Moscow Hotel. The cemeteries are closed on Thursday and Saturday. The cathedral holds services, and on Alexander Nevsky Day, 11-12 Sept., huge processions take place. Near the monastery is the Theological Seminary, reestablished in 1946, which trains 440 students for the clergy. About 100 women are taught to be teachers or choir conductors. Four cathedrals and 18 churches currently perform services in Leningrad. The Alexander Nevsky Bridge, largest bridge in the city, crosses the Neva from the monastery.

Metro stop Ploshchad Aleksandra Nevskovo brings you right to the Moscow Hotel and the monastery complex.

FINLAND STATION

The Finland Railway Station is located on the right bank of the Neva, a little east of where the cruiser *Aurora* is docked. It's also a short walk from the Liteiny (Foundry) Bridge on the Petrogradskaya side, with its beautiful railings filled with mermaids and anchors. The station, behind a towering monument to Lenin, dates back to 1870; from here Lenin secretly left from Petrograd to Finland in August 1917, after he was forced into hiding by the provisional government. A few months later he was brought back via the same locomotive to direct the October uprising. This locomotive, engine no. 293, is on display behind a glass pavilion in the back of the station by the platform area. A brass plate on the locomotive bears the inscription: "The government of Finland presented this locomotive to the government of the USSR in commemoration of journeys over Finnish territory made by Lenin in troubled times. June 13, 1957."

The monument to Lenin stands in Lenin Square. After the February 1917 Revolution overthrew the czarist monarchy, Lenin returned to Petrograd from his place of exile in Switzerland on 3 April 1917. He gave a speech from the turret of the car (now on display at the Lenin Museum) to the masses. Originally the Lenin monument was erected on the spot where he gave the speech. But during the construction of the square, the statue, portraying Lenin standing on the car's turret addressing the crowd with an outstretched hand, was moved closer to the Neva embankment, where it stands today. It was unveiled on 7 Nov., 1926. Metro stop Ploshchad Lenina lets out at Finland Station.

Taurida Palace

Crossing the Liteiny Bridge in front of the station leads to Voinova Street and the Taurida Palace at no. 47. The street was named after Ivan Voinov, who worked as a correspondent for *Pravda* and was killed on this street on 6 July 1917. The palace was built by Ivan Starov in 1789 for Prince Grigory Potemkin—a gift from Catherine the Great. Potemkin was commander-in-chief of the Russian army in the Crimea during the Turkish wars. The peninsula there was called Taurida and Potemkin was given the title prince of Taurida. One party Potemkin held in the palace (costing 200,000 rubles) used 140,000 lamps and 20,000 candles. After both he and Catherine the Great died, the new Emperor Paul I (who disliked his mother Catherine and her favorites), converted the palace into a riding house and stables. It was later renovated and became the seat of the State Duma in 1906. On 27 Feb. 1917, the left wing of the palace held the first session of the Petrograd Soviet of Workers. After Lenin returned to Petrograd in April, he addressed the Congress here on many occasions. Today it houses the Higher Party School and Party conferences. Behind the mansion are the Taurida Gardens and a small children's amusement park. The Russian poet Derzhavin wrote of the palace, "Its exterior does not dazzle the eye with carving, gilt or other sumptuous decoratons. Its merit is in its ancient, refined style; it is simple, but majestic."

Behind the gardens is the **Museum to Alexander Suvorov,** the great Russian military leader from the War of 1812; open 11 to 6 p.m., closed Wednesday. Across the street from the front of the palace is the **Kikin Palace.** Built in 1714 and one of the oldest buildings in the city, it belonged to the boyar Kikin, who plotted, along with Peter's son, Alexei, to assassinate Peter the Great. After Kikin was put to death, Peter turned the palace into Russia's first natural science museum. The collections were later moved to the Kunstkammer on Vasilyevsky Island. Today the yellow-white palace is a children's music school. The closest Metro stop is Chernyshevskaya.

THE SMOLNY

Voinova Street ends at Rastrelli Square by the monument to Felix Dzerzhinsky. Behind it, the baroque, five-domed, turquoise and white Smolny complex is truly one of Rastrelli's greatest works. Several years after Peter and Paul Fortress was founded, the tar yards, *smolyanoi dvor,* were set up at the Neva's last bend before the gulf to process tar for the shipyards. Empress Elizabeth, Peter's daughter, wanted to establish a Petersburg nunnery, and commissoned Rastrelli to build the Smolny Resurrection Convent on this bend. After Elizabeth died, the complex was never fully completed. (Elizabeth lavishly spent state funds; she had over 15,000 gowns. At her death, only six rubles were left in the treasury.) Vassily Stasov later completed the structure in the 1830s, keeping Rastrelli's original design. (When the new classicism vogue in architecture replaced baroque, Rastrelli fell into disfavor under Empress Catherine the Great and was asked to leave the country.)

Catherine set up the Institute for Young Noble Ladies in the Smolny Convent, Russia's first school for the daughters of nobility. Today the Church of the Resurrection and the former convent is the Museum for Leningrad Today and Tomorrow and the Museum of the History of the Leningrad Party; open 11 to 6, closed Wednesday. In 1806-08, Quarenghi erected additional buildings for the Smolny Institute to the right of the convent. In August 1917, the closed Institute became the headquarters for the Petrograd Bolshevik Party and the Military Revolutionary Committee. On 25 Oct. 1917, Lenin arrived at the Smolny and gave the command for the storming of the Winter Palace. On 26 Oct. the Second All-Russia Congress of Soviets gathered in the Smolny's Assembly Hall to elect Lenin the leader of the world's first "Socialist Government of Workers and Peasants," and to adopt Lenin's Decrees on Peace and Land. John Reed wrote in his book *Ten Days That Shook the World* that Lenin was "unimpressive, to be the idol for a mob, loved and revered as perhaps few leaders in history have been. A leader purely by virtue of intellect; colorless, humorless, uncompromising and detached, without picturesque idiosyncrasies—but with the power of explaining profound ideas in simple terms . . . he combined shrewdness with the greatest intellectual audacity." Lenin lived at the Smolny for 124 days before transferring the capital to Moscow. Today the places in the Smolny where Lenin lived are part of the Lenin Museum. The rest of the building houses the seat of the Leningrad Regional and City Committees of the Communist Party.

Two pavilions form the main entrances to the building. Each bears an inscription: "Soviet of Proletarian Dictatorship" and "Workers of All Countries, Unite!" A bronze monument of Lenin was set up on the 10th anniversary of the Revolution. A wide avenue leads from the Smolny Institute to Proletarian Dictatorship Square; busts of Karl Marx and Frederich Engels stand on either side of the avenue.

THEATER SQUARE

In the southwest part of the city along Glinka and Decembrists streets lies Teatralnaya Ploshchad (Theater Square). This section of land was once the location for Petersburg carnivals and fairs. In the 18th century, it was known as Ploshchad Karusel (Merry-Go-Round Square). A wooden theater was built here and later, in 1783, it was replaced by the Bolshoi Stone Theater, with over 2,000 seats. In 1836, the drama troupe moved to the Pushkin Theater and the opera remained at the Bolshoi. In 1860, Albert Kavos completed the

Mariinsky Theater (which replaced the Bolshoi), named after Maria, the wife of Alexander II. It was renamed the **Kirov Theater,** after the prominent Communist leader under Stalin, in 1935. The gorgeous five-tiered theater is decorated with blue velvet chairs, gilded stucco, ceiling paintings and chandeliers; it seats 1,700.

In the 19th century, Petersburg was the musical capital of Russia. At the Mariinsky Theater, premiers of opera and ballet were staged by Russia's most famous composers, dancers and singers. Under Petipa, Ivanov and Fokin, Russian ballet took on worldwide recognition. The Fyodor Chalyapin Memorial Room, named after the great singer, is open inside the Kirov during performances. The Kirovsky Theatre of Opera and Ballet continues to stage some of the world's finest ballets and operas; its companies tour many countries throughout the world. Performances are often sold out; check at the Intourist desk at your hotel for tickets.

Opposite the Kirov stands the **Rimsky-Korsakov State Conservatory,** Russia's first advanced school of music. The founder of the conservatory was the composer Anton Rubinstein. Some of the graduates include Tchaikovsky, Prokofiev and Shostakovich. The Conservatory was given the name of Rimsky-Korsakov, who once managed the school, in 1944. On either side of the conservatory stand the monuments to Mikhail Glinka and Rimsky-Korsakov. The Rimsky-Korsakov Museum is at 28 Zagorodny Prospekt. It's open from 11 to 5, closed Fri. and Saturday. Farther down Decembrists Street, past the Kirov, is a Jewish synagogue.

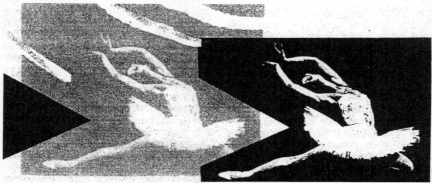

(clockwise from top) Leningrad, with the Admiralty and the Hermitage in the foreground; Catherine the Great's former palace; a Yaroslavl monastery

Glinka Street

A walk down Glinka Street leads to the Nikolsky Marine Cathedral (also functioning), built in 1753-62 by Chevakinsky in honor of St. Nicholas, the protector of seamen. Naval officers once lived in the area, thus the full name of Nikolsky Morskoi (Marine). Standing at the intersection of the Griboyedov and Kryukov canals, the blue and white church combines the old Russian five-dome tradition with the baroque. A lovely carved wooden iconostasis is inside and a four-tiered belltower stands by itself in the gardens.

Up Glinka Street in the opposite direction, the narrow Potseluyev Most (Bridge of Kisses) crosses the Moika River. To its right, the second building from the corner at no. 94 is the Palace of Culture of Educational Workers. This is an interesting spot because the last owner of the palace was the wealthy Count Yusupov, who was responsible for the assassination of Grigory Rasputin (the priest who exerted much influence in the court of Nicholas II) in the palace in 1916. Rasputin was first given poisoned cakes in the palace's basement, set up to look like a study. Nothing happened—the sugar in the cakes was thought to have neutralized the poison. Then the conspirators started shooting at Rasputin, and continued to do so as he ran from the house. Finally, they threw Rasputin's body through a hole in the ice of the Moika Canal. Later, after his body was found floating under the ice downstream, an autopsy showed that Rasputin had water in his lungs, proving he had still been alive after all the attempts to kill him. Yusupov later fled Russia.

Continuing along Glinka toward the Neva, a number of brick buildings are situated on a small triangular island. These were the storehouses for ship timber during the time of Peter the Great. Manmade canals created the small island known as Novaya Gollandiya (New Holland). The New Admiralty Canal, dug in 1717, connected the island with the Admiralty. Trade Union Boulevard was laid partly along the route of the old Admiralty Canal.

The last square before the Neva is known as Labor Square, formerly Annunciation Square. Between 1853 and 1861, a palace for the oldest son of Nicholas I was built by Stakenschneider near the square. In 1895, it was turned into the Xenia Institute for Noble Ladies, named after Xenia, the daughter of Alexander II. In 1919, it was again turned over to the Trade Union Regional Council and renamed the Palace of Labor. At no. 44 Red Fleet Embankment is the **State Museum of the History of Leningrad** (closed Wednesday) in the former Rumyantsev Mansion.

MOSCOW AVENUE

Moskovsky Prospekt runs for nearly 10 miles (16 km) in a straight line from Ploshchad Mira (Peace Square) to the airport. The avenue follows the line known as the Pulkovo Meridian (zero on old Russian maps) that led to the Pulkovo Astronomical Observatory. The square was known, in Czarist times, as Sennaya Ploshchad, a place used for public punishment of serfs. Stagecoaches also left for Moscow from here. The area was the residence of many of Dostoevsky's characters—*Crime and Punishment*'s Yeketerina Marmeladova, whose husband was killed, forced her children to perform for money near the canal. On Grazhdanskaya Ulitsa (Citizen's Street) is the "Raskolnikov House," from whose basement Raskolnikov stole the murder axe. "The houses of the murderer and his victim stood 730 paces apart." Raskolnikov knelt on the square hoping to repent for his crime.

A little past the Fontanka River is the **Moscow Triumphal Gate,** built in 1834-38 by Vasily Stasov to commemorate the Russian victories during the Russo-Turkish War of 1828-29. It was the largest cast-iron structure in the world in the mid-19th century. The gate is decorated with the Winged Victory, Glory, and Plenty and once marked the end of the city, where a road toll was collected. The closest Metro stop is Moskovskiye Vorota.

South of the gate, past the Kirov Elektrosila Factory, is the 170-acre (69-hectare) Moscow Victory Park, through which runs the Alley of Heroes. The park was laid out by tens of thousands of Leningraders after WW II in 1945. The Lenin Sports and Concert complex, seating 25,000, is located in the park. The closest Metro stop is Park Pobedy.

Farther along the prospekt on the left side is the Gothic red-white Chesma Palace and Church. Catherine the Great commissioned Felten to build it so she could have a rest stop on the way to her country residences. It was named Chesma in 1770 after the Russian victory of the Turkish fleet at Chesma Bay. The Chesma Museum houses displays on the naval battle at Chesma. It's open 10 to 5, closed Mon. and Tuesday.

Next comes Moscow Square, whose whole eastern side is lined by the House of Soviets, with a statue of Lenin at the center. Not far away is Ploshchad Pobedy (Victory Square). The **Monument to the Heroes of the Defense of Leningrad** (unveiled on 9 May 1975, 30 years after the seige) is the square's focal point. The sculptured group, called *The Victors,* looks out to where the front once ran. Pink granite steps lead down to an obelisk that stands inside a circle symbolizing the breaking of the blockade ring. An Eternal Flame is lit at the base. The ground floor of the base serves as a **Museum for the Seige of Leningrad,** open 10 to 6, closed Wednesday. Closest Metro stop is Moskovskaya.

The Green Belt of Glory is a memorial complex that stretches 145 miles (230 km) along the front line of 1941-44. Not far from the Baltic railway station, the **Narva Triumphal Gate** marks the victorious outcome of the War of 1812. Troups returning to Petersburg after the war passed through the gate.

Piskarovskoye Memorial Cemetery lies to the south of Leningrad; open 10 a.m. to 6 p.m. daily. Here are the common graves, marked only by year of burial from 1941-44, of over a half million Leningraders who died during the 900-day seige. The Leningrad poet Vera Inber wrote, "Oh, this great city! How they tortured it—from earth and sky with freezing cold, with fire, and with starvation." The central path of the cemetery leads to the **statue of the Mother Country,** holding a wreath of oak leaves, the symbol of eternal glory. Two museum pavilions are on either side of the entrance, where one realizes the horrors that faced the citizens of this city. Black-and-white photographs document the three-year blockade. The cemetery register is open at a page with the entries: "February, 1942: 18th—3,241 bodies; 19th—5,569; 20th—10,043." Another display shows a picture of 11-year-old Tanya Sevicheya and pages from her diary. "Granny died today. Mama died today. The Savichevs have died. Everybody died. Only Tanya is alive." Tanya later died after she

was evacuated from the city. Behind the statue, carved on the memorial's walls are words by the Leningrad poet, Olga Bergholts:

"Here lie the people of Leningrad,
Here are the citizens—men, women and
    children . . .
They gave their lives
Defending you, Leningrad,
Cradle of Revolution.
We cannot number all their noble names
    here,
So many lie beneath the eternal granite,
But of those honored by this stone,
Let no one forget
Let nothing be forgotten."

one of the half million killed during the Seige of Leningrad

PRACTICALITIES

ACCOMMODATIONS

Intourist Hotels

Astoria: 39 Herzen St., located by St. Isaac's Cathedral, tel. 219-1100; nearest Metro station Nevsky Prospekt. Recently renovated; one of Leningrad's oldest and most luxurious hotels. Rated Deluxe by Intourist.

Evropeiskaya: 1/7 Brodsky St., tel. 210-3295, nearest Metro station Nevsky Prospekt. Old, luxurious (recently renovated) and centrally located off of Nevsky Prospekt. Rated Deluxe by Intourist.

Gaven: 88 Sredny Prospekt on Vasilevsky Island, tel. 356-8504, nearest Metro station Primorskaya. Used mostly by visiting trade groups.

Leningrad: 5/2 Vyborgsky Embankment, tel. 542-9123, nearest Metro station Ploshchad Lenina. Modern Deluxe hotel. Located on north bank of Neva by cruiser *Aurora,* but only short hop into the city center. Ask for a view of the water.

Moskva: 2 Alexander Nevsky Square, tel. 274-9505/2051, nearest Metro Ploshchad Alexandra Nevskovo. Modern first-class hotel. Located by Alexander Nevsky Monastery, with easy access to the city center via Metro.

Olgino: Outside of town, tel. 238-3550. Modern standard hotel. Cheapest of the Intourist hotels, since it's located about 30 minutes by car or bus from the center of town. Has camping facilities in summer (must pre-book before arrival in country).

Olympia Hotel: Vasilevsky Island, nearest Metro station Primorskaya. First-class accomodations aboard a Swedish ship. Excellent, but expensive; foreign currency restaurant. Ask for a view of the water.

Pribaltiiskaya: 14 Korablestroiteley St. on Vasilevsky Island, tel. 356-0263, nearest Metro station Primorskaya. Deluxe modern hotel (built by Swedes), with bowling alley and sauna. Ask for a view of the water. Restaurants Daugava and Neva on second floor. Cafeteria-type restaurant on first floor. Top floor foreign currency bar—the back serves hot meals for foreign currency. Each floor has a small cafe. Two large *beriozkas* are outside and a smaller one inside on first floor.

Pulkovskaya: 1 Pobedy Square, tel. 264-5109; nearest Metro station Moskovskaya.

FOOD

All Intourist hotels have restaurants, cafes and bars. Swedish table smorgasbords *(Svedski Stol)* are found at the Pribaltiiskaya, Evropeiskaya, Leningrad and Moskva hotels for breakfast, lunch and dinner. This is an excellent way to get an adequate and quick meal. Outside of your hotel, many restaurants, cafes and co-operatives are located throughout the city.

Along Nevsky Prospekt

Druzhba: 15 Nevsky. The Friendship Cafe opens at 8 a.m. and serves breakfast, lunch and dinner.

Minutka: 20 Nevsky. A cafeteria serving quick snacks, soups, hot pies, desserts and coffee, cocoa and tea in a "minute."

Mercury: 22 Nevsky, tel. 311-7490. Serving pastries, ice cream and drinks.

Ogonyok: 24 Nevsky. Specializes in ice cream and drinks.

Kavkazsky: 25 Nevsky. One of the city's most popular restaurants of Caucasian dishes. Specials include the soup *kharcho,* chicken *tabak* and chakhombili, *chebureki* (small pies filled with lamb, rice and seasonings) and *shashlik.*

Literary Cafe: corner of Nevsky and the Moika Canal. Lovely restored 19th-century restaurant. (Here Pushkin met up with his second on the way to the tragic duel.) Good food, decorated with old pictures, and has music and literature recitals.

Sadko: corner of Nevsky and Brodsky next to the Evropeiskaya Hotel. Traditional Russian cooking, including *blini,* folk music, dancing and floor shows. A hard currency bar is open in the basement. Crowded with foreigners in summer, when advance reservations are needed.

Detsky: the "Children's" Cafe is at 42 Nevsky. The meals are intended for children; walls are decorated in fairy-tale motifs.

Neva: 44-46 Nevsky. Leningrad's largest restaurant, seating over 1,000. Tasty dishes are the *shchi* soup, Neva-style fish and Sever ice cream. The **Sever** (North) Cafe has good desserts; it's the best cake shop in town.

Avtomat: A self-service cafeteria at 45 Nevsky.

Moskva: 49 Nevsky. Russian cuisine with good Moscow-style stuffed meats and pancakes.

Aurora: 60 Nevsky. Milk and cheese dishes.

Blinnaya: 74 Nevsky. A cellar cafe offering Russian pancakes with a choice of fillings that include red and black caviar, sour cream, fruit.

Leningrad: 96 Nevsky. The Russian idea of a low-cal cafeteria.

Universal: 106 Nevsky.

Sadovaya (Garden) Street

Metropole: 22 Garden Street The oldest restaurant in the city is well known for the meat and fish dishes, and desserts. Next door is a shop that sells take-out food.

Lakomka: next to the Metropole. Serves a delicious variety of pastries, pies and cakes.

Baku: on Garden St. between Nevsky and Rakov streets. A popular restaurant with Azerbaijani and Caucasian cuisine. Bands, music and dancing in evenings. Reservations are usually needed.

Petrogradskaya Side

Kronwerk: A three-masted ship docked next to Peter and Paul Fortress in the Kronwerk Strait. Serves meals and drinks.

Austeria: Inside Peter and Paul Fortress near Peter's Gate. It offers dishes that were popular in the days of Peter the Great.

Primorsky: 32 Bolshoi Prospekt.

Volshebny Krai: 15/3 Bolshoi Prospekt, tel. 233-3253. Hot dishes and non-alcoholic drinks.

Vasilevsky Island

Fregat: 39/14 Bolshoi Prospekt. Offers traditional Russian dishes—many were popular in the time of Peter the Great.

Olympia: Inside a Swedish ship docked on the Gulf. Excellent food, rather expensive, pay in hard currency.

Zhemchuzhina: 2 Shkipersky Prospekt, tel. 355-2063. Azerbaijani cuisine.

Oreshek: 11 Liinaya 60. Offers desserts, drinks and snacks.

Pribaltiiskaya Hotel: Has a number of restaurants that usually require advance reservations. Try the top floor bar (in the back) that serves quick hot food of chicken and meat dishes. Must pay in foreign currency.

Fontanka Canal

Fontanka: Fontanka 77, tel. 310-0689. Very popular co-operative restaurant that offers delicious food and floor shows nightly. Expensive. Reservations recommended.

Griboyedov Canal

Chaika: 14 Griboyedov Embankment. The "Seagull" Café.

Kolomna: 162 Griboyedov Emb. Pastries and herbal teas.

Other Co-operatives

Viktoria: 190 Moskovsky Prospekt. Pies and pastries

Vodi Lagidze: 3 Belinsky St., tel. 279-1104. Serves excellent spicy food and flavored waters. (Water said to be imported from Germany and safe to drink.)

Imereti: 104 Prospekt Marxa. tel. 245-5003. Georgian cuisine.

Klassik: 202 Ligovsky Prospekt. tel. 166-0159. Open 11-9 and closed 3-4:30. Serves a varied selection of hot meals.

Ogonek: 11 B. Zelyonniya St., tel. 513-2921. Open 11-11. Dessert spot with coffee, tea and juices.

Progress: 23 Prosvesheniya Prospekt, tel. 597-

7210. Open 9-midnight. A variety of dishes, and baked and fruit desserts.

Polecye: 4 Sredneokhnsky Prospekt, tel. 224-2917. Open 12:30-10. Specializes in White Russian dishes with musical videos on TV.

Pishechnaya: 19 Razyezzhaya St., tel. 186-3427 A donut shop.

Salkhino: 8 Sovetsky St. 27/29. Georgian cuisine.

Staraya Derevnya: 72 Sabushkina Street. "Old Village" Restaurant has literary and art gatherings.

Tbilisi: 10 Sitninskaya Square, tel. 232-9391. Open 11-11. Very popular restaurant serving Georgian food.

Khachapuri: 6 Krasnoarmeisky St. 13/18. tel. 292-7377. Open 12-11. Another popular Georgian restaurant.

SHOPPING

Beriozka Shops
Hotel Pribaltiiskaya (one is inside the hotel, two other large ones are outside on either side); Hotel Leningrad; Hotel Evropeiskaya; Hotel Moskva; also at 9 Nevsky Prospekt and 26 Herzen Street.

Main Department Stores
Gostiny Dvor 35 Nevsky Prospekt; **Passazh** 48 Nevsky Prospekt; **Dom Leningradskoi Torgovli** 21-23 Zhelyabov St; **Frunzensky Univermag** 60 Moskovsky Prospekt; **Moskovsky Univermag** 205-220 Moskovsky Prospekt; **Kirovsky Univermag** 9 Stachek Sq; **Narvsky Univermag** 12-34 Geroyev (Hero) Prospekt; **Sintetika** 4 Novoizmailovsky Prospekt.

Along Nevsky Prospekt
No. 8 and 45: paintings and applied art.

No. 9: *Beriozka*

No. 13: **Mir** books published by other socialist countries.

No. 24: Galstuki tie shop and ice-cream cafe.

No. 26: souvenir shop. Outside the Literary Cafe, on the corner of Nevsky and the Moika Canal, are artists that can paint your portrait.

No: 28: **Dom Knigi**. The House of Books is the largest bookstore in Leningrad, with books, foreign language publications, posters and postcards. It used to be the Singer Sewing Company. Notice the globe on the roof.

No. 30: fabric store.

No. 34: record store; next door is the Culinary Cafe.

Down to the left, on Brodsky St., is the Evropeisky Hotel with a Beriozka, and cafe to get a quick bite to eat.

No. 35: **Gostiny Dvor**. The two-story yellow complex is the largest shopping arcade in the city. The Merchant's Yard dates from 1785. Facing the store to its left, along the side street, are a number of Commissioni second-hand stores.

No. 44: **Sever**. The best cake shop in town.

No. 48: **Passazh** department store for women.

No. 50: shop with books and postcards.

No. 52: crystal and ceramic shop.

No. 54: **Podarki** gift-shop.

No. 56: **Gastronom No. 1**. One of the oldest foodstores in Leningrad, formerly known as Yeliseyev's. It still has a lavish decor. Even though the food is lacking, it's well-worth a peek.

Across the street, in Ostrovsky Sq. with the Statue of Catherine the Great, are many artist stalls, selling paintings, portraits and local crafts.

No. 58: **Molochni** ice-cream cafe.

No. 60: sporting-goods store; next to it is a movie theater.

No. 62-64: crystal, china, embroidery, tobacco and cigarettes— *papirosi* are the ones with the long cardboard filter.

No. 66-72: breadstore, sweets, clothing store, albums, prints, reproductions and postcards.

No. 78: bookstore.

No. 92: photography goods.

No. 96: paints and varnish.

No. 114: travel wares.

No. 147: crystal.

Farmers' Market
A farmers' *rinok* (market) selling vegetables, fruit and flowers is at Kuznechny Lane, just behind Vladimirksky Metro stop, off of Vladimirsky Prospekt.

THEATERS AND CONCERT HALLS

Evening performances in theaters usually begin at 7:30, and concerts at 8:00 p.m. The time of the performance and seat number are written on the ticket. It's usually required to check your coat in

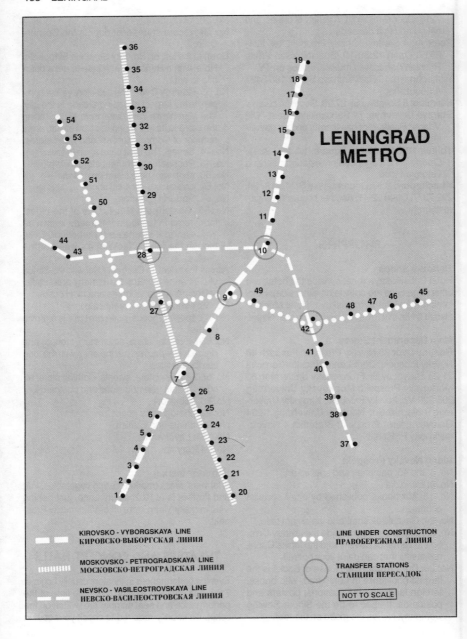

LENINGRAD
METRO

KIROVSKO - VYBORGSKAYA LINE
КИРОВСКО-ВЫБОРГСКАЯ ЛИНИЯ

MOSKOVSKO - PETROGRADSKAYA LINE
МОСКОВСКО-ПЕТРОГРАДСКАЯ ЛИНИЯ

NEVSKO - VASILEOSTROVSKAYA LINE
НЕВСКО-ВАСИЛЕОСТРОВСКАЯ ЛИНИЯ

LINE UNDER CONSTRUCTION
ПРАВОБЕРЕЖНАЯ ЛИНИЯ

TRANSFER STATIONS
СТАНЦИИ ПЕРЕСАДОК

NOT TO SCALE

the cloakroom before entering the performance. Here you can also rent opera glasses for a small charge.

Bolshoi Puppet Theater: 10 Nekrasov Street
Children's Theater: 1 Pionersky Square
Circus: 3 River Fontanka Embankment
Comedy Theater: 56 Nevsky Prospekt
Glinka Academic Capella: 20 River Moika Embankment
Gorky Academic Bolshoi Drama Theater: 65 River Fontanka Embankment
Kirov Theater: 1 Teatralnaya (Theater) Square
Komissarzhevskaya Drama Theater: 19 Rakov Street
Komsomol Theater: 4 Lenin Park
Lensoviet Theater, 12 Vladimirsky Prospekt
Maly Theater for Opera and Ballet: 1 Iskusstv (Arts) Square
Oktyabrsky Concert Hall: 6 Ligovsky Prospekt
Puppet Theater: 52 Nevsky Prospekt
Pushkin Drama Theater: 2 Ostrovsky Square
Rimsky-Korsakov Conservatory: 3 Teatralnaya (Theater) Square
Shostakovich Philharmonia: 2 Brodsky Street
Glinka Maly Philharmonia: 30 Nevsky Prospekt
Theater of Musical Comedy: 13 Rakov Street
Variety Theater: 27 Zhelyabov Street

SPORTS

Chigorin Chess Club: 25 Zhelyabov St.
Dynamo Stadium: Park Pobedy (Victory Park)
Kirov Stadium: 13 Morskoi Prospekt on Krestovsky Island
Lenin Sports and Concert Complex: 8 Gagarin Prospekt on Petrovsky Island
Palace of Culture: 42 Kirov Avenue on Vasilevsky Island
Yubileiny Sports Palace: 18 Dobrolyubov Prospekt
Winter Stadium: 11 Inzhenernaya St.

Also check at the Intourist desk for indoor and outdoor pool, and *banya* (sauna/pool) locations. One *banya* complex is on Marat Street just off Nevsky Prospekt (no. 100) and Metro stop Mayakovskaya. It's open 7 a.m. to 11 p.m., closed Mon. and Tuesday. Each part has two saunas and a small swimming pool.

GETTING AROUND

Leningrad Metro
Like the Moscow Metro, the Metro in Leningrad is a fast and economical way to travel throughout the

---

LENINGRAD METRO

1. Prospekt Veteranov
2. Leninsky Prospekt
3. Avtovo
4. Kirovsky Zavod
5. Narvskaya
6. Baltiiskaya
7. Tekhnologishesky Institut
8. Pushkinskaya
9. Vladimirskaya
10. Ploshchad Vosstaniya
11. Chernyshevskaya
12. Ploshchad Lenina
13. Vyborgskaya
14. Lesnaya
15. Ploshchad Muzhestva
16. Politekhnicheskaya
17. Akademicheskaya
18. Gradzhdansky Prospekt
19. Komsomolskaya

20. Kupchino
21. Zvyozdnaya
22. Moskovskaya
23. Park Pobedy
24. Elektrosila
25. Moskovskiye Vorota
26. Frunzenskaya
27. Ploshchad MIra
28. Nevsky Prospekt
29. Gorkovskaya
30. Petrogradskaya
31. Chornaya Rechka
32. Pionerskaya
33. Udelnaya
34. Ozerke
35. Prospekt Prosvescheney
36. Parnasskaya
37. Rybatskoye
38. Obukhovo

39. Proletarskaya
40. Lomonosovskaya
41. Elizarovskaya
42. Ploshchad Aleksandra Nevskogo
43. Vasileost Rovskaya
44. Primorskaya
45. Krasnogvardeiskaya
46. Prospekt Bolshevikov
47. Ladozhskaya
48. Krasnogvardeskaya
49. Legovskaya Prospekt
50. Sportevnay
51. Tchepostevnay
52. Krestobskaya Ostrov
53. Staray Lerevny
54. Bogatrskaya Prospekt

city, costing only five kopeks. Over 45 stations link the many sights and islands of Leningrad. The history of the Metro dates all the way back to Czar Alexander I. An engineer wanted to dig a tunnel from the city center to Vasilevsky Island. The czar responded by ordering him not to "engage in any further hare-brained schemes in the future." On 15 Nov. 1955, the first line of the Metro was opened.

Boat Tours

A number of boat tours run through Leningrad. If your tour does not include any, you can easily go on your own. Opposite the Hermitage Museum are two docks on the Neva. The first is for a boat ride along the Neva (another dock for a cruise on the Neva is opposite Decembrists' Square). Here you can buy tickets—the times are posted on the kiosk. It's a lovely cruise from the Hermitage to the Smolny Convent on a double-decker boat; the trip lasts about an hour. The second dock is for hydrofoils, the *Rockets,* to Peter's Summer Palace, Petrodvorets. The ride lasts about 25 minutes and takes you past the city out into the Gulf of Finland. (See also Petrodvorets in the "Vicinity of Leningrad" section.)

A third boat trip takes you on a tour of the Leningrad canals. This leaves from the Anichkov Bridge off of Nevsky Prospekt and cruises along the Fontanka and Moika rivers and Kryukov Canal, and lasts about 75 minutes.

Boats depart daily about every 15 minutes from May to September. Commentaries are usually in Russian only. Tickets (in rubles) are inexpensive; but often, during nice weather, they sell out quickly. It's advised to buy tickets ahead of the time you wish to leave. Refreshments are sold onboard each cruise for rubles.

VICINITY OF LENINGRAD

If you have time, go on a few excursions outside of Leningrad. Day-trips to Peter the Great's Summer Palace on the Gulf of Finland or to the towns of Pushkin and Pavlovsk are recommended!

Petrokrepost

Peter's Fortress, Petrokrepost, on a small island near the southwestern shore of Lake Ladoga, was founded by Slavs in 1323 to protect the trade waterways linking Novgorod with the Baltic. At that time, the small outpost was known as Oreshek (Nut). When Peter the Great captured the tiny fortress in 1702 from the Swedes (they took control of the lands in the 17th century), he renamed it Schlüsselburg, the Key Fortress. The town of Schlüsselburg sprang up along the left bank of the

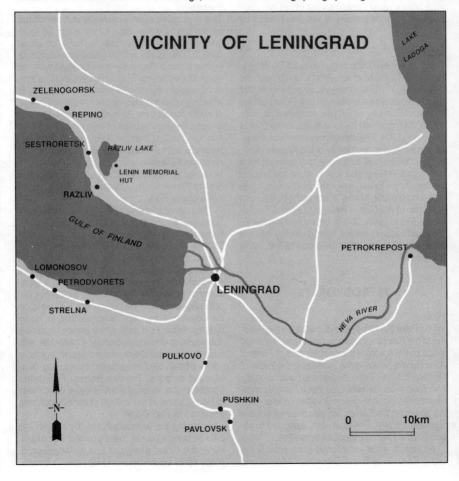

VICINITY OF LENINGRAD

LAKE LADOGA

ZELENOGORSK

REPINO

SESTRORETSK

RAZLIV LAKE

LENIN MEMORIAL HUT

RAZLIV

GULF OF FINLAND

PETROKREPOST

LOMONOSOV

PETRODVORETS

LENINGRAD

NEVA RIVER

STRELNA

PULKOVO

PUSHKIN

-N-

0   10km

PAVLOVSK

Neva, where it flows out of the lake. After the Northern War ended in 1721, Peter converted the fortress into a prison. He had his sister Maria and first wife, Eudokia Lopukhina, imprisoned here; many other Russian revolutionaries suffered similar fates. On 8 May 1887, Lenin's brother, Alexander Ulyanov, along with four others who had attempted to assassinate Czar Alexander III, were hung in the prison yard. The German name of Schlüsselburg was changed to Petrokrepost in 1944 during WW II. If you'd like to visit Petrokrepost, and it's not included in your tour, check at your hotel's travel desk; Intourist offers daily bus excursions to the fortress or you can reach it by car.

Kronstadt

When Peter the Great began to build St. Petersburg in 1703, the Northern War (1700-21) with the Swedes was in its early stages. In order to protect the sea approaches to his new city, Peter built the Kronstadt Fortress, which also contained his shipyards, on the small island of Kotlin in the Gulf of Finland in 1704. The many monuments on the island are linked to the history of the Russian fleet. Intourist offers bus excurions to Kronstadt from Leningrad. A ferry also leaves from the town of Lomonosov. On the way, take notice of the 18-mile-long (29 km) "barrier" that's being built across a section of the Gulf of Finland to control the frequent floods (over 300 in Leningrad's history). Tidal waves get swept inland during severe storms. In 1824, the water level rose 12 feet, killing 569 people.

PETRODVORETS

History

While Peter the Great was supervising the building of the Kronstadt fortress, he stayed in a small lodge on the southern shore of the Gulf of Finland. After Russia defeated the Swedes in the Battle of Poltava in 1709, Peter decided to build his summer residence, **Peterhof,** so that it not only commemorated the victory over Sweden (and of gaining access to the Baltic), but also the might of the Russian Empire. Peterhof was designed to resemble the French Palace of Versailles.

Architects were summoned from around the world: Rastrelli, Le Blond, Braunstein, Michetti and the Russian Zemtsov. Over 4,000 peasants and soldiers were brought in to dig the canals, gardens and parks in the marshy area. Soil, building materials and tens of thousands of trees were brought in by barge. Peter helped to draft the layout of all the gardens and fountains. The fountains were built by Vasily Tuvolkov, Russia's first hydraulics engineer. Over 12 miles (20 km) of canals were constructed so that 30,000 liters (7,500 gallons) of water flowed under its own pressure (without the aid of a single pump) to 144 fountains.

Fountains

The great **Cascade Fountain** in front of the palace has 17 waterfalls, 142 water jets, 66 fountains (including the two cup fountains on either side), 29-bas-reliefs, and 39 gilded statues, including the famous *Samson*—the Russians won the Battle of Poltava on St. Samson's Day. The five-ton *Samson,* surrounded by eight dolphins, is wrestling open the jaws of a lion, from which a jet of water shoots over 20 meters into the air.

Approaching the back of the palace from Red Avenue, the first fountain is known as the **Mezheumny,** with a dragon in the center pool. The **Neptune Fountain** was brought to Russia from Nuremberg, Germany. The **Oak Fountain** and **Square Ponds** are right by the walls of the palace in the Upper Park.

The northeast path leading to **Alexander Park** takes you by the Gothic Court chapel (with 43 saints along the outer walls), the **Cottage** (built in 1829 by Adam Menelaws, who designed it to resemble an aristocratic Englishman's cottage), and the **Farm.** This was also built by Menelaws as a storagehouse, but was later turned into a small summer palace by Alexander II. Following the path back around to the palace, you'll come upon the **Conservatory,** used as a greenhouse. Nearby is the **Triton Fountain,** which shows Neptune's son wrestling with a sea monster. **Chess Hill,** with a black and white checkerboard design, contains some of the best waterfalls, cascading over bronzed dragons. The two **Roman Fountains** (modeled after those at the Cathedral of St. Peter in Rome) stand at the bottom of the hill and were designed by Karl Blank.

Following the path around to the right of the palace brings you to the **Pyramid Fountain.** Peter the Great designed this water pyramid, made up of seven tiers and 505 jets. A circular seat is positioned under the **Little Umbrella Fountain.** If you're tempted to have a short rest on the bench under the umbrella, be ready to scramble—as 164 jets spray out water as soon as anyone sits down! As you scamper away, you'll approach the **Little Oak Fountain,** which has dozens of hidden jets (as do the artificial tulips) that spray as any weight approaches the oak tree. When you run off to the nearby bench to catch your breath, you'll now get completely drenched from 41 more jets! Beware of the three fir trees too!

Approaching Monplaisir, the sun fountain shoots out from a rectangular pond as 16 golden dolphins swim around shiny disks. Jets of water sprinkle out from the center column, creating the golden rays of the sun. The **Adam** and **Eve** fountains (the statues were done by the Venetian sculptor Bonazza) stand on either side of the path leading to the Gulf from the Palace.

Villa And Pavilion

While the Grand Palace was under construction, Peter designed and lived in the smaller Dutch-style villa that he called **Monplaisir** (My Pleasure), right on the Gulf of Finland. Even after the larger palace was completed, Peter preferred to stay here while he visited Peterhof. The two-story house, by the water on the other side of the palace, was known as the **Chateau de Marly,** built in 1714 in Louis XIV style—Peter visited a French king's hunting lodge in Marly. Behind it flows the Golden Hill Cascade. The other quaint two-story structure is known as the **Hermitage Pavilion.** It was built by Johann Friedrich Braunstein. The retreat was surrounded by a moat and had a drawbridge that could be raised to further isolate the guests. The first floor consisted of one room with a large dining room table that could be lifted from or lowered to servants on the ground floor; the guests placed a note on the table, rang a bell, and the table would shortly reappear with the orders. The Lion Cascade Fountains stand in front of the Hermitage.

Palaces

The original palace was built between 1714 and 1724, designed in the baroque and classical styles. It stands on a hill in the center of the Peterhof complex and overlooks the parks and gardens. Rastrelli enlarged it (1747-54) for Empress Elizabeth. After Peter's death, the palace passed on to subsequent czars. It was declared a museum after the Revolution. During WW II, the name Peterhof was changed to Petrodvorets, Peter's Palace. The palace is three stories high and attached by wings that contain the galleries. The central part contains the Exhibition Rooms, Peter the Great's Oak Study and the Royal Bedchamber. The rooms themselves have magnificent parquet floors, gilded ceilings, crystal chandeliers, and are filled with exquisite *objets d'art* from around the world. The **Crimson Room** has furniture by Chippendale; the walls of the oak study

Peter the Great's
Summer Palace

are covered by the portraits of the Empress Elizabeth, Catherine the Great and Alexander I; the **Patridge Chamber,** so named for the silk ornamental partridges that covered the walls, is filled with French silk-upholstered furniture, porcelain and clocks.

The **Portrait Gallery,** in the central hall of the palace, is filled with portraits by such painters as Pietro Rotari (the whole collection was acquired by Catherine the Great) that serves as an interesting catalog of the costumes of the period. The **White Dining Hall,** used for State dinners, is decorated in the Classical style with white molded figures on the walls and a beautiful crystal and amethyst chandelier. The table is ceremoniously laid out for 30 people with 196 pieces of English procelain. Rastrelli built the adjacent **Throne Room** for official receptions. A portrait of Catherine the Great on horseback hangs over Peter's first throne.

The **Chesma Room** commemorated the battles between the Russian and Turkish fleets in Chesma Bay in the Aegean Sea. The German artist Hackert was commissioned to paint the pictures in the room honoring the victories. Count Orlov (a squadron commander at Chesma) checked the artist's sketches and was dissatisfied with one that depicted an exploding ship. Hackert mentioned that he had never seen one. Orlov ordered a 60-cannon Russian frigate, anchored off the coast of Italy to be packed with gunpowder. Hackert had to journey to Italy to see the ship exploding. The rest of the palace is joined by numerous galleries and studies. At the east end is a Rastrelli Rococo chapel with five gilded cupolas.

Destruction And Reconstruction

Hitler invaded Russia on 22 June 1941. When, on 23 Sept. 1941, the Nazis reached Peterhof, many of the art pieces and statues had still not been evacuated. The German army spent 900 days here and destroyed the complex. Monplaisir was an artillery site, used to shell Leningrad. The Germans cut down 15,000 trees for firewood, used tapestries in the trenches, plundered over 34,000 works of art, and made off with priceless objects, including the *Samson* statue, many of which were never recovered. After the war, massive restoration work began, and on 17 June 1945, the fountains flowed once again. The head of the Hermitage, Joseph Orbelli, who lived in the Hermitage during the siege, remarked, "Even during our worst suffering, we knew that the day would come when once again the beautiful fountains of Petrodvorets would begin to spray and the statues of the park flash their golden gleam in the sunlight." There are black-and-white photographs on display in the Exhibition Room that show the extensive damage to the palace.

Leningrad poet Olga Bergholts, after visiting Peterhof after the siege, wrote:

"Again from the black dust, from the place
of death and ashes, will arise the garden as
    before.
So it will be. I firmly believe in miracles.
You gave me that belief, my Leningrad."

Getting There

The Upper and Lower parks and gardens cover about 300 acres (121 hectares) stretching around the palace to the Gulf of Finland. When it's warm and clear, it's wonderful to have a picnic (bring food) on the grounds or beach, stroll the gardens and spend the entire day. Daily tour buses run (20 miles/32 km) from Leningrad, and Intourist offers group excursions (check at the hotel service desk). An electric train also leaves from the Baltic station to the Novy Peterhof stop (35 minutes).

A much more interesting way to get there is by hydrofoil, known as the *Rocket.* This jets across the Gulf of Finland to the palace grounds in about 30 minutes. Catch one at the dock right across from the Hermitage (also opposite Decembrists' Square)—the hydrofoils run about every 20 minutes (May through September) and cost less than two rubles each way. (Intourist also offers daily group excursions. Inquire at your hotel.) Get there early to buy the ticket, since the lines tend to be long.

Besides your boat ticket, you'll also be issued a separate ticket to get into the palace grounds. Don't lose it—you need to show it when you enter the complex from the dock. Typical of the Russian love of paper, this ticket won't admit you into the palace itself! Buy *this* ticket (for a few kopeks) at the small kiosk at the end of the dock. The palace is a good 10-minute walk from the docks; if you don't have an entrance ticket, you must walk all the way back!

Also, it's a good idea to buy your return ticket as soon as you arrive at Petrodvorets. If you wait to the last minute on a crowded day, all tickets for the time you want to return may be sold out. The return-ticket kiosks are to your left across the bridge as you get off the dock. A boat number will be stamped on the back of your ticket. When on the dock, look for your boat number posted on signs.

The palace is open daily from 11 a.m. to 6 p.m. (and the fountains operate from May to September). The Grand Palace is closed on Monday and the last Tuesday of each month. Monplaisir and the Hermitage are closed on Wednesday and the last Thursday of each month. The Chateau de Marly is closed on Tuesday and the last Wednesday of each month. In June, during the White Nights, many festivals are held on the palace grounds.

LOMONOSOV

Once known as **Oranienbaum**, Lomonosov is situated only six miles (10 km) west of Petrodvorets. Peter the Great gave the lands to his close friend, Prince Alexander Menschikov, to develop. Menschikov was the first governor-general of St. Petersburg and supervised the building of the nearby Kronstadt Fortress. He turned the estate into his summer residence. Since he planted orange trees in the lower parks and grew them in hothouses, Menschikov named his residence Oranienbaum, German for "orange trees." The estate served as the country residence for later czars. Peter III and Catherine the Great expanded the buildings and grounds in the style of the times. In 1948, the name was changed to Lomonosov after the great Russian scientist, who had a glasswork factory nearby.

The estate escaped major shelling during the war and is beautifully preserved. The two-story Grand Palace (built in 1725 by architects Fontane and Shedel) stands atop a hill overlooking parks and gardens that were originally designed by Antonio Rinaldi, who also built the two pleasure pavilions, the Chinese Palace and Katalnaya Gorka (Sliding Hill). Visitors could glide on sleds along a wooden path from the third story of the pavilion and, building up speed, ride down throughout the lower parks.

Oranienbaum became the center of masqued balls and parties that entertained Russian royalty and foreign diplomats. Pushkin, Nekrasov, Dumas, Turgenev, Tolstoy, Mussorgsky and Repin were frequent guests. The estate is now a museum (buildings closed on Tuesday) and can be reached by bus, car, by a train which leaves from Leningrad's Baltic Station, or by ferry from Kronstadt.

PUSHKIN

The town of Pushkin, 15.5 miles (25 km) south of Leningrad, was formerly known as Czarskoye Selo, the Czar's Village. After the Revolution, the named was changed to Detskoye Selo (Children's Village), and many of the town's buildings were made into schools. The poet Pushkin studied at the Lyceum (1811-17). In 1937, to commemorate the 100-year anniversary of Pushkin's death, the town was renamed Pushkin.

History

The Moskovsky Prospekt was built in the early 18th century to connect the royal residence to St. Petersburg. The road continued all the way to Moscow. On the way to Pushkin, the road passes through Pulkovo Heights, where the famed **Pulkovo Observatory** is situated. It was badly damaged during the war; now restored, Pulkovo is one of the main observatories in the country. After crossing the Kuzminka River, you come to the Egyptian Entrance Gates (1830) of the city. The gates were designed by the British arthitect, Adam Menelaws, who incorporated motifs from the Egyptian temples at Karnak. To the left of the gate is a statue of Alexander Pushkin.

Peter the Great won the region between the Neva and the Gulf of Finland during the Northern War, including the area of the town. He gave these lands to Prince Menschikov, but later took them back and presented all to his wife, Catherine I. She built terraced parks and gardens and **Yekaterininsky Dvorets,** Catherine's Palace. In 1752, the Empress Elizabeth commissioned Rastrelli to renovate the palace. The beautiful baroque building stretches 900 feet (300 meters) and is decorated with statues, columns and gold ornaments.

Catherine the Great built additions to the palace. During her reign, many renowned architects, such as Cameron, Rinaldi and Quarenghi, worked in the neoclassical style on the palace. Many exhibition halls, Cameron's Green Dining Room and Chinese Blue Room are breathtaking. The walls of the Blue Room are decorated with Chinese blue silk and the Empress Elizabeth is portrayed as Flora, Goddess of Flowers. The white marble staircase leading into the palace was built in 1860 by Monighetti. On the inside walking tour, you pass through Rastrelli's Cavalier Dining Room and Great Hall. Peter the Great traded 248 personal guards with a Prussian king in exchange for panels of amber. Rastrelli built the Amber Room with these panels in 1755. During WW II, the Nazis made off with the panels, which were never found. The Picture Hall stretches the entire width of the building; of the 130 French, Flemish and Italian canvasses that were here before the war, 17 were evacuated and can be seen today. The palace chapel was begun by Rastrelli and completed by Stasov. The northeast section of the palace, in the chapel wing, contains the **Pushkin Museum,** made up of 27 halls, displaying his personal belongings and manuscripts.

Lyceum

The Lyceum is linked to the palace by an archway. It was originally built by Catherine the Great as the school for her grandsons and was expanded in 1811 for the children of the aristocracy. The classrooms were on the second floor and the dormitory on the third. The Lyceum's first open class consisted of 30 boys between 11 and 14. One of these students was Alexander Pushkin. The Lyceum is now a museum and the classrooms and laboratories are kept as they were during Pushkin's time. A room in the dormitory reads, "Door no. 14 Alexander Pushkin." Pushkin read aloud his poem "Recollections of Czarskoye Selo" on 9 June 1817, in the school's assembly hall. The outside statue of Pushkin was sculpted by Robert Bach in 1900. The church (1734-47) next to the Lyceum is the oldest building in town.

Elk Lips And Nightingale Tongues

Catherine's parks consisted of three types: the French was filled with statues and pavilions, the English had more trees and shrubs, and the Italian contained more sculpted gardens. The grounds stretch over 1,400 acres (567 hectares). Rastrelli built the Orlov column in the middle of the lake as a monument to the victory at the Battle of Chesma. The Hermitage structure was built between 1744 and 1756 to entertain the guests. No servants were allowed on the second floor. The guests wrote requests on slates; the tables were lowered and raised with the appropriate drink and dishes, including elk lips and nightingale tongues! The adjacent fish canal provided seafood for the royal banquets. The upper bath house was used by the royal family and the lower by the visitors.

Other Sights

Other buildings on the estate include the Admiralty (with a boat collection), the Grotto (once decorated with over 250,000 shells), the Cameron Gallery, the Hanging Gardens, the Agate Rooms, the Granite Terrace, Marble Bridge (made from Siberian marble), Turkish Baths (resembling a mosque) and the Milkmaid Fountain (built in 1816 by Sokolov from a fable by La Fontaine). Pushkin wrote a poem based on the fable about the sad girl who holds a piece of her milk jug that lies broken at her feet. The Alexander Palace was built by Catherine the Great (1792-96 by Quarenghi) for her grandson, the future Alexander I. Nicholas I lived here after the 1905 Revolution in St. Petersburg.

Many bus excursions run to Pushkin (check at Intourist). Another easy way to the town is by electric train from Leningrad's Vitebsky Station (from Pushkinskaya Metro to stop Detskoye Selo). From the station in Pushkin, grab a local bus or taxi to the palace. The palace is open 11 a.m. to 6 p.m., closed Tuesday. The Lyceum is closed on Thursday.

PAVLOVSK

The gay court life of Czarskoye Selo scared away most of the wildlife. So the royal family went into the nearby area of Pavlovskoye (about two miles/four km away) to hunt. Two wooden hunting lodges were known as "Krik" and "Krak." In 1777, Catherine the Great presented the villages, along with the serfs, to her son Pavel (Paul), whose first son, Alexander, had just been born. The village was renamed Pavlovsk when Paul became czar. The Scottish architect Cameron began building the palace in the 1780s and Paul turned it into his official summer residence. Pavlovsk Park was created by Pietro Gonzaga (who lived here from 1803 to 1838) and covers over 3,750 acres (1,500 hectares), making it one of the largest landscaped parks in the world, with designs such as the Valley of the Ponds and the White Birchtree. Cameron also designed the Pavilion of Three Graces, the Temple of Friendship (1782) and the Apollo

The first Russian railway was constructed between Czarskoye Selo and Pavlovsk, another royal residence, in 1834. One of the passengers who rode the first train to St. Petersburg on 31 Oct. 1837, wrote that "the train made almost one verst (a kilometer) a minute . . . 60 versts an hour, a horrible thought! Meanwhile, as you sit calmly, you do not notice the speed, which terrifies the imagination, only the wind whistles, only the steed breathes fiery foam, leaving a white cloud of steam in its wake. . . ." By 1837, the line had been extended all the way to St. Petersburg. The St. Petersburg-Moscow railroad line was built between 1843 and 1851.

Colonade (1783). Other structures include the Twelve Paths (and 12 bronze statues), Pavilion of the Monument to My Parents (of Paul I's wife), and the Mausoleum of Paul I (the murdered czar is buried in the Peter and Paul Fortress).

The architects Cameron, Brenna, Rossi, Quarenghi and Voronikhin all worked on the construction of the palace, with its 64 columns and yellow façade. The palace contains an Egyptian vestibule, Italian, French and Greek halls, library, dressing room of Empress Maria Fyodorovna and Paul I, the throne room, orchestral chambers, billiard and ball rooms and picture galleries.

The palace and grounds were virtually destroyed during the war, but have been beautifully restored. Pavlovsk is 19 miles (30 km) south of Leningrad. You can take a bus tour (check at Intourist) combining both Pushkin and Pavlovsk in the same day. You can also get there by electric train from Leningrad's Vitebsk Station (Pushinskaya Metro stop). Drivers should leave the car by the wooden bridge and walk to the palace, open from 11 a.m. to 6 p.m. and closed on Thursday and Friday. It's an enjoyable excursion all season long. There's boating in the summer and skiing, ice-skating and *troika* rides in the winter.

GATCHINA

The village of Gatchina, 28 miles (45 km) southwest of Leningrad, was first mentioned in 15th-century chronicles. In the early 18th century, Peter the Great presented his sister Natalia with a farm in the area. Later, Catherine the Great gave the villages as a present to her lover Count Orlov; he had a castle built by Rinaldi in 1781. Paul I (Catherine's son) later took control of the lands and redesigned the palace into a medieval castle. Being a paranoid czar (he was later murdered), Paul had the architect Brenna build a moat with a drawbridge, sentry boxes, toll-gates and a fortress around the castle. Gatchina Park surrounds White Lake.

Behind Long Island is Silver Lake, which never freezes over. The first Russian submarine was tested here in 1879. At the end of the lake there's a lovely little Temple to Venus on the Island of Love. The castle and grounds, badly damaged during WW II, haven't totally been restored. But it's a lovely place to walk around and here one can really notice the havoc caused by German shelling to Leningrad and the environs during WW II. The area can be reached on a bus tour or by car.

RAZLIV

Leningrad and its environs have over 300 places connected with the life of Lenin. To hide from the Provisional Government in 1917, Lenin came to the village of Razliv, 22 miles (35 km) northwest of the city on the Karelian Isthmus near the former Finnish border. Agents were searching everywhere for him and advertised a reward of 200,000 rubles in gold. Shaving off his trademark beard and wearing a wig, he ventured out in the darkness of night from the Finland railroad station to the village, and stayed in a barn owned by the Yemelyanov family. A few days later Nikolai Yemelyanov rowed Lenin across Lake Razliv and built a hut out of hay for a more secretive shelter. A haystack and hut stand on the spot where Lenin lived. There are museums in the hut and barn and a glass pavilion stands near the hut, exhibiting Lenin's personal belongings and documents. There are bus tours to Razliv (check at Intourist) and a tourist boat takes visitors across the lake. You can also get there by electric train (toward Sestroretsk) from the Finland railway station. Razliv is open from 10 a.m. to 6 p.m. and closed Wednesday.

REPINO

The road from Razliv along the Karelian Isthmus leads to Repino and the town of Sestroretsk about

20 miles (32 km) northwest of Leningrad. Repino is a small town in the resort area once known as Kurnosovo. It now bears the name of the celebrated painter Ilya Repin (1844-1930), who bought a cottage in the settlement in 1899 and made it his permanent residence. All his friends and students gathered there every Wednesday and Repin painted the rest of the week. Repin named his estate **The Penates,** after the Roman gods of home and well-being. Repin is buried on the grounds. The Penates burned down during WW II, but was totally reconstructed and is now a museum, displaying Repin's art and personal belongings. You can get there by tour bus (Intourist) or car, or by electric train from Finland station in the direction of Vyborg at the Repino stop. The estate is open from 10:30 a.m. to 5:30 p.m. and closed Tuesday.

NOVGOROD

If there is time for a few other off-the-beaten-track excursions, a visit to Novgorod and Pskov is highly recommended (especially if you don't plan to tour a few towns in the Golden Ring area). Novgorod is about a three-hour drive from Leningrad—which really gets you into the Russian countryside.

Novgorod is one of the oldest towns in all of Russia, founded almost 1,200 years ago. The first Varangian leader, Rurik, settled here. The northern Slavs named the town Novgorod, meaning "New Town," by the shores of Ilmen Lake. The town served as the main northern trade center between the Varangians and the Greeks. As it grew, it became known as Novgorod the Great. In the 12th century, there were over 200 churches. It remained a center for trade and religion well into the 15th century, when it was annexed to Moscovy.

Novgorod is a good example of an old Russian town and a treasury of Old Russian church architecture (over 30 remain), paintings (icons, frescoes and mosaics) and history (birchbark manuscripts). The town is surrounded by a *kremlin*. Its most famous structure is the Cathedral of St. Sophia (1045-50). Near the cathedral is a museum with 35 halls and 80,000 exhibitions. There's also the open-air Museum of Old Wooden Architecture.

PSKOV

Pskov is a few hours farther southwest of Novgorod. Another of Russia's most ancient towns, it was first mentioned in a chronicle in A.D. 903. Pskov began as a small outpost of Novgorod and later grew into a commercial center and developed its own school of icon painting. It's still filled with many beautiful churches and icons. Ivan the Terrible tried to annex Pskov, but the town resisted for many years before being subjugated. Rimsky-Korsakov later wrote an opera based on the uprisings called *The Maid of Pskov.* Nicholas II abdicated the throne while in his train at the Pskov station on 15 March 1917.

BOOKLIST

GENERAL HISTORY AND CURRENT AFFAIRS

Billington, James. *The Icon and the Axe: An Interpretive History of Russian Culture.* Vintage, 1966.

Binyon, Michael. *Life in Russia.* Random House, 1983.

Brown, Edward. *Russian Literature Since the Revolution.* Macmillan, 1969.

Cohen, Stephen. *Sovieticus: American Perceptions and Soviet Realities.* W. W. Norton, 1986.

deJonge, Alex. *The Life and Times of Grigorii Rasputin.* Dorset Press, 1987.

Goldman, Marshall. *Gorbachev's Challenge: Economic Reform in the Age of High Technology.* W. W. Norton, 1987.

Gorbachev, Mikhail. *Perestroika: New Thinking for Our Country and the World.* Harper & Row, 1987.

Gromyko, Andrei. *Memoirs.* Doubleday, 1990.

Hammer, Armand, and Neil Lyndon. *Hammer.* Putnam, 1987.

Hayward, Max. *Writers in Russia: 1917-1978.* Harvest, 1984.

Kaiser, Robert. *Russia: The People and the Power.* Pocket, 1976.

Lenin. *What Is To Be Done?* Written 1902, published by Penguin, 1988.

Lincoln, W. Bruce. *The Romanovs.* Dial Press, 1981.

Massie, Robert. *Nicholas and Alexandra.* Atheneum, 1967.

Massie, Robert. *Peter the Great.* Ballantine, 1980.

Massie, Suzanne. *Land of the Firebird: The Beauty of Old Russia.* Simon and Schuster, 1980.

Massie, Suzanne. *The Living Mirror: Five Young Poets from Leningrad.* Doubleday, 1972.

Medvedev, Roy. *Let History Judge.* Alfred Knopf, 1971.

Medvedev, Z & R. *A Question of Madness.* W. W. Norton, 1979.

Mirsky, D.S. *A History of Russian Literature.* Alfred Knopf, 1958.

Reed, John. *The Ten Days That Shook The World.* Written 1919, published by International, 1967.

Riasanovsky, N. *A History of Russia.* Oxford Univ. Press, 1984.

Richard & Vaillant. *From Russia to the USSR.* Independent School Press, 1985.

Riehn, Richard. *1812: Napoleon's Russian Campaign.* McGraw Hill, 1990.

Salisbury, Harrison. *Nine Hundred Days: The Seige of Leningrad.* Avon, 1970.

Smith, Hedrick. *The Russians.* Quadrangle Press, 1976.

Ulam, Adam. *The Bolsheviks.* Macmillan, 1965.

Walker, Martin. *The Waking Giant.* Sphere, 1987.

Yeltsin, Boris. *Against the Grain.* Summit Books, 1990.

PICTURE BOOKS; ART AND CULTURE

Bird, Alan. *A History of Russian Painting.* London: Oxford, 1987.

Chamberlain, Leslie. *The Food and Cooking of Russia.* London: Penguin, 1983.

Citizen Diplomats: Pathfinders in Soviet American Relations—And How You Can Join Them. Continuum, 1987.

Dancing for Diaghilev: The Memoirs of Lydia Sokolova. Mercury House, 1989.

A Day in the Life of the Soviet Union. Collins, 1987.

Gray, Camilla. *The Russian Experiment in Art 1863-1922.* Thames and Hudson, 1986.

Popova, Olga. *Russian Illuminated Manuscripts.* Thames & Hudson, 1984.

A Portrait of Tsarist Russia. Pantheon, 1989.

Robinson, Harlow. *Sergei Prokofiev: A Biography.* Paragon, 1988.

Russian Fairy Tales. Pantheon, 1973.

Russian Masters: Glinka, Borodin, Balakirev, Musorgsky, Tchaikovsky. W. W. Norton, 1986.

Saved For Humanity: The Hermitage During the Seige of Leningrad 1941-1944. Leningrad: Aurora, 1985.

Skvorecky, Josef. *Talkin' Moscow Blues.* Ecco Press, 1988.

Snowman, A. Kenneth. *Carl Fabergé: Goldsmith to the Imperial Court of Russia.* Crown, 1983.

Stanislavsky on the Art of the Stage. Translated by D. Margarshack, Hill & Wang, 1961.

Troitsky, Artemus. *Back in the USSR: The True Story of Rock in Russia.* Faber & Faber, 1987.

NOVELS AND TRAVEL WRITING

Anna Akhmatova: Poems. Trans. Lyn Coffin, Introduction by Joseph Brodsky. W. W. Norton, 1983.

The Complete Prose Tales of Alexander Sergeyevitch Pushkin. Trans. G. Aitken. W. W. Norton, 1966.

Dostoevsky, Fedor. *Crime and Punishment.* Trans. C. Garnett, Bantam, 1982.

du Plessix Gray, Francine. *Soviet Women: Walking the Tightrope.* Doubleday, 1990.

Filippov, Boris. *Leningrad in Literature.*

Gogol, Nikolai. *Dead Souls.* Trans. D. Magarshack, Penguin, 1961.

Hansson and Liden. *Moscow Women.* Random House, 1983.

Kelly, Laurence. *Moscow: A Traveller's Companion.* London: Constable & Co, 1983.

Kelly, Laurence. *St. Petersburg: A Traveller's Companion.* New York: Atheneum, 1983.

Mochulsky, K. *Dostoevsky: His Life and Work.* Princeton University Press, 1967.

Pasternak, Boris. *Dr. Zhivago.* Trans. M. Hayward. Ballantine, 1988.

The Portable Chekhov. Viking Penguin, 1968.

The Portable Tolstoy, and *War and Peace.* Penguin, 1978.

Rybakov, Anatoly. *Children of the Arbat.* Dell, 1988.

Salisbury, Harrison. *Moscow Journal.* Univ. of Chicago Press, 1961.

Solzhenitsyn, Alexander. *One Day in the Life of Ivan Denisovich.* Bantam, 1963.

Solzhenitsyn, Alexander. *The First Circle.* Harper & Row, 1968.

Solzhenitsyn, Alexander. *The Gulag Archipelago.* Harper & Row, 1973.

Taubman, W. & J. *Moscow Spring.* Summit, 1989.

Thubron, Colin. *Where Nights Are Longest.* Atlantic Monthly Press, 1983.

Turgenev, Ivan. *Fathers and Sons.* Trans. R. Matlaw. W. W. Norton, 1966.

Ustinov, Peter. *My Russia.* Little, Brown & Co, 1983.

Van Der Post, Laurens. *Journey in Russia.* Penguin, 1965.

Voinovich, Vladimir. *Moscow 2042.* Harcourt Brace Jovanovich, 1987.

Wechsberg, Joseph. *In Leningrad.* Doubleday, 1977.

Wilson, A.N. *Tolstoy Biography.* Ballantine, 1988.

FILMS AND VIDEOS AVAILABLE FOR RENTAL OR PURCHASE

National Geographic's *Inside the Soviet Circus.* 1988, and *Voices of Leningrad.* 1990.

*Durrell in Russia; Moscow: The Other Russians; Reds.*1981.

Moscow on the Hudson. 1984.

Basic Russian By Video.

Eisenstein's *Potemkin.* USSR, 1925.

October: Ten Days that Shook the World. USSR, 1927.

Alexander Nevsky. USSR, 1938.

Ivan the Terrible. USSR, 1946.

Eisenstein. USSR, 1958.

Pudovkin's *Mother.* USSR, 1926.

The End of St. Petersburg, USSR, 1927.

Vertov's *The Man with the Movie Camera,* USSR, 1928.

Petrov's *Peter the First:, Parts I, II.* USSR, 1937.

Tarkovsky's *Andrei Rublev.* USSR, 1965.

Maya Plisetskaya Dances. USSR.

Backstage at the Kirov. USSR, 1984.

Menshov's *Moscow Doesn't Believe in Tears.* USSR, 1980.

Abuladze's *Repentance.* USSR, 1987.

Pichul's *Little Vera.* USSR, 1988.

20th Century Fox. *Icons.* 1991.

INDEX

Page numbers in **boldface** indicate the primary reference.

A

Abramtsevo: 120
accommodations: 55; Leningrad
185; Moscow 111
airlines: 72-73; addresses and
phone numbers 72-73;
international flights 50;
internal flights 52
Alexandrov: 130
Alexandrov Gardens (Moscow):
84
Amusement Palace (Moscow):
91
Arbat, the (Moscow): 101-102
Archangel Cathedral (Moscow):
91
Arkhangelskoye Estate
Museum: 120
Armory Palace (Moscow): 91-92
art: 30-34; folk crafts 31-32;
icons 30-32; lacquer boxes
32-33; the modern scene 41-
43; Ilya Repin 33-34; Andrei
Rublev 31; see also music,
literature, and filmmaking

B

ballet: 36-38; Didelot 37; Petipa
37; Diaghilev 37-38; see also
music
beriozkas: 64-65; Leningrad
187; Moscow 116
Bloody Sunday: 11, 167
Bogoliubovo: 149
Bolshevik Revolution: 11, 161
Borodino: 122
Boulevard Ring, the (Moscow):
102-103
Brezhnev, Leonid: 13-14

C

Cathedral of the Annunciation
(Moscow): 91
Cathedral of the Assumption
(Moscow): 89-90
Cathedral of Saints Boris and
Gleb (Golden Ring): 136
Catherine the Great: 168
CheKa: 170

Church of the Deposition of the
Robe (Moscow): 90
circuses: 106, 119, 175
communications: 70
conduct: 70-71
consulates: see embassies and
consulates

D

Danilovsky Monastery
(Moscow): 108
Decembrists: 10, 171; Square
(Leningrad) 169-171
Donskoi Monastery (Moscow):
107-108
Dostoyevsky: 161

E

economy: 17-18
embassies and consulates: 72
Emperor Bell (Moscow): 88-89
Emperor Cannon (Moscow): 88
entertainment: Leningrad 187-
188; Moscow 118-119
etiquette: 70
Exhibition of Economic
Achievements (Moscow):
109-110

F

festivals: see holidays and
festivals
Field of Mars (Leningrad): 173-
174
filmmaking: 42-43; Moscow
International Film Festival 46
Finland Station (Leningrad):
180-181
food and drink: 49, **56-64;**
drinking 58-59; history 56;
Leningrad 185-187; menu
vocabulary 60-64; Moscow
111-115; shopping 58

G

Garden Ring, the (Moscow):
103-106; Vosstaniya Square
104-106
Gatchina: 197

getting around: 52-54; by air 52;
by bus 53; by train 52-53;
Metro 53; rent-a-car 53; taxi
53-54; Trans-Siberian Rail-
road 54; travel restrictions 71
getting there: 50-52; customs
50-51; international flights 50
glasnost: 14-15
Gogol: 176
Gogol, Nikolai: 102-103
Golden Ring, the: 4-5, 125-156;
getting there 127; history
134; introduction 125-127;
Ivanovo 143; Kostroma 142;
Palekh 144; Pereslavl-
Zalessky 131-134; Rostov
Veliky 134-136; Suzdal 150-
156; Vladimir 145-149;
Yaroslavl 137-141; Zagorsk
127-130
Gorbachev, Mikhail: 14-18
Gorky, Maxim: Museum 104
Gorky Park (Moscow): 107
Gorky Street (Tverskaya,
Moscow): 98-100;
Sovietskaya Square 98-99
government: 18-20; Communist
Party 19; congresses 20;
democratic socialism 19-20;
executive president 18
Grand Kremlin Palace: 91
GUM Department Store: 84, 116

H

health: 67
history: 6-15; Bolshevik
Revolution 11; Leonid
Brezhnev 13-14; Christianity
6-7; early days of Moscow 7-
8; early settlements 6-7;
Mikhail Gorbachev 14-18;
Adolf Hitler 12, 172; Ivan the
Terrible 8-9, 130, 133; Nikita
Khrushchev 12-13; Leningrad
4, 9, 157-161, 173, 177-178,
184; Moscow 75-78; Peter
the Great 9, 132, 161, 165,
174; revolutionary times 10-
11; Siege of Leningrad 177-

178; Josef Stalin 12; WW II 12-13

Hitler, Adolf: 12, 172

holidays and festivals: 45-46

I

icons: 30-32; and lacquer boxes 32-33

Intourist: 47, 72-73

Istra River Museum of Wooden Architecture: 122

Ivan the Terrible: **8-9,** 130, 133

Ivanovo: 143

K

Kalinin Prospekt (Moscow): 100-102; Kutuzovsky Prospekt 102

Khrushchev, Nikita: 12-13

Kideksha: 156

Klin: 122-123

Kolomenskoye Museum Preserve: 123

Kostroma: 142

Kremlin, the (Moscow): 84-92; Amusement Palace 91; Archangel Cathedral 91; Armory Palace 91-92; Cathedral of the Annunciation 91; Cathedral of the Assumption 89-90; Council of Ministers Building 87; Church of the Deposition of the Robe 90; Emperor Bell 88-89; Emperor Cannon 88; Grand Kremlin Palace 91; history 84-85; Palace of Congresses 87; Palace of Facets 90-91; Terem Palace 90

Kuibyshev Street (Moscow): 93-94

Kuskovo Palace Museum (Moscow): 123

L

lacquer boxes: 32-33

language: *see* Russian language, the

Lenin (Vladimir Ilyich Ulyanov): 11; Mausoleum 83

Lenin Hills, the (Moscow): 106-109

Leningrad: 4, 157-198; accommodations 185; airlines and airports 73; Alexander Nevsky Square 180; Arts Square 178; the

Aurora 163-164; boat tours 190; Cathedral of Our Lady of Kazan 176-177; Decembrists' Square 169-171; embassies 73; Engineer's Castle 174-175; entertainment 187-188; Field of Mars 173-174; Finland Station 180-181; food 185-187; Glinka Street 183; the Hermitage 168-169; history 9, 157-161; introduction 157-161; Kirov Islands 164; Kirov Theater 182; Kronstadt 192; Kunstkammer 165-166; Lomonosov 195; Maly Theater 178; Menshikov Palace 166; Metro 188-189; Moscow Avenue 183-184; Nevsky Prospekt 175-180; Novgorod 198; Ostrovsky Square 178; Palace Square 167-169; Pavlovsk 196-197; Peter's cottage 163; Petrodvorets 192-195; Petrokrepost 191-192; Piskarovskoye Memorial Cemetery 184; Pushkin 195-196; Pushkin Drama Theater 178-179; Pushkin-House Museum 169; Pushkin Square 165; Revolution Square 163; Rimsky-Korsakov State Conservatory 182; Royal Mint 162; St. Issac's Square 171-173; shopping 187; Siege of 12, 93, 173, **177-178,** 184; sights 161-184; the Smolny 181-182; sports 189; Taurida Palace 181; Theater Square 182; train stations 73; Vasilyevsky Island 164-167; vicinity of 191-198; Winter Palace 167-168

Lermontov, Mikhail Yurevich: 105

literature: 39-40; Museum of 96; Pushkin 39-40

Lomonosov: 195

M

mail: 70

Maly Theater (Leningrad): 178

Marx Prospekt (Moscow): 95-98; Kropotkin Street 97; Kuznetsky Most 96;

Neglinnaya Street 96-97; Petrovka Street 96

medicine: 48-49

Metro: 53; Moscow 79-81; Leningrad 188-189

money: 68; rubles 68

Moscow: 4, **75-124;** accommodations 111; airlines and airports 73; the Arbat 101-102; boat cruises 110; the Boulevard Ring 102-103; embassies 72-73; entertainment 118-119; Exhibition of Economic Achievements 109-110; food 111-115; the Garden Ring 103-106; Gorky Park 107; Gorky Street (Tverskaya) 98-100; history 75-78; Kalinin Prospekt 100-102; the Kremlin 84-92; the Lenin Hills 106-109; Marx Prospekt 95-98; Metro 79-81; Old Moscow 92-95; parks and gardens 119; Red Square 82-84; shopping 115-117; sights 82-110; Stock Exchange 94; train stations 73; University 106; vicinity of 120

Moscow Avenue (Leningrad): 183-184

music: 35-38; Mussorgsky 35; rock 'n' roll 43-44; Tchaikovsky 35-36; *see also* ballet

N

Nahabino: 123

Nevsky Prospekt (Leningrad): 175-180

Nogin Square (Moscow): 94-95

Novgorod: 198

Novodevichy Convent (Moscow): 107

O

Ostankino (Moscow): 109-110

P

Palace of Facets (Moscow): 90-91

Palekh: 144

Pasternak, Boris: 123

Paul I: 174

Pavlovsk: 196

people: 40-44

Peredelkino: 123

Pereslavl-Zalessky: 131-134; Cathedral of the Transfiguration 132-133; history 132; Museum of History and Art 133; sights 132-134
Peter the Great: **9,** 132, 161, 165, 174
Petrodvorets: 192-195
photography: film 49; restrictions 71
Piskarovskoye Memorial Cemetery (Leningrad): 184 *see also* Leningrad, Siege of
planning your trip: 47-49; food 49; what to take 48-49; when to go 48
Palekh: 144
Pskov: 198
Pushkin, Alexander: **39-40,** 176, 195-196; Drama Theater (Leningrad) 178-179; Museum 97; Pushkin-House Museum (Leningrad) 169
Pushkin Square: 99-100

R
Rasputin, Grigory: 183
Razin Street (Moscow): 94
Razliv: 197
Red Square: 82-84; Lenin Mausoleum 83; St. Basil's Cathedral 82-83
religion: 28-29; *see also* Russian Orthodox Church
Repin, Ilya: 33-34
Repino: 197-198
Rostov Veliky 134-136; Museum Preserve of Art and Architecture 136
Rublev, Andrei: **31,** 130; Museum of Religious Art 109

Russian language, the: 21-27; Cyrillic alphabet 27; vocabulary 21-26;
Russian Orthodox Church: 28-29; architecture 28-29; history 6-7, 28-29, 134

S
St. Basil's Cathedral (Moscow): 82-83
St. Issac's Square (Moscow): 171-173
shopping: 64-67; *beriozkas* 64-65; Leningrad 187; Moscow 115-117; tips 65; size conversion chart 67; vocabulary terms 65-66
Shostakovich, Dimitri: 177-178
Slavyansky Bazaar (Moscow): 93
Smolny, the (Leningrad): 181-182
Spaso-Andronikov Monastery (Moscow): 108-109
sports: Leningrad 189; Moscow 119
Stalin, Josef: 12
Suzdal: 150-156; Cathedral of the Nativity 152-153; Convent of the Intercession 155; history 150-152; Museum of 153; sights 152-156; vicinity of 156

T
taxis: 53-54
Tchaikovsky, Pyotr: **35-36,** 122-123
telephone: 70
Terem Palace (Moscow): 90
Tereshkova, Valentina: 141

Theater Square (Leningrad): 182-183
time: business hours 68; time zones 48
Tolstoy, Leo: 124; Museum 97
train: 52; stations 72-73; *see also* Trans-Siberian Railroad
transportation: *see* getting there, getting around
Trans-Siberian Railroad: 54
Tretyakov Art Gallery: 97-98
25th October Street (Moscow): 92-93

V
visas: 47-48
Vladimir: 145-149; history 145-147; sights 147-149; vicinity of 149

Y
Yaroslavl: 137-141; Church of Elijah the Prophet 139; Cosmos Museum 141; history 137; Museum of Art, History and Architecture 139; Museum of the Lay of Igor's Host 139; Museum of Old Russian Art 140; Transfiguration of Our Savior Monastery 139; vicinity of 141
Yasnaya Polyana: 124

Z
Zagorsk: 127-130; Assumption Cathedral 129; Chertogi Palace 130; history 127-128; History and Art Museum 130; Toy Museum 130; Trinity Cathedral and Monastery 129-130; vicinity of 130

ABOUT THE AUTHOR

Masha Nordbye is a writer and film producer who has traveled through more than 70 countries. She graduated from Middleday College, Vermont, with a B.A. in Russian and German Studies; she has also studied at the Johannes Guttenberg University in Mainz, Germany and at the University of Moscow. Over the past 15 years she has studied, worked, and lived in the Soviet Union. Her films in the USSR include National Geographic's "Inside the Soviet Circus" and "Voices of Leningrad," and PBS's "Villages of the North." She is the author of three other books on the Soviet Union, and now resides in Los Angeles.

Moon Handbooks—The Ideal Traveling Companions

Open a Moon Handbook and you're opening your eyes and heart to the world. Thoughtful, sensitive, and provocative, Moon Handbooks encourage an intimate understanding of a region, from its culture and history to essential practicalities. Fun to read and packed with valuable information on accommodations, dining, recreation, plus indispensable travel tips, detailed maps, charts, illustrations, photos, glossaries, and indexes, Moon Handbooks are ideal traveling companions: informative, entertaining, and highly practical.

TO ORDER BY PHONE: (800) 345-5473 • Monday-Friday • 9 a.m.-5 p.m. PST

The Pacific/Asia Series

BALI HANDBOOK by Bill Dalton
Detailed travel information on the most famous island in the world. 12 color pages, 29 b/w photos, 68 illustrations, 42 maps, 7 charts, glossary, booklist, index. 428 pages. **$12.95**

INDONESIA HANDBOOK by Bill Dalton
This one-volume encyclopedia explores island by island the many facets of this sprawling, kaleidoscopic island nation. 30 b/w photos, 143 illustrations, 250 maps, 17 charts, booklist, extensive Indonesian vocabulary, index. 1,050 pages. **$17.95**

SOUTH KOREA HANDBOOK by Robert Nilsen
Whether you're visiting on business or searching for adventure, South Korea Handbook is an invaluable companion. 8 color pages, 78 b/w photos, 93 illustrations, 109 maps, 10 charts, Korean glossary with useful notes on speaking and reading the language, booklist, index. 548 pages. **$14.95**

SOUTHEAST ASIA HANDBOOK by Carl Parkes
Helps the enlightened traveler discover the real Southeast Asia. 16 color pages, 75 b/w photos, 11 illustrations, 169 maps, 140 charts, vocabularies and suggested reading, index. 873 pages. **$16.95**

NEW ZEALAND HANDBOOK by Jane King
Introduces you to the people, places, history, and culture of this extraordinary land. 8 color pages, 99 b/w photos, 146 illustrations, 82 maps, booklist, index. 546 pages. **$14.95**

BLUEPRINT FOR PARADISE: How to Live on a Tropic Island by Ross Norgrove
This one-of-a-kind guide has everything you need to know about moving to and living comfortably on a tropical island. 8 color pages, 40 b/w photos, 3 maps, 14 charts, appendices, index. 212 pages. **$14.95**

The Americas Series

NORTHERN CALIFORNIA HANDBOOK by Kim Weir
An outstanding companion for imaginative travel in the territory north of the Tehachapis. 12 color pages, b/w photos, 69 maps, illustrations, booklist, index. 759 pages. **$16.95**

NEVADA HANDBOOK by Deke Castleman
Nevada Handbook puts the Silver State into perspective and makes it manageable and affordable. 34 b/w photos, 43 illustrations, 37 maps, 17 charts, booklist, index. Approx. 400 pages. **$12.95**

NEW MEXICO HANDBOOK by Stephen Metzger
A close-up and complete look at every aspect of this wondrous state. 8 color pages, 85 b/w photos, 63 illustrations, 50 maps, 10 charts, booklist, index. 350 pages. **$11.95**

TEXAS HANDBOOK by Joe Cummings
Seasoned travel writer Joe Cummings brings an insider's perspective to his home state. 12 color pages, b/w photos, maps, illustrations, charts, booklist, index. 483 pages. **$11.95**

ARIZONA TRAVELER'S HANDBOOK by Bill Weir
This meticulously researched guide contains everything necessary to make Arizona accessible and enjoyable. 8 color pages, 194 b/w photos, 74 illustrations, 53 maps, 6 charts, booklist, index. 505 pages. **$13.95**

UTAH HANDBOOK by Bill Weir
Weir gives you all the carefully researched facts and background to make your visit a success. 8 color pages, 102 b/w photos, 61 illustrations, 30 maps, 9 charts, booklist, index. 452 pages. **$12.95**

ALASKA-YUKON HANDBOOK by Deke Castleman, Don Pitcher, and David Stanley
Get the inside story, with plenty of well-seasoned advice to help you cover more miles on less money. 8 color pages, 26 b/w photos, 92 illustrations, 90 maps, 6 charts, booklist, glossary, index. 384 pages. **$11.95**

WASHINGTON HANDBOOK by Dianne J. Boulerice Lyons
Covers sights, shopping, services, transportation, and outdoor recreation, with complete listings for restaurants and accommodations. 8 color pages, 92 b/w photos, 24 illustrations, 81 maps, 8 charts, booklist, index. 400 pages. **$12.95**

OREGON HANDBOOK by Stuart Warren and Ted Long Ishikawa
Brimming with travel practicalities and insider views on Oregon's history, culture, arts, and activities. Color and b/w photos, illustrations, 28 maps, charts, booklist, index. Approx. 400 pages. **$12.95**

WYOMING HANDBOOK by Don Pitcher
All you need to know to open the doors to this wide-open and wild state. Color and b/w photos, illustrations, over 60 maps, charts, booklist, index. Approx. 500 pages. **$12.95**

BRITISH COLUMBIA HANDBOOK by Jane King
With an emphasis on outdoor adventures, this guide covers mainland British Columbia, Vancouver Island, the Queen Charlotte Islands, and the Canadian Rockies. 8 color pages, 56 b/w photos, 45 illustrations, 66 maps, 4 charts, booklist, index. 381 pages. **$11.95**

GUIDE TO CATALINA and California's Channel Islands by Chicki Mallan
A complete guide to these remarkable islands, from the windy solitude of the Channel Islands National Marine Sanctuary to bustling Avalon. 8 color pages, 105 b/w photos, 65 illustrations, 40 maps, 32 charts, booklist, index. 262 pages. **$9.95**

YUCATAN HANDBOOK by Chicki Mallan
All the information you'll need to guide you into every corner of this exotic land. 8 color pages, 154 b/w photos, 55 illustrations, 57 maps, 70 charts, appendix, booklist, Mayan and Spanish glossaries, index. 391 pages. **$12.95**

CANCUN HANDBOOK and Mexico's Caribbean Coast by Chicki Mallan
Covers the city's luxury scene as well as more modest attractions, plus many side trips to unspoiled beaches and Mayan ruins. Color and b/w photos, illustrations, over 30 maps, Spanish glossary, booklist, index. 257 pages. **$9.95**

BELIZE HANDBOOK by Chicki Mallan
Complete with detailed maps, practical information, and an overview of the area's flamboyant history, culture, and geographical features, *Belize Handbook* is the only comprehensive guide of its kind to this spectacular region. Color and b/w photos, illustrations, maps, booklist, index. 212 pages. **$11.95**

The International Series

EGYPT HANDBOOK by Kathy Hansen
An invaluable resource for intelligent travel in Egypt. 8 color pages, 20 b/w photos, 150 illustrations, 80 detailed maps and plans to museums and archaeological sites, Arabic glossary, booklist, index. 510 pages. **$14.95**

PAKISTAN HANDBOOK by Isobel Shaw
For armchair travelers and trekkers alike, the most detailed and authoritative guide to Pakistan ever published. 28 color pages, 86 maps, appendices, Urdu glossary, booklist, index. 478 pages. **$15.95**

MOSCOW-LENINGRAD HANDBOOK by Masha Nordbye
Provides the visitor with an extensive introduction to the history, culture and people of these two great cities, as well as practical information on where to stay, eat, and shop. 8 color pages, 36 b/w photos, 20 illustrations, 16 maps, 9 charts, booklist, index. 205 pages. **$12.95**

PHILIPPINES HANDBOOK by Peter Harper and Evelyn Peplow
Crammed with detailed information, Philippines Handbook equips the escapist, hedonist, or business traveler with thorough coverage of the Philippines's colorful history, landscapes, and culture. Color and b/w photos, illustrations, maps, charts, booklist, index. 400 pages.   **$12.95**

HAWAII HANDBOOK by J.D. Bisignani
Winner of the 1989 Hawaii Visitors Bureau's Best Guide Book Award and the Grand Award for Excellence in Travel Journalism, this guide takes you beyond the glitz and high-priced hype and leads you to a genuine Hawaiian experience. 12 color pages, 86 b/w photos, 132 illustrations, 86 maps, 44 graphs and charts, Hawaiian and pidgin glossaries, appendix, booklist, index. 879 pages.   **$15.95**

KAUAI HANDBOOK by J.D. Bisignani
Kauai Handbook is the perfect antidote to the workaday world. 8 color pages, 36 b/w photos, 48 illustrations, 19 maps, 10 tables and charts, Hawaiian and pidgin glossaries, booklist, index. 236 pages.   **$9.95**

MAUI HANDBOOK: Including Molokai and Lanai by J.D. Bisignani
"No fool-'round" advice on accommodations, eateries, and recreation, plus a comprehensive introduction to island ways, geography, and history. 8 color pages, 60 b/w photos, 72 illustrations, 34 maps, 19 charts, booklist, glossary, index. 350 pages.   **$10.95**

OAHU HANDBOOK by J.D. Bisignani
A handy guide to Honolulu, renowned surfing beaches, and Oahu's countless other diversions. Color and b/w photos, illustrations, 18 maps, charts, booklist, glossary, index. 354 pages. **$11.95**

BIG ISLAND OF HAWAII HANDBOOK by J.D. Bisignani
An entertaining yet informative text packed with insider tips on accommodations, dining, sports and outdoor activities, natural attractions, and must-see sights. Color and b/w photos, illustrations, 20 maps, charts, booklist, glossary, index. 347 pages.   **$11.95**

SOUTH PACIFIC HANDBOOK by David Stanley
The original comprehensive guide to the 16 territories in the South Pacific. 20 color pages, 195 b/w photos, 121 illustrations, 35 charts, 138 maps, booklist, glossary, index. 740 pages. **$15.95**

MICRONESIA HANDBOOK:
Guide to the Caroline, Gilbert, Mariana, and Marshall Islands by David Stanley
Micronesia Handbook guides you on a real Pacific adventure all your own. 8 color pages, 77 b/w photos, 68 illustrations, 69 maps, 18 tables and charts, index. 287 pages.   **$9.95**

FIJI ISLANDS HANDBOOK by David Stanley
The first and still the best source of information on travel around this 322-island archipelago. 8 color pages, 35 b/w photos, 78 illustrations, 26 maps, 3 charts, Fijian glossary, booklist, index. 198 pages.   **$8.95**

TAHITI-POLYNESIA HANDBOOK by David Stanley
All five French-Polynesian archipelagoes are covered in this comprehensive guide by Oceania's best-known travel writer. 12 color pages, 45 b/w photos, 64 illustrations, 33 maps, 7 charts, booklist, glossary, index. 225 pages.   **$9.95**

IMPORTANT ORDERING INFORMATION

TO ORDER BY PHONE: (800) 345-5473 · Monday-Friday · 9 a.m.-5 p.m. PST

PRICES: All prices are subject to change. We always ship the most current edition. We will let you know if there is a price increase on the book you ordered.

SHIPPING & HANDLING OPTIONS:
1) Domestic UPS or USPS 1st class (allow 10 working days for delivery): $3.50 for the 1st item, 50 cents for each additional item.
Exceptions:
 · **Moonbelt** shipping is $1.50 for one, 50 cents for each additional belt.
 · Add $2.00 for same-day handling.

2) UPS 2nd Day Air or Printed Airmail requires a special quote.
3) International Surface Bookrate (8-12 weeks delivery): $3.00 for the 1st item, $1.00 for each additional item.

FOREIGN ORDERS: All orders which originate outside the U.S.A. must be paid for with either an International Money Order or a check in U.S. currency drawn on a major U.S. bank based in the U.S.A.

TELEPHONE ORDERS: We accept Visa or MasterCard payments. Minimum order is US$15.00. Call in your order: 1 (800) 345-5473. 9 a.m.-5 p.m. Pacific Standard Time.

MOONBELTS. A new concept in moneybelts. Made of heavy-duty Cordura nylon, the Moonbelt offers maximum protection for your money and important papers. This pouch, designed for all-weather comfort, slips under your shirt or waistband, rendering it virtually undetectable and inaccessible to pickpockets. Many thoughtful features: 1-inch-wide nylon webbing, heavy-duty zipper, and a 1-inch high-test quick-release buckle. No more fumbling around for the strap or repeated adjustments, this handy plastic buckle opens and closes with a touch, but won't come undone until you want it to. Accommodates traveler's checks, passport, cash, photos. Size 5 x 9 inches. Available in black only.   **$8.95**

WHERE TO BUY THIS BOOK

Bookstores and Libraries:
Moon Publications Handbooks are sold worldwide. Please write our Sales Manager for a list of wholesalers and distributors in your area that stock our travel handbooks.

Travelers:
We would like to have Moon Publications handbooks available throughout the world. Please ask your bookstore to write or call us for ordering information. If your bookstore will not order our guides for you, please write or call for a free catalog.

MOON PUBLICATIONS INC.
722 WALL STREET
CHICO, CA 95928 U.S.A.
tel: (800) 345-5473
fax: (916) 345-6751

ORDER FORM

FOR FASTER SERVICE ORDER BY PHONE: (800) 345-5473 · 9 a.m.-5 p.m. PST
(See important ordering information on preceding page)

Name:_____ Date:_____

Street:_____

City:_____

State or Country:_____ Zip Code:_____

Daytime Phone:_____

Quantity	Title	Price

Taxable Total	
Sales Tax (6%) for California Residents	
Shipping & Handling	
TOTAL	

Ship: ☐ 1st class   ☐ UPS (no P.O. Boxes)   ☐ International Surface

Ship to: ☐ address above   ☐ other_____

_____

_____

Make checks payable to:
Moon Publications, Inc., 722 Wall Street, Chico, California 95928, U.S.A.
We Accept Visa and MasterCard
To Order: Call in your Visa or MasterCard number, or send a written order with your Visa or
MasterCard number and expiration date clearly written.

Card Number: ☐ **Visa**   ☐ **MasterCard**

☐☐☐☐ ☐☐☐☐ ☐☐☐☐ ☐☐☐☐

Exact Name on Card: ☐ same as above   expiration date:_____

☐ other_____

signature_____

33-60